Global Production

CREI Lectures in Macroeconomics

SERIES EDITORS: JORDI GALÍ, JAUME VENTURA, AND HANS-JOACHIM VOTH

Labor Markets and Business Cycles
Robert Shimer

Global Production: Firms, Contracts, and Trade Structure
Pol Antràs

Global Production

FIRMS, CONTRACTS, AND TRADE STRUCTURE

Pol Antràs

This work is published in association with the
Centre de Recerca en Economia Internacional (CREI)

PRINCETON UNIVERSITY PRESS

PRINCETON AND OXFORD

Copyright © 2016 by Princeton University Press
Published by Princeton University Press, 41 William Street,
Princeton, New Jersey 08540
In the United Kingdom: Princeton University Press, 6 Oxford Street,
Woodstock, Oxfordshire OX20 1TR

press.princeton.edu

Cover art: Image courtesy of Shutterstock

First paperback printing, 2020
Paperback ISBN 978-0-691-20903-6

The Library of Congress has cataloged the cloth edition as follows:
Antràs, Pol, 1975– author.
Global production : firms, contracts, and trade structure / Pol Antràs.
    pages cm. – (CREI lectures in macroeconomics)
Includes bibliographical references and index.
ISBN 978-0-691-16827-2 (hardcover : alk. paper) – ISBN 0-691-16827-X (hardcover : alk.
paper)   1. International trade.   2. Supply and demand.   3. Foreign trade regulation.
4. Production (Economic theory)   I. Title.
HF1379.A739 2016
382–dc23
                          2015017240

This book has been composed in Linux Libertine

Typeset by S R Nova Pvt Ltd, Bangalore, India

Printed in the United States of America

Contents

Preface

This book has grown out of the *CREI Lectures in Macroeconomics* that I delivered in Barcelona in June 2012. I am grateful to the series editor, Hans-Joachim Voth, for inviting me to deliver these lectures and for encouraging me to accept the invitation. Part of my initial reticence, I can now admit, was related to the fact that I viewed the invitation to give these prestigious lectures as a flagrant case of "home bias". At the time, the CREI Lecture series committee was composed of a coauthor of mine (Hans-Joachim Voth), one of my Ph.D. advisors (Jaume Ventura), and two of my favorite teachers during my undergraduate studies at Universitat Pompeu Fabra (Antonio Ciccone and Jordi Galí). Regardless of their motivations, it was an honor to have been selected as the 2012 CREI Lectures speaker. I am grateful for the comments and feedback I received during my lectures and also for CREI's hospitality during my many visits there.

The book is largely aimed at graduate students and researchers interested in learning about recent developments in the field of international trade. I have attempted, however, to make the style of the book a bit less terse than is standard in professional journals and graduate-level textbooks. This may alienate some technically oriented readers, but will I hope encourage some advanced undergraduate students and trade practitioners to venture into the material in this book. Chapter 1 in particular provides an overview of the topics covered in later chapters at a highly accessible level. The book contains an extensive Theoretical Appendix, which I hope will earn me the forgiveness of some mathematically inclined readers. It would be hard to sell this book as being a set of lectures in *macroeconomics*, but I hope that some of the material will appeal to researchers in that field, as well as readers interested in organizational economics and applied contract theory.

Although much of the content of this book has appeared in some form in academic journals, many chapters include new and original work. For instance, the multi-country global sourcing model introduced in Chapter 2 and further developed in Chapters 5 and 8 stems from very recent work by Antràs, Fort, and Tintelnot (2014). Similarly, I am not aware of the existence of multi-country models of limited commitment of the type developed in Chapter 3. Many of the empirical parts of the book are original as well, although they build heavily on previous work in terms of both methodology and data sources.

I have taught most of the material in these lectures at Harvard but also at Study Center Gerzensee, the London School of Economics, Penn State University, the University of Zurich, and Northwestern University. I have found that between four and five 90-minute lectures are generally sufficient to cover the contents of this book. I am grateful to all these institutions for their hospitality and to the lecture participants for many useful comments.

Although I have attempted to provide a broad overview of the topics in this lecture, the spirit of the CREI Lectures required that my own work be featured prominently in this book. For this reason, my greatest debt is to my coauthors on the papers reviewed herein, including Daron Acemoglu, Davin Chor, Fritz Foley, Teresa Fort, Esteban Rossi-Hansberg, Bob Staiger, Felix Tintelnot, Steve Yeaple, and especially Elhanan Helpman. I am also particularly grateful to my colleagues Elhanan Helpman and Marc Melitz for many stimulating discussions that have shaped my thinking on the topic of this book. My interest in the contracting aspects of global production dates back to my Ph.D. years at MIT, and I am indebted to Daron Acemoglu, Gene Grossman, Bengt Holmström, and Jaume Ventura for their encouragement during those initial phases of this intellectual adventure. I am also very grateful to the Bank of Spain for generously funding my research at that crucial early stage.

Turning my lecture slides into a book manuscript has proved to be much harder and more time-consuming than I first anticipated. Lucia Antràs, Mireia Artigot, Teresa Fort, Elhanan Helpman, Wilhelm Kohler, Marc Melitz, Felix Tintelnot, and two anonymous reviewers read different parts of the first draft and provided very useful feedback and corrections. I am also grateful to Eric Unverzagt for his careful editorial assistance.

Several colleagues have kindly shared their data for some of the empirical material in this book. These include Andrew Bernard, Davin Chor, Robert Johnson, Nathan Nunn, Mike Waugh, and Greg Wright. I have also benefited from the outstanding research assistance of Ruiqing Cao, Yang Du, Alonso de Gortari, and especially Boo-Kang Seol during various periods over which this book was written. Of course they are not responsible for any mistakes left in the manuscript. Finally, I am forever grateful to my wife Lucia and my daughters Daniela and Martina for their patience during the many hours I have spent mulling over and writing this book.

PART I

Introduction

1

Made in the World

It does not seem so long ago that I began my undergraduate studies in Economics at Universitat Pompeu Fabra (UPF), the same institution that hosts the Centre de Recerca en Economia Internacional (CREI), where these lectures were delivered. It was 1994 and I felt I lived in a truly global economy. The music I listened to and the movies I watched were mostly British or American. Most of the clothes I wore were manufactured abroad, some of them in rather exotic places such as Morocco or Taiwan. My favorite beer was Dutch. At UPF, about half of my teachers were foreign, a third of the classes were taught in English, and most of the textbooks were the same ones used in universities around the globe.

In hindsight it seems pretty clear, however, that the world had not yet witnessed the full advent of globalization. What has changed since 1994? *First* and foremost, the last two decades have brought a genuine information and communication technology (ICT) revolution that has led to a profound socioeconomic transformation of the world in which we live. The processing power and memory capacity of computers have doubled approximately every two years (as implied by Moore's law), while the cost of transmitting a bit of information over an optical network has decreased by half roughly every nine months (a phenomenon often referred to as Butter's law). The number of internet users has increased by a factor of 100, growing from around 25 million users in 1994 to more than 2,500 million users in 2012 (see World Development Indicators). As a result of these technological developments, the cost of processing and transmitting information at long distances has dramatically fallen in recent times. Consider the following example: in 2012, the 3.3GB file containing my favorite movie of 1994, *Pulp Fiction*, could be downloaded from Amazon.com in about 11 minutes and 16 seconds using a standard broadband connection with a download speed of 5 megabits per second. In 1994, downloading that same file using a dial-up connection and the state-of-the-art modem, which allowed for a maximum speed of 28.8 kilobits per second, would have kept your phone line busy for at least 33 hours and 23 minutes![1]

---

[1] Paraphrasing a memorable quote from Samuel L. Jackson's character in *Pulp Fiction*, download speeds today and in 1994 "ain't the same [*freaking*] ballpark. They ain't the same league. They ain't even the same [*freaking*] sport."

Second, during the same period, governments have continued (and arguably intensified) their efforts to gradually dismantle all man-made trade barriers. This process dates back to the initial signing of the General Agreement on Tariffs and Trade (GATT) in 1947, but it has experienced a revival in the 1990s and 2000s with the gradual expansion of the European Union, the formation of the North American, Mercosur, and ASEAN free trade agreements, the signing of a multitude of smaller preferential trade agreements under the umbrella of GATT's Article XXIV, and China's accession to the World Trade Organization (WTO), just to name a few. As a consequence, the world's weighted average tariff applied on traded manufactured goods fell from 5.14 percent in 1996 to 3.03 percent in 2010 (see World Development Indicators).[2]

Third, political developments in the world have brought about a remarkable increase in the share of world population actively participating in the process of globalization. These changes largely stemmed from the fall of communism in Eastern Europe and the former Soviet Union, but also from an ensuing ideological shift to the right in large parts of the globe. Thus, not only did former communist countries embrace mainstream capitalist policies, but these policies themselves became more friendly toward globalization, as exemplified by the deepening of trade liberalization mentioned in the last paragraph, but also by a notable relaxation of currency convertibility and balance-of-payments restrictions in several low- and middle-income countries.[3]

The Slicing of the Value Chain

One of the manifestations of these three developments in the world economy has been a gradual disintegration of production processes across borders. More and more firms now organize production on a global scale and choose to offshore parts, components, or services to producers in foreign and often distant countries. The typical "Made in" labels in manufactured goods have become archaic symbols of an old era. These days, most goods are "Made in the World."

---

[2] Technological developments since 1994 have also reduced the quality- (or time-) adjusted costs of transporting goods across countries (see Hummels, 2007), while investments in infrastructure in less developed economies have also contributed to spreading the effects of globalization across regions in those countries.

[3] The late 1990s also saw the emergence of a left-leaning anti-globalization movement, which drew particular attention during the 1999 WTO meetings in Seattle. Yet there is little evidence of this movement having led to any significant slowdown in the process of globalization (see, for instance, Harrison and Scorse, 2010).

A variety of terms have been used to refer to this phenomenon: the "slicing of the value chain," "fragmentation of the production process," "disintegration of production," "delocalization," "vertical specialization," "global production sharing," "unbundling," "offshoring," and many more (see Feenstra, 1998). I shall use these terms interchangeably throughout the book.[4]

The case of Apple's iPad 3 tablet nicely illustrates the magnitude of this new form of globalization. The slim and sleek exterior of the tablet hides a complex manufacturing process combining designs and components provided by multiple suppliers with operations in various countries. Although Apple does not disclose detailed information on its input providers, a clear picture of the global nature of the iPad 3 production process emerges when combining information from teardown reports (such as those published by isuppli.com and ifixit.com) with various press releases.[5] For instance, it is well-known that the tablet itself is assembled in China (and since 2012 also in Brazil) by two Taiwan-based companies, Foxconn and Pegatron. The revolutionary retina display is believed to be manufactured by Samsung of South Korea in its production plant in Wujiang City, China. The distinctive touch panel is produced (at least, in part) by Wintek, a Taiwan-based company that also owns plants in China, India, and Vietnam, while the case is provided by another Taiwanese company, Catcher Technologies, with operations in Taiwan and China. A third important component, the battery pack, also originates in Taiwan and is sold by Simplo Technologies and Dynapack International. Apart from these easily identifiable parts, the iPad 3 incorporates a variety of chips and other small technical components provided by various firms with headquarters and R&D centers in developed economies and manufacturing plants scattered around the world. A non-exhaustive list includes (again) Korea's Samsung, which is believed to manufacture the main processor (designed by Apple), U.S.-based Qualcomm supplying 4G modules, and Italo-French STMicroelectronics contributing key sensors.[6]

Apple's sourcing strategies are hardly an isolated example of a global approach to the organization of production. In fact, the increasing

[4] At times, I will also use the buzzword "outsourcing," but I will do so only when referring to *arm's-length* sourcing relationships, that is, instances of fragmentation in which the firms exchanging parts are not related (i.e., integrated). Outsourcing is often observed not only in foreign but also in domestic vertical relationships.

[5] Facing strong criticism over the working conditions in its suppliers' factories, Apple released a full list of its 156 global suppliers early in 2012 (see http://images.apple.com/supplierresponsibility/pdf/Apple_Supplier_List_2011.pdf). Teardown reports further faciliate a mapping between the iPad parts and their respective producers. Press releases sometimes also identify particular suppliers with specific iPad 3 components (see, for instance, Forbes's "Batteries Required?" available at http://www.forbes.com/global/2010/0607/best-under-billion-10-raymond-sung-simplo-technology-batteries-requried.html).

[6] A more extensive list can be found at: http://www.chipworks.com/en/technical-competitive-analysis/resources/blog/the-new-ipad-a-closer-look-inside/.

international disintegration of production processes has been large enough to be salient in aggregate statistics. During the 1990s and early 2000s, when this phenomenon was still in its infancy, researchers devised several approaches to measuring the quantitative importance of global production sharing.[7] Feenstra and Hanson (1996b), for instance, used U.S. Input-Output tables to infer the share of imported inputs in the overall intermediate input purchases of U.S. firms; they found that this share had already increased from 5.3 percent in 1972 to 11.6 percent in 1990. Campa and Goldberg (1997) found similar evidence for Canada and the UK, but surprisingly not for Japan, where the reliance on foreign inputs appeared to have declined between 1974 and 1993. Hummels, Ishii, and Yi (2001) instead constructed a measure of vertical specialization capturing the value of imported intermediate inputs (goods and services) embodied in a country's exported goods and found that it already accounted for up to 30% of world exports in 1995, having grown by as much as 40% since 1970.

The work of Johnson and Noguera (2012a, 2012b) constitutes the state of the art in the use of Input-Output tables to quantify the importance of global production sharing and its evolution in recent years. The main innovation of their methodology is in the attempt to compute a *global* Input-Output table from which one can back out the value-added and intermediate input contents of gross international trade flows. In particular, their VAX ratio (the value-added to gross-value ratio of exports) is an appealing inverse measure of the importance of vertical specialization in the world production: the lower is this measure, the larger is the value of imported inputs embodied in exports.[8] As is clear from Figure 1.1, their VAX ratio has declined rather significantly since 1970, with about two-thirds of the decline occurring after 1990. Johnson and Noguera (2012b) show that this decline is explained solely by increased offshoring within manufacturing. Furthermore, they find that global production sharing has grown disproportionately in emerging economies and also appears to increase following the signing of regional trade agreements.

Two limitations of the fragmentation measures discussed so far are that they rely on fairly aggregated Input-Output data and that they impose strong proportionality assumptions to back out the intermediate input component of trade. A different approach to measuring the degree to which production processes are fragmented across countries was first suggested by Yeats

---

[7] The task is complicated by the fact that data on trade flows of goods are collected on a gross output basis, without regard to the particular sources of the value added embodied in these goods.

[8] In a very recent paper, Koopman, Wang, and Wei (2014) devise a methodology that nicely nests Johnson and Noguera's (2012) VAX measure with the vertical specialization measures developed by Hummels, Ishii, and Yi (2001).

Figure 1.1 Ratio of Value Added to Gross Exports (VAX), 1970–2009. Source: Johnson
and Noguera (2012b)

(2001), and consists of computing the share of trade flows accounted for by
SITC Rev.2 industry categories that can be safely assumed to contain *only*
intermediate inputs (as reflected by the use of the word "Parts of" at the
beginning of the category description). It turns out that all these industries
are in the "Machinery and Transport Equipment" industrial group (or SITC 7).
Yeats (2001) found that intermediate input categories accounted for about 30
percent of OECD merchandise exports of machinery and transport equipment
in 1995, and that this share had steadily increased from its 26.1 percent value
in 1978. A limitation of Yeats's measure is that, by focusing on industries
composed *exclusively* of inputs, it naturally understates the importance of
input trade. This might explain why, when updating this methodology to
present times, one finds little evidence of a further increase in this share.[9]

An alternative to categorizing trade flows as *either* final goods or intermediate inputs is to attempt to calculate a more continuous measure of the
"upstreamness" of the goods being traded. This is the approach in Antràs,
Chor, Fally, and Hillberry (2012), who use Input-Output data to construct

---

[9] Other authors attempting to compute the share of intermediate inputs in world trade using
alternative methodologies have also found little evidence of a trend in the series (see, for instance,
Chen, Kondratowicz, and Yi, 2005; or Miroudot, Lanz, and Ragoussis, 2009). I have obtained
similar results when computing the relative growth of overall trade and input trade using the
classification of goods developed by Wright (2014). As argued by Johnson and Noguera (2012b),
even when taking this finding at face value, it is not necessarily inconsistent with the observed
rise in indices of vertical specialization, which better capture the use of imported inputs in
producing goods *that are exported.*

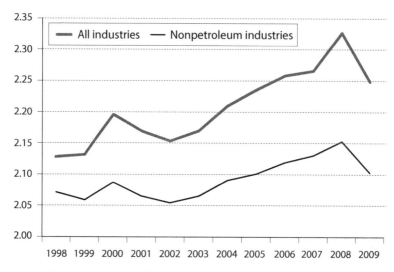

Figure 1.2 Average Upstreamness of World Exports, 1998–2009

a weighted index of the average position in the value chain at which an industry's output is used (i.e., as final consumption, as direct input to other industries, as direct input to industries serving as direct inputs to other industries, and so on), with the weights being given by the ratio of the use of that industry's output in that position relative to the total output of that industry. Intuitively, the higher this measure is, the more removed from final good use (and thus the more upstream) is that industry's output. The Data Appendix contains a lengthier discussion of the construction of this index.[10] Antràs et al. (2012) use the measure to characterize the average upstreamness of exports of different countries in 2002, but it can also be employed to illustrate how the upstreamness of world exports has evolved in recent years. As shown in Figure 1.2, world exports became significantly more upstream in recent years, particularly in the period 2002–2008. The patterns are in line with those illustrated in Figure 1.1, and also suggest an increasing predominance of input trade in world trade. Although a significant share of the observed increase in upstreamness is related to an increase the relative weight of petroleum-related industries, even when netting those out, one observes a significant upward trend in upstreamness (see Figure 1.2). Interestingly, both Figures 1.1 and 1.2 identify a disproportionate decline in global production sharing relative to the overall decline in world trade during the early years of the recent "great recession."

---

[10] This upstreamness index was independently developed by Antràs and Chor (2013) and Fally (2012), and its properties were further studied in Antràs et al. (2012).

Old and New Theories

The noticeable expansion in input trade has also captured the attention of international trade theorists eager to bridge the apparent gap between the new characteristics of international trade in the data and the standard representation of these trade flows in terms of final goods in traditional and new trade theory.

One branch of this new literature has focused on incorporating the notion of fragmentation in otherwise neoclassical models with homogeneous goods, perfectly competitive markets, and frictionless contracting. Key contributions include Feenstra and Hanson (1996a), Jones (2000), Deardorff (2001), and Grossman and Rossi-Hansberg (2008). The main idea in these contributions is that the production process (as represented by an abstract mapping between factors of production and final output) can be decomposed into smaller parts or stages that are themselves (partly) tradable. Different authors assign different labels to these parts: some refer to them as intermediate inputs, others call them vertical production stages, while others view them as tasks. Regardless of the interpretation of the process under study, a common lesson from this body of work is that the possibility of fragmentation generates nontrivial effects on productivity, and that these endogenous changes in productivity in turn deliver novel predictions for the effects of reductions in trade costs on patterns of specialization and factor prices. Antràs and Rossi-Hansberg (2009) elaborate on this broad interpretation of this branch of the literature and also offer more details on the specific results of each of these contributions.[11]

As insightful as this body of work has proven to be, it seems clear that modeling global production sharing as simply an increase in the tradability of homogeneous inputs across countries misses important characteristics of intermediate input trade. Prominent among these features is the fact that parts and components are frequently customized to the needs of their intended buyers (remember our earlier example with the iPad 3). In other words, the disintegration of the production process is more suitably associated with the growth of trade in *differentiated* (rather than homogeneous) intermediate inputs.[12]

---

[11] Another common feature of the theoretical frameworks developed in these papers is that the number of primitive factors of production is assumed to be small, and normally equal to two. Another branch of the literature has developed perfectly competitive, frictionless models in which offshoring results from the assignment of a population of a large number of heterogeneous agents into international hierarchical teams (see Kremer and Maskin, 2006, or Antràs, Garicano, and Rossi-Hansberg, 2006).

[12] Admittedly, not much evidence exists to substantiate this claim. Antràs and Staiger (2012a) offer a back-of-the-envelope quantification applying the methodology suggested by Schott (2004)

Another important characteristic of global production networks is that they necessarily entail intensive *contracting* between parties located in different countries and thus subject to distinct legal systems. In a world with perfect (or complete) contracting across borders, this of course would be of little relevance. Unfortunately, this is not the world we (or at least, I) live in. Real-world commercial contracts are incomplete in the sense that they cannot possibly specify a course of action for all contingencies that could arise during the course of a business relationship. Of course, the same can be said about domestic commercial transactions, but the cross-border exchange of goods cannot generally be governed by the same contractual safeguards that typically accompany similar exchanges occurring within borders.

Given the subject of this book, it is worth pausing to describe in more detail some of the factors that make international contract enforcement particularly problematic.

Contracts in International Trade

A first natural difficulty in contractual disputes involving international transactions is determining which country's laws are applicable to the contract being signed. In principle, the parties can include a *choice-of-law* clause specifying that any dispute arising under the contract is to be determined in accordance with the law of a particular jurisdiction, regardless of where that dispute is litigated. Nevertheless, many international contracts do not include that clause and, in any case, it is up to the court of law adjudicating a dispute to decide whether it will uphold the expressed desire of the parties. If the court is not familiar with the law specified in the contract, as may often occur in international transactions, the court might decide to rule on the basis of its own law, or may inadvertently apply the desired foreign law incorrectly.

A second difficulty relates to the fact that even when local courts are competent (in a legal sense), judges may be reluctant to rule on a contract dispute involving residents of foreign countries, especially if such a ruling would entail an unfavorable outcome for local residents. The evidence on the home bias of local courts is mixed, but even those authors advocating that a formal analysis of case law does not support the hypothesis of biases

---

to identify international trade in intermediate goods and using the "liberal" classification of Rauch (1999) to distinguish between differentiated and homogeneous goods. They find that the share of differentiated inputs in world trade more than doubled between 1962 and 2000, increasing from 10.56% to 24.85% of world trade. Behar and Freund (2011) show that during the late 1990s and 2000s, intermediate inputs traded within the EU became more sophisticated and involved more relationship-specific investments (in the sense of Nunn, 2007).

against foreigners readily admit a widespread belief of the existence of such xenophobic biases (see Clermont and Eisenberg, 2007).

A third complication with international contracts is the enforcement of remedies stipulated in the court's verdict. For instance, the court might rule in favor of a local importer that was unsatisfied with the quality of certain components obtained from an exporter, and the verdict might require the exporter to compensate the importer for any amount already paid for the components, as well as for any court or even attorney fees incurred. An issue arises, however, if the exporter does not have any assets (say bank accounts or fixed assets) in the importer's country. In that case, it is not clear that the exporter will feel compelled to accept the verdict and pay the importer.

In recent years, there have been several coordinated attempts to reduce the contractual uncertainties and ambiguities associated with international transactions. A particularly noteworthy example is the United Nations Convention on Contracts for the International Sale of Goods (or CISG), or Vienna Convention, which attempts to provide a set of uniform rules to govern contracts for the international sale of goods. The idea is that even when an international contract does not include a choice-of-law clause, parties whose places of business are in different signing countries can rely on the Convention to protect their interests in courts. As ambitious as the CISG initiative is, it has arguably fallen short of its objectives. For instance, several countries or regions (most notably Brazil, Hong Kong, India, South Africa, Taiwan, and the United Kingdom) have yet to sign the agreement. Furthermore, a few of the signing countries have expressed reservations and choose not to apply certain parts of the agreement. Finally, it is not uncommon for private parties to explicitly opt out of the application of the Convention, as allowed by its Article 6. The reluctance to unreservedly embrace the Convention has been associated with the somewhat vague language of the text, which might foster the natural inclination of judges to interpret the Convention through the lens of the laws of their own states.[13]

Another attempt to ameliorate the perceived contractibility of international transactions consists in resorting to international arbitration. More specifically, an international trade contract can include a (so-called) *forum-of-law* clause establishing that a particular arbitrator, such as the International Chamber of Commerce (ICC) in Paris, will resolve any contractual dispute that may arise between the parties. International arbitration is appealing because it avoids the aforementioned uncertainties associated with litigation

---

[13] The Institute of International Commercial Law at Pace Law School maintains a website (http://www.cisg.law.pace.edu/) with comprehensive information on the CISG, including a database of thousands of legal cases in which the Convention was invoked. The details of these cases offer a vivid account of the nature of contractual disagreements in international trade.

in national courts. It is also relatively quick and parties benefit from the fact that arbitrators tend to have more commercial expertise than a typical judge. Furthermore, arbitration rulings are confidential and are generally perceived to be more enforceable than those of national courts because they are protected by the Convention on the Recognition and Enforcement of Foreign Arbitral Awards, also known as New York Convention. Despite its attractive features, international arbitration is rarely used in practice because its cost is too high for most firms to bear.[14]

One might argue that even when explicit contracts are incomplete and perceived to be unenforceable, parties in international transactions can still resort to implicit contracting to sustain "cooperation." We shall briefly develop this idea in Chapter 3. Nevertheless, it is particularly difficult to render international commercial relationships self-enforcing. On the one hand, international parties are less likely to meet face-to-face and to transact on a repeated basis than domestic parties, in part due to distance and trade costs, but also due to shocks (such as exchange rate movements) that can quickly turn efficient relationships into inefficient ones. On the other hand, the possibility of collective or community enforcement is hampered again by distance but also by the fact that parties might have different cultural and societal values. In sum, and in the words of Rodrik (2000), "ultimately, [international] contracts are often neither explicit nor implicit; they simply remain incomplete."

Although contractual risks are also of relevance for the exchange of final goods (see Chapter 3), the detrimental effects of imperfect international contract enforcement are likely to be particularly acute for transactions involving intermediate inputs. This is so for at least two reasons. First, input transactions are often associated with relatively long time lags between the time an order is placed (and the contract is signed) and the time the goods or services are delivered (and the contract is executed). Second, parts and components often entail significant relationship-specific investments and other sources of lock-in on the part of both buyers and suppliers, which make contractual breaches particularly costly. As argued above, suppliers often customize their output to the needs of particular buyers and would find it difficult to sell those goods to alternative buyers, should the intended buyer decide not to abide

---

[14] It may be instructive to illustrate this claim with some figures. Using the arbitration cost calculator available from the ICC website, the estimated cost of arbitration (involving a single arbitrator) would be $5,401 for a $10,000 dispute (or a 54% cost-to-dispute-amount ratio), $15,425 for a $100,000 dispute, $61,094 for a $1 million dispute, and $170,799 for a $10 million dispute (or a mere 1.7% cost-to-dispute-amount ratio). It is thus little surprise that there were only 796 ICC arbitration requests in 2011 and that the amount in dispute was under one million U.S. dollars in only 22.7% of these cases (see http://www.iccwbo.org/products-and-services/arbitration-and-adr/arbitration/cost-and-payment/cost-calculator/).

by the terms of the contract. Similarly, buyers often undertake significant investments whose return can be severely diminished by incompatibilities, production line delays, or quality debasements associated with suppliers not fulfilling their contractual obligations.[15]

Firm Responses to Contractual Insecurity

When designing their global sourcing strategies, firms face two key decisions. The first concerns the *location* of the different stages in the value chain and involves deciding in which country or region firms will conduct R&D and product development, where parts and components should be produced, what is the best place to assemble the finished good, and so on. The second key decision relates to the extent of *control* that firms exert over these different production stages. For instance, firms may decide to keep these production stages within firm boundaries, thus engaging in foreign direct investment (FDI) when the integrated entity is in a foreign country. Other firms may be less inclined to keep tight control over certain stages and thus choose to contract with suppliers or assemblers at arm's length.

Neoclassical models of fragmentation focus exclusively on the first of these decisions and emphasize that fragmentation will emerge as part of a competitive equilibrium whenever firms find it cost-minimizing to break up production processes across countries. The source of the cost advantage associated with fragmentation varies by model; sometimes it stems from differences in relative factor endowments across countries (which, for instance, naturally confer comparative advantage in labor-intensive stages to relatively labor-abundant countries), while other times they are motivated by technological differences across countries.

Neoclassical models are silent on the issue of control. This is not because these models assume perfect competition, constant returns to scale, or homogeneous goods. Instead, the key assumption that renders those models (and just about *any* model in the field of International Trade) vacuous when tackling the notion of control is the assumption of perfect or complete contracting. Indeed, if firms could foresee all possible future contingencies, and if they could costlessly write contracts that specify in an enforceable manner the course of action to be taken in all of these possible contingencies,

---

[15] A third, more specific reason for which input trade might be perceived to be less contractually secure relates to the fact that Article 3 of CISG explicitly excludes from the applicability of the Convention situations in which "the party who orders the goods undertakes to supply a substantial part of the materials necessary for such manufacture or production," thus making the Convention less relevant for sustaining cooperation in global production sharing networks.

then firms would no longer need to worry about "controlling" the workers, the internal divisions, or the supplying firms with whom they interact in production. The complete contract would in fact confer *full* control to the firm regardless of the ownership structure that governs the transactions between all these producers. In other words, and as Coase (1937) anticipated more than seventy-five years ago, firm boundaries are indeterminate in a world of complete contracts.[16]

In the real world, however, contracts are very much incomplete and especially so in international transactions where, as argued above, the enforceability of contracts is particularly questionable. In response to this perceived contractual insecurity, firms spend a substantial amount of time and resources figuring out the best possible way to *organize* production in the global economy. In some cases, foreseeing that producers located in a particular country might not feel compelled to follow through with their contractual obligations, firms contemplating doing business in that country might decide to do so within their firm boundaries, either by setting up a new, wholly, or partially owned affiliate or by acquiring a controlling stake in an existing firm in that country. In some circumstances, however, the lack of contract enforceability might turn firms to independent suppliers for the procurement of parts precisely because such an arrangement might elicit the best performance from foreign producers. In other words, it is important to keep in mind that internalization is a double-edged sword: it may partly protect the integrating party from the vagaries of international contracting, but it might dilute the incentives to produce efficiently of the integrated party, which is now more tightly controlled and has less power in the relationship (cf. Grossman and Hart, 1986).

The boundaries of firms in the world economy are thus the result of the (constrained) optimal decisions of firms attempting to organize production in the most profitable way possible. A recurring theme of this book, particularly in Part III, is that much can be learned from a theoretical and empirical study of the *fundamental* forces that appear to shape whether international transactions are internalized or not, independently of the firm or sector one is studying.

Some readers might be asking themselves at this point: why should one care about the boundaries of multinational firms? Surely the fact that we can write testable models of the internalization decision is not a convincing enough argument to care about it. A first answer to this question is

---

[16] It is worth stressing that even in the presence of product differentation and market power, firm boundaries remain indeterminate when contracts are complete. For example, the often-cited double-marginalization rationale for vertical integration rests on the assumption that firms and suppliers cannot sign simple two-part tariff contracts, and as such, it also constitutes an incomplete-contracting theory of firm boundaries.

that understanding the boundaries of firms, and of multinational firms in particular, *is* interesting in its own right. Ever since the pioneering work of Ronald Coase (1937), this topic has preoccupied the minds of many distinguished economists, and constitutes one of the central themes of the field of organizational economics. A second, perhaps more compelling answer is that delineating the boundaries of multinational firms constitutes a necessary first stage for properly studying the causal implications of multinational activity on various objects of interest, such as measures of economic activity and growth, absolute and relative factor price movements, and welfare. In other words, because multinational activity is *not* randomly assigned across countries and sectors, understanding the key drivers behind such selection into multinational activity may be crucial for identification purposes. I will fall short of demonstrating this point in the current book, but I do hope that the stylized models overviewed in Part III will prove to be useful for that purpose.

Practitioners (and perhaps some academics too) might react skeptically to the idea that low-dimensional models may be able to capture the reasoning behind the complex and idiosyncratic decisions of firms in the world economy. Business school cases often highlight the peculiarities of particular organizational decisions, making it hard to envision that much can be gained from extrapolating from those particular cases. The fact that comprehensive datasets on the integration decisions of firms are not readily available might have only compounded this belief, as most empirical studies of integration decisions rely on data from specific industries or firms.[17]

A Comparative Advantage of Trade Statistics

An advantage of studying the global integration decisions of firms is that data on international transactions are particularly accessible due to the widespread existence of official records of goods and services crossing borders. For instance, it is well-known that researchers can easily access data on U.S. imports from any country of the world at the remarkably detailed ten-digit Harmonized Tariff Schedule classification system, which consists of nearly 17,000 categories.[18] A less well-known fact is that, in some countries, these same detailed country- and product-level data contain information on the

---

[17] See Baker and Hubbard (2003) for a particularly careful study using data from the trucking industry, and Lafontaine and Slade (2007) and Bresnahan and Levin (2012) for broad surveys of the empirical literature on vertical integration.

[18] Downloading these data from the NBER website, one can readily verify that in 2001 France exported $15,747 worth of frozen potatoes to the United States (HTS code 2004.10), yet none of those were French fries (HTS code 2004.10.8020)!

extent to which trade flows involve related parties or non-related parties. Most notably, the "U.S. Related-Party Trade" data collected by the U.S. Bureau of Customs and Border Protection and managed by the U.S. Census Bureau provides data on related and non-related-party U.S. imports and exports at the six-digit Harmonized System (HS) classification (which consists of over 5,000 categories) and at the origin/destination country level. This amounts to hundreds of thousands of observations *per year* on the relative prevalence of integration versus non-integration across products and countries.[19]

What do these data tell us about the global sourcing strategies of firms? The first thing that one notices when using U.S. related-party trade data is how predominant intrafirm transactions are in U.S. trade. In 2011, intrafirm imports of goods totaled $1,056.2 billion and constituted a remarkable 48.3 percent of total U.S. imports of goods ($2,186.9 billion). In fact, the share of intrafirm trade has been higher than 46.5 percent in every year since 2000. On the export side, related-party exports are also pervasive, with their share in total U.S. exports ranging from 28 percent to 31 percent in recent years. These figures illustrate the importance of multinational firms for U.S. trade.[20]

A second evident feature of the data is that the share of U.S. intrafirm imports varies widely across countries. On the one hand, in 2011 intrafirm imports equaled 0 for ten countries and territories (including Cuba), all exporting very low volumes to the United States. On the other hand, in that same year the share of intrafirm trade reached a record 89.6 percent for U.S. imports from Western Sahara. Leaving aside communist dictatorships and disputed territories, and focusing on the fifty largest exporters to the United States, Figure 1.3 illustrates that the share of intrafirm trade still varies significantly across countries, ranging from a mere 2.4 percent for Bangladesh to an astonishing 88.5 percent for Ireland.

Similarly, the share of intrafirm trade varies widely depending on the type of product being imported. Again, the raw data contain infrequently traded goods with shares equal to 0 and 100, but even when focusing on the top 20 six-digit HS manufacturing industries by importing volume, in Figure 1.4 one observes significant variation in the share of intrafirm trade,

---

[19] The U.S. Related Party Trade data are publicly available at: http://sasweb.ssd.census.gov/relatedparty/. This website permits downloading the data at the six-digit NAICS level. The finer six-digit Harmonized System (HS) data are available from the U.S. Census for a fee, but I have also made them available at http://scholar.harvard.edu/antras/books.

[20] In contrast, Atalay, Hortacsu, and Syverson (2013) study intrafirm shipments across U.S. multiplant firms and find that these constitute a very small share of total shipments, a finding that they interpret as indicating that firm boundaries are shaped by issues related to the transfer of intangible inputs, rather than of physical goods. However, as argued above, contractual insecurity in the exchange of physical inputs is much more significant in international transactions than in domestic ones, and thus firm boundaries might well be shaped by different factors in cross-border relationships than in the domestic ones in the Atalay et al. (2013) database.

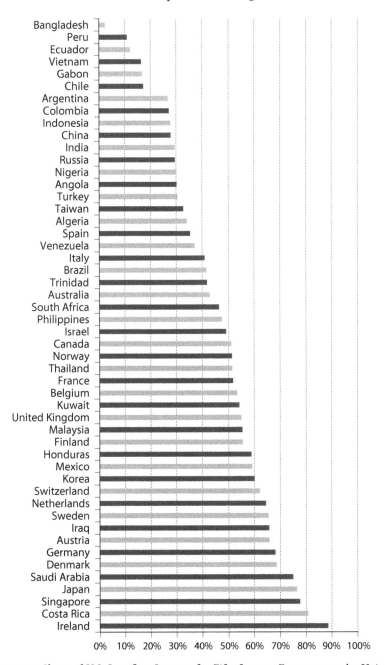

Figure 1.3 Share of U.S. Intrafirm Imports for Fifty Largest Exporters to the United States in 2011. Source: U.S. Census Related-Party Trade Database

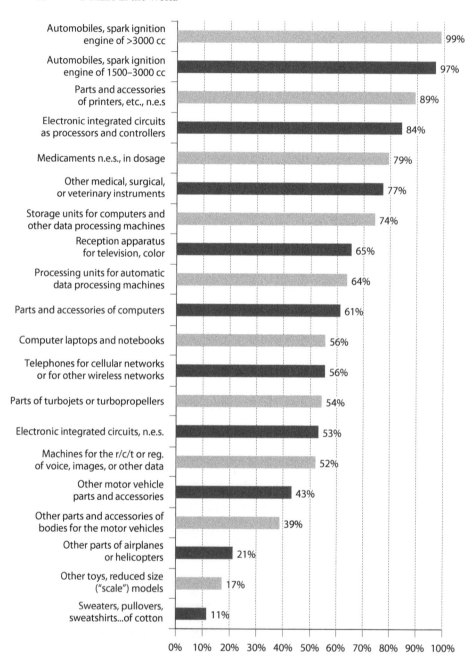

Figure 1.4 Share of U.S. Intrafirm Imports in Top Twenty Industries by U.S. Import Volume in 2011. Source: U.S. Census Related-Party Trade Database

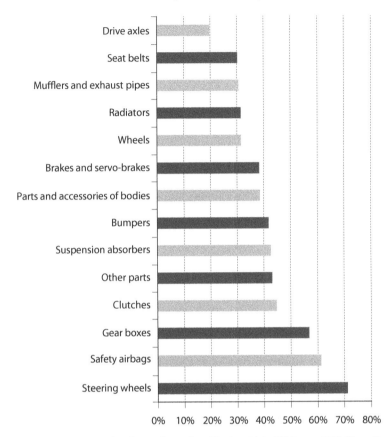

Figure 1.5 Variation in the Share of Intrafirm Trade within HS Sector 8708 (Auto Parts) in 2011. Source: U.S. Census Related-Party Trade Database

which ranges from a share of 11.4 percent for U.S. imports of sweaters, pullovers, and sweatshirts made of cotton (HS 611020) to 98.8 percent for imports of automobiles with engines of more than 3000 cc (HS 870324). This variation persists even when focusing on much narrower sectors. As shown in Figure 1.5, when analyzing imports across subcategories of the four-digit Harmonized System sector 8708 ("Parts and accessories of motor vehicles"), the share of intrafirm trade still ranges from 19.8 percent for drive axles (HS 870850) to 71.2 percent for steering wheels (HS 870894). It is thus clear that U.S.-based producers appear to source different auto parts under quite different ownership structures.

As a final illustration of the richness and variation in the data, consider the six-digit HS industry with the largest share of intrafirm imports in Figure 1.5, namely HS 870894 (steering wheels, columns, and boxes for motor vehicles).

Figure 1.6 reports the share of intrafirm trade for all fifty-six countries with positive exports to the United States in that sector. As is clear from the graph, even when focusing on a narrowly defined component, a similar pattern to that in Figure 1.3 emerges, with U.S.-based producers appearing to source particular inputs quite differently depending on the location from which these products are bought. Imports from seventeen of the fifty-six countries are exclusively transacted at arm's length, while one country (Liechtenstein) sells steering wheels to the United States almost exclusively within multinational firm boundaries. The remaining thirty-eight countries feature shares of intrafirm trade fairly uniformly distributed between 0 and 100 percent.

The large variation in the relative importance of intrafirm transactions across types of goods and countries might seem to validate the skeptics' view that the decision to integrate or outsource foreign production processes is largely driven by idiosyncratic factors that cannot possibly be captured by parsimonious models of the organization decisions of firms. If that were the case, however, not only would we observe large variation in the share of intrafirm trade, but we would also expect this variation to be uncorrelated with simple industry- or country-level variables. As first demonstrated by Antràs (2003), the evidence suggests otherwise. Chapter 8 will describe in detail several stylized facts regarding the intrafirm component of trade. As a sneak preview, Figures 1.7 and 1.8 illustrate that the share of intrafirm imports in total U.S. imports is significantly higher, the higher the U.S. capital intensity in production of the good being imported, and is also significantly higher, the higher the capital-labor ratio of the exporting country. These scatter plots suggest that, as argued above, there may indeed be some common fundamental factors that shape the integration decisions of firms across sectors and countries. The theories of internalization exposited in Chapters 6 and 7 will attempt to shed some light on these factors and will provide a valuable lens through which to study the intrafirm trade data in a more formal and structured manner.

While several features of the U.S. Related-Party Trade database make it particularly attractive to empirical researchers, it has some important limitations. Some of the shortcomings of the data relate to the extent to which the characteristics of the data permit a formal test of the theories of internalization developed later in the book, so it is convenient to postpone that discussion until after we have covered those theories in Chapters 6 and 7. Other potential limitations are more fundamental, so it is important to tackle them up front.

The U.S. database defines "related-party imports" as import transactions between parties with various types of relationships, including "any person directly or indirectly, owning, controlling or holding power to vote, 6 percent of the outstanding voting stock or shares of any organization." A first natural

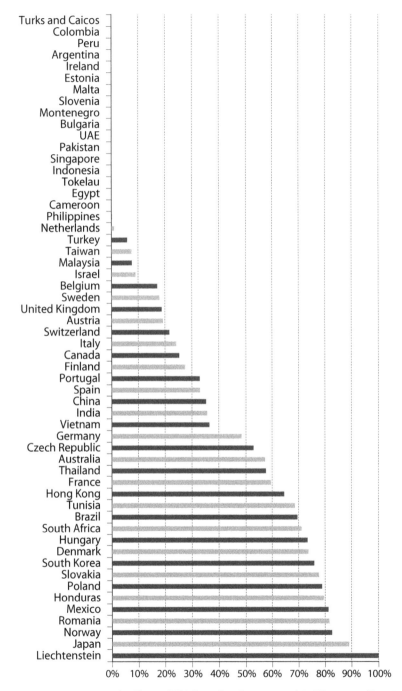

Figure 1.6 Variation in the Share of U.S. Intrafirm Imports within HS 870884 (Steering Wheels) in 2011. Source: U.S. Census Related-Party Trade Database

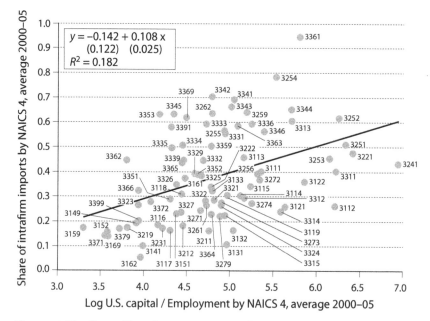

Figure 1.7 The Share of Intrafirm U.S. Imports and Capital Intensity. Source: U.S. Census Related-Party Trade Database and NBER-CES Manufacturing Industry Database

concern is that the 6 percent threshold might be too low for that "relatedness" to have any significant economic meaning, such as one of the entities having a *controlling* stake in the other entity. In practice, however, extracts from the confidential foreign direct investment dataset collected by the Bureau of Economic Analysis suggest that intrafirm trade is generally associated with one of the entities having a majority-ownership stake in the other entity. More specifically, in 2009, of all U.S. imports associated with U.S. parents purchasing goods from their affiliates, 93.8 percent involved majority-owned foreign affiliates. Similarly, majority-owned U.S. affiliates accounted for 95.5 percent of U.S. imports by all U.S. affiliates of foreign companies in 2009.[21]

A second general concern relates to overall quality of the data. In that respect, the technical documentation that accompanies the dataset stresses that the data are not subject to sampling error, since an indicator of whether the transaction involves related parties or not is required for *all* import or export transactions recorded by the U.S. Bureau of Customs and Border

[21] See Table 9 in http://www.bea.gov/scb/pdf/2011/11%20November/1111_mnc.pdf, and Table I.A.1 in http://www.bea.gov/international/pdf/fdius_2009p/I%20A1%20to%20I%20A9.pdf.

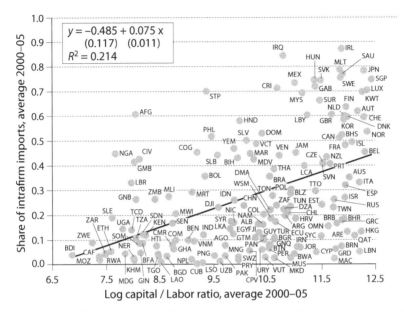

$$y = -0.485 + 0.075\,x$$
$$(0.117) \quad (0.011)$$
$$R^2 = 0.214$$

Figure 1.8 The Share of Intrafirm U.S. Imports and Capital Abundance. Source: U.S. Census Related-Party Trade Database and Penn World Tables (using perpetual inventory method of Caselli, 2005)

Protection. Despite this requirement, importers and exporters do not always report that information in their shipment documents. Luckily, these transactions are categorized on the data tables as "nonreported," so it is easily verified that these account for a very low share of trade volumes (for instance, just 1.4 percent of total imports in 2011). One might also worry about nonsampling errors related to the imputation of trade values for undocumented shipments and for low-valued transactions (which are sometimes estimated). Nevertheless, quality assurance procedures are performed at every stage of collection, processing, and tabulation, thus there is no reason to believe that these data are any less reliable than U.S. customs data on trade flows.[22]

One way to gain reassurance regarding the usefulness of the data is to see whether it delivers patterns that are consistent with what one would expect based on independent and reliable sources of data. For example, from a quick search of press releases from recent years, one learns that in 2005, Boston-based Gillette Company completed the construction of a 120 million-euro plant in Łódź (Poland), which manufactures disposable razors and other shaving products.[23] Although production was mostly directed to

[22] Ruhl (2013) provides a useful overview of alternative U.S. intrafirm trade data sources.
[23] See http://www.paiz.gov.pl/nowosci/?id_news=502.

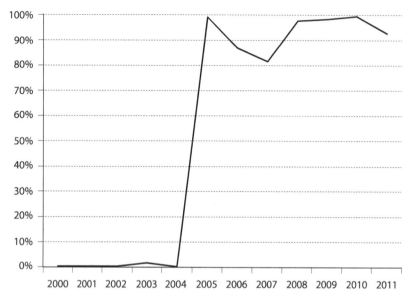

Figure 1.9 Share of Intrafirm Imports of NAICS 332211 (Razors) from Poland. Source: U.S. Census Related-Party Trade Database

the European market, it seems reasonable to assume that some of the products produced in the plant were shipped back to the United States, a transaction that would naturally occur within firm boundaries. As shown in Figure 1.9, it is reassuring to observe that the share of intrafirm imports in total U.S. imports from Poland of NAICS code 332211, which is dominated by non-electric razors and razor blades, went up dramatically around the time of the plant opening, jumping from essentially 0 percent in 2004 to close to 100 percent from 2005 onward.

Back to the Location Decision

We have emphasized above that the internalization decisions of firms in the global economy cannot be understood without appealing to contractual frictions, and we have also illustrated the importance of these frictions in the real world. It seems natural, however, to posit that imperfect contracting not only shapes the ownership structure decisions of firms but might also impact their geographical location decisions. As emphasized by neoclassical models of offshoring, profit-maximizing firms will organize production in a cost-minimizing manner, but the effective costs of doing international business are not explained solely by the factors highlighted by neoclassical theory. Certainly, other things equal, wages will tend to be relatively lower in relatively labor-abundant countries. And, other things equal, costs of production will also tend to be relatively low in countries or regions where the technologies used in production are particularly advanced. Yet, firms might be reluctant to offshore production lines to low-wage countries where suppliers are unreliable and tend not to honor their contracts, and where local courts are unlikely to effectively enforce contracts. Similarly, firms might be unwilling to operate in countries in which their advanced technologies could be effectively deployed (given the existence of local complementary factors), but in which the contractual environment might not provide enough security to firms, in terms of quality contracting but also in terms of the risk of intellectual property rights expropriation.

A key factor that makes contractual aspects important for sourcing decisions is the existence of huge variation among countries in judicial quality and contract enforcement. Empirical researchers often make use of easily accessible measures of the quality of the rule of law which are themselves based on weighted averages of various indices of the perceived effectiveness and predictability of courts in different countries. An advantage to these widely used measures, such as the "Rule of Law" variable produced by the Worldwide Governance Indicators, is that they capture broad features of the contracting environment. A disadvantage is that they are partly based on subjective assessments rather than objective measures of institutional quality. Furthermore, they may provide a useful ordinal measure of legal quality but they are less well equipped to help quantify the existence of cross-country heterogeneity in judicial quality and contract enforcement.

Djankov, La Porta, Lopez-De-Silanes, and Shleifer (2003) have proposed an ingenious alternative measure of judicial quality which is narrower in nature but more powerful in illustrating the relevance of differences in the legal system across countries. In particular, Djankov al. (2003) estimate for 109 countries the time it takes a plaintiff using an official court to evict a nonpaying tenant and to collect a bounced check. Figure 1.10 depicts the second of these two variables, which is more likely to be of relevance for firms considering doing business in a particular country. Their estimated total duration of a legal procedure aimed at collecting a bounced check ranges from 7 days in Tunisia to 1,003 in Slovenia. Even when focusing on the forty-three of the top fifty largest exporters to the United States for which they provide data, the estimated duration ranges from 39 days for the Netherlands to 645 days for Italy.

The extent of contractual insecurity not only varies across countries (or jurisdictions) but it naturally also varies depending on the characteristics of the goods being transacted. For instance, basic goods with low levels of differentiation and which are traded in relatively thick markets can be relatively safely procured even from countries with weak contracting

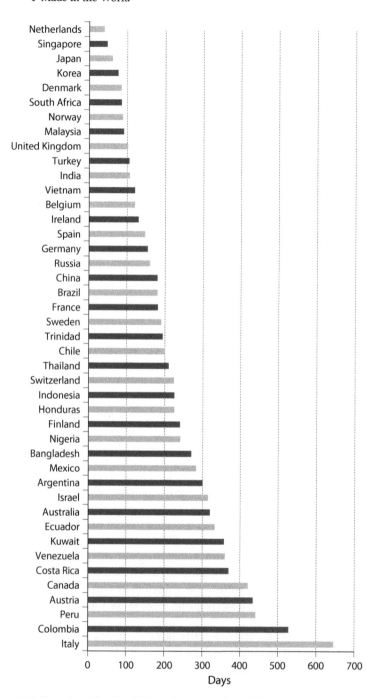

Figure 1.10 Duration of a Legal Procedure Aimed at Collecting a Bounced Check.
Source: Djankov et al. (2003)

institutions. Conversely, transactions involving highly complex or differentiated goods will tend to be much more "contract dependent," and one would expect firms to be significantly more sensitive to the institutional environment when choosing the country from which to procure those goods.

A Brief Road Map

This book will study the various ways in which the contracting environment shapes the location and internalization decisions of firms in the global economy. I will focus first on an analysis of the location decision and how it is affected by contracting factors, and only in Part III of the book will I allow firms to optimally decide the extent of control they want to exert over production processes. This does not follow the chronological order in which these topics were developed in the literature, but I will adopt this sequencing for pedagogical reasons.

Before diving into the world of incomplete contracts, it is necessary, however, to provide an overview of the "complete-contracting" frameworks that will serve as the basis or skeleton for the models to be developed in future chapters. A succinct overview of these models is offered in Chapter 2, to which I turn next. Readers familiar with Melitz's (2003) classic paper and its various extensions might want to jump straight to Part II of the book, starting in Chapter 3.

2
Workhorse Models

The field of international trade has experienced a true revolution in recent years. Firms rather than countries or industries are now the central unit of analysis. The workhorse trade models used by most researchers both in theoretical work as well as in guiding empirical studies were published in the 2000s. The purpose of this chapter is to provide a succinct account of the rich intellectual history of the field and to offer an overview of these modern workhorse models. While these benchmark frameworks ignore contractual aspects, they constitute the backbone of the models developed later in the book, so it is important to gain an understanding of their key features.

Two Centuries of Trade Theory

The recent revolution in the international trade field would perhaps not be apparent when browsing the leading undergraduate textbooks covering the basics of international trade and investment. Neoclassical trade theory still constitutes the core of what we teach college students. This should not be surprising: The concept of comparative advantage is as relevant today as it was almost two hundred years ago when David Ricardo initiated the formal modeling of foreign trade in his *Principles of Political Economy and Taxation* (1817). The first 170 years of the international trade field were largely devoted to refining Ricardo's rudimentary description of the gains from specialization. The benchmark two-good, two-country Ricardian model found in most introductory textbooks is the culmination of an intellectual endeavor to which John Stuart Mill, Frank Graham, and Lionel McKenzie contributed key advances.

Starting with the work of Eli Heckscher and his disciple Bertil Ohlin, another branch of the neoclassical theory studied models in which comparative advantage is endogenously shaped by the interaction of differences in relative factor abundance across countries and differences in relative factor intensities across sectors. The formalization of the so-called Heckscher-Ohlin model is often associated with the great Paul Samuelson, but Abba Lerner,

Ronald Jones, and Alan Deardorff should also be credited for particularly significant contributions.[1]

The core theorems of neoclassical trade theory—the Heckscher-Ohlin, the Stolper-Samuelson, and the Rybczinski theorems—are the product of these intellectual efforts. These beautiful and incredibly sharp results still shape the way most economists think about the determinants and consequences of international trade flows. Why is China the single largest exporter to the United States? How does trade with China affect the relative pay of skilled and unskilled workers in the United States? How does immigration affect sectoral employment in the United States? You would be hard-pressed to answer these questions without appealing to the insights of neoclassical theory.

Neoclassical trade models deliver sharp results but also make strong assumptions. The benchmark models assume a very low number of goods and factors, often only two of each. In higher-dimensional environments, the classical theorems become much less beautiful and much less sharp.[2] More importantly, in neoclassical models, technology is typically assumed to feature constant returns to scale and market structure is characterized by perfect competition, thus making these frameworks of limited use for firm-level studies of international trade. Indeed, in neoclassical trade theory it is not firms but rather countries that trade with each other.

Trade theory witnessed a first revolution in the late 1970s and early 1980s when a group of young trade economists, led by Paul Krugman and Elhanan Helpman, developed new models attempting to account for some empirical patterns that were hard to reconcile with neoclassical theory. Most notably, traditional theory rationalized the existence of mutually beneficial intersectoral trade flows stemming from cross-country differences in technology or endowments. In the real world, however, the bulk of trade flows occurs between countries with similar levels of technological development and similar relative factor endowments, and a significant share of world trade is accounted for by two-way flows within fairly narrowly defined sectors (i.e., "intraindustry" instead of intersectoral trade).

This new wave of research, which was dubbed "new trade theory," emphasized the importance of increasing returns to scale, imperfect competition, and product differentiation in accounting for these salient features of the data. Intuitively, even two completely identical countries will find it mutually

---

[1] A lucid exposition of neoclassical trade theory with extensive references can be found in Jones and Neary (1984).

[2] It is important to emphasize, however, that the implications of the theory for the net factor content of trade—the so-called Vanek (1968) equations—have been shown to be robust to variation in the number of goods and factors. It is no surprise then that beginning with the seminal work of Leamer (1984), empirical testing of the Heckscher-Ohlin model has largely focused on these factor content predictions (see Trefler, 1993a, 1995; Davis and Weinstein, 2001; and Trefler and Zhu, 2010).

beneficial to trade with each other as long as specializing in particular *differentiated* varieties of a sector's goods allows producers to expand their sales and operate at lower average costs, as would naturally be the case whenever technology features *economies of scale*. The relevance of *imperfect competition* for these theories stems from the simple fact that (internal) economies of scale are inconsistent with perfect competition.

A key hurdle facing the pioneers of new trade theory was the absence of a generally accepted modeling of product differentiation and imperfect competition. While there is only one way in which goods can be perfectly homogeneous, there are many ways in which products can be differentiated. Differentiation can arise because individual consumers enjoy spreading their income across different varieties of particular goods (as in the case of cultural goods), or because different consumers prefer to consume different varieties or qualities of the same good (as with tablets or cars). Even when focusing on one of these modeling approaches, there remains the issue of how to mathematically characterize product differentiation in preferences. Similarly, there is only one way in which markets can be perfectly competitive, while there are various possible approaches to modeling imperfect competition.

There are two main reasons why new trade theory was able to overcome these difficulties and become mainstream in a relatively short period of time. First, researchers quickly converged in the use of *a particular* modeling of product differentiation and market structure associated with Krugman (1979, 1980), who in turn borrowed from Dixit and Stiglitz (1977). This served the important role of providing a common language for researchers in the field to communicate among themselves. Still, the heavy use of specific functional forms in representing preferences and technology was viewed with some reservations by the old guard in the field.[3]

The second key factor in the success of new trade theory was the publication of a landmark treatise by Helpman and Krugman (1985). This concise book established the generality of most of the insights from Krugman's work and also illustrated how the new features of new trade theory could be embedded into neoclassical trade theory. As a result, these new hybrid models could explain the features of the data that motivated the new models, while at the same time preserving the validity of some of the salient results from neoclassical theory, such as the Vanek (1968) equations characterizing the factor content of trade. With the publication of this manuscript, the walls of resistance came tumbling down, new trade theory became the new paradigm,

---

[3] As an illustration of this resistance, Krugman's 1979 seminal article was rejected by the *Quarterly Journal of Economics* in 1978 and was subsequently salvaged by Jagdish Bhagwati at the *Journal of International Economics* despite two negative referee reports (see Gans and Shepherd, 1994; note however that Ethier, 2001, offers a slightly less glorifying account of Bhagwati's role in rescuing the paper at the *JIE*).

and Krugman's modeling choices gained a prominent spot in the toolbox of trade theorists (and of applied theorists in other fields).

In recent years, international trade theory has witnessed a second revolution which in many respects parallels the one witnessed thirty years ago. As in the case of new trade theory, and consistent with Kuhn's (1996) description of the structure of scientific revolutions, the need for a new paradigm was fueled by the discovery of a series of new empirical facts that were inconsistent with new trade theory models. To understand these inconsistencies, it is important to note that in Krugman-style models, all firms within a sector are treated symmetrically. Although firms produce differentiated products, they do so under a common cost function, and all varieties enter symmetrically into demand with an elasticity of substitution between any pair of varieties that is constant and common for any pair. As a result, firm behavior within an industry is "homogeneous." Furthermore, under the common assumption of iceberg (or ad valorem) trade costs, new trade theory models deliver the stark implication that all firms within a differentiated-good sector will export their output to every single country in the world.

In the 1990s, a wave of empirical papers using newly available longitudinal plant and firm-level data from various countries demonstrated the existence of significant levels of heterogeneity in revenue, productivity, factor inputs, and trade behavior across firms within sectors. In fact, in some cases, heterogeneity in performance was shown to be almost as large within sectors as across sectors (see, for instance, Bernard et al., 2003). With regard to export behavior, studies found that only a small fraction of firms engage in exporting, and that most exporting firms sell only to a few markets. This so-called extensive margin of trade has been shown to be important in order to understand variation in aggregate exports across destination markets. Several studies have also documented that exporters appear to be systematically different from non-exporters: they are larger, more productive, and operate at higher capital and skill intensities. In addition, firm heterogeneity has been shown to be of relevance for assessing the effects of trade liberalization, as those episodes appear to lead to market share reallocations toward more productive firms, thereby fostering aggregate productivity via new channels.

Access to micro-level data has also served to confirm the importance of multinational firms in world trade. For instance, according to 2009 data from the Bureau of Economic Analysis, 75 percent of the sales by U.S. firms in foreign markets is carried out by foreign affiliates of U.S. multinational enterprises (MNEs), and only 25 percent by exports from the United States (Antràs and Yeaple, 2013). Furthermore, not only do intrafirm trade flows constitute a very significant share of world trade flows (as mentioned in Chapter 1), but an important share of the volume of arm's-length international trade is accounted for by transactions involving multinational firms as buyers or sellers. For instance, data from the U.S. Census Bureau indicate that roughly

90 percent of U.S. exports and imports flow through multinational firms (Bernard et al., 2009). New trade theory did not ignore the importance of multinational firms or intrafirm trade in the world economy (see Helpman, 1984; or Helpman and Krugman, 1985, chapters 12 and 13), but by focusing on complete-contracting, homogeneous-firm models, it was unable to account for central aspects of multinational activity, such as the rationale for internalizing foreign transactions and the existence of heterogeneous participation of firms in FDI (or affiliate) sales and in global sourcing.[4]

Motivated by these new empirical findings, recent trade theory has been developed in frameworks that incorporate intraindustry firm heterogeneity. The seminal paper in the literature is that of Melitz (2003), which follows closely the structure of Krugman (1980). Although Melitz's framework features no multinational activity, no global sourcing, and no contractual frictions, it is natural to begin our incursion into theoretical territory with a variant of his model.

A Multi-Sector Melitz Model

Consider a world consisting of J countries that produce goods in $S+1$ sectors using a unique (composite) factor of production, labor, which is inelastically supplied and freely mobile across sectors. One sector produces a homogeneous good z, while the remaining S sectors produce a continuum of differentiated products. Preferences are identical everywhere in the world and given by:

$$U = \beta_z \log z + \sum_{s=1}^{S} \beta_s \log Q_s, \tag{2.1}$$

with $\beta_z + \sum_{s=1}^{S} \beta_s = 1$ and

$$Q_s = \left(\int_{\omega \in \Omega_s} q_s(\omega)^{(\sigma_s-1)/\sigma_s} \, d\omega \right)^{\sigma_s/(\sigma_s-1)}, \quad \sigma_s > 1. \tag{2.2}$$

It is worth pausing to discuss the specific assumptions we have already built into the model. The preferences in (2.1) feature a unit elasticity of substitution across sectors, so industry spending shares are constant. Within differentiated-good sectors, the preferences in (2.2) are of the Dixit-Stiglitz

---

[4] The fact that firms engaged in FDI sales and in importing appear to be distinct from other firms has been documented by, among others, Helpman, Melitz, and Yeaple (2004); and Bernard, Jensen and Schott (2009). In addition, Ramondo, Rappoport, and Ruhl (2013) have recently documented that U.S. intrafirm trade appears to be highly concentrated among a small number of large foreign affiliates.

type: There is a continuum of varieties available to consumers and these enter preferences symmetrically and with a constant, higher-than-one-elasticity of substitution between any pair of varieties. These assumptions are special, but they are standard in the international trade field. In particular, the preferences in (2.1) and (2.2) are a strict generalization of those in Krugman (1980) and Melitz (2003), which correspond to the case $\beta_z = 0$ and $S = 1$.[5] I incorporate multiple differentiated-good sectors because this will facilitate the derivation of cross-sectional predictions, while the presence of a homogeneous-good sector will simplify the general equilibrium aspects of the model. I will however consider the Krugman-Melitz, one-sector version of the model at times in the book. It would be valuable to follow the approach of Helpman and Krugman (1985) and work out the robustness of the results below to more general preference structures, but I will not attempt to do so in this book.[6]

Given (2.1), consumers in country j will optimally allocate a share β_z of their spending E_j to good z and a fraction β_s to differentiated-good sector s. I will use the subscripts i and j to refer to countries, with i denoting producing/exporting countries and j denoting consuming/importing countries. In order to keep the notation as neat as possible, I will drop the subscript s associated with differentiated-good sectors and their sector-specific parameters. Similarly, and although the model is dynamic (time runs indefinitely), I will omit time subscripts throughout since I will focus on describing stationary equilibria.

Within a representative differentiated-good sector, consumers allocate spending across varieties to maximize Q in (2.2), which gives rise to the following demand for variety ω in country j:

$$q_j(\omega) = \beta E_j P_j^{\sigma-1} p_j(\omega)^{-\sigma}, \tag{2.3}$$

where $p_j(\omega)$ is the price of variety ω, P_j is the ideal price index associated with (2.2),

$$P_j = \left[\int_{\omega \in \Omega_j} p_j(\omega)^{1-\sigma} \, d\omega \right]^{1/(1-\sigma)}, \tag{2.4}$$

and Ω_j is the set of varieties available to consumers in j.

---

[5] To be precise, the last section of Krugman (1980) develops a two-industry model featuring cross-country differences in demand patterns.

[6] As will become apparent, however, the Cobb-Douglas assumption in (2.1) is of little relevance for the main results derived in future chapters of the book. Also, the literature has developed versions of the Melitz (2003) model with alternative, specific functional forms for the aggregate industry index Q_m (see, for instance, Melitz and Ottaviano; 2008; or Novy, 2013). Relaxing the assumption of a continuum of varieties would severely complicate the analysis by introducing strategic pricing interactions across firms within an industry.

Consider next the supply side of the model. The homogeneous good is produced with labor under conditions of perfect competition, and according to a constant-returns-to-scale technology which is allowed to vary across countries. In particular, output is equal to

$$z_i = L_{zi}/a_{zi}, \tag{2.5}$$

where L_{zi} is the amount of labor in country i allocated to the production of good z, and a_{zi} is country i's unit labor requirement in that sector. The homogeneous good z is freely tradable across countries and will serve as the numéraire in the model.

The differentiated-good industries are instead monopolistically competitive. Each variety is produced by a single firm under a technology featuring increasing returns to scale, and there is free entry into each industry. The existence of internal economies of scale stems from the presence of three types of fixed costs. First, the process of entry and differentiation of a variety entails a fixed cost of f_{ei} units of labor in country i. Second, production of final-good varieties in country i entails an overhead cost equal to f_{ii} units of country i's labor. Finally, firms in country i need to incur an additional fixed "market access" cost equal to f_{ij} units of labor in order to export to country $j \neq i$. These fixed export costs capture costs associated with marketing and distributing goods in foreign markets that need to be incurred regardless of the volume exported. I will specify these costs in terms of the exporting country's labor, but not much would change if they were specified in terms of the importing country's labor. Notice that we do not assume that $f_{ij} > f_{ii}$, but the latter type of fixed costs of production need to be incurred before the firm can sell in any market.

The fixed cost parameters f_{ei}, f_{ii} and f_{ij} are common for all firms within an industry. Intraindustry heterogeneity stems from differences in the marginal cost of production faced by firms. In particular, after incurring the fixed cost of entry f_{ei}, firms learn their productivity level φ, which determines their marginal cost of production, $1/\varphi$, in terms of labor. These productivity levels are drawn independently from a cumulative distribution function $G_i(\varphi)$ which is assumed Pareto with shape parameter $\kappa > \sigma - 1$, so

$$G_i(\varphi) = 1 - \left(\frac{\underline{\varphi}_i}{\varphi} \right)^{\kappa}, \quad \text{for } \varphi \geq \underline{\varphi}_i > 0. \tag{2.6}$$

The assumption $\kappa > \sigma - 1$ is required to ensure a finite variance in the size distribution of firms.

The marginal cost of servicing foreign markets is further magnified by "iceberg" trade costs such that $\tau_{ij} > 1$ units of output need to be shipped from country i for 1 unit to make it to country j. The firm productivity parameter φ is time invariant, but firms face a common, exogenous probability $\delta \in (0, 1)$

of being subject to a (really) bad shock that would force them to exit, which keeps the value of the firm bounded for any φ.

When selling to local consumers, firms need not incur variable trade costs ($\tau_{ii} = 1$) nor market access costs in excess of the production fixed cost f_{ii}. Under the mild assumption that any firm with positive production sells some amount of output in their domestic market, we can then succinctly express the cost for a firm with productivity φ of producing q units of output in country i and selling them in country j as

$$C_{ij}(q) = \left(f_{ij} + \frac{\tau_{ij}}{\varphi} q \right) w_i. \tag{2.7}$$

Note that the formula in (2.7) applies for foreign ($i \neq j$) as well as for domestic sales ($i = j$).

This completes the description of the model. Before discussing some features of the equilibrium, it is worth briefly relating the model above to other ones in the literature. The structure of the model is most closely related to that of the multi-sector Melitz models in Arkolakis, Demidova, Klenow, and Rodríguez-Clare (2008), and Helpman, Melitz, and Rubinstein (2008).[7] The original model in Melitz (2003) corresponds to the particular case in which $\beta_z = 0$ and $S = 1$, and parameters are fully symmetric across countries, so $f_{ei} = f_e$, $f_{ii} = f$, $f_{ij} = f_X$, $\tau_{ij} = \tau$ and $L_i = L$, where L_i is the stock of labor in country i.[8] As hinted above, the seminal paper of Krugman (1980)—except for its last section—is also a special case of the framework above, in which on top of the assumptions in Melitz (2003), there are no fixed marketing costs $f_X = 0$ and the distribution of productivity $G_i(\varphi)$ is degenerate, so firms are homogeneous.[9]

Selection into Exporting

I next illustrate how this simple model is able to explain some of the firm-level exporting facts discussed above. Given the isoleastic demand in (2.3), firms will charge a price in each market in which they sell equal to a constant

---

[7] Melitz and Redding (2013a) have recently used a model with a very similar structure to navigate the literature on heterogeneous firms and trade. Chaney (2008) also develops a multi-sector Melitz framework but does not allow for free entry.

[8] The above model is less general than Melitz (2003) in that I impose that $G_i(\varphi)$ is Pareto, while he considers a general cumulative probability distribution.

[9] A hybrid model in the spirit of Helpman and Krugman (1985) could also be derived from our model (whenever $\beta_z > 0$) if we allowed sectors to use two factors of production (say capital and labor) under different factor intensities. Also, our benchmark model could easily be turned into the standard neoclassical Ricardian and Heckscher-Ohlin models by setting $\sigma \to \infty$ and all fixed costs to 0.

markup $\sigma/(\sigma - 1)$ over the marginal cost of servicing that market. As a result, the potential operating profits for a firm from i with productivity φ considering servicing a particular market j can be concisely written as

$$\pi_{ij}(\varphi) = \left(\tau_{ij} w_i\right)^{1-\sigma} B_j \varphi^{\sigma-1} - w_i f_{ij} \tag{2.8}$$

where

$$B_j = \frac{1}{\sigma} \left(\frac{\sigma}{\sigma - 1}\right)^{1-\sigma} P_j^{\sigma-1} \beta E_j. \tag{2.9}$$

The term B_j will appear repeatedly in this book and can be interpreted as a measure of market (residual) demand of country j.

Notice that $\pi_{ij}(\varphi)$ increases linearly with the transformation of productivity $\varphi^{\sigma-1}$ and that for a sufficiently low φ, $\pi_{ij}(\varphi)$ is necessarily negative. More formally, only the subset of firms from i with productivity $\varphi \geq \tilde{\varphi}_{ij}$, where

$$\tilde{\varphi}_{ij} \equiv \tau_{ij} w_i \left(\frac{w_i f_{ij}}{B_j}\right)^{1/(\sigma-1)}, \tag{2.10}$$

will find it optimal to export to country j. Other things equal, the higher are trade barriers between i and j (τ_{ij} and f_{ij}), the lower will be the share of firms in i choosing to service j. This contrasts with homogeneous firm models, in which all firms from i would sell to all possible markets j.

The model also sheds light on the fact that exporters typically appear to be more productive than non-exporters. In particular, provided that the market demand B_j does not vary too much across countries, and given that $f_{ij} > 0$ for all $j \neq i$, firms will find it relatively harder to profitably sell in foreign markets than in their local market. Furthermore, provided that $\tau^{\sigma-1} f_{ij} > f_{ii}$ for all $j \neq i$, it will necessarily be the case that a positive measure of firms sells domestically but does not export. These intuitive results regarding selection into exporting and productivity differences between exporters and non-exporters are depicted in Figure 2.1. The figure exploits the fact that firm profits $\pi_{ij}(\varphi)$ in (2.8) increase linearly with the transformation of productivity $\varphi^{\sigma-1}$. The lower slope of the export profit line reflects the large variable transport costs $\tau_{ij} > 1$ (remember that we are assuming small differences in market demand across countries). In the figure, it is also assumed that $f_{ij} > f_{ii}$, although we have noted above that $\tau^{\sigma-1} f_{ij} > f_{ii}$ is sufficient to obtain selection into exporting.[10]

---

[10] Note that no matter how low f_{ij} is, whenever B_j is identical across countries, it will never be the case that a firm from i produces *only* for a particular export market $j \neq i$. This is because in such a case, these *pure* exporters would need to incur the overhead costs f_{ii} on top of the marketing costs f_{ij}, and thus we would have $f_{ij} + f_{ii} > f_{ii}$. Lu (2011) shows that a "reverse" sorting is observed among Chinese manufacturing firms, a fact that she attributes to a particularly low value of B_j in labor-intensive industries in China relative to other countries.

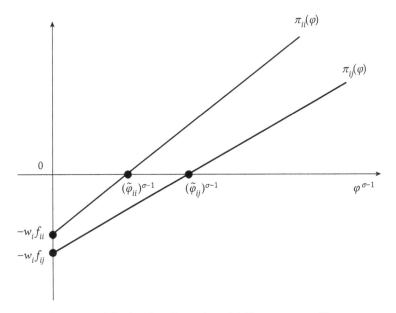

Figure 2.1 Selection into Exporting with Heterogeneous Firms

The Extensive Margin, Gravity, and Reallocation Effects

The logic behind the fact that a model with heterogeneous firms and fixed export costs can deliver selection into exporting based on productivity is hardly earth-shattering. The beauty of the Melitz (2003) model resides in the fact that, despite its simple structure, it can account for several additional features documented in empirical studies. These additional results from the model are less central for the set of results emphasized in this book, but nonetheless it is worth discussing them briefly.

Consider first the implications of the model for aggregate exports at the sectoral level. Letting X_{ij} denote aggregate exports from i to j in a representative differentiated-good sector, and denoting by N_i the measure of potential producers from i in that sector (i.e., the set of firms that have paid the fixed cost of entry $w_i f_{ei}$), we have

$$X_{ij} = N_i \int_{\tilde{\varphi}_{ij}}^{\infty} \sigma \left(\tau_{ij} w_i \right)^{1-\sigma} B_j \varphi^{\sigma-1} dG_i \left(\varphi \right), \qquad (2.11)$$

where we have used (2.8) and the fact that export revenues are a multiple σ of $\pi_{ij} \left(\varphi \right) + w_i f_{ij}$.

A first point to notice is that variation in exporting across destination markets j is composed of an extensive margin and an intensive margin. In particular, we can write

$$X_{ij} = N_{ij} \cdot \bar{x}_{ij}.$$

where $N_{ij} = (1 - G_i(\tilde{\varphi}_{ij}))N_i$ is the actual measure of firms from i selling in j (the extensive margin) and

$$\bar{x}_{ij} = \frac{1}{1 - G_i(\tilde{\varphi}_{ij})} \int_{\tilde{\varphi}_{ij}}^{\infty} \sigma \left(\tau_{ij} w_i\right)^{1-\sigma} B_j \varphi^{\sigma-1} dG_i(\varphi), \tag{2.12}$$

are average firm-level exports (the intensive margin). As first worked out by Arkolakis et al. (2008), when productivity is distributed Pareto as in (2.6), integrating (2.12) and using (2.10) to simplify, delivers

$$\bar{x}_{ij} = \frac{\kappa}{\kappa - \sigma + 1} \sigma w_i f_{ij}, \tag{2.13}$$

and thus the intensive margin is independent of variable trade costs and of market size of the destination country. In other words, the model is consistent with export volumes from i to j being lower for smaller and more distant markets, but the reason for this is very different than in homogeneous-firm models à la Krugman. It is not because firms export on average lower volumes to those markets but rather because a smaller set of firms export to those markets. As shown by Chaney (2008), this is not an immaterial distinction, since it critically affects, for instance, how the elasticity of trade flows with respect to trade frictions depends on the elasticity of substitution σ. Furthermore, as documented for instance by Bernard, Jensen, Redding, and Schott (2009), the available empirical evidence is supportive of the notion that the extensive margin accounts for a much larger share of the cross-sectional variation in trade flows than does the intensive margin.

Another remarkable feature of the model is that it delivers a modified sectoral version of the gravity equation for trade flows, which has been shown to fit the data rather well. As shown by Melitz and Redding (2013a) (see also Chapter 3 for a related derivation), in the Pareto case, aggregate exports in (2.11) can alternatively be expressed as

$$X_{ij} = \frac{Y_i}{\Theta_i} \left(\frac{\beta E_j}{P_j^{1-\sigma}}\right)^{\frac{\kappa}{(\sigma-1)}} \tau_{ij}^{-\kappa} f_{ij}^{-\frac{\kappa-(\sigma-1)}{\sigma-1}}, \tag{2.14}$$

where Y_i is the aggregate industry output in i (i.e., $Y_i \equiv \sum_j X_{ij}$) and Θ_i is a structural measure of country i's market potential in that industry.[11]

---

[11] In particular, $\Theta_i \equiv \sum_j \left(\frac{\beta E_j}{P_j^{1-\sigma}}\right)^{\frac{\kappa}{(\sigma-1)}} \tau_{ij}^{-\kappa} f_{ij}^{-\frac{\kappa-(\sigma-1)}{\sigma-1}}$.

Notice that equation (2.14) structurally justifies the use of empirical log-linear specifications for sectoral trade flows with importer-sector and exporter-sector asymmetric fixed effects and measures of bilateral trade frictions. In the one-sector models of Krugman (1980) and Melitz (2003) (i.e., $\beta_z = 0$ and $S = 1$), the model predicts that the gravity equation will hold for aggregate bilateral trade flows across countries, and as shown by Helpman et al. (2008), for estimation purposes, the model serves a very useful role in structurally correcting for the large number of bilateral zero trade flows in the data (we will cover their contribution in more detail in Chapter 3).

In this same one-sector version of the model, Arkolakis, Costinot, and Rodríguez-Clare (2012) have derived a neat formula for the welfare effects of trade in terms of two sufficient statistics: the import penetration ratio and the elasticity of imports with respect to variable trade costs. Arkolakis et al. (2012) have also shown that, remarkably, this formula is identical to the one obtained in the Anderson and van Wincoop (2003), Eaton and Kortum (2002), and Krugman (1980) models.[12]

One final aspect of the model that is worth discussing is its ability to rationalize the reallocation effects following trade liberalization documented by the empirical literature (see, for instance, Pavcnik, 2002). This is most elegantly derived in the symmetric, one-sector model of Melitz (2003) in which no parametric assumptions on $G_i(\varphi)$ are imposed. Essentially, what Melitz shows is that reductions in trade costs will not only expand the number and revenues of exporting firms, but will also (via competition effects) reduce the scale of non-exporting firms and will also lead to the exit of a set of producers that were marginally profitable before the reduction in trade costs.[13] Formally, in terms of the notation above, Melitz (2003) shows that reductions in trade costs will not only reduce $\tilde{\varphi}_{ij}$, but will also increase $\tilde{\varphi}_{ii}$ thus forcing firms with productivity marginally above $\tilde{\varphi}_{ii}$ to shut down. As discussed by Baldwin and Forslid (2010) and Arkolakis et al. (2008), under certain additional conditions, this may in turn lead to "anti-variety" effects by which the measure of varieties available to consumers decreases following trade liberalization.

The Melitz (2003) model has been extended in a variety of fruitful ways, ranging from the exploration of alternative demand systems, the introduction of Heckscher-Ohlin features into the model, the modeling of

---

[12] Because the import penetration ratio and the "trade elasticity" respond to trade opening in distinct manners in these different frameworks, their results do not necessarily imply, however, that information on the microstructure of these models is irrelevant for assessing the welfare consequences of trade liberalization (see Melitz and Redding, 2013b, for more on this).

[13] Even though the size of continuing exporters increases and that of continuing non-exporters shrinks, in the case in which $G_i(\varphi)$ is Pareto, the extensive margin responses ensure that the average size of exporters and non-exporters will remain unaffected by changes in variable trade barriers, as shown in (2.13).

multi-product firms, and many others. Several applications and extensions of the model are reviewed in Melitz and Redding (2013a). Next I will focus on an extension of the model that is particularly relevant for the study of the global organization of production, which is the central topic of this book.

Global Sourcing with Heterogeneous Firms

In the Melitz (2003) model, the only involvement of firms with foreign markets is via the exportation of final goods produced with local labor. As documented in Chapter 1, the recent process of globalization has led to a disintegration of the production process across borders in which international trade in intermediate inputs has been a dominant feature in the world economy. I next develop a simple variant of the Melitz framework in which firms not only export, but also make global sourcing decisions related to the location and quantity of inputs to buy from different countries.

In order to meaningfully study offshoring, one needs to consider multi-stage production processes, and a natural starting point is a two-stage model. With that in mind, assume that the production of varieties in the differentiated-good sectors now involves two stages, to which we will refer throughout the book as *headquarter services* and *manufacturing production*. Headquarter services may include a variety of activities such as R&D expenditures, brand development, accounting, and finance operations, but may also involve high-tech manufacturing or assembly. The important characteristic of this stage in terms of the model is that these activities need to be produced in the same country in which the entry cost f_{ei} was incurred. Manufacturing production can instead be thought of as entailing low-tech manufacturing or assembly of inputs into a final product. Crucially, we will depart from Melitz (2003) in allowing manufacturing production to be geographically separated from the location of entry and headquarter services provision. This is a highly simplified characterization of the process of offshoring, but we will work to enrich the model later in the book.

Relative to the multi-sector Melitz (2003) framework developed above, the key new decision facing firms is thus whether to maintain plant production in the same country in which entry and headquarter service provision takes place, or whether to offshore that stage. In order to simplify the model and isolate the new insights arising from the modeling of offshoring, we shall assume that there are no costs, fixed or variable, associated with exporting final goods so that the exporting decision is trivial and all firms producing final goods export them worldwide. Conversely, the decision of whether to source locally or engage in offshoring will be nontrivial: offshoring will be associated with a reduction in production costs but will also entail additional fixed and variable transportation costs that might lead some firms to opt out of that strategy.

More formally, the overall costs of producing q units of a final-good variety incurred by a firm with headquarters in country i and manufacturing production in country j (with possibly $j = i$) are given by

$$C_{ij}(q, \varphi) = f_{ij} w_i + \frac{q}{\varphi} (a_{hi} w_i)^\eta \left(\tau_{ij} a_{mj} w_j\right)^{1-\eta}. \tag{2.15}$$

As before, φ is a firm-specific productivity parameter. The parameters f_{ij}, τ_{ij}, η, a_{hi}, and a_{mj} are instead sector-specific but common across firms within a sector s, while the wage rates w_i and w_j vary only across countries. The parameters f_{ij} and τ_{ij} appeared already in the Melitz (2003) model (see equation (2.7)) but their interpretation is somewhat different in the present context. In particular, f_{ij} and τ_{ij} now reflect the fixed and variable trade costs associated with a particular sourcing strategy. Although we will often associate f_{ij} and τ_{ij} with the costs of transporting intermediate inputs across countries, these parameters can be interpreted more broadly to reflect other technological barriers associated with international fragmentation, such as communication costs, language barriers, or search costs. For these reasons, it is now natural to assume not only that $\tau_{ij} > \tau_{ii}$, but also that $f_{ij} > f_{ii}$ whenever $j \neq i$.

Relative to the specification of technology in (2.7), the new parameters are η, a_{hi}, and a_{mj}. The first of these captures the headquarter services intensity (or *headquarter intensity* for short) of the production process, and the associated primal representation of technology (leaving aside fixed costs and trade costs) is a Cobb-Douglas technology in headquarter services h and manufacturing production m:

$$q(\varphi) = \varphi \left(\frac{h(\varphi)}{\eta}\right)^\eta \left(\frac{m(\varphi)}{1-\eta}\right)^{1-\eta}, \quad 0 < \eta < 1. \tag{2.16}$$

Finally, the parameters a_{hi} and a_{mj} capture the unit labor requirements associated with headquarter service provision and manufacturing production and these are allowed to vary across sectors and countries reflecting comparative advantage considerations.

Although the benchmark model of offshoring we have developed is quite stylized, it is a generalization of a complete-contracting variant of the heterogeneous firm model in Antràs and Helpman (2004). In particular, in Antràs and Helpman (2004) it is further assumed that:

- The world consists of only two countries, North and South.
- The homogeneous good z is always produced in both countries but with a higher labor productivity in the North, thus implying that wage rates are fixed at $w^N = 1/a_{zN} > 1/a_{zS} = w^S$.

- The South features either very low productivity in producing headquarter service or very high fixed costs of entry, so that all entry and headquarter service provision occurs in the North, where $a_{hN} = 1$.
- Plant production can be done with the same physical productivity—in particular, $a_{mN} = a_{mS} = 1$—in both North and South, so offshoring to the South offers a production-cost advantage.

With these additional assumptions, and simplifying further the notation by denoting $f_{NN} = f_D$, $f_{NS} = f_O$, $\tau_{NS} = \tau$, the total cost of production associated with **D**omestic sourcing and **O**ffshoring can be written, respectively, as

$$C_D(q, \varphi) = \left(f_D + \frac{q}{\varphi} \right) w_N, \tag{2.17}$$

and

$$C_O(q, \varphi) = f_O w_N + \frac{q}{\varphi} (w_N)^\eta (\tau w_S)^{1-\eta}. \tag{2.18}$$

Selection into Offshoring

We can now study the implications of the above framework for the selection of firms into offshoring. I will focus here on the simplified two-country framework in Antràs and Helpman (2004) since it has featured prominently in the literature, but at the end of the chapter I will discuss how the results can be extended to a multi-country environment.

In light of the cost functions in (2.17) and (2.18), and given that firms charge a price for the final good equal to a constant markup $\sigma/(\sigma - 1)$ over the marginal cost of production, the potential operating profits for a Northern firm with productivity φ associated with Domestic sourcing and Offshoring can be expressed as

$$\pi_D(\varphi) = (w_N)^{1-\sigma} B\varphi^{\sigma-1} - f_D w_N \tag{2.19}$$

and

$$\pi_O(\varphi) = \left((w_N)^\eta (\tau w_S)^{1-\eta} \right)^{1-\sigma} B\varphi^{\sigma-1} - f_O w_N, \tag{2.20}$$

respectively, where

$$B = \frac{1}{\sigma} \left(\frac{\sigma}{(\sigma - 1) P} \right)^{1-\sigma} \beta (w_N L_N + w_S L_S)$$

and P is the common price index in (2.4) in each country, given costless international trade in final goods.

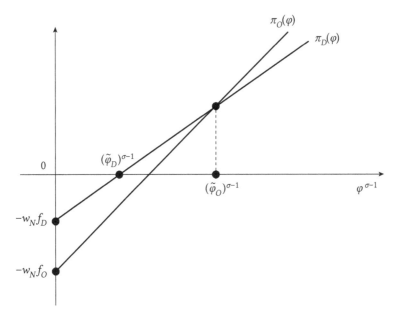

Figure 2.2 Equilibrium Offshoring Sorting with High Wage Differences

As in Melitz (2003), the profit functions $\pi_D(\varphi)$ and $\pi_O(\varphi)$ are linearly increasing in the transformation of productivity $\varphi^{\sigma-1}$ and for a sufficiently low φ, both of these profit levels necessarily take negative values. Hence, upon observing their productivity, the least productive firms in an industry will optimally decide not to produce. Furthermore, the fact that $f_O > f_D$ ensures that for sufficiently low levels of productivity, we have $\pi_D(\varphi) > \pi_O(\varphi)$, and offshoring is not a viable option in situations in which domestic sourcing might be profitable. In fact, whenever

$$f_O > \left(\frac{w_N}{\tau w_S} \right)^{(1-\eta)(\sigma-1)} f_D, \tag{2.21}$$

there always exists a subset of firms in the industry that find it optimal to opt out of offshoring and decide instead to source locally in the North. In order for some firms within the industry to find it optimal to offshore, it is necessary to assume that offshoring trade costs τ are low enough to ensure that $w_N > \tau w_S$. This case is depicted in Figure 2.2, which is also drawn under the implicit assumption that condition (2.21) holds.[14]

---

[14] Notice that, unlike in exporting models, we do not need to make additional assumptions regarding differences in market size across countries to draw Figure 2.2.

TABLE 2.1 Trading Premia in U.S. Manufacturing, 1997

	Exporter Premia	Importer Premia
Log Employment	1.50	1.40
Log Shipments	0.29	0.26
Log Value-Added per Worker	0.23	0.23
Log TFP	0.07	0.12
Log Wage	0.29	0.23
Log Capital per Worker	0.17	0.13
Log Skill per Worker	0.04	0.06

Source: Bernard, Jensen and Schott (2009), table 8.

As shown by Figure 2.2, the model features selection into offshoring by which only the most productive firms within an industry find it worthwhile to pay the fixed costs of fragmentation to benefit from the lower production costs associated with manufacturing in the South.[15] In particular, offshoring is the preferred option only for firms with productivity $\varphi \geq \tilde{\varphi}_O$, where

$$\tilde{\varphi}_O \equiv \left(\frac{f_O - f_D}{B} \frac{w_N}{\left((w_N)^\eta (\tau w_S)^{1-\eta} \right)^{1-\sigma} - (w_N)^{1-\sigma}} \right)^{1/(\sigma-1)}.$$

The sorting pattern in Figure 2.2 is consistent with the evidence on selection into importing in Bernard, Jensen, Redding, and Schott (2007), who show that not only U.S. exporting firms but also U.S. importing firms appear to be more productive than purely domestic producers. Their results are reproduced in Table 2.1, which shows that U.S. manufacturing plants engaged in importing employ more workers, sell more, are more productive, pay higher wages, and are more capital- and skill-intensive than plants that do not source abroad.

More specifically, firms that import appear to be 12 percent more productive than firms that do not, while the productivity advantage of exporting plants is only 7 percent. Furthermore, according to Bernard et al. (2007), only 14 percent of U.S. manufacturing plants report positive imports (versus 27 percent of plants reporting positive exports), which is again suggestive of the existence of significant fixed costs of importing.

One might be concerned that the patterns observed by Bernard et al. (2007) do not necessarily support the sorting pattern implied by the theory because it is unclear whether the goods that firms are importing are intermediate inputs, rather than finished goods. In the latter case, one might worry that

---

[15] In the much less interesting case in which $w_N < \tau w_S$, no firm in the industry finds it optimal to offshore and if this condition holds for all sectors of the economy, then the South is fully specialized in the production of the homogeneous good z.

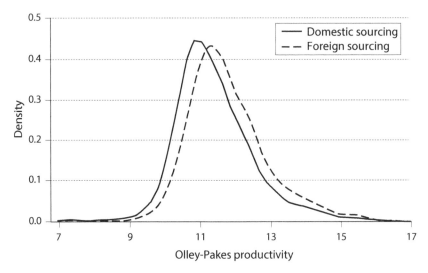

Figure 2.3 Selection into Offshoring in Spain

Table 2.1 is simply picking the role of large intermediaries (wholesalers or retailers) in bringing consumer goods into the United States. The fact that the importer premia reported in Table 2.1 correspond to the operations of U.S. *manufacturing* firms should, however, dispel that concern. Furthermore, recent work by Fort (2014) using U.S. Census data demonstrates that a similar sorting pattern is observed when focusing on imports of contract manufacturing services, which cover exclusively offshoring of inputs that are customized to specific U.S. firms' production needs. More specifically, Fort (2014) finds that U.S. firms that offshore contract manufacturing services feature on average 13 percent higher valued-added labor productivity than U.S. firms in the same six-digit NAICS that purchase those services only domestically.

Figure 2.3 provides further confirmation of the superior performance of offshoring firms with 2007 data from the Spanish Encuesta sobre Estrategias Empresariales (ESEE). The dataset distinguishes between firms that purchase inputs only from other Spanish producers and firms that purchase inputs from abroad. More details on this dataset will be provided in Chapter 8. As is clear from Figure 2.3, the distribution of productivity of firms that engage in foreign sourcing is a shift to the right of that of firms that only source locally.[16]

---

[16] Total factor productivity is computed according to the Olley and Pakes (1996) methodology, which attempts to correct for simultaneity biases associated with how variable input demand is shaped by total factor productivity.

Determinants of the Prevalence of Offshoring

We can next use this simple model of global sourcing to study the determinants of the relative prevalence of offshoring in an industry. For instance, consider computing the share of spending on *imported* manufacturing inputs over total manufacturing input purchases in a particular industry. Given the Cobb-Douglas technology in (2.16) and the CES preferences in (2.1), manufacturing input purchases will constitute a share $(\sigma - 1)(1 - \eta)/\sigma$ of revenue for all firms, while revenue itself will be a multiple σ of firm operating profits (defined as revenue minus variable costs). Using the profit functions (2.19) and (2.20) and cancelling common terms, we can thus express the share of imported manufacturing input purchases in a given industry as

$$
\Upsilon_O = \frac{\left(\frac{w_N}{\tau w_S}\right)^{(1-\eta)(\sigma-1)} \int_{\tilde{\varphi}_O}^{\infty} \varphi^{\sigma-1} dG(\varphi)}{\int_{\tilde{\varphi}_D}^{\tilde{\varphi}_O} \varphi^{\sigma-1} dG(\varphi) + \left(\frac{w_N}{\tau w_S}\right)^{(1-\eta)(\sigma-1)} \int_{\tilde{\varphi}_O}^{\infty} \varphi^{\sigma-1} dG(\varphi)}.
$$

Particularly sharp results can be obtained when assuming that the distribution of firm productivity is Pareto as in equation (2.6), in which case we obtain

$$
\Upsilon_O = \frac{\left(\frac{w_N}{\tau w_S}\right)^{(1-\eta)(\sigma-1)}}{\left(\frac{\tilde{\varphi}_O}{\tilde{\varphi}_D}\right)^{\kappa-(\sigma-1)} - 1 + \left(\frac{w_N}{\tau w_S}\right)^{(1-\eta)(\sigma-1)}}, \tag{2.22}
$$

where

$$
\frac{\tilde{\varphi}_O}{\tilde{\varphi}_D} = \left[\frac{f_O/f_D - 1}{(w_N/\tau w_S)^{(1-\eta)(\sigma-1)} - 1}\right]^{1/(\sigma-1)}. \tag{2.23}
$$

As indicated by equations (2.22) and (2.23), the prevalence of offshoring is naturally increasing in the wage gap (w_N/w_S) and decreasing in fragmentation barriers $(f_O/f_D, \tau)$. These comparative statics are quite intuitive. Note that the elasticity of substitution σ and the parameter κ governing the thickness of the right tail of the Pareto distribution also have an impact on the prevalence of offshoring in an industry. The intuition for these effects is analogous to that in Helpman, Melitz, and Yeaple (2004). In particular, the Pareto parameterization of productivity combined with CES preferences imply that the distribution of sales of all active firms is also Pareto with shape parameter $\kappa/(\sigma - 1)$. As a result, a decrease in κ raises the sales and input purchases of firms with productivity $\varphi > \tilde{\varphi}_O$—i.e., firms that find offshoring optimal, relative to the sales and input purchases of firms with productivity $\varphi \in (\tilde{\varphi}_D, \tilde{\varphi}_O)$—i.e., firms that source domestically. Because the standard deviation of the logarithm of sales by all active firms in the industry is equal to $(\sigma - 1)/\kappa$, this result can be interpreted as indicating that the prevalence of offshoring should be higher in industries with a larger dispersion in firm size.[17]

Note that the elasticity of substitution σ affects positively the share of imported inputs for an additional reason—see the exponent of $w_N/(\tau w_S)$ in (2.22) and (2.23). The intuition for this effect is simpler: the more substitutable final-good varieties are, the more elastic will demand be and the higher will be the incentive of firms to engage in a costly investment (in this case offshoring) to reduce the marginal cost of input provision from w_N down to τw_S.

Back to the Multi-Country Model

Having worked with a simplified two-country model to build intuition, we can now go back to the multi-country environment in which the overall costs of producing q units of a final-good variety faced by a firm with headquarters in country i and manufacturing production in country j are given by equation (2.15). Given CES preferences over final-good varieties, it is then straightforward to show that the operating profits associated with that sourcing strategy are given by

$$\pi_{ij}(\varphi) = \left((a_{hi} w_i)^{\eta} \left(\tau_{ij} a_{mj} w_j \right)^{1-\eta} \right)^{1-\sigma} B \varphi^{\sigma-1} - f_{ij} w_i, \qquad (2.24)$$

where market demand B is now given by

$$B = \frac{1}{\sigma} \left(\frac{\sigma}{(\sigma - 1) P} \right)^{1-\sigma} \beta \sum_j w_j L_j$$

and P is the common price index (2.4) for final-good varieties in each country.

Equation (2.24) illustrates again that the profit levels associated with different sourcing strategies are all linear in $\varphi^{\sigma-1}$ and thus the sourcing decision of firms can be analyzed with graphs analogous to that in Figure 2.2. Of course, with multiple countries the range of possible sorting patterns is much more complex, but we can still derive some general results.

For instance, as long as $f_{ij} > f_{ii}$ for all $j \neq i$, so domestic sourcing is the sourcing strategy associated with the lowest fixed costs, the model can only deliver a positive amount of offshoring in an industry whenever

---

[17] Other measures of industry firm size dispersion, such as the Theil index, also vary monotonically with $(\sigma - 1)/\kappa$.

$\tau_{ij}a_{mj}w_j < a_{mi}w_i$ for some country $j \neq i$. Importantly, in such a case, if firms sourcing domestically and abroad coexist within an industry, then firms that offshore are necessarily larger and more productive than firms that source domestically. In sum, under the plausible condition $f_{ij} > f_{ii}$ for all $j \neq i$, the model continues to predict selection into offshoring based on productivity in a manner consistent with the U.S. import premia in Table 2.1 and with the evidence from Spain depicted in Figure 2.3.

It is also noteworthy that in contrast to the simple two-country model above, this multi-country extension of the model can easily generate two-way intermediate input trade flows across countries. For instance, a given country i can feature a high manufacturing productivity level $1/a_{mj}$ in some industries and a very low one in others. In the former type of industries, this country i may well export inputs to firms with headquarters located in other countries (particularly when country i's productivity in headquarter provision is low in that industry), while it may well import manufacturing inputs in the latter type of industries.[18]

With multiple countries, firms not only decide whether to offshore manufacturing production or not but also choose the optimal location of production among all possible ones. It is evident that, other things equal, firms based in country i will be drawn to locations j entailing low fixed costs of sourcing f_{ij} and low variable costs of manufacturing, as summarized by $\tau_{ij}a_{mj}w_j$. Some highly productive firms might, however, be drawn to locations with high sourcing fixed costs as long as those locations offer a particularly favorable marginal cost of input manufacturing.

Figure 2.4 depicts a possible equilibrium in a world of four countries— a "Home" country i and three "Foreign" countries j, k, and l. Domestic sourcing is the lowest fixed cost sourcing strategy, and as argued above, this is the preferred option for the least productive among the active firms in the industry. Offshoring to country l entails high fixed costs and also high variable costs (perhaps due to high transportation costs τ_{il} or high productivity-adjusted manufacturing wages $a_{ml}w_l$), and thus no firm finds it optimal to import inputs from l. Country j offers the largest marginal cost savings when offshoring there, but the fixed costs of fragmentation are high there, so only the most productive firms within an industry find it optimal to import inputs from j. Finally, country k is associated with moderate fixed costs of offshoring and offers a cost advantage relative to domestic sourcing, so a subset of middle-productivity firms chooses it as their optimal location of manufacturing input production.

---

[18] From this discussion, it should be obvious that the two-country model developed above failed to deliver two-way input trade flows because of its assumptions on technology (e.g., ruling out headquarter services provision in the South), and not because it featured only two countries.

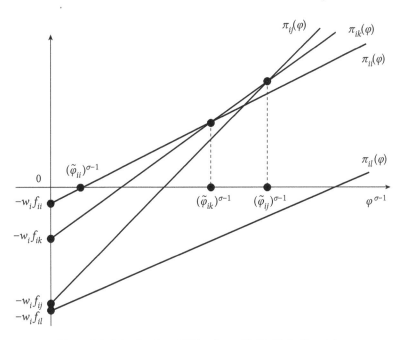

Figure 2.4 Selection into Offshoring with Multiple Countries

Naturally, the example illustrated in Figure 2.4 is rather special and, of greater concern, very different sorting patterns could emerge with mild changes in the key productivity and cost parameters. To illustrate this sensitivity, consider the case in which all foreign countries share the same level of offshoring fixed costs or $f_{ij} = f_{iO}$ for all $j \neq i$. It is then clear that, conditional on finding it optimal to offshore, firms headquartered in country i will offshore manufacturing to the location j that minimizes marginal costs, or $j^* = \arg\min_j \{\tau_{ij} a_{mj} w_j\}$. Small changes in any of these parameters could thus lead to discontinuous jumps in the prevalence of imports of inputs from particular countries.

Another limitation of this multi-country model is that it is not well designed to aggregate all firm decisions within an industry in order to guide empirical analyses of the determinants of the relative prevalence of offshoring to particular countries depending on some fundamental parameters of those countries. For similar reasons, the model is not a particularly useful tool for quantitative analysis, particularly when envisioning a more realistic world with multiple inputs.

Fortunately, below we will be able to make some progress on these limitations by borrowing some techniques from the work of Antràs, Fort, and

Tintelnot (2014), who in turn build on the seminal paper by Eaton and Kortum (2002).[19]

Bringing Eaton and Kortum (2002) inside the Firm

Imagine now that the manufacturing stage of production entails the procurement of a continuum of measure one of inputs indexed by v, rather than just one input as assumed so far. I let these inputs be imperfectly substitutable with each other with a constant and symmetric elasticity of substitution equal to $\sigma_\rho > 1$. Very little will depend on the particular value of σ_ρ. The cost function associated with producing q units of a final-good variety faced by a firm with headquarters in country i is now given by

$$C_{i\{j(v)\}_{v=0}^1}(q,\varphi) = w_i \sum_{j \in \mathcal{J}_i(\varphi)} f_{ij} + \frac{q}{\varphi}(a_{hi}w_i)^\eta$$

$$\times \left(\int_0^1 \left(\tau_{ij(v)} a_{mj(v)}(v)\, w_{j(v)} \right)^{1-\sigma_\rho} dv \right)^{(1-\eta)/(1-\sigma_\rho)}, \quad (2.25)$$

where $j(v)$ corresponds to the country in which input v is produced and $\mathcal{J}_i(\varphi) = \{\hat{j} : j(v) = \hat{j} \text{ for some } v\}$ is the set of locations from which this firm with productivity φ sources inputs.

I will depart from the previous model in allowing the manufacturing productivity parameters $1/a_{mj(v)}$ to be *firm-specific*, and following Eaton and Kortum (2002), in treating them as the realization of random variables rather than as being deterministic. More formally, by paying the fixed cost f_{ij} of offshoring to country j, a firm headquartered in country i gains the ability of having *any* input v produced in that country j under an input-specific inverse unit labor requirement $1/a_{mj}(v)$ drawn (independently from other inputs) from the Fréchet distribution

$$Pr(a_{mj}(v) \geq a) = e^{-T_j a^\theta}, \quad \text{with } T_j > 0 \text{ and } \theta > \sigma_\rho - 1.$$

As in Eaton and Kortum's (2002) model, T_j governs the industry-level state of technology in country j, while θ determines the variability of productivity draws across inputs, with a lower θ fostering the emergence of comparative advantage *within* input subsectors across countries.

---

[19] Antràs, Fort, and Tintelnot (2014) draw inspiration from Tintelnot (2013), who studies the location of final-good production of multi-product multinational firms in a framework that does not feature trade in intermediate inputs. Garetto (2013) also applies the Eaton and Kortum (2002) framework to a global sourcing environment, but does so in a two-country model and with other goals in mind.

In order to simplify matters, it is assumed that firms only learn their particular realization of $1/a_{mj}(v)$ after they have incurred all sunk costs of off-shoring. Hence, regardless of the different amounts that firms paid to have the ability to source from particular countries, the choice of location of production of any input v will simply solve $j^*(v) = \arg\min_{j(v) \in \mathcal{J}_i(\varphi)} \{\tau_{ij} a_{mj}(v) w_j\}$. Remember that the set $\mathcal{J}_i(\varphi)$ from which $j^*(v)$ is chosen corresponds to the set of countries in which a firm from country i with productivity φ paid the associated fixed costs of offshoring f_{ij}. I will refer to $\mathcal{J}_i(\varphi)$ as the *sourcing strategy* of a firm headquartered in i with productivity φ.

Because this model has many moving parts, it is worth pausing to review the timing of events. Firms in a given sector s (subscripts omitted) initially pay a fixed cost of entry $f_{ei} w_i$ to enter country i and gain the ability to later produce headquarter services there at a unit labor cost equal to $a_{hi} w_i$. After paying this entry cost, firms learn their core productivity φ which affects firm productivity in a Hicks-neutral manner. Firms next select a set of countries $\mathcal{J}_i(\varphi)$ from which to be able to import inputs and pay all fixed offshoring costs $w_i \sum_{j \in \mathcal{J}_i(\varphi)} f_{ij}$. Once those countries have been selected, the firm observes the vector of input-location-specific productivity draws $\{a_{mj}(v)\}_{v \in [0,1]}$ for each $j \in \mathcal{J}_i(\varphi)$. The firm then decides from which country to buy a particular input v, after which headquarter services and manufacturing inputs are produced, and the final good is assembled and sold in world markets.

We have obviously made the model significantly more complicated than it originally was. Some readers might then be wondering: to what effect? To understand the purpose of this added structure, consider first the choice of location of manufacturing inputs, once all offshoring fixed costs have been paid. As argued above, at that point, a firm headquartered in i with productivity φ simply solves $j^*(v) = \arg\min_{j(v) \in \mathcal{J}_i(\varphi)} \{\tau_{ij} a_{mj}(v) w_j\}$. The beauty of the Fréchet distribution (see Eaton and Kortum, 2002) is that the probability that a given location j is chosen for any input v to be used by a firm headquartered in i with productivity φ is simply given by

$$\chi_{ij}(\varphi) = \frac{T_j \left(\tau_{ij} w_j\right)^{-\theta}}{\Theta_i(\varphi)}, \qquad (2.26)$$

where

$$\Theta_i(\varphi) \equiv \sum_{k \in \mathcal{J}_i(\varphi)} T_k \left(\tau_{ik} w_k\right)^{-\theta} \qquad (2.27)$$

summarizes the *sourcing capability* of firm φ from i. With a continuum of inputs, $\chi_{ij}(\varphi)$ corresponds to the fraction of inputs sourced from j conditional on the sourcing strategy $\mathcal{J}_i(\varphi)$. Even more remarkably, the distribution of the actual price paid for any input v turns out to be independent of the actual source j of those inputs (again, see Eaton and Kortum, 2002, for details), which implies that $\chi_{ij}(\varphi)$ in (2.26) also corresponds to country j's share of all manufacturing input purchases by a firm with sourcing strategy $\mathcal{J}_i(\varphi)$.

I hope the reader is beginning to appreciate that the extra machinery is starting to pay off. According to expression (2.26), and conditional on the set of active locations $\mathcal{J}_i(\varphi)$, sourcing decisions at the level of the firm now vary smoothly with the key parameters of the model. Furthermore, each country's market share in a firm's purchases of intermediates corresponds to this country's contribution to the sourcing capability $\Theta_i(\varphi)$ in (2.27). Countries in the set $\mathcal{J}_i(\varphi)$ with lower wages w_j, more advanced technologies T_j, or lower distance from country i are predicted to have higher market shares in the intermediate input purchases of firms based in country i.

Although it might seem that the core productivity parameter φ no longer plays a relevant role in the model, it is important to stress that the set of "activated" offshoring locations $\mathcal{J}_i(\varphi)$ is endogenous and will naturally be a function of that core productivity level. To see this, let us then turn to studying the determination of the set $\mathcal{J}_i(\varphi)$.

After choosing the lowest cost source of supply for each input v, the overall cost function associated with producing q units of a final-good variety can be written, after some nontrivial derivations, as

$$C_i(q, \varphi, \mathcal{J}_i(\varphi)) = w_i \sum_{j \in \mathcal{J}_i(\varphi)} f_{ij} + \frac{q}{\varphi} (a_{hi} w_i)^\eta (\gamma \Theta_i(\varphi))^{-(1-\eta)/\theta}, \qquad (2.28)$$

where $\gamma = \left[\Gamma \left(\frac{\theta + 1 - \sigma_\rho}{\theta} \right) \right]^{\theta/(1-\sigma_\rho)}$ and Γ is the gamma function.[20] Note that the addition of a new location to any potential set of active locations necessarily lowers the marginal cost faced by firms. Intuitively, an extra location grants the firm an extra cost draw for all varieties $v \in [0, 1]$. It is thus natural that greater competition among suppliers will reduce the expected minimum sourcing cost $\tau_{ij^*} a_{mj^*}(v) w_{j^*} = \min_{j(v) \in \mathcal{J}_i(\varphi)} \{ \tau_{ij} a_{mj}(v) w_j \}$ per intermediate. In fact, the addition of a country to $\mathcal{J}_i(\varphi)$ lowers the expected price paid for *all* varieties v, and not just for those that are ultimately sourced from the country being added to $\mathcal{J}_i(\varphi)$.[21]

Following analogous steps as in the previous models to solve for the profit function associated with the cost function in (2.25), we can express the profits associated with the optimal sourcing strategy of a firm from country i with

---

[20] These derivations are analogous to those performed by Eaton and Kortum (2002) to solve for the aggregate price index in their model of final-good trade.

[21] Hence, the addition of an input location decreases costs and increases revenue-based productivity for reasons quite distinct than in the love-for-variety frameworks in Halpern, Koren, and Szeidl (2011); Goldberg, Khandelwal, Pavcnik, and Topalova (2010); and Gopinath and Neiman (2013).

productivity φ as the solution to the following problem:

$$\pi_i(\varphi) = \max_{\mathcal{J}_i(\varphi)} \left\{ (a_{hi}w_i)^{-\eta(\sigma-1)} (\gamma\Theta_i(\varphi))^{(\sigma-1)(1-\eta)/\theta} B\varphi^{\sigma-1} - w_i \sum_{k\in\mathcal{J}_i(\varphi)} f_{ik} \right\}.$$
(2.29)

As is clear from equation (2.29), when deciding whether to add a new country l to the set $\mathcal{J}_i(\varphi)$, the firm trades off the reduction in costs associated with the inclusion of that country in the set $\mathcal{J}_i(\varphi)$ against the payment of the additional fixed cost $w_i f_{il}$.

The problem in (2.29) is not straightforward to solve because the decision to include a country j in the set $\mathcal{J}_i(\varphi)$ naturally interacts with the decision to add any other country j'. For this reason, although the larger is the core productivity level φ, the higher will the marginal benefit of adding a location to any given set $\mathcal{J}_i(\varphi)$, it is not necessarily the case that the set $\mathcal{J}_i(\varphi)$ is "increasing" in φ. Or, more precisely, the choice of locations $\mathcal{J}_i(\varphi_0)$ of a firm with productivity φ_0 is not necessarily a strict subset of the set of locations $\mathcal{J}_i(\varphi_1)$ chosen by a firm with a higher productivity level $\varphi_1 > \varphi_0$. For example, a highly productive firm from i might pay a large fixed cost to be able to offshore to a country l with a particularly high value of $T_l(\tau_{il}w_l)^{-\theta}$, after which the marginal incentive to add further locations might be greatly diminished whenever $(\sigma-1)(1-\eta) < \theta$.[22]

As I show in the Theoretical Appendix, however, these complications do not arise whenever $(\sigma-1)(1-\eta) \geq \theta$, in which case the addition of a location to the set of active locations does not decrease the marginal benefit of adding further locations. As a result, one can show that the number of locations to which a firm offshores is a monotonically increasing function of productivity φ, and even more strongly, that $\mathcal{J}_i(\varphi_0) \subseteq \mathcal{J}_i(\varphi_1)$ for $\varphi_1 \geq \varphi_0$. The model thus delivers a "pecking order" in the extensive margin of offshoring that is reminiscent of the one typically obtained in models of exporting with heterogeneous firms, such as in Eaton, Kortum, and Kramarz (2011). Furthermore, for a sufficiently low value of core productivity φ, the only profitable location of input production might be one associated with a low fixed cost of sourcing. Under the maintained assumption that $f_{ij} > f_{ii}$ for all $j \neq i$—so domestic sourcing is the sourcing strategy associated with the lowest fixed costs—the model thus continues to deliver selection into offshoring based on firm core productivity.

The more tractable case with $(\sigma-1)(1-\eta) \geq \theta$ is more likely to apply whenever demand is elastic and thus profits are particularly responsive

---

[22] The difficulties in solving for $\mathcal{J}_i(\varphi)$ are nicely discussed in Blaum, Lelarge, and Peters (2013) in a model of input trade with very different features. It is worth pointing out, however, that one can easily show that the endogenous sourcing potential $\Theta_i(\varphi)$ is necessarily increasing in φ regardless of parameter values.

to variable cost reductions (high σ), and whenever input efficiency levels are relatively heterogeneous across markets (low θ), so that the expected reduction in costs achieved by adding an extra country into the set of active locations is relatively high. Naturally, this scenario is also more likely whenever headquarter intensity η is low, and thus changes in the cost of the input bundle cost have a relatively high impact on profits. Antràs, Fort, and Tintelnot's 2014 structural estimation of the model suggests that $\sigma - 1$ is significantly larger than θ, and thus this more tractable scenario also appears to be the more plausible one.

We can obtain sharper characterizations of the solution to the sourcing strategy problem in (2.29) by making further specific assumptions. For instance, when the fixed cost of offshoring is common for all foreign countries, so $f_{ij} = f_{iO}$ for all $j \neq i$, then regardless of the value of $(\sigma - 1)(1 - \eta)/\theta$, it is clear that locations j associated with a high value of $T_j \left(\tau_{ij} w_j\right)^{-\theta}$ will necessarily be more attractive than locations associated with low values of this term. In such a case, and regardless of the value of $(\sigma - 1)(1 - \eta)/\theta$, one could then rank foreign locations $j \neq i$ according to their value of $T_j \left(\tau_{ij} w_j\right)^{-\theta}$, and denote by $i_r = \left\{ i_1, i_{2,...}, i_{j-1} \right\}$ the country with the r-th highest value of $T_j \left(\tau_{ij} w_j\right)^{-\theta}$. Having constructed i_r, it then follows that for any firm with productivity φ from i that offshores to at least one country, $i_1 \in \mathcal{J}_i(\varphi)$; for any firm that offshores to at least two countries, we have $i_2 \in \mathcal{J}_i(\varphi)$, and so on. In other words, not only does the extensive margin increase monotonically with firm productivity, but it does so in a manner uniquely determined by the ranking of the $T_j \left(\tau_{ij} w_j\right)^{-\theta}$ terms.

Even with variation of fixed costs of offshoring, a similar sharp result emerges in the knife-edge case in which $(\sigma - 1)(1 - \eta) = \theta$. In that case, the addition of an element to the set $\mathcal{J}_i(\varphi)$ has no effect on the decision to add any other element to the set, and the same pecking order pattern described previously applies, but when one ranks foreign locations according to the ratio $T_j \left(\tau_{ij} w_j\right)^{-\theta}/f_{ij}$. This result is analogous to the one obtained in standard models of selection into exporting featuring constant marginal costs, in which the decision to service a given market is independent of that same decision in other markets.

After having solved the sourcing strategy problem in (2.29), it is straightforward to compute the aggregate volume of intermediate inputs from any country j in the industry under consideration. These imports are given by

$$M_{ij} = (\sigma - 1)(1 - \eta)\, \widetilde{B} N_i \int_{\tilde{\varphi}_{ij}}^{\infty} \chi_{ij}(\varphi)\, \Theta_i(\varphi)^{(\sigma-1)(1-\eta)/\theta}\, \varphi^{\sigma-1}\, dG_i(\varphi), \quad (2.30)$$

where N_i is the measure of final-good entrants in country i, $\chi_{ij}(\varphi)$ is given in (2.26), $\widetilde{B} = (a_{hi} w_i)^{-\eta(\sigma-1)} \gamma^{(\sigma-1)(1-\eta)} B$, and $\tilde{\varphi}_{ij}$ is the productivity of the least productive firm from i offshoring to j. As long as a higher value of $T_j \left(\tau_{ij} w_j \right)^{-\theta}$ is associated with a (weakly) higher probability that country j belongs to the set $\mathcal{J}_i(\varphi)$, it is then clear from (2.30) that a high value of $T_j \left(\tau_{ij} w_j \right)^{-\theta}$ leads to a large volume of imports from that country j on account of both the intensive and extensive margins of trade.

Interestingly, in the special case in which the fixed costs of offshoring are low enough to ensure that all firms acquire the capability to source inputs from *all* countries, equation (2.30) reduces to a modified version of the gravity equation, analogous to that in Eaton and Kortum (2002). To see this, note that whenever $\mathcal{J}_i(\varphi) = \{1, 2, \ldots, \mathcal{J}\}$ for all φ and i, (2.30) can be written as

$$M_{ij} = (\sigma - 1)(1 - \eta)\, \widetilde{B} N_i \left(\bar{\Theta}_i \right)^{(\sigma-1)(1-\eta)/\theta} \chi_{ij} \int_{\underline{\varphi}_i}^{\infty} \varphi^{\sigma-1}\, dG_i(\varphi), \qquad (2.31)$$

where

$$\bar{\Theta}_i \equiv \sum_{k=1}^{\mathcal{J}} T_k \left(\tau_{ik} w_k \right)^{-\theta}$$

and

$$\chi_{ij} = \frac{T_j \left(\tau_{ij} w_j \right)^{-\theta}}{\bar{\Theta}_i}.$$

Defining $A_i = \sum_j M_{ij}$ as the total absorption of intermediate inputs by firms in i, and $Q_j = \sum_l M_{lj}$ as the total production of intermediates in country j, it is straightforward to verify that (2.31) in fact reduces to

$$M_{ij} = \frac{\left(\tau_{ij} \right)^{-\theta} \frac{A_i}{\bar{\Theta}_i}}{\sum_l \left(\tau_{lj} \right)^{-\theta} \frac{A_l}{\bar{\Theta}_l}} Q_j,$$

which is analogous to equation (11) in Eaton and Kortum (2002).

When the extensive margin (or sourcing capability $\Theta_i(\varphi)$) varies across firms, such a neat expression no longer applies. This suggests that one might be able to infer the importance of the firm-level extensive margin (and of cross-country variation in the fixed costs of offshoring) from observed deviations from the traditional gravity equation. This is one of the approaches explored by Antràs et al. (2014) in their study of the extensive margin of offshoring of U.S. firms.

Further Reading

This concludes my overview of the key benchmark models of international trade I will be building on in future chapters. Although most of the papers I have discussed are quite recent, there already exist a number of useful reviews of this literature. For instance, three of the chapters in the forthcoming fourth volume of the *Handbook of International Economics*, namely Melitz and Redding (2013a), Antràs and Yeaple (2013), and Costinot and Rodríguez-Clare (2013), cover these models in significant detail.[23] The multi-country model of global sourcing is more novel and originates in Antràs, Fort, and Tintelnot (2014), where it is used to interpret and structurally estimate the extensive margin of U.S. imports.

With this machinery at hand, we are now ready to begin our theoretical exploration of the implications of contractual imperfections for the global organization of production.

---

[23] Other useful surveys of this literature include Helpman (2006); Redding (2011); and Bernard, Jensen, Redding, and Schott (2012).

PART II

Location

3

Contracts and Export Behavior

Noble Group Limited is a global supply chain manager of agricultural and energy products, metals, and minerals.[1] In January 2004, the firm had arranged to export Brazilian soybeans to soybean crushers in China. The contracts signed in January fixed a price for the transaction, even though the delivery was only scheduled to occur in April of that same year. Unfortunately for the buyers in China, prospects for a bumper soybean crop led to a 20 percent decline in soybean prices between January and April. The associated drop in the price of crushed soybeans implied that the Chinese crushers would be operating at substantial losses were they to honor the high prices fixed in their January contracts with Noble. As a result, Chinese buyers began searching for ways to nullify their January contract with Noble. Perhaps not coincidentally, that same month Chinese port authorities discovered a discoloration among a handful of red beans on a 60,000-ton soybean shipment from Brazil, which they claimed indicated the presence of carboxin, a slightly toxic fungicide. Although such discoloration (at least in small quantities) is not unusual in traded soybeans, the Chinese government proceeded to institute a ban on *all* soybean shipments from Brazil, thereby effectively voiding the contract that Noble had signed with the Chinese soybean crushers. As a result, Noble was left with millions of dollars' worth of stranded cargo. Noble eventually found other buyers for its shipments, but the incident cost the company around $25 million in demurrage losses.

This unfortunate incident of Noble Group in China exemplifies the contractual insecurity that producers face in their international transactions, the sources of which were explained in Chapter 1.[2] In the three chapters of this part of the book, I will discuss the implications of introducing contractual imperfections in the benchmark models developed in Chapter 2. In this chapter, I will develop simple imperfect-contracting variants of the Melitz (2003) model of exporting and will also discuss empirical evidence suggestive of the role of these frictions as determinants of the structure of international trade

---

[1] The following discussion builds on Foley, Chen, Johnson, and Meyer (2009).

[2] Interestingly, and in line with the internalization response to contractual insecurity highlighted in Chapter 1, in 2005 Noble Group acquired four soybean processing plants in China.

flows. In Chapter 4, I will introduce contractual frictions into the two-country model of global sourcing developed in Chapter 2, and will use several variants of this stylized model to shed light on the basics of how imperfect contract enforcement shapes the sourcing decisions of firms. Finally, in Chapter 5, a multi-country version of this global sourcing model will be developed to guide an empirical analysis of the relevance of contractual factors for the global sourcing decisions of U.S. firms.

Contracting in the Melitz Model

As derived in Chapter 2, in the Melitz (2003) model firms set the volume of output sold and the price charged in each market in a profit-maximizing manner and, as a result, the profits that a firm from country i with productivity φ anticipates obtaining in country j are given by

$$\pi_{ij}(\varphi) = (\tau_{ij} w_i)^{1-\sigma} B_j \varphi^{\sigma-1} - w_i f_{ij}, \tag{3.1}$$

where

$$B_j = \frac{1}{\sigma} \left(\frac{\sigma}{\sigma-1}\right)^{1-\sigma} P_j^{\sigma-1} \beta E_j, \tag{3.2}$$

and E_j is aggregate spending in country j.

It is worth pausing to discuss some key and often overlooked assumptions needed for a firm from i with productivity φ to *actually* realize the profit flow in equation (3.1) when choosing to export in country j. First, it is necessary for the firm to have complete information regarding all variables relevant for profits, including its own productivity level φ and the level of (residual) demand implicit in the term B_j. Second, equation (3.1) implicitly assumes that the firm can expand its production in order to meet foreign demand by costlessly hiring additional labor (or the composite factor of production) at a market wage rate w_i which is independent of the firm's operational decisions. Third, the firm is assumed to be able to costlessly contract with a local distributor or importer (an agent, an employee, or a firm) that will collect the sales revenue in country j and will hand them over to the exporter in i.[3]

Some interesting recent work in the field of international trade has been devoted to studying the implications of relaxing the first two assumptions mentioned above. On the one hand, Segura-Cayuela and Vilarrubia (2008), Albornoz, Calvo Pardo, Corcos, and Ornelas (2012), and Nguyen (2012) have

---

[3] Although I will abstract from such a possibility below, one could imagine that the fixed cost of exporting $w_i f_{ij}$ partly reflects the remuneration of the importer for his or her services.

all fruitfully incorporated foreign demand uncertainty in heterogeneous firm frameworks.[4] On the other hand, a voluminous recent literature, which includes the work among others of Helpman, Itskhoki, and Redding (2010) and Amiti and Davis (2012), has studied the implications of imperfect labor markets for the exporting decision, the structure of international trade, and the effect of trade liberalization on labor markets, wage inequality, and unemployment. As interesting as these contributions are, a treatment of these topics is beyond the scope of the current book. Instead, I will hereafter focus on relaxing the third of the assumptions mentioned above, namely, that the contracting between exporters and local distributors or importers is frictionless and allows the exporter to capture the full surplus from the transaction.

Before discussing the implications of contractual imperfections in the Melitz (2003) framework, it is necessary to introduce contracting into the framework and this requires us to be a bit more explicit about the agents involved in the model. For simplicity, in this chapter I will restrict attention to situations in which each export transaction involves only two agents, the exporting firm F in country i and the importer M in country j. One can think of the fixed cost of exporting $w_i f_{ij}$ as partly capturing the cost incurred by the exporter in order to be able to contract with importers from j. For the time being, I will also focus on discussing simple contracts taking the following form: at some initial date t_0, the exporting firm F agrees to ship an amount of goods equal to q_{ij}, and in exchange the importer simultaneously agrees to pay the exporter an amount s_{ij} at some later date t_1, perhaps corresponding to the time at which the good is received or perhaps when it has been sold and revenue has been collected. In order to avoid introducing non-essential parameters, I set the discount rate between dates t_0 and t_1 to 0. Contracts with alternative timings of payments will be discussed below.

It simplifies the exposition to assume that the opportunity cost of the importer's time is 0, so that the net surplus associated with firm F with productivity φ exporting in country j continues to be given by

$$\pi_{ij}(\varphi) = \left(p_{ij}(\varphi) - \frac{\tau_{ij}}{\varphi} w_i \right) q_{ij}(\varphi) - w_i f_{ij}, \tag{3.3}$$

with $q_{ij}(\varphi) = \beta E_j P_j^{\sigma-1} p_j(\varphi)^{-\sigma}$ as dictated by the demand schedule faced by the exporting firm. In the absence of contractual frictions, the contract will set the quantity of goods $q_{ij}(\varphi)$ shipped to country j and the associated price $p_{ij}(\varphi)$ to maximize the joint surplus in (3.3), thereby leading to the joint profit

---

[4] Conversely, models in which firms learn their productivity level φ over time, as in the seminal work of Jovanovic (1982), have not been extensively used in international trade environments.

flow given by

$$\pi_{ij}(\varphi) = \left(\tau_{ij} w_i\right)^{1-\sigma} B_j \varphi^{\sigma-1} - w_i f_{ij}, \tag{3.4}$$

which coincides with (3.1). Only when this joint profit flow is expected to be positive will the exporter decide to invest in being able to export to j.

Even if contracting is frictionless, whether the exporter F is able to realize that entire profit flow in (3.4) will depend on the relative bargaining power of the exporter and the importer. Given the zero reservation value of importers, the equilibrium in the Melitz (2003) framework corresponds to the case in which exporters have all the bargaining power, in the sense that they are assumed to be able to credibly make a take-it-or-leave-it offer to importers when contracting with them. To see this more formally, notice that the optimal contract from the point of view of the exporter will solve the exporter's profit subject to the importer's participation constraint, or

$$\max_{q_{ij}(\varphi), s_{ij}(\varphi)} \quad s_{ij}(\varphi) - \frac{\tau_{ij}}{\varphi} w_i q_{ij}(\varphi) - w_i f_{ij}$$

$$\text{s.t.} \quad p_{ij}\left(q_{ij}(\varphi)\right) q_{ij}(\varphi) - s_{ij}(\varphi) \geq 0, \tag{3.5}$$

with $p_{ij}(q_{ij}(\varphi)) = (\beta E_j P_j^{\sigma-1})^{1/\sigma} q_{ij}(\varphi)^{-1/\sigma}$. Quite naturally, the exporter will find it optimal to make the importer's participation constraint bind, thus implying that $q_{ij}(\varphi)$ will maximize joint profits and the exporter will end up capturing the profit flow in (3.4), as assumed in the Melitz framework.

The assumption that exporters have all the bargaining power is perhaps a natural one to make given that the model is not explicit about the role of importers in facilitating trade. If these agents have a zero opportunity cost and add no value to exports, why should they be remunerated? In the real world, however, intermediaries serve a central role in linking demand and supply by, among others, alleviating search frictions (see Antràs and Costinot, 2011) and providing quality assurance (see Bardhan, Mookherjee, and Tsumagari, 2013; or Tang and Zhang, 2012). It is therefore natural that they capture a share of the gains from international trade. Although important, a treatment of international trade intermediation is beyond the scope of this book.

Contractual Frictions in the Melitz Model

As simple as the contract discussed above is, our discussion of international contract enforcement in Chapter 1 and the above account of Noble Group's soybean misadventures in China suggests that even those simple contracts are not fully enforceable in the real world. To fix ideas, I will next develop a simple model featuring one such source of contractual insecurity, namely a limited commitment problem on the part of the importer along the lines of the seminal work of Hart and Moore (1994) and Thomas and Worrall (1994).

The lack of commitment on the part of the importer is captured by assuming that at t_1, and before he transfers the collected sale revenue to the exporter, this importer is presented with an opportunity to divert some cash flows away from the exporter. In an extreme case, this might reflect the possibility of the importer absconding with the exporter's goods and attempting to sell them on the side, perhaps at a discount. More generally, the assumption reflects the notion that the initial contract might not compel the parties to honor its terms, thereby tempting the importer to deviate from the contract by underreporting the amount of revenues actually collected, perhaps claiming that those lower revenues were due to the low quality of the goods the exporter shipped. To simplify matters, I will let the share of diverted revenues be a common constant $1 - \mu_{ij} \in [0, 1]$ for all pairs of agents shipping goods from i to j, but later I will briefly discuss the case in which this parameter might vary with productivity.

The parameter μ_{ij} captures the extent to which the importer feels constrained in defaulting on its contractual commitments with exporters from i and thus it is natural to treat this parameter as a measure of the degree of contract enforcement in country j. The fact that the share μ_{ij} also depends on the exporting country i implies that the level of international contract enforcement is allowed to potentially be a function of the nationality of the two agents in the transaction, reflecting perhaps the effects of legal similarity (e.g., common versus civil law countries), a common language, or proximity (cultural or geographical).

I realize that the above modeling of contractual institutions is exceedingly simplistic, with the great complexities and nuances of this type of institution being reduced to a single parameter μ_{ij} capturing the "stealing" possibilities of agents residing in the importing country. I will stick to this simple framework for most of this chapter, but let me briefly expand on different mechanisms that might jointly contribute to a country offering a low level of contractual security to firms exporting to it. First, in some institutional environments, agents might face more opportunities to deviate from the initial contract than in other environments. This might be partly due to social norms, but is also explained by the legal environment which might determine how complete formal contracts tend to be. Let us denote by $1 - \rho_{ij}$ the probability with which a "default" opportunity arises for a j-importer transacting with an i-exporter (before we assumed $\rho_{ij} = 0$). When such an opportunity to default does not arise, the importer will necessarily honor the initial contract and deliver all sale revenue to the exporter. When a default opportunity arises, however, the importer will assess the legal ramifications of a contractual breach, and will optimally decide whether to default or not. The legal consequences of a default are in turn shaped by the probability with which a court of law will rule against a misbehaving importer (denoted by λ_{ij}) and by the amount of damages that it will be required to pay in such an eventuality. It is convenient to model these damages as a multiple d_{ij} of the sale revenues the importer had diverted from the exporter.

Notice that if d_{ij} or λ_{ij} are high enough such that $d_{ij}\lambda_{ij} > 1$, the importer will never default on the exporter and thus the exporter will be able to achieve the same profit flow as in the case with no contractual frictions (see equation (3.4)). Conversely, when $d_{ij}\lambda_{ij} < 1$, if the exporter insisted on demanding the entire sale revenue, the importer would optimally choose to fully default on the exporter because by doing so, it could obtain an expected payoff equal to a multiple $(1 - \rho_{ij})(1 - \lambda_{ij}d_{ij}) > 0$ of revenue.

Below, I will focus on the more interesting scenario in which $d_{ij}\lambda_{ij} < 1$. In such a case, the exporter is left, *in expectation*, with a share

$$\mu_{ij} \equiv \rho_{ij} + (1 - \rho_{ij})\lambda_{ij}d_{ij} \tag{3.6}$$

of sale revenue. This expression for μ_{ij} summarizes how the prevalence of default opportunities, the competence of courts in ruling against deviating parties, and the size and enforceability of damages jointly shape the perceived contractual security associated with different countries. Equation (3.6) also illustrates how even in situations in which contracts include choice-of-law and forum-of-law clauses (see Chapter 1), thus potentially making ρ_{ij} and λ_{ij} insensitive to j, the importing country institutions may still matter by shaping the extent to which damages set by international courts of law or arbitrators are enforced.

Later in this chapter, I will return to the general formulation of μ_{ij} in (3.6), but for the time being I will focus on the reduced form interpretation of $1 - \mu_{ij}$ as capturing the share of sale revenues that importers from j are able to divert from exporters from i.

Implications of Contractual Insecurity

How does the lack of commitment affect contracting between the exporter and the importer? The key new constraint facing the exporter when designing the initial contract is that any remuneration to the importer lower than $(1 - \mu_{ij})p_{ij}(q_{ij}(\varphi))q_{ij}(\varphi)$ would necessarily lead the importer to divert cash flows. As a result, the optimal contracting problem now incorporates a new incentive compatibility (IC) constraint which is necessarily tighter than the participation constraint in the previous optimal contracting program in (3.5).

Formally, and maintaining the assumption that the exporter makes a take-it-or-leave-it offer to the importer, we now have that the date-0 quantity shipped $q_{ij}(\varphi)$ and the date-1 payment $s_{ij}(\varphi)$ solve

$$\max_{q_{ij}(\varphi),s_{ij}(\varphi)} \quad s_{ij}(\varphi) - \frac{\tau_{ij}}{\varphi} w_i q_{ij}(\varphi) - w_i f_{ij}$$

$$\text{s.t.} \quad p_{ij}\left(q_{ij}(\varphi)\right) q_{ij}(\varphi) - s_{ij}(\varphi) \geq 0$$

$$p_{ij}\left(q_{ij}(\varphi)\right) q_{ij}(\varphi) - s_{ij}(\varphi) \geq \left(1 - \mu_{ij}\right) p_{ij}\left(q_{ij}(\varphi)\right) q_{ij}(\varphi),$$

with $p_{ij}(q_{ij}(\varphi)) = (\beta E_j P_j^{\sigma-1})^{1/\sigma} q_{ij}(\varphi)^{-1/\sigma}$. It is straightforward to see that $s_{ij}(\varphi)$ will now be set to exactly satisfy the (tighter) incentive compatibility constraint, thus implying that the exporter will now only capture a share μ_{ij} of revenues, and will choose $q_{ij}(\varphi)$ such that

$$\pi_{ij}(\varphi) = \max_{q_{ij}(\varphi)} \left\{ \mu_{ij} \left(\beta E_j P_j^{\sigma-1}\right)^{1/\sigma} q_{ij}(\varphi)^{(\sigma-1)/\sigma} - \frac{\tau_{ij}}{\varphi} w_i q_{ij}(\varphi) - w_i f_{ij} \right\}.$$

Solving this problem, the profit function for the exporter can be written as

$$\pi_{ij}(\varphi) = \mu_{ij}^{\sigma} \left(\tau_{ij} w_i\right)^{1-\sigma} B_j \varphi^{\sigma-1} - w_i f_{ij}. \tag{3.7}$$

Comparing equations (3.1) and (3.7), it is clear that imperfect contracting reduces the profitability of selling in country j, and the more so the lower is μ_{ij}. The reason for this is twofold: first, the exporter now shares part of the profits obtained in country j with an importer there, and second, the exporter naturally responds to this rent dissipation by reducing the desired amount of goods to ship to country j.

The Margins of Trade, Gravity, and Welfare

We now turn to a more formal study of the effects of contract enforcement on the intensive and extensive margins of trade and on aggregate bilateral trade flows across countries. In analogy to the benchmark model with perfect contracting, from equation (3.7) we now have that only firms from i with productivity $\varphi > \tilde{\varphi}_{ij}$ will find it optimal to export to country j, where

$$\tilde{\varphi}_{ij} \equiv \tau_{ij} w_i \left(\frac{w_i f_{ij}}{\mu_{ij}^{\sigma} B_j}\right)^{1/(\sigma-1)}. \tag{3.8}$$

Clearly, for fixed w_i and B_j, the lower is μ_{ij}, the lower will be the measure of firms exporting to country j, and thus the extensive margin of trade is negatively affected by weak contract enforcement. This is illustrated in Figure 3.1 with the shift in the export productivity threshold from $\tilde{\varphi}_{ij}$ to $\tilde{\varphi}_{ij'}$.

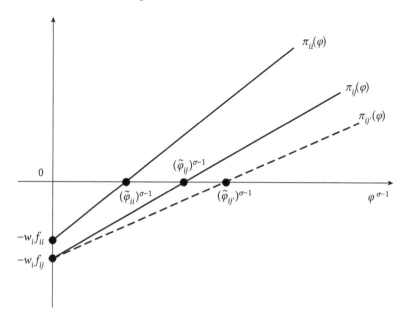

Figure 3.1 Selection into Exporting with Contractual Frictions

Next, aggregating across all firms from i, we find

$$X_{ij} = N_i \int_{\tilde{\varphi}_{ij}}^{\infty} \sigma \mu_{ij}^{\sigma} \left(\tau_{ij} w_i\right)^{1-\sigma} B_j \varphi^{\sigma-1} dG_i(\varphi), \qquad (3.9)$$

which, as in Chapter 2, we can decompose into an extensive margin N_{ij}, namely the measure of firms from i that export in j, and an average intensive margin $\bar{x}_{ij}$, corresponding to the average export volume across the active exporters:

$$X_{ij} = N_{ij} \cdot \bar{x}_{ij}. \qquad (3.10)$$

Whenever firm-level productivity is drawn from a Pareto distribution, we can integrate equation (3.9) and use (3.8) to express $\bar{x}_{ij}$ as

$$\bar{x}_{ij} = \frac{\kappa}{\kappa - \sigma + 1} \sigma w_i f_{ij}, \qquad (3.11)$$

just as in Chapter 2. Equation (3.11) then indicates that, in the particular Pareto case, the average intensive margin turns out to be unaffected by the degree of contractual enforcement. It is important to emphasize, however, that this does not imply that the intensive margin of trade *at the firm level* is unaffected by the quality of contracting institutions μ_{ij}. In fact, if a firm were to sell in two markets that differed only in their level μ_{ij}, then the firm would necessarily sell more in the market with better contract enforcement (a higher μ_{ij}), a prediction consistent with the empirical results of Araujo, Mion, and Ornelas (2012), who study the effect of the quality of contracting institutions on the cross-section of firm-level export volumes of firms based in Belgium. The insensitivity of $\bar{x}_{ij}$ to μ_{ij} in equation (3.11) is explained by the fact that countries with better contract enforcement attract a disproportionately larger set of relatively smaller exporters.

We can next follow the steps suggested in Melitz and Redding (2013a) to express aggregate sectoral exports from i to j in (3.10) in a slightly more familiar way. In particular, note first that the measure of active exporters in j is given by $N_{ij} = N_i \left(1 - G_i \left(\tilde{\varphi}_{ij}\right)\right)$. Thus, plugging (3.11) and the value of the threshold in (3.8) into (3.10), and invoking the Pareto distribution, we have

$$X_{ij} = N_i \left(\frac{\varphi_i}{\tau_{ij} w_i}\right)^\kappa \left(\frac{\mu_{ij}^\sigma B_j}{w_i f_{ij}}\right)^{\kappa/(\sigma-1)} \frac{\kappa}{\kappa - \sigma + 1} \sigma w_i f_{ij}. \tag{3.12}$$

Next, aggregating over all markets in which firms from i sell (including their domestic market), we can express the aggregate sale revenue obtained by firms in country i as

$$Y_i = \sum_j X_{ij} = N_i \left(\frac{\varphi_i}{w_i}\right)^\kappa \left(\frac{1}{w_i}\right)^{\kappa/(\sigma-1)} \frac{\kappa}{\kappa - \sigma + 1} \sigma w_i \Theta_i \tag{3.13}$$

where

$$\Theta_i \equiv \sum_j B_j^{\frac{\kappa}{\sigma-1}} \tau_{ij}^{-\kappa} f_{ij}^{-\frac{\kappa-(\sigma-1)}{(\sigma-1)}} \mu_{ij}^{\sigma\kappa/(\sigma-1)} \tag{3.14}$$

is a measure of country i's market potential (see Redding and Venables, 2004). Plugging equation (3.13) back into (3.12) finally delivers

$$X_{ij} = \frac{Y_i}{\Theta_i} B_j^{\frac{\kappa}{\sigma-1}} \tau_{ij}^{-\kappa} f_{ij}^{-\frac{\kappa-(\sigma-1)}{(\sigma-1)}} \mu_{ij}^{\sigma\kappa/(\sigma-1)}. \tag{3.15}$$

This expression is analogous to equation (2.14) in Chapter 2 except for the last term involving the parameter μ_{ij} (remember that B_j is given by equation (3.2)).

Equation (3.15) demonstrates that even after introducing contractual frictions, the model continues to deliver a modified sectoral version of the gravity equation for trade flows. This feature can again serve to motivate the widespread use of empirical log-linear specifications of trade flows with exporter and importer fixed effects and measures of bilateral trade frictions. The main new lesson one derives from (3.15) is that such log-linear specifications should include a bilateral measure of the level of contractual security in transactions between producers in country i and country j. We will shortly refer back to equation (3.15) when we review the empirical literature on the effects of institutional quality on trade flows. But before doing so, it is worth addressing one more theoretical matter related to the policy implications of the model.

Implications for Policy

It may appear that the effect of contractual insecurity in the current model is isomorphic to the effect of standard variable trade costs τ_{ij} in the benchmark model without contractual frictions. In particular, if one were to define a broad, contract-inclusive measure of trade frictions as

$$\tilde{\tau}_{ij} \equiv \frac{\tau_{ij}}{\mu_{ij}^{\sigma/(\sigma-1)}} > \tau_{ij},$$

it is straightforward to verify that all the equations above exactly correspond to those derived in the benchmark model in Chapter 2 with $\tilde{\tau}_{ij}$ replacing τ_{ij}. One is thus tempted to conclude that, apart from serving to motivate the inclusion of contracting institutions in standard empirical models of export participation, the explicit modeling of contractual frictions has little bearing on the workings of the benchmark model. Such a conclusion is however not warranted because, as mentioned above, contractual frictions not only reduce the profitability of exporting for producers in country i but also transfer exporting surplus to importers from country j. In other words, contractual insecurity not only reduces the overall gains from international trade, but also shapes how those gains are distributed across countries.

This distinction has important bearings for the relationship between contract enforcement and welfare. For instance, in the special case in which there is only one sector in the economy, Demidova and Rodríguez-Clare (2013) have shown that unilateral reductions in variable trade frictions by a small open economy are always welfare enhancing, while the same would not always be true for an increase in μ_{ij} in the framework developed in this chapter. The reason for this is that, although country j would become a more attractive location for foreign exporters if it instituted a higher μ_{ij}, the share of sale proceeds accruing to producers in j would also diminish in that event. For a high enough value of μ_{ij}, the balance of these two effects can be shown to be necessarily negative. This result is analogous to that in Demidova and Rodríguez-Clare (2009) and Felbermayr, Jung, and Larch (2013), who show that in a one-sector Melitz (2003) model, each country's unilaterally optimal import tariff is positive. An implication of this result is that countries have a *unilateral* incentive to create some amount of contractual insecurity for producers attempting to sell in their markets. Naturally, however, and as in the case of tariff wars, the unilateral optimality of contractual insecurity is associated with a globally inefficiently low level of contract enforcement.

Preliminary Empirical Evidence

The gravity equation has been one of the most widely used empirical models of international trade since being introduced by Tinbergen (1962). It is thus not surprising that it has been employed to study the effect of contracting institutions on bilateral international trade flows. The work of Anderson and Marcouiller (2002) is a pioneering study in this literature. Anderson and Marcouiller (2002) start by imposing a model of bilateral trade flows very similar to that in equation (3.15), although not derived from a theoretical model, as we have done above.[5] Following their approach, we next note that if one takes a country, say the United States, as a reference country, one can use equation (3.15), together with the definition of B_j in (3.2), to derive:

$$\frac{X_{ij}}{X_{iUS}} = \left(\frac{P_j^{\sigma-1} E_j}{P_{US}^{\sigma-1} E_{US}} \right)^{\frac{\kappa}{\sigma-1}} \left(\frac{\tau_{ij}}{\tau_{iUS}} \right)^{-\kappa} \left(\frac{f_{ij}}{f_{iUS}} \right)^{-\frac{\kappa-(\sigma-1)}{(\sigma-1)}} \left(\frac{\mu_{ij}}{\mu_{iUS}} \right)^{\sigma\kappa/(\sigma-1)}. \quad (3.16)$$

Equation (3.16) shows that the ratio of exports of country i to market j relative to the exports of this same country i to the United States is a function of the relative demand or absorption in the two importing countries, as well as different terms capturing the ratio of trade barriers associated with shipping goods from i to j relative to shipping them from i to the United States. The main advantage of this approach is that the ratio X_{ij}/X_{iUS} nets out the effect of the exporter country's term Y_i/Θ_i in (3.15) that is common for all destinations j.

Anderson and Marcouiller (2002) estimate a log-linear version of equation (3.16) in which relative bilateral traditional trade barriers (variable and fixed) are proxied by a common border ratio, a common language ratio, a distance ratio, and a tariff ratio. The key contract enforcement ratio is proxied by a "composite security" index that corresponds to the average score obtained by each importing country in survey-based measures of transparency and contract enforcement relative to the average score obtained by the United States in those same measures. Note, in particular, that Anderson and Marcouiller (2002) assume that the contractual security experienced by exporters in country j relative to that experienced by exporters to the United States is common for all exporters, regardless of their country of origin i. This seems

---

[5] Anderson and Marcouiller (2005) do study the theoretical links between contractual insecurity and trade flows, but their framework does not predict a gravity equation in trade flows.

to be a restrictive assumption given that one would imagine that differences in legal proximity could make this ratio vary with i, as allowed by (3.15), and so we will revisit this assumption shortly in this chapter. A last important hurdle in estimating equation (3.16) is finding suitable proxies for the first term involving the aggregate spending ratio E_j/E_{US} and the price index ratio P_j/P_{US}. The former ratio is proxied with relative measures of GDP, while the latter is approximated with weighted sums of the physical trade cost ratios, in analogy with the "remoteness" variable often present in gravity-style estimations. This is perhaps the least satisfactory element of their empirical design because mismeasurement of these importer-specific terms could lead to important biases in the estimates of the effects of the quality of the importer's contracting institutions on trade flows. We will return to this issue below.

With these caveats in mind, the key results of Anderson and Marcouiller (2002), which use 1996 data for forty-eight importing countries, are reproduced in Table 3.1. Column (1) presents the results of a benchmark gravity equation without institutional variables. As expected, higher relative GDP levels and lower relative traditional trade barriers of any sort are all associated with higher relative export volumes into these countries. When introducing the relative "composite security" index in column (2), this variable has a large and statistically significant effect on relative bilateral trade flows. In column (3), Anderson and Marcouiller confirm the robustness of their results to the use of a Tobit to deal with the large number of zeros in their sample. Although it is not obvious from the nonstandardized point estimates in Table 3.1, the estimates of Anderson and Marcouiller (2002) imply that the effect of weak contracting institutions on trade flows is of a similar order of magnitude as the effect of import tariffs.

As hinted earlier, two obvious limitations of the Anderson and Marcouiller (2002) study is the insensitivity of their contractual insecurity measure to characteristics of the exporting country and the econometric treatment of the demand terms B_j. These limitations are in fact related to each other. The standard way to address the second concern is to control for these importer-country absorption terms with importer-specific fixed effects. This approach is, however, not feasible when the key explanatory variable of interest varies only across importing countries and thus would be subsumed in the importer fixed effect. This problem clearly applies to Anderson and Marcouiller's (2002) proxy for contractual insecurity. Notice, conversely, that this is not an issue for standard measures of trade barriers, which are defined at the exporter-importer level. A potential way to address both of these limitations is thus to construct a measure of contractual security that is a function of both the exporter and importer country.

What factors might result in particularly high contractual enforcement in transactions between two specific countries i and j? A natural candidate

TABLE 3.1 Importer Contracting Institutions and Relative Exports

	(1)	(2)	(3)
Log GDP ratio	0.855**	0.866**	0.911**
	(0.042)	(0.038)	(0.040)
Relative composite security		0.285**	0.279**
		(0.073)	(0.081)
Log common border ratio	0.794**	0.747**	0.665**
	(0.155)	(0.163)	(0.186)
Log common language ratio	0.327**	0.336**	0.358**
	(0.080)	(0.082)	(0.109)
Log distance ratio	−1.109**	−1.095**	−1.133**
	(0.058)	(0.056)	(0.056)
Log adjusted tariff ratio	−2.973	−4.814*	−4.699*
	(1.992)	(2.343)	(2.327)
Number observations	2135	2135	2159
R-squared	.69	.70	
Log likelihood			−3865

Source: Reproduced from table 5 in Anderson and Marcouiller (2002). Robust standard errors with clustering by importer in parentheses. The regressions also include a log of GDP per capita ratio and remoteness variables for language, border, and distance. +, *, ** denote 10, 5, 1% significance.

might be a simple measure of whether the exporter and importer country share a common legal origin or not, because that legal relatedness might facilitate the resolution of contractual disputes. A few papers in the literature have explored the role of a common legal origin in affecting bilateral trade flows across countries. Below I focus on the particular contribution of Helpman, Melitz, and Rubinstein (2008) because their estimation equation is derived from the Melitz (2003) model in a similar manner as we derived equation (3.15) above, and because their estimation technique allows one to disentangle the effects of particular explanatory variables on both the intensive and extensive margins of trade.

From a theoretical perspective, the only new feature in the framework developed by Helpman et al. (2008) is the introduction of an upper bound in the distribution from which firms draw their productivity level. In the specific Pareto case, we now have that

$$G_i(\varphi) = \frac{1 - \left(\underline{\varphi}_i/\varphi\right)^{\kappa}}{1 - \left(\underline{\varphi}_i/\bar{\varphi}_i\right)^{\kappa}}, \quad \text{for } \bar{\varphi}_i \geq \varphi \geq \underline{\varphi}_i > 0. \tag{3.17}$$

The immediate implication of this assumption for our contracting model is that if for some exporting country i, no exporting firm draws a productivity level higher than the threshold $\tilde{\varphi}_{ij}$ defined in (3.8), then bilateral exports from i to j will be zero. This is also easy to see when writing these aggregate bilateral exports as in (3.9), but with the upper limit on the probability distribution:

$$X_{ij} = N_i \int_{\tilde{\varphi}_{ij}}^{\bar{\varphi}_i} \sigma \mu_{ij}^{\sigma} \left(\tau_{ij} w_i\right)^{1-\sigma} B_j \varphi^{\sigma-1} dG_i(\varphi).$$

Defining aggregate (sectoral) output in i as $Y_i = \sum_j X_{ij}$ and also

$$V_{ij}\left(\tilde{\varphi}_{ij}\right) \equiv \int_{\tilde{\varphi}_{ij}}^{\bar{\varphi}_i} \varphi^{\sigma-1} dG_i(\varphi),$$

bilateral exports from i to j can be expressed as

$$X_{ij} = \frac{Y_i}{\tilde{\Theta}_i} B_j \tau_{ij}^{1-\sigma} \mu_{ij}^{\sigma} V_{ij}\left(\tilde{\varphi}_{ij}\right) \tag{3.18}$$

where

$$\tilde{\Theta}_i = \sum_j \mu_{ij}^{\sigma} \left(\tau_{ij}\right)^{1-\sigma} B_j V_{ij}\left(\tilde{\varphi}_{ij}\right).$$

Equation (3.18) is again a modified version of the gravity equation and it is easily verified that when $\bar{\varphi}_i \to \infty$, (3.18) coincides with (3.15) after plugging the value of $\tilde{\varphi}_{ij}$ in (3.8) into $V_{ij}\left(\tilde{\varphi}_{ij}\right)$.

Equation (3.18) nicely illustrates the existence of an omitted-variable bias in standard gravity-style estimation methods. Even when one partials out the terms $Y_i/\tilde{\Theta}_i$ and B_j with exporter and importer fixed effects, respectively, standard techniques do not take into account the term $V_{ij}\left(\tilde{\varphi}_{ij}\right)$ capturing the extensive margin of trade from i to j.[6] This omission is likely associated with an upward bias in the elasticity of trade flows to institutional quality because, as indicated by the threshold equation (3.8), μ_{ij} has a negative effect on the threshold $\tilde{\varphi}_{ij}$, thus reducing $V_{ij}(\tilde{\varphi}_{ij})$.

Helpman et al. (2008) develop a two-step estimation procedure to deal with these biases. In a first stage, a Probit selection equation is derived from the model, and the estimates of this equation are used to structurally construct a control variable for the second stage, which is a log-linear model with exporter and importer fixed effects, and various measures of bilateral trade barriers.[7] For the procedure to work, one needs an explanatory variable that

---

[6] The relevance of these biases is clear from the fact that the *direct* elasticity of trade flows to the index of contractual security is lower in equation (3.18) than in equation (3.15).

[7] The first stage estimates are also used to include a more standard Heckman-correction term for selection in the second stage.

enters the first stage (the extensive margin of trade), but not the second stage. Helpman et al. (2008) argue that the cost of creating a business in a particular country satisfies this condition (they also suggest a common religion variable that allows estimation on a larger sample of countries in their sensitivity analysis).

For our purposes, the most relevant feature of Helpman et al.'s (2008) results is that their first and second stages include a variable that is equal to 1 whenever the exporter and importer share a common legal origin as defined by La Porta, Lopez-de Silanes, Shleifer, and Vishny (1999). These authors classify the legal origin of a large cross-section of countries as being either German, Scandinavian, British, French, or Socialist. As argued above, it seems natural that, other things being equal, producers located in countries sharing a common legal origin will perceive a higher degree of contractual security when transacting with each other than with producers located in countries with different legal origins. Despite the obvious coarseness of this variable, I will interpret the effect of this variable as reflecting the effect of the contracting institutions term μ_{ij} in specification (3.18).

Table 3.2 reproduces some of the main results in the Helpman et al. (2008) study. The trade data are for 1986 and cover 158 countries. The first column in the table reports the result of the first stage, in which a Probit model is used to predict the probability of positive trade flows from i to j. Not surprisingly, a lower distance and sharing a common language are both positively correlated with the probability that two countries trade with each other. Interestingly, the same is true for the common legal origin variable, and the standardized coefficients indicate that the effect of legal institutions is almost half as large as that of a common language. Somewhat perhaps surprisingly, zero trade flows appear to be more prevalent for countries that share a land border, perhaps reflecting the incidence of wars. Regulation costs, in turn, appear to have a negative effect on the extensive margin of trade.[8]

Column (2) of Table 3.2 presents the results of a benchmark gravity estimation of the intensive margin of trade that does not correct for the biases identified above. With the exception of the common border variable (which now positively impacts trade flows), the remaining coefficients have the same sign as in the Probit regressions. The effect of a common legal origin on trade flows is positive, large, and highly statistically significant. One might worry, however, that the omitted-variable bias discussed above would lead us to overestimate the effects of contractual security on the intensive margin of trade. The results in column (3), which present the second stage

---

[8] The original regressions in Helpman et al. (2008) include six additional controls: whether both countries are islands, whether they are both landlocked, whether they have colonial ties, whether they are members of the same currency union, whether they belong to the same FTA, and a measure of religious proximity. I do not report these coefficients to save space.

TABLE 3.2 Legal Origin and Bilateral Trade Flows

	(1) Probit	(2) Benchmark	(3) NLS
Distance	−0.213**	−1.167**	−0.813**
	(0.016)	(0.040)	(0.049)
Share a land border	−0.087	0.627**	0.871**
	(0.072)	(0.165)	(0.170)
Share a common legal origin	0.049**	0.535**	0.431**
	(0.019)	(0.064)	(0.065)
Share a common language	0.101**	0.147+	−0.030
	(0.021)	(0.075)	(0.087)
Regulation costs ($ amount)	−0.108**	−0.146	
	(0.036)	(0.100)	
Regulation costs (days and procedures)	−0.061*	−0.216+	
	(0.031)	(0.124)	
Firm heterogeneity correction term			0.840**
			(0.043)
Sample selection correction			0.240*
			(0.099)
Observations	12,198	6,602	6,602
R-squared	0.573	0.693	

Source: Reproduced from table II in Helpman et al. (2008). Robust standard errors clustered by country pair (bootstrapped for NLS). Regressions also include exporter and importer fixed effects as well as six other controls (island, landlocked, colonial ties, currency union, FTA, religion). Marginal effects at sample means and pseudo R^2 reported for Probit. +, *, ** denote 10, 5, 1% significance.

in the Helpman et al. (2008) procedure, confirm that such biases exist but the coefficient on legal origins is reduced by only about 20 percent and remains large and highly significant. We can conclude from these results that, consistently with the simple model we have developed above, contractual insecurity has a significant negative effect on bilateral trade flows and that such effect operates through an extensive margin as well as an intensive margin.

Responses to Contractual Insecurity

Our theoretical and empirical results so far illustrate that exporters will respond to the perceived contractual insecurity associated with servicing certain foreign markets by reducing their sales or by simply opting out from selling in those markets. As explained in Chapter 1, in practice firms can resort to alternative means to alleviate such contractual insecurity. We will next discuss three of these mechanisms: investing in contract enforcement, repeated interactions with importers, and demanding prepayment from importers.

Investing in Contract Enforcement

Consider first the possibility of firms investing in enhancing the contractibility of their transactions. This might involve hiring legal counsel to design the initial contract in a way that makes it more likely to be enforced, or it might be associated with resorting to international arbitration, which would typically also provide the exporter with more contractual security. Without delving into the details of these different legal mechanisms, let us suppose that if a firm from i were to invest a fixed amount $w_i f_c$ of resources in improving contractibility, the share of revenues that an importer from j would be able to divert would be reduced from $1 - \mu_{ij}$ to $1 - \bar{\mu}_{ij}$ with $\bar{\mu}_{ij} > \mu_{ij}$. The assumption that legal expenses are independent of the volume of sales is a strong one, but the results below will continue to go through as long as there is a fixed cost component to these costs, which seems a plausible assumption to make in this setting.

Following analogous derivations as those in the previous model, it is then straightforward to verify that firms from i will optimally choose to invest in contractibility whenever

$$\bar{\mu}_{ij}^{\sigma} \left(\tau_{ij} w_i\right)^{1-\sigma} B_j \varphi^{\sigma-1} - w_i f_c > \mu_{ij}^{\sigma} \left(\tau_{ij} w_i\right)^{1-\sigma} B_j \varphi^{\sigma-1},$$

which can alternatively be expressed as

$$\varphi^{\sigma-1} > \left(\varphi_{ij^c}\right)^{\sigma-1} \equiv \frac{w_i f_c}{\left(\bar{\mu}_{ij}^{\sigma} - \mu_{ij}^{\sigma}\right) \left(\tau_{ij} w_i\right)^{1-\sigma} B_j}.$$

In words, only the largest, most productive exporters will find it optimal to incur additional legal expenses to reduce their contractual insecurity. This might explain, for instance, why arbitration cases at the International Chamber of Commerce rarely involve disputes over amounts lower than 1 million U.S. dollars (see footnote 14 in Chapter 1). The selection of exporters into enhanced contractibility is depicted in Figure 3.2. The figure also shows that the endogenously higher contractibility of large exporters will tend to lead to a more skewed distribution of exports than in the version of the model in which the parameter μ_{ij} is common for all firms within an industry.

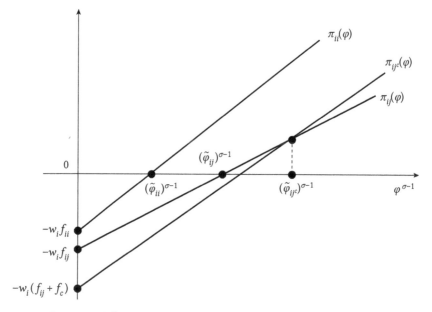

Figure 3.2 Selection into Exporting with Endogenous Contractibility

Repeated Interactions

In the previous setup in which the exporter and the importer transact only once, it is optimal for importers to divert revenue from the exporter if the contract is not perceived to be enforced. I next briefly explore how the incentives of importers to misbehave might be affected by repeated interactions with a given exporter, and how this affects the dynamics of exporting volumes. In doing so, I build on the work of Araujo, Mion, and Ornelas (2012) and Antràs and Foley (2013). To emphasize the differences with the static model, let us assume that the exporter and importer perceive their business relationship to be infinitely repeated. Assume also that importers come in two types: some of them are very patient and discount the future at a very low rate, while the rest are myopic and care only about current payoffs. At the beginning of each period t, the exporter and importer sign an agreement that binds the exporter to ship an amount $q_{ijt}(\varphi)$ of output to the importer in j in exchange for a payment from the importer once the goods have been sold.

With probability $1 - \rho_{ij}$, however, the importer is presented with an opportunity to divert all sale revenue and pay nothing to the exporter at the end of the period. We thus adopt here the probabilistic version of contract enforcement discussed earlier in the chapter and that led to expression (3.6) for μ_{ij}, but for simplicity I set $d_{ij}\lambda_{ij} = 0$, so that the exporter is left with a zero payoff in case of default. Provided that the discount rate of patient importers is sufficiently low, the folk theorem implies that a trigger-strategy equilibrium exists in which patient importers never choose to default, while myopic importers always do so when an opportunity arises.[9]

To generate nontrivial dynamics, we assume that whether an agent is patient or myopic is private information to that agent. The exporter forms beliefs on the type of the particular importer they are dealing with based on the bilateral transaction history with that importer and on a public signal reflecting the prevalence of patient importers in the population. I will denote this public signal by ξ_0 and I will treat it as an exogenous parameter, although in Araujo, Mion, and Ornelas (2012) it is endogenized by specifying a process of matching between exporters and importers.

Notice that a new importer will initially be assigned a probability ξ_0 of being patient, which is associated with a probability $\xi_0 + (1 - \xi_0)\rho_{ij}$ of the contract being enforced in this initial period. With a history of no defaults, the exporter's belief on the importer's type will improve over time, while an incidence of a default will immediately reveal the importer to be a myopic type. Denoting by ξ_t the particular posterior probability assigned to the importer being patient, repeated application of Bayes' rule delivers

$$\xi_t = \frac{\xi_0}{\xi_0 + (1 - \xi_0)\left(\rho_{ij}\right)^t} \tag{3.19}$$

when there have been no defaults up to length t, and $\xi_t = 0$ otherwise. As a result, the perceived probability of the contract signed at t being enforced is given by $\xi_t + (1 - \xi_t)\rho_{ij}$, and naturally rises with a history of no defaults. Having determined this time-varying level of contractual insecurity, the rest of the equilibrium is analogous to that of the static model with the share of revenue accruing to exporters given by

$$\mu_{ij}(t) = \xi_t + (1 - \xi_t)\rho_{ij}.$$

Hence, all firm-level equilibrium expressions continue to hold with $\mu_{ij}(t)$ replacing μ_{ij} throughout.

This extension of the model delivers several empirical predictions for the effects of weak contracting institutions on firm-level exports. As in the static model developed above, the extensive margin of trade continues to be negatively impacted by low institutional quality (low ρ_{ij}). This is because firms are less inclined to begin selling in weak institutions countries, but

---

[9] Of course, this requires that the importer obtains some positive payoff when it chooses to honor the contract. Still, for a discount factor close enough to 1, this required payoff can be made arbitrarily close to 0. This limiting case is considered here for simplicity.

also because the probability of an export relationship being discontinued is higher the lower is the probability of contracts being enforced. The effects of low formal contract enforcement on the intensive margin of trade are richer. The perceived initial probability of default is given by $(1 - \xi_0)(1 - \rho_{ij})$, and thus export relationships in weak contracting environments (countries with low ρ_{ij}) will tend to begin at low volumes. Nevertheless, the negative effect of weak contracting on the intensive margin of trade is predicted to be attenuated over time, resulting in firm-level export volumes that should rise over time.

Araujo et al. (2012) study the effects of importer-country characteristics on the cross-section of firm-level exports of Belgian firms over the period 1995–2008 and find broad support for these predictions. Other things being equal, export entry is higher and export exit is lower in countries with better contracting institutions. Initial firm-level export volumes are increasing in contract enforcement, while firm-level export growth is on average positive. Interestingly, however, this positive growth in exports appears to be faster in countries with weak contracting institutions. The simple model developed above provides a simple rationale for this fact: in countries with high default rates contractual insecurity will be lower, but the exporter will be able to learn the type of the importer at a faster rate than in an environment in which a very low default rate prevents myopic importers from defaulting. Formally, differentiation of (3.19) indicates that for a low enough t, the growth in ξ_t over time t is necessarily decreasing in ρ_{ij}.[10]

Choice of Payment Method: Exporter Institutions Matter

So far, we have discussed the role of investments in contractibility and repeated interactions in reducing the extent of contractual insecurity faced by exporters. If the *only* contractual friction in international transactions was the risk of importer default, then a simple solution to this problem would be for the exporter to demand pre-payment from the importer before shipping the goods. Formally, a simple modification of the static contract we have considered so far would suffice to resolve the inefficiencies associated with contractual insecurity: instead of the payment s_{ij} occurring at t_1, the exporter could insist that it was made at t_0. With this simple modification, the exporter would not need to worry about the payment s_{ij} satisfying an incentive compatibility constraint for the importer and could thus choose s_{ij} to satisfy exactly the importer's participation constraint. The problem would

---

[10] Araujo et al. (2012) endogenize the prior ξ_0, and show that the differentially lower growth of exports in high contract enforcement countries actually holds true for *all* values of t in that case.

thus reduce to that in (3.5), which we have shown above delivers payoffs identical to those in the Melitz (2003) model without contractual frictions.

Although 'cash-in-advance' transactions are not infrequent in international trade (see Antràs and Foley, 2013, for evidence from a U.S.-based exporter), the available evidence suggests that the majority of international transactions are conducted on open account (or post-shipment payment) terms.[11] These type of transactions roughly correspond to the timing of payments we have assumed so far. A natural question is then: why are cash-in-advance terms not used more often if they effectively eliminate the risk of importer default?

The key for answering this question is that not only exporters but also importers are exposed to the risk of counterparty misbehavior in international transactions. In particular, a standard concern for importers in cash-in-advance transactions is that, after being paid, the exporter might no longer have the incentive to ship goods in the most advantageous manner for importers, thus intentionally or unintentionally reducing the amount of sale revenues that the importer would obtain when selling the goods in their local market. I next briefly develop a simple model of exporter misbehavior along the lines of the model of limited commitment by importers developed above.[12] The model will serve to illustrate the role of exporter-country institutions in shaping the different margins of international trade.

Suppose that the exporter and importer sign the following simple cash-in-advance contract. At t_0, the exporting firm F agrees to ship an amount of goods equal to q_{ij} in exchange for an amount s_{ij} to be paid upon signing the contract at t_0. After receiving the goods, the importer sells them in her local market and she keeps the collected sale revenue. As argued above, without any type of frictions, the exporter could set an initial payment $s_{ij}(\varphi)$ equal to the sale revenue collected by the importer at time t_1, i.e., $p_{ij}(q_{ij}(\varphi))q_{ij}(\varphi)$, thus attaining the frictionless profit flow in (3.4).

Imagine, however, that shortly after signing the contract at t_0, the exporter is presented with an opportunity to deviate from the initial contract in a way that would reduce its costs of production but would also reduce the expected revenues collected by the importer at t_1. Such a deviation might entail shirking in quality-enhancing investments or in the use of shipping methods that best ensure the quality of goods when they reach the importer's

---

[11] For instance, using the World Bank Enterprise Survey database, Hoefele, Schmidt-Eisenlohr, and Yu (2013) find that the average share of sales on open account terms for the firms in the sample is in excess of 80%.

[12] Financial constraints faced by the importer might be another factor limiting the use of cash-in-advance contracts. Manova (2012) has found indeed that bilateral trade flows are depressed by low quality of financial institutions in importing countries, even though that was not the focus of her study.

market. For the time being, consider the case in which exporter misbehavior takes the extreme form of the exporter incurring no variable production costs and the importer not receiving goods or receiving totally worthless goods. Below, I will consider much less extreme cases. Faced with this opportunity to misbehave, the exporter will consider the legal implications of such a deviation before cheating on the importer. Suppose that if the exporter were to deviate, the importer could sue the exporter in the latter's country, and the court of law in the exporter's country would rule in favor of the importer with probability λ_{ij}^{exp}. Such a ruling would in turn result in the exporter being asked to pay the importer an amount in damages equal to a multiple d_{ij}^{exp} of the payment stipulated in the initial contract, i.e., s_{ij}. When $\lambda_{ij}^{exp} d_{ij}^{exp} > 1$, the exporter would never be tempted to cheat on the importer, so we will focus below on the more interesting case in which $\lambda_{ij}^{exp} d_{ij}^{exp} < 1$. In the latter case, in order for the exporter not be tempted to misbehave, the payment stipulated in the initial contract needs to satisfy the following incentive compatibility (IC) constraint:

$$s_{ij}(\varphi) - \frac{\tau_{ij}}{\varphi} w_i q_{ij}(\varphi) \geq \left(1 - \lambda_{ij}^{exp} d_{ij}^{exp}\right) s_{ij}(\varphi). \tag{3.20}$$

Note that it is in the exporter's own interest to ensure that the initial contract satisfies this IC constraint because otherwise the importer would anticipate misbehavior with probability one, and he or she would not be willing to pay *any* amount of money to the exporter in the initial period, thus leaving both agents with a zero payoff.

Using equation (3.4) and the fact that revenues are a multiple σ of operating profits, it is straightforward to verify that provided that $\lambda_{ij}^{exp} d_{ij}^{exp} \geq (\sigma - 1)/\sigma$, the constraint in (3.20) will be slack when evaluated at the unconstrained profit-maximizing output level $q_{ij}(\varphi)$, and thus the exporter will still be able to achieve the unconstrained profit flow in (3.4). Conversely, when courts punish deviating agents with a low enough probability or when damages are low enough or unenforceable, so that $\lambda_{ij}^{exp} d_{ij}^{exp} < (\sigma - 1)/\sigma$, the exporter will no longer be able to achieve the unconstrained profit flow in (3.4). Instead, the quantity of output being shipped will need to adjust to ensure that equation (3.20) holds, and the exporter will find it optimal to make that constraint exactly bind. Furthermore, one can show that the exporter will never find it optimal to demand an ex ante payment lower than the total sale revenues collected by the importer at t_1, so $s_{ij}(\varphi) = p_j(q_{ij}(\varphi)) q_{ij}(\varphi)$, and from equations (3.20) we can infer that

$$p_j(q_{ij}(\varphi)) = \frac{\tau_{ij} w_i}{\lambda_{ij}^{exp} d_{ij}^{exp} \varphi}. \tag{3.21}$$

Using (3.21) together with $q_{ij}(\varphi) = \beta E_j P_j^{\sigma-1} p_j^{-\sigma}$ and the definition of B_j in (3.2), we can then express the profits of the exporter as

$$\pi_{ij}(\varphi) = \mu_{ij}^{exp} \left(\tau_{ij} w_i\right)^{1-\sigma} B_j \varphi^{\sigma-1} - w_i f_{ij}, \qquad (3.22)$$

where

$$\mu_{ij}^{exp} = \begin{cases} 1 & \text{if } \lambda_{ij}^{exp} d_{ij}^{exp} \geq (\sigma - 1)/\sigma \\ \sigma \left(1 - \lambda_{ij}^{exp} d_{ij}^{exp}\right) \left(\dfrac{\sigma \lambda_{ij}^{exp} d_{ij}^{exp}}{\sigma-1}\right)^{\sigma-1} < 1 & \text{if } \lambda_{ij}^{exp} d_{ij}^{exp} < (\sigma - 1)/\sigma. \end{cases}$$

$$(3.23)$$

Note that μ_{ij}^{exp} is (weakly) increasing in $\lambda_{ij}^{exp} d_{ij}^{exp}$, and that $\mu_{ij}^{exp} = 1$ only when $\lambda_{ij}^{exp} d_{ij}^{exp} \geq (\sigma - 1)/\sigma$. Hence, in the range of parameter values in which the exporter is tempted to misbehave, the profits the exporter will end up obtaining will necessarily be lower than in the unconstrained problem.

Equation (3.22) illustrates that limited commitment problems on the part of the exporter end up affecting the profitability of exporting in a similar manner as limited commitment problems on the importer side. In fact, equation (3.21) is identical to (3.7) except for the term μ_{ij}^{exp} in (3.21) instead of μ_{ij}^σ in (3.7). The superscript *exp* in the contracting term in (3.21) serves to emphasize that the quality of the *exporter* country's contracting institutions is now key in shaping the profitability of exporting, the intensive and extensive margins of trade, and bilateral trade flows across countries. Of course, one could argue, as we did in the importer limited commitment case, that agents could make use of choice-of-law or choice-of-forum contractual clauses to partly isolate the security of a transaction from weak contracting institutions in the exporting country. Nevertheless, and as explained in Chapter 1, even when disputes are adjudicated by foreign courts, the enforceability of damages is ultimately an issue related to the local legal environment in the exporting country, and particularly whether that country has signed the New York convention.

I will next provide an overview of the empirical work linking bilateral trade flows to the quality of the exporter country's contracting institutions, but before doing so I should briefly address two further theoretical points. First, and although it is obvious to see that all equilibrium conditions with exporter limited commitment will be identical to those in (3.7) through (3.15) with μ_{ij}^{exp} replacing μ_{ij}^σ, there is one important, subtle difference in the general equilibrium implications of the two models. Because in this second model, importers always end up with a net payoff of zero, the effects of a low μ_{ij}^{exp} are not isomorphic to an import tariff in the importing country, but instead are analogous to those of an iceberg trade cost. An implication of this difference is that, at least in the one-sector version of the model, improvements in the quality of contracting institutions in a small exporting country will always be beneficial for the importing country (see Demidova and Rodríguez-Clare, 2013). A second point worth making is that our model of exporter misbehavior can easily be extended to the case in which the exporter's temptation to deviate from the contract entails reducing marginal costs by a certain fraction ν_{ij}^{exp} where we now allow $\nu_{ij}^{exp} < 1$. In such a case, the exporter's incentive compatibility constraint becomes

$$\lambda_{ij}^{exp} d_{ij}^{exp} s_{ij}(\varphi) \geq \nu_{ij}^{exp} \frac{\tau_{ij}}{\varphi} w_i q_{ij}(\varphi),$$

and the same expressions (3.21) through (3.23) apply, but with $\lambda_{ij}^{exp} d_{ij}^{exp} / \nu_{ij}^{exp}$ replacing $\lambda_{ij}^{exp} d_{ij}^{exp}$ throughout. Clearly, exporter profits will be higher in that case, but as long as $\lambda_{ij}^{exp} d_{ij}^{exp} / \nu_{ij}^{exp} < (\sigma - 1)/\sigma$, contractual frictions continue to reduce the profitability of exporting.

Exporter-Country Institutions: Empirical Evidence

Earlier in the chapter we discussed the empirical work of Anderson and Marcouiller (2002) establishing a link between bilateral trade flows and the quality of the importer's contracting institutions. It is clear that the empirical strategy in that paper is not applicable to the study of the effects of exporter-country institutions, since the relative exports specification in (3.16) effectively partials out exporter-specific variables. Berkowitz, Moenius, and Pistor (2006) propose instead a more traditional log-linear gravity specification which can be motivated by a simple variant of equation (3.15) with μ_{ij}^{exp} replacing μ_{ij}^{σ}:

$$X_{ij} = \frac{Y_i}{\Theta_i} B_j^{\frac{\kappa}{\sigma-1}} \tau_{ij}^{-\kappa} f_{ij}^{-\frac{\kappa-(\sigma-1)}{(\sigma-1)}} \left(\mu_{ij}^{exp}\right)^{\kappa/(\sigma-1)}. \tag{3.24}$$

In order to control for the unobserved multilateral resistance term Θ_i and the price index implicit in B_j, Berkowitz et al. (2006) introduce exporter and importer fixed effects. The authors' measure of the quality of contracting institutions is an average of a country's index of rule of law, expropriation risk, corruption in government, and bureaucratic quality as computed by the International Country Risk Guide. This variable is computed for the exporter and the importer in each pair of trading partners and both variables are introduced in the regression, thus allowing for both importer and exporter country institutions to affect bilateral trade flows. In order for the country fixed effects not to absorb these institutional variables, Berkowitz et al. (2006) use data from 1982 to 1992 and exploit time-series variation in both bilateral trade flows and the perceived quality of contracting institutions.

TABLE 3.3 Exporter and Importer Contracting Institutions and Bilateral Exports

Type of Goods Included	(1) Overall	(2) Overall	(3) Complex	(4) Simple
GDP importer	0.81**	−0.15	0.08	−1.06*
	(0.02)	(0.29)	(0.30)	(0.42)
GDP exporter	0.76**	−0.19	0.32	−1.38**
	(0.02)	(0.29)	(0.30)	(0.42)
Distance	−1.16**	−1.03**	−0.98**	−1.26**
	(0.04)	(0.04)	(0.04)	(0.06)
Adjacent	0.35*	0.40**	0.44**	0.27
	(0.14)	(0.15)	(0.17)	(0.18)
Links	0.42**	0.45**	0.54**	0.18
	(0.10)	(0.10)	(0.11)	(0.15)
Language similarities	0.09	1.00**	1.28**	0.11
	(0.18)	(0.17)	(0.19)	(0.28)
Remoteness	0.58**	1.79*	0.74	6.69**
	(0.10)	(0.78)	(0.77)	(1.22)
Quality of importer legal institutions	0.61**	0.05	−0.44**	0.66**
	(0.11)	(0.10)	(0.10)	(0.15)
Quality of exporter legal institutions	0.91**	0.36**	0.93**	−0.53**
	(0.13)	(0.11)	(0.11)	(0.15)
Country dummies	No	Yes	Yes	Yes
Time dummies	No	Yes	Yes	Yes
Number of clusters (country pairs)	2792	2792	2755	2550
R-squared	0.70	0.77	0.79	0.38
Number observations	23,564	23,564	22,669	18,948

Source: Reproduced from tables 2 and 3 in Berkowitz et al. (2006). Robust standard errors (within-group clustering) in parentheses. Regressions also include exporter and importer GDP per capita and a constant. +, *, ** denote 10, 5, 1% significance.

Their specifications also include time fixed effects and controls for GDP, GDP per capita, and various measures of proximity between the exporter and the importer, including a measure of the remoteness related to whether a pair of countries are close to each other but distant from the rest of the world.

The first two columns of Table 3.3 reproduce the results obtained by Berkowitz et al. (2006) when running their specification with and without the country and year fixed effects, respectively. As is clear from column (1), when ignoring these fixed effects, all variables affect bilateral trade flows in the expected way, and the institutional quality variables related to both the exporter and the importer are highly statistically significant, with exporter institutions appearing to matter more than importer institutions. When introducing the exporter, importer, and year fixed effects in column (2), a first noteworthy fact is that the effect of GDP on bilateral trade flows vanishes. This is not entirely surprising since the fixed effects were supposed to control for terms in the gravity equation involving GDP. More relevant for the current discussion is the fact that the variable capturing the quality of contracting institutions in the exporting country remains both positive and highly statistically significant, while the importer country institutional quality variable remains positive but loses its statistical significance.

I will soon discuss a set of additional results in the Berkowitz et al. (2006) paper that anticipated the voluminous literature on the institutional determinants of comparative advantage. Before doing so, however, I will draw on the work of Waugh (2010) and briefly outline an alternative way to identify the potential role of contracting institutions in shaping bilateral trade flows across countries. Let us return to the modified gravity equation in (3.24), and note that we can use it to express the ratio of exports from i to j to the domestic absorption of the importing country j as:

$$\frac{X_{ij}}{X_{jj}} = \frac{Y_i/\Theta_i \, \tau_{ij}^{-\kappa} \, f_{ij}^{-\frac{\kappa-(\sigma-1)}{(\sigma-1)}} \left(\mu_{ij}^{exp}\right)^{\kappa/(\sigma-1)}}{Y_j/\Theta_j \, \tau_{jj}^{-\kappa} \, f_{jj}^{-\frac{\kappa-(\sigma-1)}{(\sigma-1)}} \left(\mu_{jj}^{exp}\right)^{\kappa/(\sigma-1)}}. \tag{3.25}$$

Next suppose that within-country or domestic barriers to trade— technological and contractual—do not vary significantly across countries, so we can set $\tau_{jj} = \tau_d$, $f_{jj} = f_d$, and $\mu_{jj}^{exp} = \mu_d$ for all j. This is a strong assumption, so I will return to it below. Assume also that transportation barriers are symmetric across countries, so $\tau_{ij} = \tau_{ji}$ and $f_{ij} = f_{ji}$ for any two countries i and j. Conversely, and as long as $i \neq j$, let μ_{ij}^{exp} be *only* a function of the quality of the exporter-country institutions, in the spirit of our discussion above. Let us thus simply denote $\mu_{ij}^{exp} = \mu_i$. Taking logs of (3.25) then delivers

$$\ln\left(\frac{X_{ij}}{X_{jj}}\right) = \alpha + \Psi_i - \Psi_j - \kappa \ln \tau_{ij} - \frac{\kappa - (\sigma - 1)}{\sigma - 1} \ln f_{ij} + \frac{\kappa}{\sigma - 1} \ln \mu_i, \tag{3.26}$$

where $\Psi_i = \ln(Y_i/\Theta_i)$. A key feature of equation (3.26) is that when regressing the left-hand side on exporter and importer fixed effects, and empirical proxies for the bilateral trade costs between i and j (distance, language, and so on), the only reason for a country's fixed effect as an exporter to be different from that as an importer is for μ_i to be less than 1, i.e., for contract enforcement to be imperfect.

Waugh (2010) runs the specification in (3.26) with data on bilateral trade flows and domestic absorption for seventy-seven countries in 1996. His findings indicate the existence of very significant asymmetries in a country's fixed effect as an exporter and as an importer, and he shows that these asymmetries are correlated with income per capita. He interprets his results

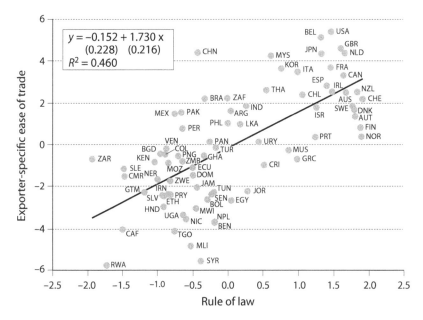

Figure 3.3 Inferred Exporter-Specific Ease of Exporting and the Rule of Law

as suggesting that poor countries face much larger trade barriers when exporting than rich countries do. Waugh (2010) associates this asymmetry to an exporter-specific term in iceberg trade barriers (so $\tau_{ij} \neq \tau_{ji}$), while above I have ascribed these asymmetries to differences in export-country contract enforcement across countries. Admittedly, this is quite arbitrary, but as Figure 3.3 indicates there exists a very significant positive correlation between the implied measure of $\frac{\kappa}{\sigma-1} \ln \mu_i$ one backs out from the data and the "Rule of Law" measure from the Governance Matters III Database, which is a standard proxy for contract enforcement (see Nunn, 2007, for details). Furthermore, the implied effect of contract enforcement on trade flows is remarkably large. For example, if the quality of contracting institutions in Guatemala were to increase to the level of those in Ecuador —which corresponds to an increase of 0.65 standard deviations in the rule of law measure—Guatemalan exports relative to the domestic absorption of an average importing country would increase by 118 percent.

In order to extract the exporter-specific trade impediment from data on trade flows and domestic absorption, we have made strong assumptions. For instance, it seems reasonable that countries with poor institutions will also feature particularly weak contract enforcement in domestic transactions. It is apparent from (3.25), however, that this would tend to restore the symmetry between the fixed effect of a country as an exporter and as an importer, and thus this would presumably work to attenuate the strong positive correlation observed in Figure 3.3, rather than provide an alternative explanation for it.

Hopefully, the reader will view the evidence reviewed so far as suggestive of the relevance of contracting institutions as a determinant of bilateral trade flows across countries. It would be quite a stretch, however, to claim that the results in Table 3.3 or Figure 3.3 come anywhere close to identifying a causal effect of contracting institutions on trade flows. A particularly important concern is that we have ascribed to contractual institutions an effect that might in reality be caused by other country characteristics that happen to be correlated with the quality of this type of institution.[13]

Berkowitz et al. (2006) acknowledge the potential existence of omitted-variable biases in their estimates and suggest an ingenious identification strategy based on the notion that contracting institutions are likely to have a differential effect on different types of goods. More specifically, it seems natural to suppose that the type of contractual difficulties highlighted in this chapter are more likely to apply to complex goods than to simple goods. In fact, it is rather simple to extend the above model of exporter misbehavior to formalize this insight. For that purpose, assume that whether the exporter will be presented with an opportunity to misbehave or not occurs with a probability ρ which is a function of the type of good being traded. In particular, assume that ρ is higher for complex, less contractible goods than for simple, homogeneous goods. Provided that both producers know whether such misbehavior is possible or not before they sign the initial contract (but not before the fixed exporting cost is incurred), it is straightforward to show that the equilibrium of the model will be identical to that above, but with

$$\tilde{\mu}_{ij}^{exp} \equiv \rho + (1 - \rho)\,\mu_{ij}^{exp}$$

replacing μ_{ij}^{exp} throughout. It is then clear that the effect of better contract enforcement on profitability, firm-level exports, bilateral exports, and so on is lower, the higher is ρ, i.e., the more complex goods are.

In order to test this prediction, Berkowitz et al. (2006) employ the Rauch (1999) classification of goods into differentiated and homogeneous and run their specification on each set of goods separately. Their results are repro-duced in columns (3) and (4) of Table 3.3. A striking feature of their findings is that high levels of contract enforcement in the exporting country are shown to increase exports of complex goods but at the same time they *reduce* exports of simple goods. Conversely, and somewhat puzzlingly, good contracting institutions in the importing country enhance imports of simple goods, but reduce those of complex goods!

---

[13] For example, the positive relationship in Figure 3.3 remains positive but loses its statistical significance when controlling for income per capita.

In order to rationalize their findings, Berkowitz et al. (2006) argue that the quality of contracting institutions will not only affect the security with which international transactions are conducted, but will also shape the efficiency with which the traded goods are produced, thus becoming a source of comparative advantage. Viewed from that perspective, their results in columns (3) and (4) are less surprising. They simply might reflect that countries with strong contracting institutions gain comparative advantage in complex (contract-intensive) goods, and as a result they tend to feature disproportionately high levels of exports of these complex goods and disproportionately low levels of imports of simple goods.

Domestic Institutions and Comparative Advantage

The idea that the quality of domestic institutions may constitute a source of comparative advantage has featured prominently in the trade literature in recent years. The vast literature on the topic is reviewed in Nunn and Trefler (2013a), so I will only sketch a few key contributions here. The earliest papers in that literature were closest in spirit to the work of Berkowitz et al. (2006). Nunn (2007), Levchenko (2007), and Costinot (2009) all explored how domestic contracting institutions shape productivity differentially across sectors depending on characteristics of those sectors. They each proposed a measure of contract intensity different from the dichotomous one used by Berkowitz et al. (2006), and each showed that the effect of contracting institutions on trade flows was disproportionately higher in the industries identified to be relatively contract-intensive.

I will next briefly overview Nunn's paper because it has been the most influential one in this literature. In Chapter 5, I will perform empirical tests closely related to those in Levchenko (2007), so I will provide more details on his work at that point. Nunn (2007) proposes as a proxy for contract intensity a measure of the proportion of an industry's intermediate inputs that are relationship-specific. To construct that proportion, he builds on the classification of goods developed by Rauch (1999), which distinguishes between goods sold on organized exchanges, those with reference prices in trade publications, and all residual goods, which are assumed to be differentiated or customized. More specifically, Nunn uses U.S. Input-Output Use tables to construct an industry's use of intermediate inputs provided by other industries, and then infers the extent to which these inputs are customized from Rauch's classification of goods.

The resulting least and most contract-intensive industries according to Nunn's (2007) definition are reproduced in Table 3.4. The ordering of industries appears sensible. For instance, the two least contract-intensive industries are "poultry processing" and "flour milling", which indeed use

TABLE 3.4 The Ten Least and Ten Most Contract-Intensive Industries

10 Least Contract-Intensive: Lowest z_i^{rs1}		10 Most Contract-Intensive: Highest z_i^{rs1}	
0.024	Poultry processing	0.810	Photogr. & photoc. equip. manuf.
0.024	Flour milling	0.819	Air & gas compressor manuf.
0.036	Petroleum refineries	0.822	Analytic laboratory instr. manuf.
0.036	Wet corn milling	0.824	Other engine equipment manuf.
0.053	Aluminum sheet, plate, & foil manuf.	0.826	Other electronic component manuf.
0.058	Primary aluminum production	0.831	Packaging machinery manuf.
0.087	Nitrogenous fertilizer manuf.	0.840	Book publishers
0.099	Rice milling	0.851	Breweries
0.111	Prim. nonferrous metal	0.854	Musical instrument manuf.
0.132	Tobacco stemming & redrying	0.872	Aircraft engine & parts manuf.

Source: Reproduced from table II in Nunn (2007).

highly homogeneous inputs (chickens and wheat, respectively), while the most contract-intensive industry is aircraft manufacturing, which requires the use of highly customized inputs.

With this industry measure of contract intensity at hand, Nunn (2007) then uses international trade data for 146 countries and 222 industries in 1997 to explore whether countries with better contract enforcement appear to feature disproportionately large levels of exports in contract-intensive sectors. As a proxy for the level of contract enforcement in a particular country, Nunn (2007) uses the "Rule of Law" variable from the Governance Matters III Database, which consists of a weighted average of seventeen measures of judicial quality and contract enforcement. Nunn's specifications are of the form

$$\ln(X_{si}) = \alpha_s + \alpha_i + \beta_1 z_s \mu_i + \beta_2 h_s H_i + \beta_3 k_s K_i + \gamma c_s C_i + \varepsilon_{si},$$

where X_{si} denotes total exports in industry s from country i to all other countries in the world, z_s is contract intensity in industry s, μ_i is a measure of the quality of contract enforcement in (the exporting) country i, H_i and K_i denote country i's endowments of skilled labor and capital, and h_s and k_s are the skill and capital intensities of production in industry s. The term $c_s C_i$ represents a vector of control interactions of industry and country characteristics, while α_s and α_i denote industry fixed effects and country fixed effects, respectively.

Table 3.5 reproduces the benchmark results in Nunn (2007). The first two columns demonstrate that the interaction of contract intensity and judicial quality has a positive and statistically significant effect on exports, which is suggestive of the importance of contracting variables for the structure of

TABLE 3.5 The Determinants of Comparative Advantage

	(1)	(2)	(3)	(4)
Judicial quality interaction	0.289**	0.318**	0.326**	0.296**
	(0.013)	(0.020)	(0.023)	(0.024)
Skill interaction			0.085**	0.063**
			(0.017)	(0.017)
Capital interaction			0.105**	0.074+
			(0.031)	(0.041)
Log income × value added				−0.137*
				(0.067)
Log income × intraindustry trade				0.546**
				(0.056)
Log income × TFP growth				−0.010
				(0.049)
Log income × capital				0.021
				(0.018)
Log income × input variety				0.522**
				(0.103)
R-squared	0.72	0.76	0.76	0.76
Number of observations	22,598	10,976	10,976	10,816

Source: Reproduced from table IV in Nunn (2007). Regressions also include country and industry fixed effects. Standardized beta coefficients reported. Standard errors in parentheses. +, *, ** denote 10, 5, 1% significance.

international trade flows. Column (2) features a lower number of observations than column (1) because the sample is restricted to those countries and industries for which suitable proxies for factor abundance and intensities are available. The addition of these Heckscher-Ohlin interactions in column (3) has a negligible impact on the estimate of β_1, while the standardized beta coefficients in that column indicate that the effect that judicial quality has on the pattern of trade is greater than the combined effects of both capital and skilled labor. The inclusion of additional controls in column (4) has little impact on these conclusions. Nunn (2007) presents several robustness tests and also attempts to deal with endogeneity concerns by using legal origin as an instrument for judicial quality and by using propensity score techniques.

Building on the insights of this empirical literature on the effects of contracting institutions, other researchers have explored the role of other types of institutions in shaping comparative advantage across sectors. Manova (2008, 2012), for instance, explores the role of the quality of financial institutions in shaping the extensive and intensive margin of trade. Her empirical strategy builds on the seminal work of Rajan and Zingales (1998), who categorized sectors into more or less financially dependent depending on their external finance requirements. Relatedly, Cuñat and Melitz (2012) study how differences in the flexibility of labor market institutions across countries affect comparative advantage by building an industry-level measure of the importance of within-sectoral reallocations of labor as a response to shocks. In a very nicely executed study, Chor (2010) attempts to disentangle the partial effect of each of these institutional determinants of comparative advantage in a unified empirical model.

Despite the recent focus in the literature on the role of *domestic* contracting institutions in shaping trade flows, it is not a warranted conclusion from these studies that *international* contract enforcement is irrelevant for explaining trade flows across countries. First, the aforementioned findings of Helpman et al. (2008) regarding the effect of having a common legal origin on aggregate bilateral trade flows are hard to rationalize in models in which international contract enforcement is perfect. Second, apart from their results discussed above, Berkowitz et al. (2006) also found that the effects of exporter and importer legal quality appear to be significantly affected by whether or not countries have ratified the New York convention. For instance, their estimates indicate that for the case of complex goods, the quality of exporter institutions matters disproportionately more when the export partner has not yet signed the New York convention and thus international enforcement of damages is more doubtful. For a third illustration of the importance of imperfect international contract enforcement, I next briefly return to the choice of payment-method decision faced by exporters and importers when negotiating their initial contracts.

Back to Trade Finance

So far we have illustrated how the quality of importer country institutions shapes the profitability and structure of exports whenever contracts are associated with post-shipment payment (or simply, open account) terms, while the quality of exporter country institutions plays a similar role in cash-in-advance transactions. Obviously, this constitutes a simplistic description of the effect of institutions on exporting. It seems natural, for instance, that exporter country institutions will matter even in open account terms to the extent that the consequences of exporter misbehavior might manifest themselves long after the goods have been received by the importer, or even after these goods have been sold to local consumers. Similarly, importer country institutions might affect the profitability of cash-in-advance transactions to the extent that they shape the financing costs faced by exporters. Intuitively, in countries where defaults are not sufficiently punished, not only exporters but also banks will shy away from extending credit to importers.

An active literature in international trade has explored the determinants of the choice of payment mode in international transactions, with a special emphasis on the role of weak contracting institutions. This literature includes, among others, the work of Amiti and Weinstein (2011), Antràs and Foley (2013), Ahn (2011), Hoefele et al. (2013), Olsen (2013), and Schmidt-Eisenlohr (2013). Antràs and Foley (2013) in particular focus on the role of importer country institutions, while allowing these to affect the profitability of both open account transactions (via default risk) as well as cash-in-advance transactions (via financing costs). Their key theoretical finding is that in the plausible case in which local banks in the importing country are better able than exporters to pursue financial claims against importers, one would expect exports to locations characterized by weak contractual enforcement to be more likely to occur on cash-in-advance as opposed to open account terms.[14]

One of the main challenges in studying the financing arrangements used to support international trade is that detailed data on how different types of transactions are financed are not readily available. Antràs and Foley (2013) overcome this dearth of data by analyzing detailed transaction-level data from a single U.S.-based firm that exports frozen and refrigerated food products, primarily poultry. The data cover roughly $7 billion in sales to more than 140 countries over the 1996–2009 period and contain comprehensive information on the financing terms used in each transaction. A key advantage of the dataset is that by focusing on the sales of a single exporter based in the United States, any institution-driven variation in the choice of payment mode must be ascribed to importer-country institutions or, following our broader interpretation of the parameter μ_{ij} in (3.6), to legal proximity between the United States and the importing country.

Antràs and Foley (2013) find robust evidence that variation in importer country contract enforcement has a strong effect on the method of payment offered to importers. Figure 3.4 reproduces the results in Figure 3 of their paper. For each of the proxies of contractual enforcement in the figure, the share of transactions occurring on cash-in-advance share is strikingly lower in strong contract enforcement countries than in weak contract enforcement countries. For instance, in Common law countries, 4.0 percent of sales occur on cash-in-advance terms and 79.8 percent of sales occur on open account terms, while in civil law countries these shares are 63.8 percent and 20.4 percent. Similarly stark differences appear when the sample is split using measures of contract viability from International Country Risk Guide (ICRG), payment delay (also from ICRG), and the enforceability of contracts (from Knack and

---

[14] Antràs and Foley (2013) also consider the possibility of exporters and importers resorting to letters of credit, but these financial instruments mediate a small share of world trade in modern times (see also Olsen, 2013, for more on letters of credit).

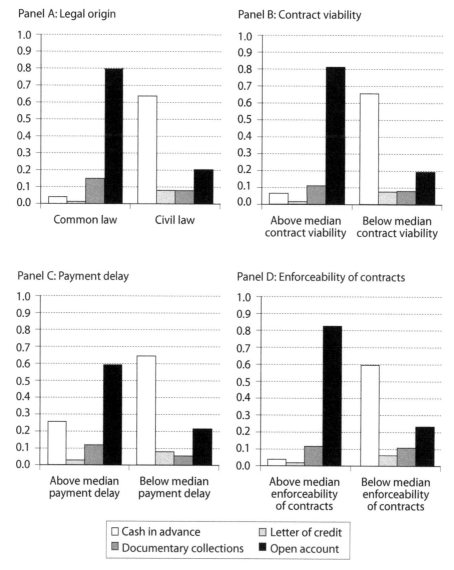

Figure 3.4 Financing Terms and the Enforcement of Contracts

Keefer , 1995). Antràs and Foley (2013) show that these patterns persist after controlling for several country-level variables as well as product fixed effects. Consistent with the results of the dynamic model of repeated interactions developed earlier in this chapter, they also find that first-time buyers are disproportionately more likely to be demanded to prepay for their purchases, but that as the exporter establishes a relationship with an importer, the share of cash-in-advance transactions falls smoothly over time.

In a recent paper, Hoefele et al. (2013) have employed information from the World Bank Enterprise Survey to study the effects of variation in *exporting* country institutions on the choice of trade finance by firms. Consistent with the models developed in this chapter, Hoefele et al. (2013) find that the use of cash-in-advance terms is more prevalent in exporting countries with strong contracting institutions, in which exporter misbehavior is less of a concern.

The Road Ahead

This chapter has explored both theoretically as well as empirically the significance of weak contract enforcement for the export decisions of firms and, more broadly, for the structure of international trade flows. The focus, however, has been on how contractual frictions affect the international *exchange* of goods. As explained in Chapter 1, the rapid growth in intermediate input trade has been one of the most prominent developments in the world economy in recent years. At the same time, the contractual relationships that support the phenomenon of offshoring are much more intricate than those that support the mere shipment of goods across countries. Thus, weak contract enforcement has the potential to affect the global organization of production in more profound ways than we have studied so far. In the next chapter, we will begin to explore these more complex contractual aspects of global sourcing.

4

Contracts and Global Sourcing

In his highly entertaining book, *Poorly Made in China*, Paul Midler (2009) describes his experiences as an offshoring consultant in China, where his command of Chinese made him a particularly valuable asset for American companies eager to outsource in that country. The bulk of Midler's book is centered around his work in assisting the chief operating officer of Johnson Carter, a U.S. personal care import company, in his negotiations with King Chemical, a Chinese manufacturer located outside Guangzhou (the names in the book are fictitious but the stories are genuine). Johnson Carter is in the business of supplying large chain stores in the United States with house-brand shampoo and soaps.

Midler's book vividly illustrates just how irrelevant formal outsourcing contracts can prove to be in China, reflecting the old Chinese adage that "signing a contract is just the first step in the real negotiations." Chinese manufacturers—and King Chemical in particular—appear to attract clients by offering very low prices in order to secure contracts. After locking in U.S. buyers, in this case, Johnson Carter, they work to devise numerous ways to increase their profit margins. These maneuvers often involve reductions of material costs, last-minute price increases, or even the use of the client's designs to sell the same products to alternative buyers at higher prices. In one particular instance, and after a contract order had been signed, King Chemical sought to reduce the money they spent on plastic by secretly switching to thinner bottles which were much more likely to collapse when squeezed. In another instance, Midler discovered that King Chemical was filling the bottles with significantly less soap than the 850 milliliters they had agreed on. Arbitrary price increases were particularly frustrating to Johnson Carter, as King Chemical's price hikes were typically poorly justified and were invariably demanded right after the U.S. company had secured a large order from a U.S. retailer, at which point the U.S. company had no time to turn to an alternative Chinese manufacturer. These last-minute price spikes were hardly specific to King Chemical. As Midler writes," 'Price go up!' was the resounding chorus heard across the manufacturing sector" in China.

The goal of this chapter is to initiate the analysis of the implications of weak contract enforcement for the international organization of production.

With that goal in mind, I will start by going back to the benchmark two-country model of global sourcing developed in Chapter 2, and I will highlight the contracting assumptions underlying the results of that model. I will then introduce a model of contractual frictions that will shed light on the effect of contracting institutions on the intensive and extensive margins of intermediate input trade. Next, I will develop a series of extensions of the model that will open the door for model-based empirical tests of the effects of contracting considerations on the offshoring decisions of firms. In Chapter 5, I will develop a multi-country version of the model and will present suggestive evidence based on U.S. import data of the empirical relevance of the concepts highlighted in this chapter.

A Brief Recap of the Global Sourcing Model

Let us now go back to the model of global sourcing with heterogeneous firms introduced in Chapter 2. To build intuition, I will initially focus on the simple two-stage, two-country offshoring model inspired by the work of Antràs and Helpman (2004). Before transitioning to the empirics, it will prove useful to extend the model to a multi-country environment as outlined toward the end of Chapter 2, but I defer any discussion of multi-country environments until Chapter 5.

I will not review the benchmark global sourcing model in great detail, but it may be useful to remind the reader of a few of its key features. We are largely concerned with the behavior of firms in a differentiated-good sector in which final goods are produced by combining two stages, headquarter services and manufacturing production, under a Cobb-Douglas technology. Firms differ in their productivity level, which as in Melitz (2003) is only revealed upon paying a fixed cost of entry. There are two countries, the North and the South. The North has comparative advantage in entry and headquarter services, so these stages always occur there. Conversely, the South has comparative advantage in manufacturing production, and absent any fixed costs of offshoring, all firms would want to fragment production and combine Northern headquarter services and Southern manufacturing production. But offshoring is however costly and entails a fixed cost of f_O units of Northern labor, while Northern production of manufacturing goods entails a lower fixed cost equal to $f_D < f_O$ units of Northern labor.

Overall, the total cost of production associated with **D**omestic sourcing in the North and **O**ffshoring to the South are given, respectively, by

$$C_D(q, \varphi) = \left(f_D + \frac{q}{\varphi} \right) w_N,$$

and

$$C_O(q, \varphi) = f_O w_N + \frac{q}{\varphi}(w_N)^\eta (\tau w_S)^{1-\eta},$$

where φ is a firm-specific productivity parameter throughout the book, w_i denotes the wage rate in country $i = N, S$, τ reflects variable costs of offshoring (input trade costs, communications costs,...), and η represents the headquarter intensity of production.

Assuming further, and for simplicity, that trade in final goods is free, we then used the demand equation (2.3) to derive the operating profits associated with each of the two sourcing strategies available to firms in the North. In particular, a Northern firm with productivity φ would obtain a profit flow equal to

$$\pi_D(\varphi) = (w_N)^{1-\sigma} B\varphi^{\sigma-1} - f_D w_N \qquad (4.1)$$

when sourcing domestically, and a profit flow equal to

$$\pi_O(\varphi) = \left((w_N)^\eta (\tau w_S)^{1-\eta}\right)^{1-\sigma} B\varphi^{\sigma-1} - f_O w_N, \qquad (4.2)$$

when offshoring the manufacturing stage of production to the South. In these equations, market demand B is given by

$$B = \frac{1}{\sigma}\left(\frac{\sigma}{(\sigma-1)P}\right)^{1-\sigma} \beta(w_N L_N + w_S L_S).$$

As in our discussion of the export profit functions in the Melitz (2003) model, the realization of the entire profit flow (4.2) by the Northern final-good producer rests on strong assumptions, including having information on all parameters of the model, and frictionless contracting between producers (and between producers and workers). Below, I will maintain the assumption that all the parameters of the model are deterministic and common knowledge to all producers, and that labor markets work competitively and efficiently. This will focus our attention on the implications of weak contracting enforcement between Northern headquarters and Southern manufacturing plants. A discussion of contracting issues requires a more detailed discussion of the agents involved in production and the timing of events, a task to which I turn next.

Microeconomic Structure and Contracting

We shall begin by assuming that there are only two agents relevant for contracting in the production of each final-good differentiated variety. On the one hand, there is the final-good producer—agent F—who is in charge of

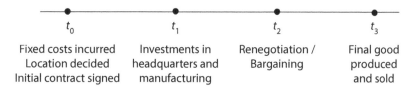

Figure 4.1 Timing of Events

incurring all fixed costs of production (including entry) and who also controls the provision of headquarter services. On the other hand, manufacturing production is controlled by a manager—agent M—in that production facility. Both agents have an outside opportunity that delivers them an income level which, for simplicity, I normalize to 0.

I next describe the timing of events, which is also illustrated in Figure 4.1. At some initial date t_0, the final-good producer F incurs the fixed cost of entry $w_N f_e$, upon which the productivity level φ is revealed, and F decides whether to have the manufacturing stage of production controlled by a Northern or a Southern manager. At the end of this same period, F approaches a manager M in the chosen location and offers him or her a formal sourcing contract (details below). This initial stage is followed by an investment stage t_1, at which F produces headquarter services and M undertakes manufacturing production. I assume for now that these investments occur simultaneously, but we will contemplate models with sequential production below. Once the investments have been incurred and before the manager M hands over the manufactured goods to the final-good producer F, we shall consider the possibility that the terms in the initial contract are renegotiable and bargained over at stage t_2. Finally, the terms of this renegotiation (or of the initial contract in the absence of renegotiation) are executed at a final stage t_3, when the final good is also produced and sold.

I will first illustrate that a seemingly simple initial contract might suffice for F to be able to attain the "frictionless" levels of operating profits in (4.1) and (4.2). To fix ideas, let us consider the case in which, at t_0, F has decided to approach a Southern manufacturer (we will later study the location choice). Suppose then that in the initial contract, F offers the Southern manager a contract that stipulates a quantity m^c of manufacturing production to be provided by M in exchange for a fee s^c received by M. Assume also that the initial contract includes a clause such that if any party deviates from this initial contract, the other party is entitled to arbitrarily large damages. With that clause, F can be assured that any level of manufacturing services stipulated in the initial contract will be honored by the manager. As a result, F can safely choose $h^c(\varphi)$, $m^c(\varphi)$ and $s^c(\varphi)$ to solve the following problem, where the constraint reflects the participation constraint of the Southern manager:

$$\max_{h(\varphi),m(\varphi),s(\varphi)} \quad p(q(\varphi))q(\varphi) - w_N h(\varphi) - w_N f_O - s(\varphi)$$

$$\text{s.t.} \quad s(\varphi) - \tau w_S m(\varphi) \geq 0. \tag{4.3}$$

Naturally, F will set $s^c(\varphi)$ in the initial contract to make the participation constraint of the manager M exactly bind, and as a result, F will choose $h^c(\varphi)$ and $m^c(\varphi)$ to maximize the overall surplus from the relationship, thus resulting in profit-maximizing investments and a profit flow identical to that in equation (4.2) above. Note that the timing of events, investments, or payments is quite irrelevant for this result.

Incomplete Contracts and Weak Contract Enforcement

As simple as the above contract may seem, it is hard to imagine that agents will in fact be able to (1) write such a type of contract, and (2) find a court of law to enforce it. More specifically, note that the initial contract needs to specify the level of m, which corresponds to the value or services obtained from the manufacturing stage of production. It does not merely reflect, in particular, the number of physical units of manufacturing goods. This distinction is crucial and carries important consequences. Consider our above anecdotal evidence from Midler's book *Poorly Made in China*. Johnson Carter presumably signed a contract with King Chemical for the provision of a certain number of bottles of soap in exchange for a certain amount of money (or price per bottle). It is hard to imagine, however, that the formal contract specified a variety of characteristics of the product which were clearly relevant for how the combination of Johnson Carter's "headquarter services" and King Chemical's manufactured goods was to translate into sale revenues in U.S. retail chains. For instance, the contract almost surely did not indicate the plastic content of the bottles or the chemical composition of the soap. Flimsy bottles or abrasive soap would each lead to a low value of m in the model, no matter how large the number of bottles actually manufactured.

The general lesson here is that while certain aspects of manufacturing, such as the number of units of goods to be produced, the price per unit, or the date of the delivery are relatively easy to incorporate into a formal written contract, many other aspects of production are not. And, crucially, these noncontractible elements of production are often key in shaping the quality of goods or their compatibility with other parts of the production process.

Beyond the obvious incompleteness of real-life commercial contracts, there still remains the issue of contract enforcement. Even if two expert parties were able to design a highly comprehensive contract specifying what each party is supposed to contribute to production and making explicit what defines high or low quality or compatibility, it is still questionable that a court of law will be able to understand such a contract and enforce it properly. And even when it does, in international transactions there still remains the uncertainty over the cross-border enforcement of damages (see Chapters 1 and 3 for a discussion of this issue). A natural response of the contracting parties is thus to shy away from specifying too harsh penalties for deviations from highly detailed clauses in written contracts. In Midler's soap bottles examples, Johnson Carter presumably could have insisted on the initial contract specifying the plastic content of bottles or that each bottle contained exactly 850 milliliters of soap, but it is somewhat hard to believe that a court of law would be able to verify whether that contract had been honored or not.

In sum, as simple as it might have seemed, the type of contract that we have considered so far is in fact too complicated to realistically discipline the behavior of agents. If such a contract is not feasible or enforceable, then what type of contracts are? One could envision the possibility that the initial contract would at least specify all the characteristics of the contractible aspects of production, while stipulating large penalties for deviations from that contract, thus ruling out the possibility of any ex-post renegotiation. It is not hard to see, however, that these types of contracts will typically deliver unappealing outcomes. For instance, imagine that the initial contract were to stipulate the number of physical units of m to be traded as well as their price in a binding manner, and without allowing M or F to renegotiate those terms upon observing the quality of the manufactured goods. In such a case, M would have every incentive to produce the inputs m in the least-cost possible manner, which would typically result in a low quality level of those goods. Foreseeing these debasements in quality, F would not be willing to offer a particularly large price for those goods in the initial contract, and the overall surplus of such a contractual relationship would end up being quite low and possibly zero, if M were to produce useless goods. In these circumstances, F might be better off offering a less complete contract at the initial stage, as we will show below.

Another possibility would be for the initial contract to specify a simple sharing rule for the sale revenue obtained by F when selling the final good to consumers. Even if the initial contract did not specify the quality characteristics of the manufactured inputs in a binding manner, it seems natural that the incentives of M to skim on quality will be attenuated when his or her profits are a function of the willingness of consumers to pay for goods that embody those manufactured inputs. Whenever certain aspects of the investments in h and m remain noncontractible, however, these types of revenue-sharing contracts will not lead to the frictionless levels of investment and profits of the complete-contracting environment, a result reminiscent of Holmstrom's (1982) moral-hazard-in-teams problem. As a result, even when revenue-sharing arrangements are feasible and enforceable, we will see that in some cases it may well be in the interest of the parties to opt out of them in the initial contract. Needless to say, the appeal of these contracts is further diminished whenever they are not perfectly enforceable, perhaps due to manipulation by the agent collecting revenues, who may be tempted to underreport them. Gennaioli (2013) has studied optimal contracting in a model with potentially biased judges, and has shown that the enforcement risk generated by these biases often leads parties to write simple contracts that are not contingent on revenues.

Borrowing tools from the mechanism design literature, an important body of theoretical work has proposed a variety of ingenious *mechanisms* to restore efficiency in environments in which the contracting parties (i) have symmetric information, (ii) can commit not to renegotiate an initial contract, and (iii) can resort to a third party (presumably a court of law or arbitrator) to enforce off-the-equilibrium-path penalties (see, for instance, Aghion, Dewatripont, and Rey, 1994; or Maskin and Tirole, 1999). This literature is often criticized for suggesting somewhat convoluted contracts that are not observed in the real world. I find that criticism unconvincing: after all, one could have similarly criticized some key contributions to the auction theory literature, and yet they have subsequently had an enormous impact in real-world auctions (see, for instance, Milgrom, 2000). My main reservation with mechanism-design resolutions to incomplete contracting is that they rely on the ability of a third party to enforce contracts, and as argued repeatedly in this book, this is a real sticking point when studying the international organization of production.

"Totally Incomplete" Contracts

Given the discussion above and for pedagogical reasons, I will begin by considering environments in which, when contracts are incomplete, they are so in a rather extreme way. With that in mind, consider the following definition:

> A contract is said to be "*totally incomplete*" whenever no aspect of the contract is perceived to be enforceable, with the possible exception of a lump-sum transfer exchanged at the time of the agreement.

For reasons discussed in Chapter 1, it seems natural to assume that certain contracts that are feasible or enforceable in domestic transactions might not be feasible or enforceable in international transactions. To illustrate the implications of this asymmetry, I will consider first the case in which contracting is complete or perfect in the domestic sourcing relationships, while contracting is *totally incomplete* in offshoring relationships. Later in the chapter, I will consider environments with partial contractibility under each of these two sourcing options.

With complete contracting in domestic sourcing, we have demonstrated above that F will be able to design a contract such that the levels of headquarter services h and manufacturing production m are set at their joint-profit maximizing level, thus resulting in the frictionless profit flow $\pi_D(\varphi)$ in equation (4.2).

Let us next consider the more interesting implications of incomplete contracting in offshoring relationships. What happens when the initial contract does not stipulate the levels of h or m nor a payment to be paid to the manufacturer M contingent on the volume of m produced or contingent on sale revenues? In that case, the only option left for the parties is to decide on the terms of exchange at t_2 (remember the timing of events in Figure 4.1). The next question is then: how should one model this bargaining/contracting stage? Given that we have assumed above that the final-good producer makes a take-it-or-leave-it offer to the manager at t_0, it might seem natural to maintain that assumption for stage t_3. This would, however, ignore what Oliver Williamson famously termed the "fundamental transformation" (see, for instance, Williamson, 1985). This transformation refers to the fact that even though the final-good producer might have chosen a particular manager M from a competitive fringe of managers, once the investments h and m have been incurred, a contractual separation is likely to prove costly to both parties. To the extent that parties feel "locked-in" with each other, the initial competitive environment at t_0 has thus been fundamentally transformed into one of bilateral monopoly.

As explained in Chapter 1, in the global sourcing environments that we are considering in this book, there are several natural sources of *lock-in* between final-good producers and suppliers. First, manufacturing inputs are often customized to their intended buyers and cannot easily be resold at full price to alternative buyers. Second, certain types of headquarter services are also designed with particular suppliers in mind, and it would prove costly to reuse these services with alternative suppliers. Third, even though we have abstracted from modeling them in the initial period, search frictions are particularly relevant in international environments and they likely make ex-post separations particularly costly for both final-good producers and suppliers, who would at the very least suffer from delays in obtaining a return on their investments.

In sum, in the presence of lock-in effects, incomplete contracting leads to a situation of bilateral monopoly in which the terms of exchange between

F and M will only be determined ex-post (at t_2), after these agents have incurred investments that are by then sunk and have a relatively lower value outside that particular business relationship. The combination of incomplete contracting and lock-in effects leads to what is often referred to as a *hold-up problem*, which in our particular context is two-sided. More specifically, on one end, F will try to push down the price paid for M's manufacturing input, realizing that M might be inclined to accept a reduced price due to the lower value of those inputs for alternative buyers. At the same time, however, M will try to raise the price of m as much as possible, knowing that it might also be in F's best interest to accept a relatively high price if that avoids having to search for a new supplier.

In deciding how assertively to bargain, each party takes into account that a too aggressive offer might lead the other party to refuse to trade, an outcome that is not appealing given the lower value of the sunk investments outside the relationship. As a result, even when bargaining is efficient and trade takes place in equilibrium, the *possibility* of a disagreement and associated failure to trade implies that F and M will tend to have lower incentives to invest in h and m than in the complete contracting case, in which circumstance the initial contract ensures that trade will occur. In more technical terms, with incomplete contracting, the payoff obtained by each party in the ex-post negotiations will put a positive weight on *off-the-equilibrium path* situations in which the return to each party's investments is lower than on the equilibrium path.

In the literature, it is common to characterize the ex-post bargaining at t_2 using the Nash bargaining solution and assuming symmetric information between F and M with regard to all parameters of the model. In such a case, each party ends up with a payoff equal to the value of their outside option (their payoff under no trade) plus a share of the ex-post gains from trade, which correspond to the difference between the sum of the agents' payoffs under trade and their sum under no trade. For the time being, I will assume that the outside option for each party is equal to 0. In other words, I am assuming that the manufactured input m is fully specialized to F and thus useless to other producers, while headquarters h are also fully tailored to the supplier M and could not be productively combined with inputs provided by other manufacturers. I will also consider the case of *symmetric* Nash bargaining, which implies that F and M share *equally* the ex-post gains, which with zero outside options equal sale revenues. Obviously, these are restrictive assumptions, but I will consider more general environments below.

In sum, with symmetric Nash bargaining, each party will anticipate obtaining a payoff equal to one-half of sale revenue at t_2, and thus the levels of $h(\varphi)$ and $m(\varphi)$ will be set at t_1 to solve

$$\max_{h} \quad \frac{1}{2} p(q(\varphi)) q(\varphi) - w_N h \qquad (4.4)$$

and

$$\max_{m} \frac{1}{2} p\left(q\left(\varphi\right)\right) q\left(\varphi\right) - \tau w_S m, \tag{4.5}$$

respectively, where

$$q\left(\varphi\right) = \varphi \left(\frac{h}{\eta}\right)^{\eta} \left(\frac{m}{1-\eta}\right)^{1-\eta} \tag{4.6}$$

and $p\left(q\left(\varphi\right)\right) = B^{1/\sigma} \sigma \left(\sigma - 1\right)^{-(\sigma-1)/\sigma} q\left(\varphi\right)^{-1/\sigma}.$[1]

For comparability with the complete-contracting case, I will assume again that at t_0 there is a competitive fringe of potential managers M willing to work for each final-good producer F at a reservation wage equal to 0. Each F then decides the terms of the initial contract and makes a take-it-or-leave-it offer to one of those managers. Because the initial contract is allowed to include a lump-sum transfer between parties, F can set the transfer such that the participation constraint of M exactly binds. So, as with complete contracts, F ends up with a profit level equal to

$$\pi_O\left(\varphi\right) = p\left(q\left(\varphi\right)\right) q\left(\varphi\right) - w_N h\left(\varphi\right) - \tau w_S m\left(\varphi\right) - w_N f_O. \tag{4.7}$$

The key difference, however, is that the levels of $h(\varphi)$ and $m(\varphi)$ can no longer be set in the initial contract in an enforceable manner. As a result, $h(\varphi)$ and $m(\varphi)$ are no longer set to maximize $\pi_O\left(\varphi\right)$ in (4.7), but instead are chosen simultaneously and non-cooperatively by F and M to solve programs (4.4) and (4.5), respectively.

Analogous to the way we studied contractual frictions in Chapter 3 and to our formulation of the complete-contracting program in (4.3), a compact way to represent the ex-ante problem faced by the final-good producer under "totally incomplete" contracts is:

$$\max_{h(\varphi), m(\varphi), s(\varphi)} \quad \tfrac{1}{2} p\left(q(\varphi)\right) q(\varphi) - w_N h(\varphi) - w_N f_O - s(\varphi)$$

$$\text{s.t.} \quad s(\varphi) + \tfrac{1}{2} p\left(q(\varphi)\right) q(\varphi) - \tau w_S m(\varphi) \geq 0 \tag{4.8}$$

$$h(\varphi) = \arg\max_h \{\tfrac{1}{2} p\left(q(\varphi)\right) q(\varphi) - w_N h(\varphi)\}$$

$$m(\varphi) = \arg\max_m \{\tfrac{1}{2} p\left(q(\varphi)\right) q(\varphi) - \tau w_S m(\varphi)\}.$$

A simple comparison of (4.3) and (4.8) shows that the effect of incomplete contracting is captured by the addition of the last two constraints, which

[1] It should be noted that I am assuming that the agreement in t_2 is always enforced. Enforcement might become an issue if the parties exchange the goods at t_2 and the payment occurs at t_3, but not if the payment occurs at t_2, simultaneously with the exchange of goods.

represent incentive compatibility constraints faced by both F and M. Because the bargaining payoffs of each agent put a positive weight (in this case, 1/2) on an off-the-equilibrium-path zero return to producing in h and m, it is naturally the case that the hold-up problem discussed above leads to inefficiently low investment levels at t_1, and consequently, results in depressed overall profits as well.

Solving formally program (4.8) delivers a volume of profits that F anticipates obtaining when choosing foreign sourcing at t_0 equal to

$$\pi_O = \left((w_N)^\eta (\tau w_S)^{1-\eta}\right)^{1-\sigma} B\Gamma_O \varphi^{\sigma-1} - w_N f_O, \tag{4.9}$$

where

$$\Gamma_O = (\sigma + 1)\left(\frac{1}{2}\right)^\sigma < 1 \quad \text{for } \sigma > 1. \tag{4.10}$$

Note that expression (4.9) is identical to the complete-contracting expression (4.2) except for the term Γ_O, which is necessarily lower than 1. Hence, this term reflects the loss of efficiency due to incomplete contracting. Furthermore, for the relevant range $\sigma > 1$, Γ_O is a decreasing function of σ. Thus in environments with tougher competition (i.e., lower markups), the profit losses from incomplete-contracting frictions are relatively larger (see the Theoretical Appendix for a formal proof). Intuitively, the last two constraints in (4.8) suggest that the effect of incomplete contracting on the choice of h and m is analogous to a doubling of the marginal cost of each of these stages, and this will tend to reduce profits more, the more price elastic demand is. This marginal cost inflation only becomes irrelevant in the limiting case $\sigma \to 1$, since in that case a firm's market share is independent of its cost.

Choice of Location and Prevalence of Offshoring

Having computed the anticipated profits associated with domestic sourcing and offshoring, we can next study the choice of location of the final-good producer in the initial period t_0. Note from equations (4.1) and (4.9) that we can write these profit functions succinctly as

$$\pi_\ell(\varphi) = \psi_\ell B\varphi^{\sigma-1} - w_N f_\ell \quad \text{for } \ell = D, O,$$

with

$$\frac{\psi_D}{\psi_O} = \frac{1}{\Gamma_O}\left(\frac{w_N}{\tau w_S}\right)^{-(1-\eta)(\sigma-1)}. \tag{4.11}$$

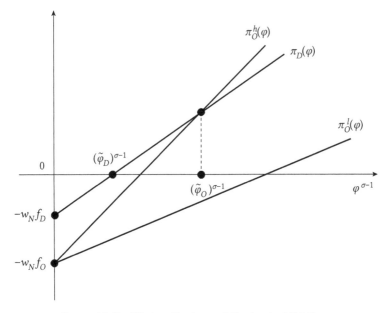

Figure 4.2 Equilibrium Sorting and Contractual Frictions

As in the benchmark models reviewed in Chapter 2, the profit functions $\pi_D(\varphi)$ and $\pi_O(\varphi)$ are linearly increasing in the transformation of productivity $\varphi^{\sigma-1}$, with the relative slope of the two functions now being governed by the ratio ψ_D/ψ_O. Figure 4.2 depicts these functions for the case in which wage differences across countries are high so that $\psi_D < \psi_O$ (see the line π_O^h), and the case in which wage differences are sufficiently low to imply $\psi_D > \psi_O$ (see the line π_O^l). In the latter case, no firm finds it optimal to offshore in the South, while in the former case, only the most productive firms will. The key difference with the complete-contracting case is that, other things equal, firms will now find it less profitable to offshore to the South due to the term Γ_O in (4.11).

Let us now aggregate the decisions of the various firms in a sector and study the determinants of the relative importance of offshoring in different industries. As in Chapter 2 and with an eye to the empirical applications in Chapter 5, it seems natural to focus on the share of spending on *imported* manufacturing inputs over total manufacturing input purchases in a particular industry as a measure of the prevalence of offshoring. Because contracts are complete in domestic transactions, for all firms sourcing domestically, input purchases constitute a share $(1 - \eta)(\sigma - 1)/\sigma$ of revenue and a multiple $(1 - \eta)(\sigma - 1)$ of operating profits (defined as revenue minus variable costs).

Matters are trickier in the case of foreign intermediate inputs, since one needs to take a stance on how these inputs are priced. One possibility is to assume that the headquarter H's spending on inputs corresponds to the payment obtained by the manufacturing manager M in the ex-post bargaining at t_2, which in the model above is simply $\frac{1}{2}$ of revenue and a share $\sigma/(\sigma + 1)$ of operating profits. Alternatively, one could appeal to the existence of the ex-ante lump-sum transfer $s(\varphi)$ at t_0 to argue that H is *effectively* purchasing inputs at marginal cost and thus total spending on foreign inputs is instead given by $\tau w_S m(\varphi)$. From the first-order condition of the program in the last constraint of program (4.8), this corresponds to a share $\frac{1}{2}(1 - \eta)(\sigma - 1)/\sigma$ of sale revenue or a share $(1 - \eta)(\sigma - 1)/(\sigma + 1)$ of operating profits.

I do not want to take a strong stance on a particular pricing practice so I will instead take the more agnostic approach of assuming that foreign inputs are priced such that these input expenditures constitute the same multiple $(1 - \eta)(\sigma - 1)$ of operating profits as in the case of domestic input purchases. I do not believe that this assumption is crucial for the results derived below, but it will significantly simplify the derivations.

Assuming a Pareto distribution of productivity, we can then follow similar steps as in the derivation of equations (2.22) and (2.23) to solve for the share Υ_O of imported manufacturing input purchases in a given industry as

$$\Upsilon_O = \frac{\Gamma_O \left(\frac{w_N}{\tau w_S} \right)^{(1-\eta)(\sigma-1)}}{\left(\frac{\tilde{\varphi}_O}{\tilde{\varphi}_D} \right)^{\kappa-(\sigma-1)} - 1 + \Gamma_O \left(\frac{w_N}{\tau w_S} \right)^{(1-\eta)(\sigma-1)}}, \tag{4.12}$$

where

$$\frac{\tilde{\varphi}_O}{\tilde{\varphi}_D} = \left[\frac{f_O/f_D - 1}{\Gamma_O \left(\frac{w_N}{\tau w_S} \right)^{(1-\eta)(\sigma-1)} - 1} \right]^{1/(\sigma-1)}. \tag{4.13}$$

These expressions are analogous to equations (2.22) and (2.23) in Chapter 2 except for the presence of the term $\Gamma_O < 1$.

As is clear from these equations, the prevalence of offshoring is naturally increasing in the term Γ_O, and is thus reduced by the presence of contractual frictions. The remaining comparative statics are analogous to those in the complete-contracting case. The share of imported inputs is increasing in wage differences (w_N/w_S) and productivity dispersion ($1/\kappa$) and decreasing in (relative) fragmentation barriers (f_O/f_D, τ) and headquarter intensity (η). Conversely, the overall effect of the elasticity of substitution on the share Υ_O is now ambiguous. As in the complete-contracting case, a higher σ makes offshoring more prevalent by reducing the Pareto shape parameter $\kappa/(\sigma - 1)$ for firm sales and by increasing the percentage gain from a reduction in marginal costs of labor from w_N down to τw_S. Nevertheless, as mentioned above in our discussion of equation (4.10), a larger σ now also aggravates the inefficiencies caused by incomplete contracting, hence reducing Υ_O.

Extensions of the Basic Model

So far, our analysis has illustrated that weak contract enforcement across countries will tend to reduce the profitability associated with firms engaging in global sourcing strategies and will thus lead to a larger reliance on domestic intermediate inputs. We have illustrated this insight with a highly stylized framework with many simplifying assumptions, and as a result the model has not delivered any particularly valuable empirical predictions other than the intuitive negative effect of weak contracting on offshoring. I will next turn to studying more general environments that relax some of the strong assumptions above. This will serve to verify the robustness of the key comparative statics emphasized so far, and also to develop a richer set of comparative statics that are better suited to guide empirical work on the contractual determinants of the global sourcing decisions of firms.

I will consider six basic extensions of the model: (i) a generalization of the bargaining process at t_2, (ii) the possibility of restrictions on ex-ante transfers at t_0, (iii) environments with partial contractibility at t_0, (iv) investments at t_1 that are only partially relationship-specific, (v) global sourcing decisions with multiple suppliers, and (vi) sequential production in which the investments of different suppliers occur at different points in time. In each of these cases, we will confirm that the basic insights obtained so far continue to apply to those more general environments, but we will obtain sharper predictions about the differential effect of contractual institutions on firm profitability across firms, sectors, and countries.

To be as succinct as possible, I will focus on outlining how each of these extensions affects and enriches the determination of the term Γ_O in (4.9) capturing the inefficiencies associated with incomplete contracting in offshore relationships. I will also develop variants of the model in which contractual frictions reduce the profitability of domestic sourcing via an analogous term Γ_D which is also shaped by the parameters of the model in ways to be discussed below. In the next chapter, I will return to the aggregation of firms' decisions to illustrate how Γ_O and Γ_D jointly affect the share of imported manufacturing input purchases in a given industry as in equation (4.12). This will serve to motivate my discussion of the empirical evidence based on U.S. import data.

Generalized Nash Bargaining and Revenue-Sharing Contracts

In our basic model above, we have assumed that F and M share the ex-post gains from trade equally at t_2. In some circumstances, it may make sense to assume that the primitive bargaining power of final-good producers might be higher (or perhaps lower) than that of supplying managers. The large literature on non-cooperative models of bargaining emanating from the seminal work of Rubinstein (1982) has uncovered several potential determinants of primitive bargaining power. It is well-known, for instance, that relatively impatient or risk-averse agents will tend to have relatively low bargaining power, and the same will be true about agents for which a bargaining delay might be particularly costly for reasons other than impatience, such as credit constraints (see, for instance, Rubinstein, 1982, or Roth, 1985).

Rather than developing any of these microfoundations in great detail, let me just assume that the final-good producer F obtains a share β of the ex-post gains from trade, with the manager M obtaining the remaining share $1 - \beta$. This is often referred to as the *generalized* Nash bargaining solution. With the maintained assumption that the investments incurred to produce h and m are fully relationship-specific, β and $1 - \beta$ will also correspond to the shares of revenue obtained by F and M, respectively, in their ex-post negotiations at t_2. Below, we will develop variants of the model in which the division of revenue will be shaped by factors other than primitive bargaining power.

It should be clear by now that with complete contracting, the particular bargaining solution adopted to characterize the t_2 stage is irrelevant, and thus the profits associated with domestic sourcing are still given by (4.1). Conversely, when solving for the equilibrium associated with offshoring, one needs to replace the term $1/2$ in (4.4) and the second constraint in (4.8) with β, and the term $1/2$ in (4.5) and the third constraint in (4.8) with $1 - \beta$. Naturally, the larger is β, the lower will tend to be the underinvestment in the provision of headquarter services, but the larger will be the underinvestment in the provision of manufacturing services.

Solving for the equilibrium profits obtained by F under generalized Nash bargaining, delivers a profit flow identical to that in equation (4.9), but with

$$\Gamma_O = \Gamma_\beta \equiv (\sigma - (\sigma - 1)(\beta\eta + (1 - \beta)(1 - \eta))) \left(\beta^\eta (1 - \beta)^{1-\eta}\right)^{\sigma-1}. \quad (4.14)$$

It is straightforward (though somewhat tedious) to verify that, regardless of the value of the primitive bargaining power β, incomplete contracting still necessarily reduces the profitability of offshoring, i.e., $\Gamma_\beta < 1$ for $\sigma > 1$.[2] Furthermore, in the Technical Appendix I show that the size of these contractual distortions continues to be increasing in the elasticity of demand

---

[2] This is a special case of the proof of Proposition 1 in Antràs and Helpman (2008). The result can also be proven more directly by noting that Γ_β was derived from an optimization problem that is more constrained than the one that delivered the profit flow in (4.2), and the latter profit flow can be obtained from (4.9) by setting $\Gamma_\beta = 1$.

(or $\partial\Gamma_\beta/\partial\sigma < 0$). The main novelty in (4.14) is that the level of contractual frictions is no longer only shaped by the elasticity of substitution σ, but now also depends on headquarter intensity η and on the bargaining power parameter β. The effects of these parameters on the level of Γ_β are non-monotonic and interact closely with each other. More specifically, it can be shown that Γ_β is decreasing in η when $\beta < 1/2$, while it is increasing in η when $\beta > 1/2$.[3] Notice also that when $\eta \to 0$, $\Gamma_\beta \to (\sigma - (\sigma - 1)(1 - \beta))(1 - \beta)^{\sigma-1}$ and thus Γ_β is a decreasing function of β, while when $\eta \to 1$, $\Gamma_\beta \to (\sigma - (\sigma - 1)\beta)\beta^{\sigma-1}$, and Γ_β is instead an increasing function of β. In other words, whether increases or decreases in the bargaining power of the final-good producer increase or decrease profits also crucially depends on the level of headquarter intensity. Intuitively, and as argued above, when β increases, the underinvestment in headquarter services is alleviated, while the underinvestment in manufacturing production is aggravated. Whether the net effect is positive or negative naturally depends on the intensity with which these two stages are combined in production. In fact, straightforward calculations show that there exists a unique value β^* that maximizes Γ_β, and it satisfies

$$\frac{\beta^*}{1 - \beta^*} = \sqrt{\frac{\eta}{1 - \eta}\frac{\sigma - (\sigma - 1)(1 - \eta)}{\sigma - (\sigma - 1)\eta}}. \tag{4.15}$$

In line with our intuition above, this profit-maximizing level of β^* is an increasing function of headquarter intensity η.

This result also shed lights on the implications of the model when allowing for revenue-sharing contracts to be signed at t_0. In particular, imagine a situation in which the ex-ante contract was not "totally incomplete" but rather was allowed to include a division rule contingent on the volume of revenue generated at t_3. Denoting revenue by $R = p(q)q$ and the sharing rule by $\beta(R)$, the optimal initial contract would now solve (I am omitting the argument φ in all functions for simplicity):

$$\max_{h,m,s,\beta(R)} \quad \beta(R)R - w_N h - w_N f_O - s$$

$$\text{s.t.} \quad s + (1 - \beta(R))R - \tau w_S m \geq 0$$

$$h = \arg\max_h\{\beta(R)R - w_N h\}$$

$$m = \arg\max_m\{(1 - \beta(R))R - \tau w_S m\}.$$

If one restricts attention to linear sharing rules where $\beta(R)$ is independent of R, then the above discussion indicates that the optimal contract will set $\beta(R) = \beta^*$, where β^* is given in (4.15). Even with this more complete initial contract,

---

[3] The proof is straightforward but cumbersome, so I relegate it to the Theoretical Appendix.

the frictionless profit flow in (4.2) cannot possibly be attained because remember that Γ_β in (4.14) is less than 1 for any $\beta \in (0, 1)$. Importantly, this conclusion is not specific to the case of linear sharing rules. As shown by Holmstrom (1982), for general sharing rules $\beta(R)$ satisfying budget balance, the resulting investment levels h and m will continue to differ from the efficient ones, and the equilibrium profits associated with offshoring will necessarily fall short of those under complete contracts.

Limitations on Ex-Ante Transfers: Financial Constraints

So far, I have assumed that F and M are allowed to freely exchange lump-sum transfers when signing the initial contract at t_0. This transfer can be inferred from the participation constraint of the manager M, which implies

$$s(\varphi) = \tau w_S m(\varphi) - \frac{1}{2} p(q(\varphi)) q(\varphi).$$

Plugging the equilibrium values of $m(\varphi)$ and $q(\varphi)$ it is straightforward to show that $s(\varphi) \leq 0$ and thus the optimal contract calls for the manager M to post a bond in order to be able to transact with the final-good producer F. In practice, it is not obvious that supplying firms will be willing or able to make that initial transfer. This is due to at least two reasons. First, managers might worry that the final-good producer will disappear after period t_0 without incurring the fixed cost of offshoring or investing in headquarter services.[4] Second, depending on the financial environment in the manager's country, it may be hard for M to raise from financiers the full amount of cash $s(\varphi)$ stipulated in the contract we have considered so far. We next explore the implications of the existence of constraints on these ex-ante transfers.

To fix ideas, consider the case in which M can pledge to external financiers in his domestic economy at most a share ϕ of the net income it receives from transacting with F. I will not specify the source of these financial frictions, but they could stem from a limited commitment friction on the part of M along the lines of the models we have explored in Chapter 3. The equilibrium under financial constraints can again be reduced to a program analogous to that in (4.8), but with the additional constraint

$$-s(\varphi) \leq \phi \left[\frac{1}{2} p(q(\varphi)) q(\varphi) - \tau w_S m(\varphi) \right].$$

---

[4] It can be shown, however, that if the manager insists that the fixed cost of offshoring be incurred prior to the payment $s(\varphi)$, the final-good producer would no longer have an incentive to abscond with the transfer.

This constraint is tighter than the original participation constraint in (4.8) and will bind in equilibrium. Solving the program, we then find that F again obtains a payoff equal to that in equation (4.9), but now with

$$\Gamma_O = \Gamma_\phi \equiv (\sigma + \phi - (\sigma - 1)(1 - \phi)\eta) \left(\frac{1}{2}\right)^\sigma. \qquad (4.16)$$

It is straightforward to see that Γ_ϕ is increasing in ϕ and attains the symmetric Nash bargaining value of $(\sigma + 1)(1/2)^\sigma$ when financial constraints disappear, i.e., $\phi = 1$. A first implication is thus that the profitability of offshoring will be increasing in the quality of financial contracting in the manager's foreign country, as summarized by the parameter ϕ. Intuitively, offshoring is now not only associated with distorted investments, but it also entails a loss of rents for the final good producer F. It is interesting to note that Γ_ϕ is also decreasing in headquarter intensity. This is due to the fact that headquarter services are complementary to manufacturing production, and the higher is η, the larger are the rents that M obtains in the ex-post bargaining at t_2 relative to the costs of production he or she incurs at t_1. Consequently, the larger is η, the larger is the loss of rents for F associated with a low ϕ. For the same reason, we observe in (4.16) that an increase in improvement in the quality of financial contracting will have a differentially large positive effect on the profitability of offshoring in production processes with high headquarter intensity (i.e., $\partial\left(\partial\Gamma_\phi/\partial\phi\right)/\partial\eta > 0$).[5]

Partial Contractibility

It is obviously unrealistic to assume, as we have done so far, that contracts in international transactions are "totally incomplete". It seems natural that some aspects of production can be specified in a contract in a manner that contracting parties feel confident that those aspects of the contract will be enforced. Moreover, it is also unrealistic to assume, as we have done so far, that contracts in domestic transactions are complete. Surely some aspects of production are nonverifiable or certain contracts are perceived to be hard to enforce in domestic transactions. I next incorporate partial contractibility into our global sourcing model following the approach in Antràs and Helpman (2008).

It will prove useful to assume that the production of headquarter services and manufacturing inputs now entails a continuum of processes or activities,

---

[5] It is also worth pointing out that, under plausible parametric restrictions, in this extension of the model too, higher demand elasticities are associated with larger incomplete-contracting distortions (see the Technical Appendix for details).

all of them carried out at t_1. A fraction of these processes is assumed to be ex-ante contractible, in the sense that contracts specifying how those processes should be carried out can be designed in a way that a court of law can verify their fulfillment and penalize any deviation from what was stipulated in the contract. Conversely, the complementary fraction of processes is noncontractible and contracts specifying these activities would fail to discipline their provision at t_1.

There are two main determinants of the degree to which the overall production process is contractible. First, a low fraction of contractible activities could reflect technological factors that make it particularly hard to write down enforceable contracts disciplining the behavior of the agents engaged in production. For instance, the production of new and high-tech goods is more contractually demanding than that of more traditional and standardized goods. Second, even focusing on the same production process, it seems reasonable to assume that the fraction of contractible activities will vary across countries reflecting international variation in the quality of contracting institutions. In other words, certain types of contracts are perceived to be enforceable in some environments but perhaps not in others.

To further illustrate these two determinants, it may be useful to consider the following analogy to refereeing in (European) football. There are some rules in football that are almost trivial to enforce, such as ensuring that each team has no more than eleven players on the pitch or preventing a team from performing more than three substitutions. On the other hand, other rules are much trickier to enforce, such as calling a close offside infraction or deciding whether the entire ball crossed the goal line in a ghost-goal situation. It is thus not surprising that players anticipate the former rules to be properly enforced with a much higher likelihood than the latter ones. At the same time, the quality of the referees is also obviously critical in predicting whether the rules will be correctly applied or not. Skilled referees (or linesmen) make fewer mistakes in enforcing these rules than incompetent ones.

In order to formally introduce partial contractibility into the framework, we now let headquarter services h and manufacturing production m be a Cobb-Douglas aggregate of the services of a continuum of measure one of activities, so

$$h = \exp\left[\int_0^1 \log h(i)\, di\right] \tag{4.17}$$

and

$$m = \exp\left[\int_0^1 \log m(i)\, di\right]. \tag{4.18}$$

Our key new assumption is that activities related to input $k = h, m$ in the range $[0, \mu_{kj}]$ (with $0 \le \mu_{kj} \le 1$) are contractible in country $j = N, S$, in the sense that the characteristics of these activities can be fully specified in advance in an enforceable ex-ante contract involving a manufacturer M from country j. Hence, the initial contract is no longer "totally incomplete" because in addition to a lump-sum transfer between F and M, it also specifies the level of contractible activities to be carried out at t_1. The remaining activities in the range $(\mu_{kj}, 1]$ continue to be noncontractible as in our benchmark model and F and M decide on the terms of exchange for those activities only after they have been produced. Because the initial contract does not compel any of the two parties to provide a positive amount of these noncontractible tasks, the threat point for each party in the negotiations at t_2 is to withhold the services from those activities, which in light of the Cobb-Douglas production technologies (4.6), (4.17), and (4.18), and our maintained assumption that all investments are fully relationship-specific, would lead to a zero payoff for both parties.[6] Thus each agent ends up capturing a constant share of sale revenues, and for simplicity, I will now revert back to the assumption of symmetric Nash bargaining, so that the two parties end up sharing evenly total sale revenues.

The symmetry assumptions on technology built into (4.17) and (4.18) allows us to simplify the problem of the firm conditional on having selected a location $j = N, S$, to the choice of an ex-ante transfer s, a common value h_c for all contractible headquarter activities, a common value h_n for all noncontractible headquarter services, and analogous values m_c and m_n for contractible and noncontractible manufacturing tasks, respectively. Formally, we can now write the problem (ignoring fixed costs) as

$$\max_{h_c, h_n, m_c, m_n, s} \quad \tfrac{1}{2}R - w_N \left(\mu_{hj} h_c + \left(1 - \mu_{hj}\right) h_n \right) - s$$

$$\text{s.t.} \quad s + \tfrac{1}{2}R - c_j \left(\mu_{mj} m_c + \left(1 - \mu_{mj}\right) m_n \right) \geq 0 \qquad (4.19)$$

$$h_n = \arg\max_h \{ \tfrac{1}{2}R - w_N \left(1 - \mu_{hj}\right) h_n \}$$

$$m_n = \arg\max_m \{ \tfrac{1}{2}R - c_j \left(1 - \mu_{mj}\right) m_n \},$$

where revenue is given by

$$R = B^{1/\sigma} \sigma (\sigma - 1)^{-(\sigma-1)/\sigma} \varphi^{(\sigma-1)/\sigma}$$

$$\times \left(\frac{(h_c)^{\mu_{hj}} (h_n)^{1-\mu_{hj}}}{\eta} \right)^{(\sigma-1)\eta/\sigma} \left(\frac{(m_c)^{\mu_{mj}} (m_n)^{1-\mu_{mj}}}{1-\eta} \right)^{(\sigma-1)(1-\eta)/\sigma} \qquad (4.20)$$

and where $c_j = w_N$ when $j = N$ and $c_j = \tau w_S$ when $j = S$.

---

[6] An implicit assumption in the analysis is that these noncontractible tasks are not yet fully embodied into the manufactured inputs at the time of bargaining.

This problem is somewhat tedious to solve, so I will not go over the derivations here. The interested reader can find the details in the Theoretical Appendix, where I reproduce the derivations in Antràs and Helpman (2008), where we solved the same problem for a general division of revenue (β_h, β_m), rather than $(1/2, 1/2)$. Using these results, we find that, in the case of domestic sourcing, the profits obtained by F are now given by

$$\pi_D(\varphi) = (c_N)^{1-\sigma} \, B\Gamma_D(\mu_N) \, \varphi^{\sigma-1} - f_D w_N,$$

where

$$\Gamma_D(\mu_N) = \left(\frac{\sigma}{\sigma - (\sigma - 1)(1 - \mu_N)} + 1 \right)^{\sigma-(\sigma-1)(1-\mu_N)} \left(\frac{1}{2} \right)^{\sigma} \tag{4.21}$$

and

$$\mu_N \equiv \eta\mu_{hN} + (1 - \eta)\mu_{mN}.$$

The derived parameter μ_N measures the average contractibility associated with domestic sourcing and is a weighted sum of the contractibility of headquarter services and manufacturing.

F's profits under foreign sourcing can be similarly computed, resulting in

$$\pi_O = \left((w_N)^{\eta} (\tau w_S)^{1-\eta} \right)^{1-\sigma} B\Gamma_O(\mu_S) \, \varphi^{\sigma-1} - w_N f_O,$$

with

$$\Gamma_O(\mu_S) = \left(\frac{\sigma}{\sigma - (\sigma - 1)(1 - \mu_S)} + 1 \right)^{\sigma-(\sigma-1)(1-\mu_S)} \left(\frac{1}{2} \right)^{\sigma} \tag{4.22}$$

and

$$\mu_S \equiv \eta\mu_{hS} + (1 - \eta)\mu_{mS}.$$

As in the simpler models developed above, the term $\Gamma_\ell(\mu_j)$ captures the contractual frictions associated with the sourcing options $\ell = D$ and $\ell = O$, which entail manufacturing in country $j = N$ and country $j = S$, respectively. Differentiation of (4.21) and (4.22) demonstrates that each of these terms is increasing in their associated index of contractibility (see the Theoretical Appendix). Hence, as in our simpler model above, contract incompleteness reduces the profitability of production but the effect is now smoothly shaped by the partial contractibility parameters μ_{hj} and μ_{mj} for $j = N, S$. In fact, our initial model is a special case of the current one, with complete contracting in domestic sourcing (so $\mu_{hN} = \mu_{mN} = 1$), and "totally incomplete contracts" in foreign sourcing (or $\mu_{hS} = \mu_{mS} = 0$).[7]

---

[7] This is easily verifed by plugging these values of μ_{hj} and μ_{mj} for $j = N, S$ into the profit functions above and comparing them with (4.1) and (4.9).

Our notation associates the relevant degree of contractibility in foreign sourcing with the quality of contractual institutions in the South. In particular, agents engaged in this type of sourcing strategy perceive that the quality of Southern institutions will be the key one determining the extent to which contracts specifying certain aspects of production, including headquarter service provision, will be enforced. This is a strong assumption to make. One would expect that the contractual insecurity of offshoring relationships would be a function of both the Northern and Southern institutions and perhaps their legal similarity, as argued in Chapter 3 when studying the exporting decision. Nevertheless, by using this notation, I seek to stress the notion that the quality of contracting institutions in the country where manufacturing takes place will be an important determinant of the profitability of offshore transactions. I will later appeal to this result when discussing the empirical evidence in Chapter 5. Of course, as I discussed in Chapter 3, parties can seek to insulate a given transaction from weak contract enforcement in "the South" by including choice-of-law and forum-of-law clauses (see Chapter 1). Still, Southern institutions will likely remain crucial in determining the degree to which damages set by international courts of law or arbitrators are enforced.

Notice that equations (4.21) and (4.22) not only illustrate the positive effect of better contract enforcement on profitability, but they also shed light on the differential effect of such an improvement on institutions depending on other features of the environment. For instance, tedious differentiation of these expressions delivers the intuitive result that an increase in the reduced-form aggregate contractibility μ_j for $j = N, S$, will have a disproportionately larger effect on profitability whenever σ is high, that is, when the final-good producer faces a particularly competitive environment.[8] Intuitively, the higher the price elasticity the final-good producer faces, the costlier the investment inefficiencies associated with weak contracting will prove to be. Apart from this interaction effect, in the Theoretical Appendix, we also show that the elasticity of demand continues to have an unambiguous negative effect on $\Gamma_\ell\left(\mu_j\right)$ in this more general framework.

When inspecting how the terms μ_N and μ_S are shaped by the con-tractibility of the different process of production, it is also evident that improvements in contractibility will interact with the headquarter intensity of production depending on the source of these changes in contractibility. For instance, if improvements in Southern institutions affect disproportionately the contractibility of manufacturing, then this version of the model predicts that these improvements will have a disproportionate effect on profitability in sectors with low headquarter intensity. Conversely, if Southern institutions disproportionately affect the extent to which F will capture the full marginal

---

[8] More precisely, in the Theoretical Appendix we establish that $\partial\left(\partial\ln\Gamma_\ell/\partial\mu_j\right)/\partial\sigma > 0$.

return from his or her investments in headquarter services, then the model predicts a larger impact of improved contracting on headquarter-intensive sectors.

Partial Relationship Specificity

Although relationship-specific investments are pervasive in economic transactions, the assumption of *full* relationship specificity in our basic model is extreme. Even when particular transactions end up not occurring, suppliers can generally recoup part of the cost of their investment, perhaps by reselling their goods to alternative buyers. Similarly, contractual breaches by suppliers may reduce the overall profitability of headquarter services, but will generally not render them useless. A proper modeling of partial relationship specificity would require the introduction of a secondary market for inputs as well as of the negotiations between final-good producers and suppliers in that market, which in turn might depend on the outside options of agents in a tertiary market, and so on (see, for instance, Grossman and Helpman, 2002). The main idea would then be that the lower is the degree of specificity, the larger is the value of inputs in the secondary markets and thus the lower should be the incentive of agents to underinvest. I will next consider a reduced form version of such a model.

In particular, assume that there indeed exists a second market for inputs in which the manager M can obtain a price $p_m^s(\varphi)$ for each unit of m, while the final-good producer F anticipates obtaining a monetary return $p_h^s(\varphi)$ per unit of headquarter services. These constitute the outside options for each party at the bargaining stage t_2 we have studied above. I will assume that the agents perceive these secondary market transaction prices $p_h^s(\varphi)$ and $p_m^s(\varphi)$ as unaffected by their actions and in particular their investment levels.

Assuming again symmetric Nash bargaining, the payoff obtained by final-good producer will now be given by $p_h^s(\varphi)h + \frac{1}{2}\left(R - p_h^s(\varphi)h - p_m^s(\varphi)m\right)$, while the supplier will obtain $p_m^s(\varphi)m + \frac{1}{2}\left(R(\varphi) - p_h^s(\varphi)h - p_m^s(\varphi)m\right)$. As a result, the levels of investments $h(\varphi)$ and $m(\varphi)$ at t_1 will satisfy the following first-order conditions:

$$\frac{1}{2}\left(\frac{\partial R(\varphi)}{\partial h} + p_h^s(\varphi)\right) = w_N$$

$$\frac{1}{2}\left(\frac{\partial R(\varphi)}{\partial m} + p_m^s(\varphi)\right) = \tau w_S. \tag{4.23}$$

Consider next the determination of the prices $p_h^s(\varphi)$ and $p_m^s(\varphi)$. In a frictionless environment *without* any relationship specificity, one would expect that this secondary market would provide a thick market for each input and that, in equilibrium, the price commanded by these inputs would correspond to the monetary value of their marginal product. In that case, we would have $p_k^s(\varphi) = \partial R(\varphi)/\partial k$ for $k = h, m$, and the corresponding investments in (4.23) would coincide with the efficient ones under complete contracts. In other words, in the absence of relationship specificity of investments, weak contract enforcement is irrelevant as the hold-up problem disappears. Conversely, in the other extreme case with full relationship specificity, we instead have $p_h^s(\varphi) = p_m^s(\varphi) = 0$, and the model collapses back to our basic model.[9]

In order to consider environments with partial relationship specificity, assume then that the secondary market price commanded by each input is a share $1 - \epsilon$ of the actual value of the marginal product of this input, so that larger values of ϵ are associated with larger degrees of customization or relationship specificity. As is clear from equation (4.23), this then corresponds to the case in which F and M choose investments h and m while anticipating obtaining a share $\beta_h = \beta_m = 1 - \epsilon/2$ of the actual value of the marginal return to these investments.

The rest of the equilibrium of this variant of the model is as in our basic model. Notice in particular that the parties will still find it efficient to reach an agreement at t_2 and thus the secondary market is never used in equilibrium.[10] Overall, the equilibrium can be solved in a manner analogous to the program in (4.19), but with $1 - \epsilon/2$ replacing $1/2$ in the second and third constraints.[11]

As mentioned before, Antràs and Helpman (2008) solved this program for a general division of revenue (β_h, β_m), so we can just plug $\beta_h = \beta_m = 1 - \epsilon/2$ into their equilibrium equations (see the Theoretical Appendix). This yields a level of profits associated with domestic sourcing ($\ell = D$ and $j = N$) and foreign sourcing ($\ell = O$ and $j = S$) equal to

$$\pi_\ell = \left(c_j\right)^{1-\sigma} B \Gamma_\ell \left(\mu_j, \epsilon\right) \varphi^{\sigma-1} - w_N f_\ell,$$

with

$$\Gamma_\ell \left(\mu_j, \epsilon\right) = \left(1 + \frac{\frac{\epsilon}{2}}{1 - \frac{\epsilon}{2}} \frac{\sigma}{\sigma - (\sigma - 1)\left(1 - \mu_j\right)}\right)^{\sigma - (\sigma-1)(1-\mu_j)} \left(1 - \frac{\epsilon}{2}\right)^{\sigma}, \quad (4.24)$$

---

[9] The setup I am developing is admittedly special in that I am allowing the value of the marginal product of the manufacturer's investment m in the secondary market to be a function of the productivity level φ of the final-good producer with whom it initially contracted. This might reflect the fact that the secondary market is thick for any level of φ or perhaps that the supplier is able to assimilate F's technology while producing m.

[10] More specifically, given the concavity of the revenue function, we necessarily have that $R(\varphi) > (1 - \epsilon/2) \left(\frac{\partial R(\varphi)}{\partial h} h + \frac{\partial R(\varphi)}{\partial m} m\right)$.

[11] Despite the fact that F and M do not each receive a share $1 - \epsilon/2$ of revenue, their investments are determined *as if they did*.

and where remember that $\mu_j = \eta\mu_{hj} + (1 - \eta)\mu_{mj}$ for $j = N, S$, and $c_j = w_N$ when $j = N$ and $c_j = \tau w_S$ when $j = S$. As in the model with full relationship specificity, it continues to be the case that improvements in contractibility are associated with larger values of $\Gamma_\ell(\mu_j, \epsilon)$. Similarly, the negative effect of σ on $\Gamma_\ell(\mu_j, \epsilon)$ and the positive "interaction" effect $\partial(\partial \ln \Gamma_\ell/\partial \mu_j)/\partial \sigma > 0$ continue to apply in this more general environment (see the Theoretical Appendix).

The main new feature of expression (4.24) is that the inefficiencies derived from incomplete contracting are now increasing in the degree of specificity ϵ in the sense that $\Gamma_\ell(\mu_j, \epsilon)$ decreases in ϵ. This intuitive result is not immediate from inspection of equation (4.24), but it can be verified by analyzing the partial derivative $\partial \ln \Gamma_\ell(\mu_j, \epsilon)/\partial \epsilon$. The reader is referred to the Theoretical Appendix for the mathematical derivations, which also demonstrate that the cross-partial derivative $\partial(\ln \partial \Gamma_\ell(\mu_j, \epsilon)/\partial \epsilon)/\partial \mu_j$ is positive. In other words, the positive effect of higher quality of contracting institutions on firm profitability is predicted to be disproportionately higher in production processes with high degrees of specificity ϵ. Or, put differently, the model seems to be consistent with the fact that countries with weak contracting environments appear to export manufactured goods featuring relatively low levels of specificity, as empirically shown by Nunn (2007). I will further illustrate this result in Chapter 5, when I develop a multi-country version of the model.

Multiple Inputs and Multilateral Contracting

So far, I have focused on situations in which F is concerned only with the provision of one input. In modern manufacturing processes, final-good producers instead combine intermediate inputs provided by various suppliers. I will next return to the version of the global sourcing model introduced in Chapter 2, in which the manufacturing stage of production entails the procurement of a continuum of measure one of inputs indexed by v, all produced simultaneously at t_1. Assuming that the services from these stages are imperfectly substitutable with each other with a constant and symmetric elasticity of substitution equal to $\sigma_\rho \equiv 1/(1 - \rho)$, we can now write the production function as

$$q(\varphi) = \varphi \left(\frac{h}{\eta}\right)^\eta \left(\frac{\left[\int_0^1 m(v)^\rho \, dv\right]^{1/\rho}}{1 - \eta}\right)^{1-\eta}. \qquad (4.25)$$

Note that if one interprets $q(\varphi)$ as the *quality-adjusted* volume of output, this formulation is perfectly consistent with the notion that, from an engineering point of view, all stages might be essential. For example, producing a car requires four wheels, two headlights, one steering wheel, and so on, but the value of this car for consumers will typically depend on the services obtained from these different components, with a high quality in certain parts potentially making up for inferior quality in others.

I will assume that the various inputs are not only symmetric in technology but are also produced with the same marginal cost in a given location. Manufacturing also continues to entail fixed costs that depend on the location of this activity but I assume that these fixed costs are independent of the number of inputs produced in a location. For this reason, it is natural to focus on symmetric equilibria in which all manufacturing inputs are produced in the same location.

Headquarter service provision continues to be controlled by the final good producer, agent F. To obtain the various intermediate inputs, F now needs to contract with a continuum of managers $M(v)$, each controlling one input. If all the aspects associated with the production of the different inputs could be specified in an enforceable manner in an initial contract, then it is straightforward to show that the resulting profit functions for the final-good producer associated with domestic sourcing and offshoring would be exactly identical to those of the single manufacturing input model. These profit flows are given by equations (4.1) and (4.2). Note that, given our symmetry assumptions and complete contracting, these profit flows are independent of the value of the input substitution parameter ρ. As we will next demonstrate, this parameter will play a much more relevant role in the presence of contractual frictions.

Consider now the case of partial contractibility introduced above, in which some of the characteristics of production are contractible, while others are not. Specifically, headquarter services h and each manufacturing input $m(v)$ are a Cobb-Douglas aggregate of the services of a continuum of measure one of activities, as in equations (4.17) and (4.18), and only a share μ_{hj} and μ_{mj} of those activities are contractible when manufacturing takes place in country $j = N, S$. Note that, for simplicity, the share μ_{mj} is common for all inputs v. The terms of exchange related to the noncontractible activities are only decided at t_2, after they have been performed but not yet embodied into production. The threat point for each party in the negotiations at t_2 is to withhold the services from those activities.

The key novel feature of this richer environment is that the ex-post negotiations at t_2 are now multilateral, rather than bilateral. How should one model this ex-post bargaining? One possible way would be to apply Nash bargaining to our multilateral setup with each agent obtaining their outside option plus a share of the difference between joint surplus under cooperation and the sum of outside options (see, for instance, Osborne and Rubinstein, 1990, p. 23). With zero outside options, and hence full relationship specificity, this would amount to all agents obtaining a constant share of revenues. This would lead, however, to a situation analogous to a moral hazard in teams problem (see Holmstrom, 1982) with an arbitrarily large number of agents. In such a case, the agents would have no incentive to invest in noncontractible tasks and revenue would be zero. In sum, a minimal amount of contractual frictions would be sufficient to drive production efficiency to zero.

This extreme result is in part due to our Cobb-Douglas assumptions in (4.17) and (4.18) but it also reflects the limitations of the Nash bargaining solution in multi-agent environments. In particular, this solution does not allow for situations of *partial cooperation* in which even if one supplier rejects an agreement, the other agents are still allowed to cooperate with each other and obtain some surplus. For this reason, in multilateral bargaining setups it is customary to adopt the Shapley value as the solution concept characterizing the equilibrium of these negotiations. In a bargaining game with a finite number of players, each player's Shapley value is the average of her contributions to all coalitions that consist of players ordered below her in all feasible permutations.[12]

A complication arises from the fact that, in our environment, we have a continuum of agents bargaining over surplus. Acemoglu, Antràs, and Helpman (2007) resolve this issue by considering a discrete-player version of the game and computing the *asymptotic* Shapley value of Aumann and Shapley (1974). I will next develop an alternative, heuristic derivation of this Shapley value.

First note that agent F is an *essential* player in the bargaining game and thus a supplier $M(v)$'s marginal contribution is equal to zero when being added to a coalition that does not include the firm. When that coalition does include the firm and a measure n of suppliers, the marginal contribution of supplier v is equal to $\Delta R(v, n) = \partial R(\varphi, n)/\partial n$, where $R(\varphi, n) = p(q(\varphi, n))q(\varphi, n)$ and $q(\varphi, n)$ is as in (4.25) but with the integral running up to n rather than 1. Using Leibniz's rule and invoking symmetry, this marginal contribution can

---

[12] More formally, in a game with M players, let $g = \{g(1), \ldots, g(M)\}$ be a permutation of $1, 2, \ldots, M$, and let $z_g^j = \{j' \mid g(j) > g(j')\}$ be the set of players ordered below j in the permutation g. Denoting by G the set of feasible permutations, and by $v : G \to \mathbb{R}$ the value (or surplus generated) of the coalition consisting of any subset of the M players, the Shapley value of player j is then

$$s_j = \frac{1}{(M+1)!} \sum_{g \in G} \left[v\left(z_g^j \cup j\right) - v\left(z_g^j\right) \right].$$

be succinctly written as

$$\Delta R(v, n) = \frac{(\sigma - 1)(1 - \eta)}{\sigma\rho} R(\varphi) \left(\frac{m_n(v)}{m_n(-v)} \right)^\rho n^{\frac{(\sigma-1)}{\sigma\rho} - 1}, \qquad (4.26)$$

where $m(-v)$ represents the (symmetric) investments of all suppliers other than v. Note that in deriving this expression we also have imposed, without loss of generality, a symmetric choice for contractible manufacturing tasks, or $m_c(v) = m_c$ for all v.

The Shapley value of $M(v)$ is the average of $M(v)$'s marginal contributions to coalitions that consist of players ordered below $M(v)$ in all feasible orderings. A supplier that has a measure n of players ordered below him or her has a marginal contribution of $\Delta R(v, n)$ if the firm is ordered below him or her – which occurs with probability n –, and 0 otherwise. Averaging over all possible orderings of the players and using the above formula for $\Delta R(v, n)$ we obtain the following payoff for supplier $M(v)$:

$$P_m(v) = \int_0^1 n\Delta R\left(v', n\right) dv' = \frac{(\sigma - 1)(1 - \eta)}{(\sigma - 1)(1 - \eta) + \sigma\rho} R(\varphi) \left(\frac{m_n(v)}{m_n(-v)} \right)^\rho. \quad (4.27)$$

A number of features of (4.27) are worth noting. First, in equilibrium, all suppliers invest equally in all the noncontractible activities, and thus each receives a share $(\sigma - 1)(1 - \eta)/((\sigma - 1)(1 - \eta) + \sigma\rho)$ of revenue, leaving F with the residual share $\sigma\rho/((\sigma - 1)(1 - \eta) + \sigma\rho)$. The bargaining power of the firm is thus naturally increasing in the substitutability of inputs as governed by ρ, since the suppliers' bargaining threats are less effective in that case. Second, and although in equilibrium suppliers end up with an equal share of sale revenue, equation (4.27) indicates that suppliers perceive their non-contractible investments to have a non-negligible (i.e., measurable) effect on their payoffs, and thus the moral-hazard-in-teams, zero-investment result mentioned above does not apply here. Third, the degree of substitutability ρ crucially impacts the marginal return to suppliers' investments by shaping the degree to which increases in the investments of a given supplier affect output. Intuitively, when inputs are highly complementary (low ρ), the marginal return to increasing the production of one input v while holding the rest fixed is particularly low.

Having solved for the division of surplus at t_2, the rest of the equilibrium is as in previous models. In particular, the program is analogous to that in (4.19), but with $\beta_h = \sigma\rho/((\sigma - 1)(1 - \eta) + \sigma\rho)$ replacing $1/2$ in F's choice of h and with each supplier $M(v)$ choosing $m_n(v)$ to maximize $P_m(v) - c_j\left(1 - \mu_{mj}\right) m_n(v)$. In equilibrium, the latter choice is isomorphic to that of a single supplier choosing a *common* m_n for all v to maximize $\beta_m R(\varphi) - c_j\left(1 - \mu_{mj}\right) m_n$ with

$\beta_m = \rho\sigma/((\sigma - 1)(1 - \eta) + \sigma\rho)$.[13] Thus we can apply the general formula in Antràs and Helpman (2008) (see the Theoretical Appendix) to express the level of contractual frictions $\Gamma_\ell(\mu_j, \rho)$ associated with manufacturing taking place in country j as

$$\Gamma_\ell(\mu_j, \rho) = \left(1 + \frac{1}{\rho}\frac{(\sigma - 1)(1 - \eta)}{\sigma - (\sigma - 1)(1 - \mu_j)}\right)^{\sigma-(\sigma-1)(1-\mu_j)} \left(\frac{\rho\sigma}{\rho\sigma + (\sigma - 1)(1 - \eta)}\right)^\sigma,$$

(4.28)

again with $\mu_j = \eta\mu_{hj} + (1 - \eta)\mu_{mj}$ (where $j = N$ when $\ell = D$ and $j = S$ when $\ell = O$).

The generality of the results in Antràs and Helpman (2008) allows us to conclude, without having to differentiate this expression, that $\Gamma_\ell(\mu_j, \rho)$ is again increasing in the degree of contractibility μ_j and decreasing in the elasticity of demand σ.[14] In addition, the positive effect of contract enforcement affects high-substitutability sectors disproportionately, or $\partial(\partial\ln\Gamma_\ell/\partial\mu_j)/\partial\sigma > 0$.

The main novelty of equation (4.28) is that the degree of input substitutability is now a key determinant of the extent to which contractual frictions depress the profitability of production. Straightforward differentiation demonstrates that $\Gamma_\ell(\mu_j, \rho)$ is increasing in ρ, and thus contractual frictions are lower, the more substitutable inputs are. Intuitively, investments tend to be less distorted in that case because a higher level of ρ (i) provides more ex-post surplus to F thus enhancing the investments in headquarter services by F, and (ii) increases the sensitivity of suppliers' ex-post payoffs to their own investments. Naturally, a high ρ also reduces the share of ex-post surplus accruing to suppliers, but given the functional forms, this is a dominated effect in the model.

Differentiation of (4.28) also demonstrates (see the Theoretical Appendix) that $\partial(\partial\ln\Gamma_\ell(\mu_j, \rho)/\partial\mu_j)/\partial\rho < 0$ and thus the effect of an improvement in contractual institutions has a differentially larger effect in sectors featuring higher input complementarities. The model thus suggests that, other things equal, foreign sourcing to countries with particularly weak contract enforcement should be more prevalent in sectors with higher substitutability between inputs. We will further formalize and test this result in Chapter 5.

---

[13] This follows from noting that β_m must be such that $\rho P_m(v) = \beta_m \frac{(\sigma-1)(1-\eta)}{\sigma} R(\varphi)$ whenever $m_n(v) = m_n$ for all v.

[14] This latter comparative static result would appear to be complicated by the fact that the bargaining weights β_h and β_m are now endogenous and a function of σ. But since $\Gamma_\ell(\mu_j, \rho)$ in (8.17) is increasing in β_h and β_m, and each of these two shares is decreasing in σ, this does not affect the sign of the derivative $\partial\ln\Gamma_\ell/\partial\sigma$.

Sequential Production

The variant of the model with multiple suppliers that I have developed above assumes that all stages of production are performed simultaneously. In real-life manufacturing processes, there is often a natural sequencing of stages. First, raw materials are converted into basic components, which are next combined with other components to produce more complicated inputs, before themselves being assembled into final goods. Antràs and Chor (2013) develop a sequential production variant of the model with a continuum of inputs we have just studied. The key new feature of their analysis is that the relationship-specific investments made by suppliers in upstream stages can affect the incentives of suppliers involved in downstream stages, thereby generating investment inefficiencies that vary systematically along the value chain.

The model developed by Antràs and Chor (2013) turns out to be very tractable but some of the details of the analysis are somewhat intricate, so I refer the reader to the paper and its Supplemental Appendix for many details. Antràs and Chor (2013) assume a production technology analogous to (4.25) but with $v \in [0, 1]$ indexing the position of an input in the value chain, with a larger v corresponding to stages further downstream (closer to the final end product). Although they develop extensions with headquarter services and partial contractibility, I will focus below on their benchmark model in which $\eta = 0$ and in which all investments are noncontractible.

The final-good producer F plays two roles in the model. On the one hand, it is in charge of assembling the measure one of sequentially produced inputs into a final good valued by consumers. Second, it sequentially negotiates with suppliers once their stage input has been produced and the firm has had a chance to inspect it. It is simplest to consider the case in which this negotiation at stage v is treated independently from the bilateral negotiations that take place at other stages (see Antràs and Chor, 2013, for alternative formulations). Because each intermediate input v is assumed compatible only with the firm's output, the supplier's outside option at the bargaining stage is 0. Hence, the quasi-rents over which the firm and the supplier negotiate are given by the incremental contribution to total revenue generated by supplier v at that stage. In light of (4.20) and (4.25), this incremental contribution is given by

$$\Delta R(v) = \frac{(\sigma - 1)}{\sigma \rho} B^{1/\sigma} \sigma (\sigma - 1)^{-(\sigma-1)/\sigma} \varphi^{(\sigma-1)/\sigma}$$

$$\times \left(\int_0^v m(u)^{(\sigma_\rho - 1)/\sigma_\rho} \, du \right)^{(1 - \sigma_\rho/\sigma)/(\sigma_\rho - 1)} m(v)^\rho, \qquad (4.29)$$

where you recall that $\sigma_\rho = 1/(1 - \rho)$. Assume that the share of these quasi-rents accruing to F are given by $\beta(v)$. Below, I will allow this share to be affected by the location of manufacturing production.

Notice that if $\sigma > \sigma_\rho$, then the investment choices of suppliers are *sequential complements* in the sense that higher investment levels by prior suppliers increase the marginal return of supplier v's own investment $m(v)$. Conversely, if $\sigma < \sigma_\rho$, investment choices are *sequential substitutes* because high values of upstream investments reduce the marginal return to investing in $m(v)$. Because the supplier at position v chooses $m(v)$ to maximize $(1 - \beta(v))\Delta R(v) - c_j m(v)$, equation (4.29) illustrates the trickle-down effect that upstream investment inefficiencies can have on downstream stages.

Exploiting the recursive structure of the model, Antràs and Chor (2013) show that if agent F is able to use ex-ante transfers to extract all surplus from suppliers, then the overall profits obtained by a final-good producer with productivity φ when all inputs are produced under a marginal cost equal to j are given by

$$\pi_j = \left(c_j\right)^{1-\sigma} B\Gamma_j\left(\{\beta(v)\}_{v=0}^1\right)\varphi^{\sigma-1}$$

where

$$\Gamma_\ell\left(\{\beta(v)\}_{v=0}^1\right) = \frac{(\sigma - 1)}{(\sigma_\rho - 1)}\left(\frac{\sigma_\rho}{\sigma}\right)^{\frac{\sigma - \sigma_\rho}{\sigma_\rho - 1}}\int_0^1\left\{\left(\frac{\sigma_\rho}{1 - \beta(v)} - (\sigma_\rho - 1)\right)\right.$$
$$\left.\times (1 - \beta(v))^{\sigma_\rho}\left[\int_0^v(1 - \beta(u))^{\sigma_\rho-1}\,du\right]^{\frac{\sigma - \sigma_\rho}{\sigma_\rho - 1}}\right\}dv. \qquad (4.30)$$

In the case of a symmetric bargaining power at all stages, so $\beta(v) = \beta$ for all v, equation (4.30) reduces to

$$\Gamma_\ell\left(\{\beta(v)\}_{v=0}^1\right) = \left(\frac{\sigma_\rho}{\sigma}\right)^{\frac{\sigma - \sigma_\rho}{\sigma_\rho - 1}}\left(\frac{\sigma_\rho}{1 - \beta} - (\sigma_\rho - 1)\right)(1 - \beta)^\sigma.$$

This expression in turns collapses to the single-supplier index of contractual frictions in equation (4.14) when $\sigma = \sigma_\rho$ (and $\eta = 0$, of course). This is intuitive since in that knife-edge case, the payoff to a supplier is independent of other suppliers' investments, and the trickle-down effects mentioned above become irrelevant.

More interesting implications from the modeling of sequential production can be obtained when allowing the bargaining share $\beta(v)$ to vary along the value chain and across manufacturing locations. To build intuition, it is instructive to consider first the case in which the (infinite-dimensional) vector of $\beta(v)$'s is chosen to maximize F's profits. Antràs and Chor (2013) show that this seemingly complicated problem can be reduced to a standard calculus of variation problem which delivers the surprisingly simple Euler-Lagrange condition

$$\frac{\partial \beta^*(v)}{\partial v} = \frac{1 - \sigma_\rho/\sigma}{\sigma_\rho - 1} v^{\frac{-\sigma_\rho(\sigma-1)}{(\sigma_\rho-1)\sigma}}.$$

The key implication of this expression is that the relative size of the input and final-good elasticities of substitution σ_ρ and σ governs whether the incentive for F to retain a larger surplus share increases or decreases along the value chain. Intuitively, when σ is high relative to σ_ρ, investments are sequential complements, and high upstream values of $\beta(v)$ are particularly costly since they reduce the incentives to invest not only of these early suppliers but also of all suppliers downstream. Conversely, when σ is small relative to σ_ρ, investments are sequential substitutes, and low values of $\beta(v)$ in upstream stages are now relatively detrimental, since they reduce the incentives to invest for downstream suppliers, who are already underinvesting to begin with.[15]

This result has interesting implications for the choice between domestic and foreign sourcing whenever these sourcing strategies are associated with different levels of contract enforcement or with different bargaining shares for F in its negotiations with suppliers. To see this, consider first the case in which contracting in domestic Northern transactions is complete, while foreign sourcing is associated with totally incomplete contracting. Our results above then suggest that, in the sequential complements case ($\sigma > \sigma_\rho$), foreign sourcing is particularly unappealing in upstream stages. Thus, if domestic and foreign sourcing coexist along the value chain, then only relatively downstream inputs will be offshored.[16] Conversely, in the sequential substitutes case, ($\sigma < \sigma_\rho$) one would expect relatively upstream stages to be offshored. In sum, the model predicts that the "upstreamness" of an input should be a relevant determinant of the extent to which it is procured from foreign suppliers, with the sign of that dependence being crucially shaped by the relative size of σ and σ_ρ.

---

[15] Imposing two boundary conditions on the Euler-Lagrange equation, the optimal stage-v bargaining share can in fact be solved in closed form, and is given by $\beta^*(v) = 1 - v^{\frac{\sigma_\rho/\sigma-1}{\sigma_\rho-1}}$. In the sequential complements case ($\sigma > \sigma_\rho$) this implies $\beta^*(v) < 0$ for all v, so F has an incentive to allocate to suppliers more than their entire incremental contribution. This extreme result does not apply when F cannot extract all surplus from suppliers via ex-ante lump-sum transfer or when the model includes headquarter service provision (see Antràs and Chor, 2013, for details). Importantly, in those cases, it continues to be true that the sign of $\partial \beta^*(v)/\partial v$ is determined by the relative size of σ and σ_ρ, and $\partial \beta^*(v)/\partial v > 0$ whenever $\sigma > \sigma_\rho$.

[16] This result can be proved in a manner analogous to Proposition 2 in Antràs and Chor (2013). See also the Theoretical Appendix for a related proof of a result in the transaction-cost model in Chapter 6.

Note, however, that very different results might arise if domestic and foreign sourcing do not differ significantly in their contractibility, but are associated with F obtaining a higher share of surplus under domestic sourcing than under offshoring, i.e., $\beta_D(v) > \beta_O(v)$, as suggested for instance by Antràs and Helpman (2008). In such a case, offshoring would be relatively more appealing in upstream stages in the sequential complements case, and relatively more appealing in downstream stages in the sequential substitutes case. We will explore the empirical relevance of these different scenarios in the next chapter.

Summary and Implications for Policy

This chapter has explored the determinants of the global sourcing decisions of firms in the presence of incomplete contracting frictions in vertical relationships. The different variants of our global sourcing model have delivered a rich set of comparative statics and have also provided tools for testing these predictions with data on intermediate input trade. In the next chapter, I will test the empirical success of the model with detailed data on U.S. imports by product and source country. In the process, and given the cross-country dimension of the data, it will prove necessary to develop a multi-country version of the model.

Before proceeding to the empirical analysis, it is worth pointing out that the framework developed in this chapter not only delivers novel positive predictions, but also carries important normative implications. Although research on the role of trade policy in a world where firms make organizational decisions under incomplete contracts is at an embryonic stage, a first attempt in this direction is provided by my joint work with Robert Staiger.

In Antràs and Staiger (2012a), we consider a two-country framework in the spirit of the global sourcing model developed in this chapter, in which international trade transactions involve significant lock-in effects and in which, due to incomplete contract enforcement, prices tend to be bilaterally negotiated and are thus not fully disciplined by market-clearing conditions. In the paper, we show that the existence of hold-up inefficiencies gives rise to a role for trade policy to actively encourage input trade volume across borders. Furthermore, because contractual insecurity affects international transactions disproportionately, these optimal trade interventions satisfy Bhagwati and Ramaswami's (1963) targeting principle and are the optimal method of addressing contractual frictions. A similar point was made in a contemporaneous paper by Ornelas and Turner (2012).

Perhaps more interestingly, in Antràs and Staiger (2012a, 2012b) we demonstrate that, even in the absence of hold-up inefficiencies, the fact that prices are bilaterally (or multilaterally) negotiated has profound implications for the optimal design of trade agreements. In particular, when prices are not fully disciplined by market-clearing forces, trade policy–induced changes in local prices can have spillover effects in other countries, even when they hold constant international (untaxed) prices. This in turn leads to predictions quite distinct from those of the traditional terms-of-trade theory of trade agreements, as exposed for instance in Bagwell and Staiger (1999, 2001). As opposed to the traditional "shallow integration" approach of the GATT (now WTO), which is often justified based on the terms-of-trade theory, we instead argue that it is necessary to achieve "deep integration" involving direct negotiations over both border *and* behind-the-border policies. As a corollary, we argue that the growing prevalence of offshoring and of trade in customized goods and services is likely to make it increasingly difficult for governments to rely on traditional GATT/WTO concepts and rules (such as market access, reciprocity, and non-discrimination) to help them solve their trade-related problems.

5

Contracts and Sourcing: Evidence

In Chapter 3, I reviewed several empirical studies exploring the significance of weak contract enforcement for the export decisions of firms and for the structure of international trade flows. It has become customary to appeal to this empirical literature when motivating the role of contractual frictions in the global sourcing decisions of firms. As demonstrated in Chapter 4, however, imperfect contracting affects the international organization of production in ways distinct from those in which it shapes exporting decisions. This was illustrated by the different variants of the global sourcing model developed in Chapter 4, which highlighted the importance of various factors for predicting the differential effect of weak contracting on trade flows of different types of intermediate inputs.

The goal of this chapter is to develop empirical tests of this global sourcing model using detailed data on U.S. imports by product and source country. I will first use the import data aggregated across source countries to explore the determinants of the cross-industry variation in the extent to which U.S. firms rely on domestically produced inputs versus foreign inputs in their production processes. This specification is motivated by equation (4.12) in Chapter 4, which solved for the share of spending on imported manufacturing inputs over total manufacturing input purchases in a particular industry. The equation related this share to several parameters of the model including trade costs, productivity dispersion, demand elasticities, and the level of contractual enforcement as captured by Γ, which in turn was shown to depend on institutional variables as well as on other primitive parameters of the model. Below, I will review some of the key predictions of the models in Chapter 4 before assessing their empirical validity.

I will next exploit the cross-country dimension of U.S. import data to provide richer tests of the model. Before doing so, however, it is necessary to develop a multi-country version of the model that illustrates how cross-country variation in institutional quality shapes the relative propensity of U.S. firms to source particular types of inputs from different countries. This model will build on the multi-country model of sourcing developed toward the end of Chapter 2 and will deliver an explicit formula relating the volume of U.S. imports of a particular input v from a particular country j to trade costs between the United States and j, the wage rate in j, an aggregate measure of labor productivity in j, and an index Γ_j of contractual efficiency in j that is analogous to the parameter Γ derived in the two-country sourcing models in Chapter 4. Crucially, the (re)derivation of Γ_j will highlight the differential effect of weak contracting on U.S. imports of different products depending on particular characteristics of the product being traded and of the industry purchasing those inputs. This will motivate empirical tests along the lines of Nunn (2007) and Levchenko (2007), which will relate U.S. imports of a particular input v from a particular country j to the interaction of industry and country characteristics, while controlling for product and country-year fixed effects.

In order to build intuition on this difference-in-differences approach, consider the following motivating example. Chile and Argentina are two countries that are fairly equidistant to the United States, and had very similar levels of physical capital per worker and of educational attainment in the period 2000–2005.[1] Nevertheless, Chile is recorded as having a significantly higher level of contract enforcement than Argentina does, with the difference in their "rule of law" being 1.90 standard deviations in the underlying measure. In fact, over 2000–2005, Chile was ranked 22nd out of 134 countries in terms of this measure of institutional quality, while Argentina was ranked 95th.

Perhaps for this reason, and despite the fact that both population and GDP in Argentina over that period were more than twice as large as in Chile, the latter country actually featured larger manufacturing exports to the United States than the former (US $2.58 billion vs. $2.38 billion), a difference that persists after netting out manufacturing exports related to some key primary products in these two countries, such as copper, petroleum, and aluminium. The higher market share of Chile versus Argentina in U.S. imports is, however, very weak evidence of the importance of contract enforcement for trade flows, as there might be a myriad of alternative country characteristics that distinguish these two countries and that might be relevant for their differential exports to the United States.

To better identify the causal role of institutions on trade patterns, one can exploit the cross-industry variation in the data to see whether the depressing effect of bad institutions on trade is disproportionately large precisely in the type of industries in which the theory suggests the effect should be disproportionately large. We shall term these industries "contract intensive" and we will use the models developed in Chapter 4 to suggest different proxies for contract intensity.

---

[1] Out of 134 countries with data on these variables, the differences in these variables across these two countries were 0.09 standard deviations for distance, 0.02 for physical capital, and 0.10 for average years of schooling.

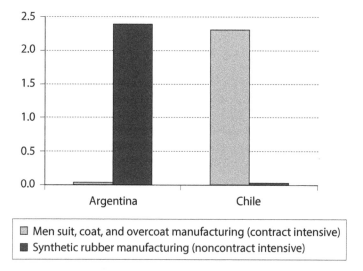

Figure 5.1 Industry Market Share in U.S. Imports Relative to Average Market Share

As an example, consider two manufacturing industries with very different levels of Nunn's (2007) input relationship-specificity measure discussed in Chapter 3. On the one hand, in the six-digit North American Industry Classification System (NAICS) industry 315222 (Men's and Boys' Cut and Sew Suit, Coat, and Overcoat Manufacturing), Nunn (2007) estimates that 75 percent of that industry's intermediate inputs are relationship-specific. On the other hand, in the NAICS six-digit industry 325212 (Synthetic Rubber Manufacturing), this same percentage is only 19 percent. This suggests that the former industry is much more contract intensive than the latter, and thus U.S. buyers might be particularly inclined to purchase this industry's manufactured goods from Chile relative to Argentina. The logic of comparative advantage suggests in turn that Argentina should be a more attractive source than Chile of low contract-intensive goods, such as synthetic rubber manufacturing.

Figure 5.1 confirms this logic by plotting Argentina's and Chile's market share in each of these two industries, while normalizing these shares by each country's aggregate market share in U.S. manufacturing imports. As is clear from the figure, Argentina exports virtually no men's suits, coats, and overcoats to the United States, while its market share in synthetic rubber is 2.4 times its aggregate market share. Conversely, Chile features virtually no exports of synthetic rubber to the United States, while its market share in men's suits, coats, and overcoats is 2.3 times its aggregate market share.

Of course, skeptical readers might argue that this is just a conveniently chosen example, so I will develop empirical tests below that exploit this identification strategy in a more systematic manner using *all* available U.S.

import data. Before specifying these tests, I will briefly discuss some of the pros and cons of using U.S. import data to test our global sourcing model.

Using U.S. Import Data: Pros and Cons

The variants of the global sourcing model developed in Chapter 4 focus on the decisions of firms regarding the location from which intermediate inputs are sourced. Hence, firm-level data would appear to be the ideal laboratory for testing these models. Nevertheless, firm-level data on the sourcing decisions of firms are not readily available, and most of the datasets that have been used for this purpose in the literature do not provide a sufficiently rich picture of the variation in the sourcing decisions of firms across inputs and locations.[2] I will instead conduct tests at the product level that exploit the extent to which different types of manufactured goods are sourced from particular foreign countries or from domestic producers in the United States. It is important to emphasize that these tests are well grounded in theory. As demonstrated in Chapters 2 and 4, and further illustrated below, by solving for the sectoral equilibrium in which a continuum of differentiated final-good producers make sourcing decisions, one can aggregate these producers' decisions and obtain predictions for the relative market share of all countries (including the United States) in the purchases of the different intermediate inputs sourced by U.S.-based firms. In sum, I will use *sectoral*-level data to test *sectoral*-level predictions.

Although the empirical analysis in this chapter could have been conducted with product-level trade data from multiple countries, I will restrict the analysis to import data from a single country, the United States. I do so to facilitate a comparison with the intrafirm trade empirical analysis in Chapter 8, but also because data availability would constrain me from performing some of the sensitivity tests described below for other countries. I will employ U.S. import data for the period 2000–2011 collected by the U.S. Bureau of Customs and Border Protection and publicly available from the U.S. census website. Although the data are available at the extremely detailed ten-digit Harmonized Tariff Schedule classification system (featuring nearly 17,000 good categories), I will work with more aggregated data to be able to match the trade data with a host of other industry-level variables that are only available at more aggregated levels (more on this below).[3] The regressions below will exploit variation on import volumes associated with up to 390

[2] Some datasets, such as the Spanish Encuesta sobre Estrategias Empresariales (ESEE) employed in other parts of the book, only record the firm-level sum of imported inputs aggregated across inputs and foreign sources.

[3] As described in the Data Appendix, I do, however, use the ten-digit data to isolate the intermediate input component of U.S. imports.

manufacturing sectors, 232 countries, and 12 years, which results in up to 1,085,760 observations. Many specifications will, however, feature fewer observations due to data limitations on some key explanatory variables, as will be explained in more detail.

Mapping the rich theoretical predictions from the models in Chapter 4 to U.S. import data poses at least three additional difficulties. First, the theory demonstrates that characteristics of *both* the final-good producing firm (such as the elasticity of demand it faces) and the inputs being purchased (such as their relationship specificity) are relevant for the choice of location from which inputs are sourced. Unfortunately, publicly available U.S. trade statistics are reported based *only* on the sector or industry category of the good being transacted and do not contain information on the sector that is purchasing the good. To give a specific example, while one observes U.S. imports of synthetic rubber (NAICS 325212) from Argentina, a breakdown of these import volumes into those purchased by plants manufacturing footwear, plastic bottles, or tires is not available to researchers. Nevertheless, as described in Antràs and Chor (2013), one can use information from U.S. Input-Output Tables to provide an educated guess of such a breakdown.

A second limitation of U.S. product-level import data is that they do not identify precisely the end use of the good being imported, and thus it is not straightforward to distinguish between import flows corresponding to intermediate inputs and those corresponding to finished products. For instance, although part of U.S. imports of men's suits and coats (NAICS 315222) can certainly be treated as inputs bought by U.S. manufacturing and service firms in a variety of sectors (this is an informed guess based on inspection of the U.S. Input-Output Use Tables), one would expect that a significant share of U.S. imports in this sector constitute finished products sold to consumers perhaps via the retail sector. The mapping between the latter type of imports and the models in Chapter 4 is certainly a bit of a stretch and generates additional problems in the measurement of the characteristics of these buying sectors. For this reason, in the tests below I will implement the methodology developed by Wright (2014) to attempt to isolate the intermediate input component of U.S. imports.

A third key concern with U.S. import data relates to the fact that even when one is confident that an import flow into the United States reflects the exchange of an intermediate input, this does not ensure that such a flow is associated with an importing decision of the headquarters of a firm based in the United States, as the models in Chapter 4 focus on. In particular, it is natural to imagine that some of these transactions are related to the headquarters or parent of a foreign multinational company shipping intermediate inputs to one of its affiliates in the United States. Nunn and Trefler (2013*b*) have suggested a correction for this phenomenon that uses data from Bureau van Djik's Orbis Database to identify the set of countries for which this concern might be particularly salient. I will explain this correction in more detail below and will implement it in some robustness tests.

An additional limitation of using U.S. import data is that they only capture those sourcing decisions that entail goods being shipped back to the United States. In practice, some large U.S. firms have global value chains in which parts and components are shipped across foreign locations and then only shipped back to the United States after being assembled abroad, as is the case of the iPad 3 discussed in Chapter 1. For this reason, U.S. imports generally underrepresent the involvement of U.S. firms in global sourcing strategies. I will not attempt to correct for these third-market effects in the empirical exercises to be performed below, but at the same time it is not clear to me in which direction this phenomenon biases the results to be shown.

I have thus far focused on describing some limitations of U.S. import data when serving as a proxy for the relative propensity of U.S. firms to source particular types of inputs from particular countries. Empirically testing the models in Chapter 4 will also require constructing variables related to some of the key parameters driving these decisions in those models. This will naturally raise additional challenges, but it is best to postpone their discussion until we have revisited the main theoretical predictions to be tested.

Cross-Industry Tests: Complete-Contracting Model

I will begin by implementing empirical tests of the variants of the two-country sourcing model in Chapter 4. Although the ultimate goal of this exercise is to explore the contractual determinants of the global sourcing decisions of firms, it will prove useful to first devote some time to an empirical analysis of the benchmark version of the model with complete contracts.

Remember from Chapter 2 that, assuming a Pareto distribution of productivity across producers, we solved for an industry equilibrium in which the share of spending on *imported* manufacturing inputs over total manufacturing input purchases in a particular industry is given by

$$\Upsilon_O = \frac{\left(\frac{w_N}{\tau w_S}\right)^{(1-\eta)(\sigma-1)}}{\left(\frac{\tilde{\varphi}_O}{\tilde{\varphi}_D}\right)^{\kappa-(\sigma-1)} - 1 + \left(\frac{w_N}{\tau w_S}\right)^{(1-\eta)(\sigma-1)}}$$

where

$$\frac{\tilde{\varphi}_O}{\tilde{\varphi}_D} = \left[\frac{f_O/f_D - 1}{\left(\frac{w_N}{\tau w_S}\right)^{(1-\eta)(\sigma-1)} - 1}\right]^{1/(\sigma-1)}.$$

TABLE 5.1 The Ten Industries with the Least and Most Offshoring Intensity

10 Least Offshoring Intensive: Lowest Υ_O		10 Most Offshoring Intensive: Highest Υ_O	
.000	Ready-Mix Concrete Manufacturing	.899	Luggage Manufacturing
.001	Fluid Milk Manufacturing	.905	Men's & Boys' Cut and Sew Shirt
.002	Manifold Business Forms Printing	.919	Men's & Boys' Cut and Sew Shirt
.002	Rolled Steel Shape Manufacturing	.924	Plastics, Foil, & Coated Paper Bag
.002	Manufactured Mobile Home Manuf	.926	Infants' Cut and Sew Apparel Ma
.003	Sheet Metal Work Manufacturing	.936	Fur and Leather Apparel Manuf
.003	Guided Missile & Space Vehicle Ma	.952	All Other General Purpose Mach
.004	Poultry Processing	.959	Jewelers' Material and Lapidary
.005	Ice Cream and Frozen Dessert Ma	.966	Women's Footwear (exc. Athletic)
.005	Soybean Processing	.996	Other Footwear Manufacturingskip

Sources: U.S. Census, NBER-CES Manufacturing database, and Annual Survey of Manufactures

As discussed in Chapter 2, the share of imported inputs Υ_O is predicted to increase in wage differences (w_N/w_S), productivity dispersion ($1/\kappa$), and the elasticity of substitution σ, and to decrease in (relative) fragmentation barriers (f_O/f_D, τ) and headquarter intensity (η). We can write this succinctly as

$$\Upsilon_O = \Upsilon_O \left(\underset{+}{w_N/w_S}, \underset{-}{\tau}, \underset{-}{f_O/f_D}, \underset{+}{\kappa}, \underset{+}{\sigma}, \underset{-}{\eta} \right). \tag{5.1}$$

Consider now a particular type of input v that is purchased by firms in different sectors of the Northern economy, which in our empirical application we will associate with the United States. The extent to which U.S. firms procure this input domestically or from foreign sources is then shaped by the key parameters of the model, as summarized in (5.1). Other things equal, the relative importance of imports in the total sales of that input should be higher whenever the input can be produced relatively more cheaply abroad and whenever it can be imported with relatively low trade barriers. Furthermore, equation (5.1) suggests that the relative prevalence of imports of input v should be higher whenever sectors purchasing that input feature high degrees of productivity dispersion, high price elasticities of demand, or low levels of headquarter intensity.

A simple way to proxy for the share Υ_O for input v is by computing the ratio of U.S. imports to total U.S. absorption in that particular industrial product v, where U.S. absorption is defined as the sum of shipments by U.S. producers of that good v plus U.S. imports minus U.S. exports of that good. This measure is closely related to what the literature refers to as an import penetration ratio, but I will work to attempt to refine the measure to better capture intermediate input shipments rather than total shipments.

The left panel of Table 5.1 reports the ten industries with the lowest average offshoring share Υ_O over the period 2000–11. The right panel of this same table reproduces the ten industries with the highest offshoring shares over the same period 2000–11. These shares are computed by combining import and export data from the U.S. Census website with total shipments data from the NBER-CES Manufacturing database (for 2000–09) and from the Annual Survey of Manufacturing (for 2010–11). Although all the data are available at the six-digit NAICS level, small adjustments were necessary to deal with minor changes in industrial classifications over time (see the Data Appendix for details). For a few industries and years, the share Υ_O turns out to be either negative or higher than one. This is due to the fact that, for 3.3 percent of the observations (156 out of 4,680), the recorded value of total shipments bizarrely falls short of the value of U.S. exports.[4] I drop these few observations when computing the averages in Table 5.1.

As is clear from Table 5.1, most sectors in the left panel of the table produce goods that are relatively difficult or expensive to ship across borders. Conversely, most sectors in the right panel belong to the apparel sector, which are associated with low trade costs and much lower production costs abroad than in the United States. It is also clear from Table 5.1 that many of the sectors with high offshoring shares appear to produce almost exclusively final goods, which helps motivate our attempt below to restrict the analysis to imports of intermediate inputs.

Having computed these offshoring shares for the period 2000–11, Table 5.2 presents a simple set of benchmark regressions that attempt to explain these shares using cross-industry variation in (i) freight costs and U.S. tariffs to capture trade frictions; (ii) various proxies for headquarter intensity; (iii) a measure of within-industry productivity dispersion; and (iv) a proxy for the elasticity of demand σ. To better interpret the quantitative importance of the results, all the coefficients in the regressions tables correspond to "beta" coefficients. Furthermore, because the industry controls do not vary across countries or years, I cluster the standard errors at the industry level. Before discussing the results, let me briefly outline the data sources while relegating most details to the Data Appendix.

Sectoral measures of freight costs were downloaded from Peter Schott's website (see Schott, 2010, for further documentation), while tariff data correspond to applied tariffs from the World Integrated Trade Solution (WITS) database maintained by the World Bank. Both of these trade cost variables are averaged across exporting countries and over all years in 2000–11 in which they were available. With regard to headquarter intensity, I follow the bulk of the literature and proxy for it with measures of capital, skill, and R&D intensity of U.S. manufacturing firms. More specifically, capital intensity and skill intensity were computed from the NBER Manufacturing Database, while

---

[4] This in turn might be explained by how the Annual Survey of Manufactures allocates shipments across industry categories for multi-product firms, or by the fact that some exports of manufactured goods are conducted by non-manufacturing firms which add value to them before shipping.

R&D intensity corresponds to the logarithm of the average R&D expenditures to sales ratio as computed by Nunn and Trefler (2013b) using the Orbis database. The measure of productivity dispersion is obtained from Nunn and Trefler (2008), who constructed it based on the standard deviation of log trade flows within the Harmonized System ten-digit sub-industries associated with a sector. Finally, the elasticity of demand was computed based on the widely used U.S. import demand elasticities for Harmonized System (HS) ten-digit products computed by Broda and Weinstein (2006).[5]

Having discussed the variables included and their sources, we can now turn to describing the results in Table 5.2. I begin in column (1) with a simple regression of offshoring shares on trade costs and proxies for headquarter intensity, using all available data, which corresponds to 390 industries and 12 years, for a total of 4,680 observations. Column (1) confirms that industries with large freight and insurance costs are associated with lower offshoring shares, as predicted by the theory. The effect is significant both in statistic and economic terms: an increase in one standard deviation of transport costs reduces the offshoring share by 0.22 standard deviations. Conversely, the evidence for a negative effect of man-made trade barriers is much weaker, as the coefficient on tariffs is actually positive, though statistically and economically insignificant. This puzzling result might be explained by a reverse-causality bias, as political-economy theories of tariff formation emphasize a positive effect of import penetration ratios on the desired level of protection of a sector. Ideally, one would attempt to correct for this simultaneity bias along the lines of Trefler (1993b), but I will leave this for future research. This is in part because, despite the existence of an endogeneity bias, some of the refined specifications below will record a negative and significant effect of tariffs. The remaining three coefficients of column (1) of Table 5.2 confirm a negative effect of the three measures used to proxy headquarter intensity, but the statistical significance of each of these coefficients is very low.

In column (2), I repeat the same regression but dropping the 156 observations for which the offshoring share Υ_O falls outside the interval $[0, 1]$. This improves the fit of the regression, but affects the estimates only slightly, with the exception of capital intensity, which now appears to be close to significant at standard confidence levels. From now on, I work with the sample of observations with $\Upsilon_O \in [0, 1]$. In column (3), I break up the effect of capital intensity into the independent effect of capital equipment and

---

[5] All of the variables used in regressions in Table 5.2 were either downloaded at or converted into the six-digit NAICS classification at which the international trade was available in its original form, as explained in more detail in the Data Appendix. The entire dataset and Stata program codes used in the empirical analysis in this chapter and in Chapter 8 are available for download at http://scholar.harvard.edu/antras/books.

TABLE 5.2 Determinants of U.S. Offshoring Shares

Dep. Var.: $\frac{Imp}{Imp+Shipments-Exp}$	(1)	(2)	(3)	(4)	(5)	(6)
Freight Costs	-0.217**	-0.271**	-0.280**	-0.275**	-0.025**	-0.052**
	(0.041)	(0.044)	(0.045)	(0.044)	(0.004)	(0.009)
Tariffs	0.038	0.046	0.015	0.012	0.001	0.003
	(0.073)	(0.089)	(0.073)	(0.075)	(0.006)	(0.010)
Log(R&D/Sales)	-0.027	-0.004	0.025	0.023	-0.001	-0.008
	(0.052)	(0.051)	(0.051)	(0.051)	(0.005)	(0.010)
Log(Skilled/Unskilled)	-0.000	-0.023	-0.043	-0.045	-0.002	-0.006
	(0.000)	(0.048)	(0.049)	(0.049)	(0.005)	(0.010)
Log(Capital/Labor)	-0.049	-0.082				
	(0.042)	(0.053)				
Log(Capital Equip/Labor)			-0.484**	-0.466**	-0.037**	-0.074**
			(0.121)	(0.120)	(0.010)	(0.015)
Log(Capital Struct/Labor)			0.411**	0.393**	0.032**	0.067**
			(0.115)	(0.114)	(0.010)	(0.016)
Productivity Dispersion				-0.002	0.003	0.007
				(0.086)	(0.006)	(0.020)
Elasticity of Demand				0.050	0.002	0.005
				(0.063)	(0.005)	(0.006)
Sample Restrictions	None	$\Upsilon_O \in [0,1]$	$\Upsilon_O \in [0,1]$	$\Upsilon_O \in [0,1]$	$\Upsilon_O \in [0,1]$	$\Upsilon_O \in [0,1]$
Fixed Effects	Year	Year	Year	Year	Ctr/Year	Ctr/Year
Observations	4,680	4,524	4,524	4,524	1,085,537	312,929
R-squared	0.063	0.092	0.140	0.142	0.203	0.196

Standard errors clustered at the industry level in all columns. [+], [*], [**] denote 10, 5, 1% significance.

capital structures. Interestingly, equipment intensity appears to have a very significant negative effect on offshoring shares, while structures affect these shares positively. Both effects are highly significant in both economic and statistical terms. This result is intuitive if one interprets headquarter intensity as representing the relative importance of the type of capital investments for which the "North" appears to have the largest comparative advantage. Indeed, Mutreja (2013) documents that cross-country dispersion in capital equipment is much larger than the dispersion in capital structures and that the ratio of equipment to structures is much higher in rich than in poor countries.[6] The effects of productivity dispersion and the elasticity of demand on offshoring shares are analyzed in column (4) of Table 5.2. The coefficients on these variables are small in magnitude and are imprecisely estimated.

In columns (5) and (6) of Table 5.2, I exploit the full cross-sectoral *and* cross-country variation of the import data. I first compute sectoral offshoring shares at the exporter-country level, by replacing total sectoral imports in the numerator of Υ_O with sectoral imports from a particular country j. I then study the cross-product variation in Υ_O within particular exporting countries by introducing source-country-year fixed effects into the regressions. Later in the chapter, I will motivate in more detail the benefits of exploiting the cross-country dimension of the data for identification purposes. For the time being, it suffices to point out that one might be concerned that the patterns we observed in columns (1)–(4) reflect the attractiveness of particular countries as sources of imports and the fact that these locations are particularly good at producing goods that happen to be cheap to transport or feature a high equipment capital intensity. By introducing source-country-year fixed effects, one is then better able to isolate the effect of sectoral-level characteristics on the relative propensity to offshore or source from domestic producers.

In column (5), I use the full sample of 1,085,760 offshoring shares, except for the mere 223 observations (0.02%) for which Υ_O remains either negative or higher than one. A simple comparison of columns (4) and (5) indicates that the qualitative nature of the results is largely unaffected by the use of country-specific offshoring shares. Note, however, that the (beta) coefficients are around ten times smaller than in the purely cross-sectoral regressions, and broadly suggest a rather small economic significance of the industry covariates. Part of the reason for this is that 71.1 percent of the country/industry/year observations feature zero imports into the United

---

[6] Using data from the Annual Survey of Manufactures (2002–2010), I have further experimented with breaking up capital equipment into expenditures on (i) automobiles and trucks for highway use, (ii) computers and peripheral data processing equipment, and (iii) all other machinery and equipment computers. The effect of autos and 'other equipment' is negative and significant, while that of computers is positive and very significant. The fact that there appears to exist a higher propensity to offshore in sectors that make more intensive use of computers is interesting and intuitive.

States (thus implying $\Upsilon_O = 0$), and hence the simple OLS (linear probability) model I have specified does not ensure the best possible fit of the data. In column (6), I restrict the sample to those observations for which imports flows are positive, and the coefficients roughly double in size relative to those in column (5). I realize, of course, that this is not the proper econometric way to handle the zeroes in the data. In my (weak) defense, however, this approach is fairly standard in the literature.

Overall, the results in Table 5.2 provide mixed evidence in favor of our benchmark global sourcing model with complete contracting. On the one hand, we are able to confirm the negative effect of freight costs and certain proxies of headquarter intensity (most notably, capital equipment) on offshoring shares. On the other hand, the negative effect of other plausible proxies for headquarter intensity appears to be much less precisely estimated. In addition, productivity dispersion and the elasticity of demand affect offshoring shares positively as predicted by the theory, but both the economic and the statistical significance of these results are very small.

Cross-Industry Tests: Sample Restrictions

At some level, it should not be too surprising that the empirical evidence is mixed. After all, earlier in this chapter I highlighted three serious caveats associated with the use of U.S. imports in the construction of offshoring shares. Let me next briefly outline how one can refine the above tests to partially address these limitations.

Consider first the concern that the import data identify only the sector to which the good being transacted belongs. This led me to correlate the degree to which the purchases of an industrial sector's goods come from abroad versus the United States with characteristics of that same sector. In light of our global sourcing model, this seems the natural thing to do when studying the effect of freight costs and tariffs, but it is less justifiable for headquarter intensity, and simply erroneous with regard to the elasticity of demand. More specifically, the headquarter intensity parameter η captures the relative importance of the inputs provided by U.S. headquarters and their suppliers, and thus it would seem more appropriate to construct measures of headquarter intensity of the industry *buying* those inputs. Even more clearly, the parameter σ shaping Υ_O in (5.1) is related to the elasticity of demand in the industry buying and not selling those inputs. Unfortunately, the U.S. Census Related-Party data, and publicly available trade statistics more generally, do not contain information on the industry classification of the importing firm. Still, following the approach in Antràs and Chor (2013), one can use interindustry flow data from the U.S. input-output tables to compute industry variables (e.g., proxies for η and σ), related to the *average* industry buying inputs belonging to a particular industry category. The interested reader is referred to the Data Appendix for more details on the construction of these "buyer" variables.

Although one could construct a buyer version of the Nunn and Trefler (2008) productivity dispersion measure, taking a weighted average of a series of dispersion measures is less likely to provide an accurate measure of the dispersion of the *average* buying industry. Furthermore, as pointed out by Nunn and Trefler (2013b), the comparative static relating offshoring shares to the parameter κ will apply regardless of whether size dispersion stems from productivity dispersion across buyers or across sellers. While the latter type of heterogeneity is missing in the model, it could easily be introduced. For these reasons, I follow Nunn and Trefler (2008) in restricting attention to productivity dispersion measures associated with the sector to which the good being imported belongs.

The need to filter the data through an Input-Output table forces me to abandon the use of the NAICS six-digit industry classification (at which the trade data are reported) and switch to 2002 Input-Output industry codes (IO2002), which is a slightly coarser classification. As a result, I am left with data on 253 IO2002 manufacturing industries instead of the 390 NAICS industries in Table 5.2.[7] Column (1) of Table 5.3 reports cross-industry results analogous to those in column (4) of Table 5.2 but with the IO2002 classification instead of NAICS classification. Comparing these two columns, we see that the change in industry classification has a relatively modest effect on the estimates. Freight costs continue to have a negative and significant effect on offshoring shares, while the evidence for the other parameters of the model is mixed. The main differences in the two columns are that the negative effect of equipment capital intensity is now statistically significant only at the 7 percent level, and that the effect of R&D intensity now appears positive and significant at the 10 percent level.[8]

In column (2) of Table 5.3, I introduce buyer versions of the elasticity of demand and of the proxies for headquarter intensity. The above discussion might have given the impression that the mismeasurement of some key determinants of offshoring shares was responsible for the mixed performance of the model in Table 5.2. Nevertheless, introducing buyer industry variables into the regression only has a minor effect on the estimates. In fact, the coefficient on capital equipment is slightly reduced and loses even more of

---

[7] As explained in the Data Appendix, late in the production of this book, Davin Chor alerted me to the fact that one IO2002 industry appears to have an unrealistically high R&D intensity. Fortunately, the results were found to be virtually unaffected when excluding this industry from the analysis. Such an outlier does not appear in the NAICS-level dataset.

[8] The total number of observations (2986) corresponds to $253 \times 12 = 3,036$ minus 50 observations (1.6%) for which Υ_O falls outside the interval $[0, 1]$.

TABLE 5.3 Refined Determinants of U.S. Offshoring Shares

Dep. Var:: $\frac{Imp}{Imp+Shipments-Exp}$	(1)	(2)	(3)	(4)	(5)	(6)
Seller Industry Freight Costs	-0.315**	-0.295**	-0.269**	-0.273**	-0.025**	-0.054**
	(0.058)	(0.056)	(0.058)	(0.053)	(0.005)	(0.012)
Seller Industry Tariffs	-0.025	-0.013	-0.083*	-0.088**	-0.007**	-0.012
	(0.068)	(0.068)	(0.031)	(0.029)	(0.002)	(0.008)
Log(R&D/Sales)	0.088[+]	0.095	0.033	0.034	0.006	0.007
	(0.053)	(0.072)	(0.085)	(0.082)	(0.008)	(0.016)
Log(Skilled/Unskilled)	-0.021	-0.036	0.054	0.039	0.004	-0.009
	(0.062)	(0.073)	(0.073)	(0.072)	(0.007)	(0.016)
Log(Capital Equip/Labor)	-0.293[+]	-0.221	-0.113	-0.141	-0.005	-0.048
	(0.161)	(0.163)	(0.152)	(0.155)	(0.014)	(0.031)
Log(Capital Struct/Labor)	0.261[+]	0.108	0.085	0.113	0.003	0.037
	(0.151)	(0.150)	(0.148)	(0.151)	(0.013)	(0.029)
Productivity Dispersion	0.016	0.048	0.093	0.118[+]	0.016*	0.031*
	(0.071)	(0.064)	(0.069)	(0.069)	(0.007)	(0.015)
Elasticity of Demand	-0.023	-0.042	-0.032	-0.045	-0.005	-0.004
	(0.072)	(0.082)	(0.080)	(0.084)	(0.005)	(0.019)
Sample Restrictions	$\Upsilon_O\in[0,1]$	$\Upsilon_O\in[0,1]$	W	W+NT	W+NT	W+NT[+]
Fixed Effects	Year	Year	Year	Year	Ctr/Year	Ctr/Year
Buyer vs Seller Industry Controls	Seller	Buyer	Buyer	Buyer	Buyer	Buyer
Observations	2,986	2,986	2,510	2,513	582,811	148,879
R-squared	0.149	0.148	0.147	0.156	0.200	0.198

W and NT stand for the Wright (2014) and Nunn and Trefler (2013b) sample corrections. Standard errors clustered at the industry level. [+] , [*] , [**] denote 10, 5, 1% significance.

its significance, and overall, freight costs is the only variable that appears to statistically affect offshoring shares.[9]

Let us now tackle the second limitation of U.S. product-level import data related to the fact that it does not explicitly distinguish between final goods and intermediate inputs. So far, I have included all U.S. imports of manufacturing goods in the construction of offshoring shares, but it seems sensible to attempt to restrict the sample to intermediate input purchases. In part, this is because the model we have laid out is one in which a U.S. final-good manufacturer is deciding on the optimal location of production of the inputs it combines in production. In response to this, one might argue that it would suffice to relabel some of the objects in the theory to make the model apply to a U.S. retailer deciding on whether to offshore the production of the manufacturing goods it markets. However, this would make it impossible (with available data) to construct average buyer versions of some of the key determinants of offshoring shares, since I only have access to data on U.S. manufacturing firms. For these reasons, it is worth putting some effort into purging final-good purchases from the data.

In order to do so, I build on the methodology developed by Wright (2014). I relegate most details to the Data Appendix, but in a nutshell, Wright's (2014) approach employs a U.S. Census industry concordance between ten-digit HS codes and five-digit End-Use codes to categorize highly disaggregated commodities into final goods and intermediate inputs. With that information, one can then remove from the sample all ten-digit HS codes associated with final-good production, and then reaggregate the data to the IO2002 level to have a proxy for intermediate input import and export flows.[10]

Implementing this methodology naturally reduces the volume of trade differentially across industries and also leads to the loss of observations associated with industries that are composed *entirely* of final goods, such as IO 2002 industry 335222 (Household Refrigerator and Home Freezer Manufacturing). The Data Appendix contains the full list of dropped final-good industries.[11] This procedure can be used to compute imports and exports of intermediate inputs, but the offshoring share formula also requires that we

---

[9] The correlation between the buyer and seller versions of these key industry variables is high and ranges from 0.74 for capital buildings to 0.89 for the elasticity of demand. This, in turn, partly reflects the disproportionate importance of within-industry commodity flows in Input-Output tables.

[10] I follow Wright (2014) in also removing industries that purely process raw materials so we can more comfortably treat inputs as differentiated.

[11] A sector is dropped whenever it comprises zero aggregate imports of intermediate inputs in each year with an offshoring share in $[0, 1]$. There are 39 industries for which this is true (see Table B.1 in the Data Appendix). Column (3) of Table 5.3 drops 526 observations, which is more than $39 \times 12 = 468$ because 58 additional observations have offshoring shares outside the interval $[0, 1]$.

TABLE 5.4 The Ten Industries with the Least and Most *Corrected* Offshoring Intensity

10 Least offshoring intensive: lowest Υ_O		10 Most offshoring intensive: highest Υ_O	
.000	Ready-Mix Concrete Manufacturing	.651	Computer Storage Devices
.004	Support Activities for Printing	.661	Metal Cutting Machine Tools
.006	Asphalt Paving Mix. & Block Manuf	.664	Electr. Capacitors & other Inductors
.007	Textile and Fabric Finishing Mills	.668	Electronic Connectors
.007	Concrete Pipe/ Brick / Block Manuf	.748	Optical Instruments & Lens
.008	Sign Manufacturing	.764	Doll, Toy, Game Manufacturing
.015	Asphalt Shingle & Coating Materials	.773	Leather & Hide Tanning & Finishing
.015	Ornamental & Architectural Metal	.831	Other General Purpose Machinery
.016	Motor Vehicle Body Manufacturing	.838	Pulp Mills
.017	Paperboard Mills	.882	Audio & Video Equipment Manuf

Source: U.S. Census, NBER-CES Manufacturing database, Annual Survey of Manufactures, and a sample adjustment based on Wright (2014)

adjust U.S. shipments in order to constrain these to reflect U.S. intermediate input sales. I do so by multiplying U.S. shipments in each industry by the average "Wright" factor applied to trade flows in that industry over 2000–11. Before discussing the effects of implementing this refinement on the estimates, in Table 5.4 I report the ten sectors with the lowest and highest Wright-corrected average offshoring share Υ_O over the period 2000–11. It is reassuring to compare these sectors with those in Table 5.1 and notice that most of the consumer good sectors in that earlier table are no longer in the sample.

The results of applying this filter to our empirical model explaining offshoring shares are shown in column (3) of Table 5.3. A first noteworthy result is that the effect of tariffs is six times larger than in column (2) and is now statistically significant at the 5 percent level. Furthermore, the effect of productivity dispersion doubles in size and is close to significant at the 10 percent level. On the negative side, the effect of the buyer proxies of headquarter intensity and the elasticity of demand continue to have an imprecisely estimated impact on offshoring shares, and even the sign of some of these coefficients is the opposite of that implied by the model.

In column (4) of Table 5.3, I experiment with one additional refinement of the empirical test. Our discussion above regarding the effects of "buyer" headquarter intensity, productivity dispersion, and demand elasticities relied on an interpretation of U.S. intermediate input imports as being associated with U.S. headquarters importing goods from foreign suppliers. A nontrivial share of these imports, however, consists of shipments from foreign headquarters to their U.S. affiliates or to U.S. unaffiliated parties. Arguably, the rationale for these transactions might not be best interpreted through the lens of the models developed in Chapters 2 and 4. For this reason, in column (4), I follow Nunn and Trefler (2013*b*) in checking the robustness of our results to a restricted sample that better fits the spirit of our global sourcing model. More specifically, Nunn and Trefler (2013*b*) use data from Bureau van Djik's Orbis Database to identify all subsidiary headquarter pairs in which either the subsidiary or the headquarter are from the United States. They find that there are only eighteen countries (see their table 4) such that the share of pairs for which the U.S. firm is the parent is below 75 percent. Furthermore, only for five of these eighteen countries is this share below 50 percent. It is thus advisable to present results in which these five countries (Iceland, Italy, Finland, Liechtenstein, and Switzerland) are removed from the sample. I have also experimented with dropping all eighteen countries with a share below 75 percent and the results are not materially changed.[12]

As is clear from column (4) of Table 5.3, this Nunn-Trefler correction has a qualitatively similar effect as the previous refinements. The negative effect of tariffs and the positive effect of productivity dispersion are larger and more precisely estimated than in previous columns (and the latter effect is now significant at the 10% level), but supporting evidence for a negative effect of buyer headquarter intensity and positive effect of demand elasticities on offshoring remains elusive.

In the last two columns of Table 5.3, I return to the use of both cross-industry and cross-country variation in offshoring shares, while applying the Wright and Nunn-Trefler corrections to trade flows and U.S. shipments in the construction of the shares. Again, the specifications include country-year fixed effects, so the purpose here is to compare offshoring shares across industries, while controlling for time-varying unobserved country characteristics. Arguably, even when one is interested in purely cross-industry variation, it is advisable to fit the data through this straighter jacket. Similarly to Table 5.2, in column (5) I include all (Wright and Nunn-Trefler adjusted) offshoring shares in the interval $[0, 1]$, while in column (6) I drop all observations in column (5) with zero U.S. imports and thus zero offshoring shares.[13] As in Table 5.2, the results are qualitatively similar to the regressions exploiting only the cross-industry dimension of the data, although the economic size of these effects is greatly reduced, while their statistical significance is generally enhanced. Note, in particular, that the effect of buyer productivity dispersion is now

---

[12] The full list of 18 countries includes Iceland, Italy, Finland, Liechtenstein, Switzerland, Sweden, Taiwan, Belgium, Bermuda, Norway, Denmark, Korea, Japan, Spain, Israel, Austria, France, and Germany.

[13] To make sense of the number of observations in column (5), note that the sample now excludes 5 countries and 39 industries, and 125 of the remaining offshoring shares are lower than 0 or higher than 1. We thus have $(232 - 5) \times (253 - 39) \times 12 - 125 = 582,811$ observations.

significant at the 5 percent level in both columns (5) and (6).[14] The results on the elasticity of demand and headquarter intensity remain mixed, although the effect of capital equipment in column (6) is negative and very close to significant at the 10 percent level.

Put together, the estimates in Table 5.3 provide supporting evidence for some of the key predictions of the benchmark complete-contracting benchmark model. In particular, offshoring shares appear to be significantly higher for goods that are relatively cheap to transport (due to low trade costs or low tariffs) and for goods purchased by sectors featuring high productivity dispersion. We have also found some evidence for a negative effect of some proxies of "buyer" headquarter intensity on offshoring shares, though these effects are not particularly robust. Disappointingly, we have found little evidence suggesting a positive effect of buyer demand elasticities on offshoring shares. We next turn to the incomplete-contracting version of the global sourcing model to see whether one can make sense of the mixed effects of the tests performed above, and to formally test the distinctive predictions that arise from the modeling of contractual frictions.

Cross-Industry Tests: Incomplete-Contracting Model

Recall that toward the beginning of Chapter 4, I derived a formula—see equations (4.12) and (4.13)—for the share of spending on imported manufacturing inputs over total manufacturing input purchases in a particular industry in the presence of contractual frictions. I did so, however, under the strong assumptions of complete contracting in the North, "totally" incomplete contracting in the South, a single input, symmetric bargaining, and no financial constraints. As I show in the Theoretical Appendix, this formula can be readily extended to *all* the variants of the model developed in Chapter 4. In those variants of the model, I expressed firm profits under domestic sourcing and under offshoring as

$$\pi_D(\varphi) = (w_N)^{1-\sigma} B\Gamma_D\varphi^{\sigma-1} - f_D w_N$$

and

$$\pi_O(\varphi) = \left((w_N)^{\eta}(\tau w_S)^{1-\eta}\right)^{1-\sigma} B\Gamma_O\varphi^{\sigma-1} - f_O w_N,$$

respectively, where Γ_D and Γ_O denote the levels of contractual efficiency associated with domestic sourcing and offshoring, respectively. The general

---

[14] It is worth stressing that the standard errors in these regressions are clustered conservatively at the industry level.

formula for the share of offshored intermediate inputs is then given by

$$\Upsilon_O = \frac{\frac{\Gamma_O}{\Gamma_D} \left(\frac{w_N}{\tau w_S} \right)^{(1-\eta)(\sigma-1)}}{\left(\frac{\tilde{\varphi}_O}{\tilde{\varphi}_D} \right)^{\kappa-(\sigma-1)} - 1 + \frac{\Gamma_O}{\Gamma_D} \left(\frac{w_N}{\tau w_S} \right)^{(1-\eta)(\sigma-1)}}, \qquad (5.2)$$

where

$$\frac{\tilde{\varphi}_O}{\tilde{\varphi}_D} = \left[\frac{f_O/f_D - 1}{\frac{\Gamma_O}{\Gamma_D} \left(\frac{w_N}{\tau w_S} \right)^{(1-\eta)(\sigma-1)} - 1} \right]^{1/(\sigma-1)}. \qquad (5.3)$$

In a manner analogous to the complete-contracting case, we can summarize the dependence of the share Υ_O on the parameters of the model by

$$\Upsilon_O = \Upsilon_O \left(\underset{+}{w_N/w_S}, \underset{-}{\tau}, \underset{-}{f_O/f_D}, \underset{+}{\kappa}, \underset{-}{\sigma}, \eta, \underset{+}{\Gamma_O/\Gamma_D} \right), \qquad (5.4)$$

where the only novel feature relative to (5.1) is the positive dependence of Υ_O with respect to Γ_O/Γ_D.

Although the same formulas (5.2) and (5.3) apply to all the variants of the global sourcing model, it is important to emphasize that the particular values of Γ_D and Γ_O (and how they are shaped by parameters) differ across the various extensions of the model. For reasons that will become clear later in this chapter, the discussion in Chapter 4 was centered around the effects of the deep parameters of the model on the *level* of Γ_D and Γ_O, rather than on the ratio Γ_O/Γ_D. Nevertheless, the Theoretical Appendix contains detailed derivations and proofs of how various parameters affect the ratio Γ_O/Γ_D under the plausible assumption that offshore transactions are associated with a lower degree of contractibility than domestic transactions.

Table 5.5 summarizes some of the key comparative statics associated with the levels of contractual efficiency as well as their ratio. Notice first that a higher elasticity of demand σ of the buying industry is associated with lower contractual efficiency, with the effect being disproportionately large for offshoring relationships relative to domestic ones.[15] Hence, the distortions generated by incomplete contracting appear to be aggravated by a high degree of competition in final-good markets. Next, note that for reasons discussed in Chapter 4, the effect of headquarter intensity η on these indices of contractibility and their ratio is ambiguous.[16] Naturally, when assessing the effects of the elasticity of demand σ and headquarter intensity η on offshoring

---

[15] To be precise, in Chapter 4 we showed that in the extension with limitations on ex-ante transfers, this negative effect required making a mild parametric assumption.

[16] For instance, in the version of the model with generalized Nash bargaining, the primitive bargaining power parameter β was key for determining the sign of the dependence of contractual efficiency with respect to headquarter intensity η.

TABLE 5.5 Effect of Parameters on Γ_O, Γ_D, and Γ_O/Γ_D

	σ	η	ϕ	μ_S	ϵ	ρ
Γ_D	−	Ambiguous	0	0	−	+
Γ_O	−	Ambiguous	+	+	−	+
Γ_O/Γ_D	−	Ambiguous	+	+	−	+

shares Υ_O, one also needs to take into account the *direct* effects of these parameters in equations (5.2) and (5.3), as summarized in (5.4). The overall effect of σ and η on offshoring shares turns out to be ambiguous because it is the balance of two effects of opposite (or potentially opposite) sign.

These theoretical ambiguities might explain why, in the regressions in Table 5.3, the empirical proxies for these two parameters did not appear to affect offshoring shares in a robust way as predicted by the complete-contracting benchmark model. Conversely, buyer productivity dispersion $1/\kappa$ and trade costs τ have no indirect effect on offshoring shares working through the size of contractual frictions, and thus the model continues to predict in an unambiguous way the positive effect of dispersion and the negative effect of trade frictions that we confirmed empirically in the last columns of Table 5.3.

Apart from offering a potential rationale for the mixed results in Table 5.3, the incomplete-contracting version of our global sourcing model demonstrates that offshoring shares should also be shaped by certain novel variables that affect profitability only through their effect on the size of contractual inefficiencies. As indicated in Table 5.5, the model predicts that offshoring shares Υ_O should be increasing in the ability of the final-good producer to extract rents from suppliers (ϕ), in the degree of contractibility associated with offshoring (μ_S), and in the degree to which the imported input is substitutable with other inputs in production (ρ). Conversely, offshoring shares should be lower whenever the input being purchased features a relatively high level of customization (ϵ).

I will next attempt to incorporate the effect of these variables into the cross-industry empirical specifications that I developed in Table 5.2 and 5.3. Before doing so, I must briefly discuss how to empirically proxy for these contractual determinants of offshoring shares (see the Data Appendix for more details).

In Chapter 4 we have related the parameter ϕ to the extent to which suppliers face financial constraints that inhibit their ability to make upfront payments to final-good producers. The most widely used industry-level proxies for the importance of financial constraints are the external financial dependence measure of Rajan and Zingales (1998) and the asset tangibility measure of Braun (2002). The idea behind these variables is that financial constraints will be tighter in sectors in which firms' internal cash flows are not a significant source of funding or in which firms' assets are largely intangible and cannot be used as collateral.

The recent empirical literature on trade and contracting institutions has proposed various sector-level proxies for the extent to which contractual frictions reduce production efficiency. Anecdotally, three of these measures originate from the Ph.D. theses of three of the brightest young researchers in international trade. In Chapter 3, I described in some detail the input specificity measure developed by Nunn (2007), which I will use extensively below. In a contemporaneous paper, Levchenko (2007) suggested an alternative measure of contractual dependence based on the degree to which firms in a sector use a large number of intermediate inputs in production. More precisely, Levchenko's (2007) measure consists of a sector's Herfindahl index of intermediate input use, computed from U.S. Input-Output Tables for 1992. Also, in the mid-2000s, Costinot (2009) devised a third alternative measure of contractibility related to the complexity of production, as captured by the average training time required to be qualified to work in that sector (based on PSID survey questions). A fourth and final measure of contractibility I will experiment with below is the one proposed by (the also bright and young!) Bernard, Jensen, Redding, and Schott (2010), which builds on the idea that products that are shipped across borders through intermediaries (such as wholesalers) are indirectly revealed to be more contractible. More specifically, their index is computed with U.S. census data as a weighted average of the wholesale employment share of firms importing a particular product. I will for now run with the idea that each of these four measures constitutes an empirical proxy for the degree of contractibility associated with offshoring (μ_S), but below I will highlight some caveats related to that interpretation.[17]

In order to explore the role of the degree of customization ϵ in shaping offshoring shares, I will again build on the methodology of Nunn (2007), but will instead build a measure of the average specificity of the good being transacted rather than of the inputs used in the production of that good. More precisely, and following Antràs and Chor (2013), for each IO2002 sector, I calculate the fraction of ten-digit HS constituent codes classified by Rauch (1999) as neither reference-priced nor traded on an organized exchange (under Rauch's "liberal" classification).

The model also suggests that the degree of input substitutability ρ, which was irrelevant in the complete-contracting framework, should have a positive effect on offshoring shares. Because I will be restricting the sample to imports of intermediate inputs, a simple approach to proxy for ρ is to use the demand elasticity of the good being imported, as estimated by Broda and Weinstein (2006), since this should capture how substitutable that input is vis-à-vis other inputs. To better capture input substitution rather than differentiation by

---

[17] As described in the Data Appendix, each of these four sectoral measures of contract intensity were normalized so that higher levels imply higher contractibility or lower dependence on formal contract enforcement.

country of origin, I follow Antràs and Chor (2013) in using demand elasticities estimated at the three-digit industry level rather than at the ten-digit product level (see the Data Appendix for more details).

Finally, in Chapter 4, I developed a global sourcing model with sequential production that illustrated the potential role of downstreamness in the offshoring decision. I have not included that comparative static in Table 5.5 because the sign of that effect depends on the environment in subtle ways, but below I will explore the effect of downstreamness in some specifications. To do so, I will employ the measure of downstreamness developed by Antràs and Chor (2013) and overviewed in the Data Appendix.

In Table 5.6, I report the results of introducing these nine variables (the two proxies for ϕ, the four for μ_S, plus those for ϵ, ρ, and downstreamness) into the specifications in Table 5.3. For simplicity, I focus on incorporating them into the Wright- and Nunn-Trefler-corrected regressions in columns (4), (5), and (6) of Table 5.3, and I do not report the coefficients on the variables already included in that table. These coefficients are, however, virtually unaffected by the inclusion of these contractually motivated variables.[18]

In the first three columns of Table 5.6, I report the results of adding these nine new variables *one at a time* to the regressions in columns (4), (5), and (6) of Table 5.3. Thus, although nine coefficients appear in each column, each of them is produced by a different regression. As is clear from the table, these nine variables have a small and imprecisely estimated effect on offshoring shares. In fact, of the twenty–seven coefficients in those three first columns of Table 5.6, only four are statistically significant at the 5 percent level. Furthermore, the sign of these coefficients is frequently the opposite from the one predicted by theory and different proxies for the same variable often appear with opposite signs. For instance, we expect all four proxies of μ_S to appear with a positive coefficient, but close to half of those estimates are negative. Similarly, asset tangibility has a negative effect on offshoring shares, whereas the model predicts this effect to be positive (since the more tangible the assets, the lower should financial constraints ϕ be).

In columns (4), (5), and (6) of the table I report the results of regressions analogous to those in columns (1), (2), and (3), but in which a single proxy for financial constraints, a single proxy for contractibility, and the proxies for ϵ, ρ, and downstreamness are all included *in the same* specification. I choose to include Rajan and Zingales's financial dependence measure and Nunn's input relationship-specificity measure because they are the most widely used empirical proxies for financial constraints and contractibility. The results in the table speak for themselves and I will not attempt to sugarcoat them. Only one of those coefficients (for downstreamness in column (6))

---

[18] The interested reader can consult the whole set of regression coefficients by accessing the data and programs available online at http://scholar.harvard.edu/antras/books.

TABLE 5.6 Contractual Determinants of U.S. Offshoring Shares

Dep. Var.: $\frac{Imp}{Imp+Shipments-Exp}$	(1)	(2)	(3)	(4)	(5)	(6)
Financial Dependence	-0.010	-0.004	-0.004	-0.037	-0.000	-0.002
	(0.078)	(0.009)	(0.018)	(0.079)	(0.009)	(0.019)
Asset Tangibility	-0.179**	-0.009	-0.021			
	(0.069)	(0.008)	(0.017)			
Nunn Contractibility	-0.096	-0.005	-0.011	-0.037	-0.000	0.002
	(0.060)	(0.007)	(0.016)	(0.086)	(0.008)	(0.016)
Levchenko Contractibility	-0.118*	-0.000	0.004			
	(0.049)	(0.009)	(0.021)			
Costinot Contractibility	0.130+	0.008	0.018			
	(0.067)	(0.006)	(0.013)			
BJRS Contractibility	0.078	0.006	0.022			
	(0.071)	(0.006)	(0.013)			
Specificity	0.116*	0.006	0.013	0.083	0.003	0.003
	(0.055)	(0.006)	(0.014)	(0.080)	(0.008)	(0.016)
Input Substitutability	-0.019	-0.003	-0.012	0.008	-0.002	-0.010
	(0.064)	(0.005)	(0.011)	(0.062)	(0.006)	(0.013)
Downstreamness	0.096	0.009	0.031*	0.055	0.009	0.032+
	(0.084)	(0.007)	(0.016)	(0.094)	(0.008)	(0.017)
Sample Restrictions	W+NT Year	W+NT Ctr/Year	W+NT Ctr/Year	W+NT Year	W+NT Ctr/Year	W+NT Ctr/Year
Observations	2,513	582,811	148,879	2,513	582,811	148,879
R-squared	≃ 0.15	≃ 0.19	≃ 0.20	0.168	0.200	0.199

Standard errors clustered at the industry level. +, *, ** denote 10, 5, 1% significance. The sign ≃ indicates that this value is roughly the average R-squared across specifications.

appears statistically significant. I have also experimented with simultaneously including all nine contractual variables in the same regression, and the results were equally disappointing.

Overall, the results in Table 5.6 provide no evidence in support of our contracting models of global sourcing. Next I discuss why that might be so, and how one can use alternative approaches to more cleanly evaluate the model.

Limitations and Alternative Approaches

The industry-level tests performed so far have failed to provide much supportive evidence for the importance of contractual factors in determining the global sourcing decisions of U.S. firms. The fact that the earlier tests of the benchmark complete-contracting model did not deliver much more robust results suggests, however, that perhaps part of the blame for this rests on the approach we have followed so far. Indeed, the low R^2 in the above regressions indicates that most of the variation in offshoring shares is explained by "omitted" factors. These omitted characteristics might well be correlated with the industry variables included in the regressions above, thus creating biases that have the potential to explain the poor results obtained so far.

Recent empirical literature in international trade has been well aware of these potential biases and has developed alternative strategies to identify the role of factor endowments and institutional factors in shaping comparative advantage and trade flows across countries. A particularly dominant approach builds on the seminal work of Rajan and Zingales (1998) and exploits the idea that industry characteristics should have a differential effect on trade flows (and on input flows in our context) across countries, depending on characteristics of these countries. This difference-in-difference approach was first applied in a trade context by Romalis (2004), who cast the Heckscher-Ohlin model as predicting an effect of capital intensity on export flows that is disproportionately large for physical capital–abundant countries. As mentioned in Chapter 3, the recent empirical literature on institutions and trade has emphasized, in a similar vein, that differences in contracting institutions across countries should have a differential effect on trade flows in different sectors, depending on certain characteristics of these sectors.

In econometric terms, this approach advocates the inclusion of both country and industry fixed effects in regressions predicting trade flows, and tests the validity of models by inspecting the effect of interactions terms composed of industry and country characteristics. From an empirical point of view, adapting this methodology to the global sourcing environment I have been studying is relatively straightforward, particularly given my use of variation both across sectors and countries in some of my specifications above. From a theoretical point of view, this approach is also feasible because the different variants of our global sourcing model deliver comparative statics relating offshoring shares to interactions of parameters, which one might associate with country or industry characteristics. For instance, in Chapter 4, I showed that the positive effect of offshore contractibility μ_S on offshoring shares should be higher whenever the buyer's demand elasticity σ or the degree of customization ϵ are high, or whenever input substitutability ρ is low. It seems natural to associate offshore contractibility at least partly to the quality of contractual institutions in the exporting country, while the parameters σ, ϵ, and ρ can be thought of as being industry characteristics, as in the regressions above. Hence, our global sourcing model implies that the interaction of source country contract enforcement with proxies for σ, ϵ, and ρ, should have predictive power for U.S. imports of particular intermediate inputs from particular source countries.

As natural as this approach may appear, it is, however, not firmly grounded in the two-country model of global sourcing I have developed in Chapter 4. Before returning to the data, I will briefly describe a multi-country version of this global sourcing model that provides a semi-structural interpretation of the tests to be performed below.

Multi-Country Framework

Toward the end of Chapter 2, I discussed how to extend the two-country complete-contracting global sourcing model to a multi-country environment. The key for tractability was to follow Eaton and Kortum (2002) in modeling labor productivity as the realization of an extreme-value Fréchet random variable. In order to characterize the intensive and extensive margins of global sourcing, it also proved convenient to consider a richer environment in which production required the completion of a continuum of stages, with each of these stages being potentially produced in a different country. Adapting that framework to an incomplete-contracting environment raises important challenges, so I will instead focus on a version of the model in which each final-good producer procures only one input (as in the two-country model). Furthermore, I will restrict the analysis to a variant of the model in which the firm-level extensive margin of offshoring is not operative.

Let us now discuss the assumptions of the model in more detail. I consider a framework with J countries in which final-good producers in every country combine locally produced headquarter services with a manufacturing input that can be procured from any of the J countries. To build intuition, let us consider first the complete-contracting version of the model. As in equation (2.24) in Chapter 2, the operating profits associated with a firm based in i

using an input manufactured in country j are given by

$$\pi_{ij}(\varphi) = \left((a_{hi}w_i)^\eta (\tau_{ij}a_{mj}w_j)^{1-\eta}\right)^{1-\sigma} B\varphi^{\sigma-1} - f_{ij}w_i, \qquad (5.5)$$

where B is now given by

$$B = \frac{1}{\sigma}\left(\frac{\sigma}{(\sigma-1)P}\right)^{1-\sigma} \beta \sum_{j\in\mathcal{J}} w_j L_j$$

and P is the common price index (2.4) for final-good varieties in each country. Remember the parameters a_{hi} and a_{mj} capture the unit labor requirements associated with headquarter service provision and manufacturing production, and they are allowed to vary across countries. Furthermore, while a_{hi} is a technological parameter common across firms based in i, the manufacturing productivity parameters $1/a_{mj}$ for all j are assumed to be firm-specific and drawn from a Fréchet distribution as in Eaton and Kortum (2002), so that

$$Pr(a_{mj} \geq a) = e^{-T_j a^\theta}, \quad \text{with } T_j > 0.$$

These Fréchet draws are assumed to be independent across firms and locations, and also orthogonal to core productivity φ.

As in Chapter 2, a firm obtains a productivity draw from a given country j only after paying the fixed cost f_{ij} of sourcing from country j. I will simplify matters relative to Chapter 2 by assuming that the fixed costs of sourcing f_{ij} are small enough that all firms from i find it profitable to incur these costs and draw a parameter a_{mj} from each country $j \in \mathcal{J}$. This is obviously a strong assumption, but it is worth emphasizing that it does not imply that firms will buy inputs from all countries in the world. In fact, because they only require a single input for production, firms will only buy inputs from a single market. As mentioned before, this will shut down the extensive margin of sourcing at the firm level.

Because firms only learn their particular realizations of $1/a_{mj}$ for each $j \in \mathcal{J}$ after they have incurred all sunk costs of offshoring, the choice of location of production of the single manufacturing input will simply maximize the first term of the profit function in (5.5), which is analogous to choosing $j^* = \arg\min_{j\in\mathcal{J}} \{\tau_{ij}a_{mj}w_j\}$. Importantly, this is true for all firms in i regardless of their core productivity φ. Appealing to the properties of the Fréchet distribution, we can then conclude that all firms from i will source inputs from country j with probability

$$\chi_{ij} = \frac{T_j\left(\tau_{ij}w_j\right)^{-\theta}}{\sum_{l\in\mathcal{J}} T_l\left(\tau_{il}w_l\right)^{-\theta}}. \qquad (5.6)$$

Since there is a continuum of firms in i, we can then apply the law of large numbers to conclude that χ_{ij} in (5.6) will also constitute the share of inputs purchased by firms in i that originate in j. Less trivially, but again following in a straightforward manner from the results in Eaton and Kortum (2002), the distribution of the actual price paid for any input is independent of the actual source j of that input, and thus χ_{ij} in (5.6) also corresponds to country j's share of all manufacturing input purchases by firms from i.

With this machinery in hand, we can now reintroduce contractual frictions into this multi-country version of the model. Notice that apart from the initial vector of sunk costs of sourcing f_{ij}, all production decisions of and negotiations between final-good producers and suppliers are performed with knowledge of the realization of the vector of cost draws a_{mj}. It is then straightforward to verify that, in all versions of the global sourcing model developed in Chapter 4, the operating profits (net of sunk costs) associated with input manufacturing in a given location j can be written as

$$\pi_{ij}(\varphi) = \left((a_{hi} w_i)^\eta \left(\tau_{ij} a_{mj} w_j \right)^{1-\eta} \right)^{1-\sigma} \Gamma_{ij} B \varphi^{\sigma-1}, \tag{5.7}$$

where $\Gamma_{ij} < 1$ summarizes the reduction in profitability associated with incomplete contracting in the different versions of the model. For instance, in the version of the model with partial contractibility, we have from equation (4.22) that

$$\Gamma_{ij} = \left(\frac{\sigma}{\sigma - (\sigma - 1)\left(1 - \mu_{ij}\right)} + 1 \right)^{\sigma - (\sigma-1)\left(1-\mu_{ij}\right)} \left(\frac{1}{2} \right)^\sigma,$$

where μ_{ij} corresponds to the degree of contractibility associated with firms from i sourcing inputs from j.

Even though we have focused on a single-input version of the model, this multi-country version of the model can easily accommodate an extension with a continuum of inputs as long as these inputs are all produced in the same country j under the same labor productivity a_{mj}, in which case the index of contractual efficiency Γ_{ij} becomes (see equation (4.28))

$$\Gamma_{ij} = \left(1 + \frac{1}{\rho} \frac{(\sigma - 1)(1 - \eta)}{\sigma - (\sigma - 1)\left(1 - \mu_{ij}\right)} \right)^{\sigma - (\sigma-1)\left(1-\mu_{ij}\right)} \left(\frac{\rho\sigma}{\rho\sigma + (\sigma - 1)(1 - \eta)} \right)^\sigma. \tag{5.8}$$

Given that Γ_{ij} is not stochastic, it affects the profit function in equation (5.7) in a manner analogous to the trade cost τ_{ij} and the wage rate w_j, and we can use steps analogous to the ones above for the complete-contracting case to conclude that the share of intermediate input purchases sourced from country j is given by

$$\chi_{ij} = \frac{T_j \left(\tau_{ij} w_j \Gamma_{ij}^{1/(1-\eta)(1-\sigma)} \right)^{-\theta}}{\sum_{l \in \mathcal{J}} T_l \left(\tau_{il} w_l \Gamma_{il}^{1/(1-\eta)(1-\sigma)} \right)^{-\theta}}. \quad (5.9)$$

Hence, conditional on transport costs, technological productivity, and wage costs, locations associated with worse perceived contract enforcement from the point of view of firms from i will tend to sell a relatively lower share of the intermediate inputs purchased by firms from country i.[19]

Empirical Implementation of the Multi-Country Model

In order to transition back to the empirical exploration of the model, it will prove useful to reintroduce input subscripts v and express the offshoring share χ_{ijv} associated with input v as

$$\chi_{ijv} = \frac{T_{jv} \left(\tau_{ijv} w_{jv} \Gamma_{ijv}^{1/(1-\eta_v)(1-\sigma_v)} \right)^{-\theta}}{\sum_{l \in \mathcal{J}} T_{lv} \left(\tau_{ilv} w_{lv} \Gamma_{ilv}^{1/(1-\eta_v)(1-\sigma_v)} \right)^{-\theta}}, \quad (5.10)$$

where I will write Γ_{ijv} as

$$\Gamma_{ijv} = \Gamma \left(\sigma_v, \eta_v, \epsilon_v, \rho_v, \phi_{ij}, \mu_{ij} \right). \quad (5.11)$$

For simplicity, I omit time subscripts throughout, although remember that the estimation uses annual data for 2000–11. Notice from equation (5.10) that I am allowing the absolute advantage parameter T_{jv} and the wage rate w_{jv} to vary not only across countries but also across products. These features would complicate the general equilibrium of the model, but I have restricted attention to industry equilibria, so this cross-sectoral variation can be introduced at little cost. Similarly, I am allowing trade costs (or tariffs) τ_{ijv} to vary across both countries and sectors. Note also that the index of contract efficiency Γ_{ijv} associated with firms from i sourcing from country j inputs of type v is written in (5.11) as a function of product characteristics $(\sigma_v, \eta_v, \epsilon_v, \rho_v)$ and country-pair characteristics (ϕ_{ij}, μ_{ij}).

These choices are not without loss of generality and warrant some discussion. I view it as natural to assume that headquarter intensity η_v and specificity ϵ_v are largely sectoral characteristics, independent of the country that exports an input. Similarly, the parameters σ_v and ρ_v govern

---

[19] As in the two-country model, one needs to take a stance on how inputs are priced in an incomplete-contracting framework. To derive equation (5.9), I assume as in Chapter 4 that input expenditures constitute the same multiple of operating profits in all countries.

substitutability across final goods and inputs, and although these could presumably vary across countries, the data I am using to proxy for them (from Broda and Weinstein, 2006) provide a unique sectoral estimate based on U.S. import data. Conversely, I will for the most part treat the degree of financial constraints ϕ_{ij} and contractibility μ_{ij} as country (or country-pair) characteristics. In some specifications, I will, however, allow the effect of financial constraints and contractibility to be expressed as an interaction of a sector-specific component and a country-pair-specific component, so we can write these as $\phi_{ijv} = \phi_v \times \phi_{ij}$ and $\mu_{ijv} = \mu_v \times \mu_{ij}$.

It might be useful to employ equations (5.10) and (5.11) to illustrate some of the limitations of the cross-industry empirical tests developed earlier in this chapter. Above, we argued that the inclusion of source-country-year fixed effects helped isolate the effect of sectoral-level characteristics on offshoring shares. Indeed, if the inclusion of country-year fixed effects completely partialled out the effect of any country-level variable on offshoring shares χ_{ijv}, then all that would be left for identification would be the cross-sectoral variation in the data. It is pretty clear from the formula for χ_{ijv} in (5.10), however, that demeaning offshoring shares within countries (and years) will not eliminate the effects of country-level variables, since these effects interact with industry-level variables. This is true even when we consider a log-transformation of offshoring shares, in which case we can rewrite (5.10) as

$$\ln \chi_{ijv} = \ln T_{jv} - \theta \ln w_{jv} - \theta \ln \tau_{ijv} + \frac{\theta}{(1 - \eta_v)(\sigma_v - 1)} \ln \Gamma_{ijv} + \alpha_{iv}, \quad (5.12)$$

where α_{iv} is an importer/product fixed effect given by

$$\alpha_{iv} = -\ln \left(\sum_{l \in \mathcal{J}} T_{lv} \left(\tau_{ilv} w_{lv} \Gamma_{ilv}^{1/(1-\eta)(1-\sigma)} \right)^{-\theta} \right).$$

Only when T_{jv}, w_{jv}, τ_{ijv}, and Γ_{ijv} can all be decomposed into the product of a sector-specific term and a country-specific term, will country-year fixed effects effectively partial out the effect of country-level variables. Nevertheless, it should be clear from the formulas for Γ_{ijv}—such as equation (5.8)—that this decomposability is not a feature satisfied by the index of contractibility Γ_{ijv}. As demonstrated in Chapter 4 and also in the Theoretical Appendix, the partial derivative of $\ln \Gamma_{ijv}$ with respect to industry characteristics is generally affected by country-level variables, such as μ_{ij} or ϕ_{ij}.

In light of these interaction effects, I will next present the results of empirical specifications that include both product and country-year fixed effects and judge the validity of our global sourcing model based on the predicted effect of the interaction of sector and country characteristics. More specifically, we can express the specification equation as

$$\ln \chi_{ijv} = \alpha_{iv} + \alpha_{ij} + \beta \mathbf{Z}_{ij}\mathbf{z}_v + \gamma \ln \tau_{ijv} + \delta \ln \Gamma_{ijv} + \varepsilon_{ijv}. \qquad (5.13)$$

Because in the empirical application we are fixing the importing country to be the United States, the terms α_{iv} and α_{ij} in this expression are effectively sector- and exporting-country-year fixed effects. The effect of technological or factor endowments differences as sources of comparative advantage is captured by the interaction terms $\mathbf{Z}_{ij}\mathbf{z}_v$, that of trade frictions (freight costs and tariffs) is represented by $\ln \tau_{ijv}$, while the vector $\ln \Gamma_{ijv}$ summarizes the effect of interactions of the primitive parameters of the model on the logarithm of the index of contractual efficiency Γ_{ijv}. In light of our results in Chapter 4 and the Theoretical Appendix, we can write $\ln \Gamma_{ijv}$ in terms of the following interaction terms (and predicted effects):

$$\ln \Gamma_{ijv} = \Phi \left(\underset{-}{\mu_{ij} \times \rho_v}, \underset{+}{\mu_{ij} \times \sigma_v}, \underset{+}{\mu_{ij} \times \epsilon_v}, \underset{\text{ambiguous}}{\mu_{ij} \times \eta_v}, \underset{+}{\phi_{ij} \times \eta_v} \right). \qquad (5.14)$$

Although the log-linear specification in (5.13) is quite standard in the literature, it has the downside of dropping all the observations with zero import flows. I have also experimented with linear specifications in which the dependent variable is the share χ_{ijv} instead of its logarithm. The qualitative results I obtained in those regressions were similar to those reported below, but the R^2 were orders of magnitude smaller than in log-linear specifications. Given that the model I have used to motivate the empirical analysis does not feature an extensive margin of offshoring, and thus captures variation only across positive trade flows, I will focus on discussing the results of the log-linear specification.

A Brief Detour into Previous Empirical Studies

Before formally testing our global sourcing model, I briefly discuss the results of running specifications analogous to the one in (5.13), but with a number of institutional interactions that have been suggested in the literature in recent years (rather than those suggested by the global sourcing model developed in this book). The goal of this exercise is to document that the results obtained by other authors continue to apply when studying the determinants of U.S. imports, even when restricting the analysis to U.S. imports of intermediate inputs using the sample restrictions described above.

The specifications to be discussed below are most closely related to the work of Nunn (2007) and Levchenko (2007). More specifically, I follow Nunn (2007) in studying log-linear specifications in which trade flows are projected on sectoral and country-year fixed effects, together with Heckscher-Ohlin interactions associated with physical capital and skilled labor and a series of institutional interactions. By focusing on U.S. imports across sectors and countries (rather than worldwide exports of individual countries), I follow the approach in Levchenko (2007). The key novelties of the analysis below are that (i) similar to Chor (2010), I experiment with the inclusion of a wide set of institutional interactions; and (ii) I attempt to capture the effect of these variables on the global sourcing decisions of U.S. firms, rather than on overall U.S. imports.[20]

I experiment below with the inclusion of four interactions associated with contracting institutions, two related to financial institutions, and one reflecting the role of labor-market institutions. Although I do not theoretically motivate these specifications, the contracting and financial interactions can be thought of as corresponding to the effect of ϕ_{ijv} and μ_{ijv} in the global sourcing model, whenever these are expressed as an interaction of a sector-specific component and a country-pair-specific component ($\phi_{ijv} = \phi_v \times \phi_{ij}$ and $\mu_{ijv} = \mu_v \times \mu_{ij}$).

The four contract enforcement interactions correspond to the product of the exporter's rule of law averaged over 2000–05 (from the Worldwide Governance Indicators) with the contract intensity measures created by Nunn (2007), Levchenko (2007), Costinot (2009), and Bernard et al. (2010), all of which were described above. These industry variables were normalized so that higher values of these variables are associated with lower dependence on formal contract enforcement (see the Data Appendix).[21] Following Manova's (2012) work, the two financial institutions' interactions are the product of the exporter's log private credit to GDP ratio averaged over 2000–05 (from the World Development Indicators), with the external financial dependence measure of Rajan and Zingales (1998) and the asset tangibility measure of Braun (2002) (also discussed above). Finally, the labor-market institutions interaction corresponds to the one developed by Cuñat and Melitz (2012), which is the product of the labor-market flexibility measure developed by Botero, Djankov, La Porta, Lopez-de Silanes, and Shleifer (2004) and a measure of average firm-level sales volatility in an industry (which captures the need for labor reallocations across firms within a sector). In addition, all specifications will include two Heckscher-Ohlin interactions that are constructed with standard measures of physical capital and skilled labor intensity and relative abundance, as described in the Data Appendix. In Table 5.7, I do not report the coefficient on these Heckscher-Ohlin interactions, but they generally appear

---

[20] See Nunn and Trefler (2013a) for an overview of the literature on trade and institutions.

[21] In the regressions including Costinot's product complexity measure, I follow Costinot (2009) in always including as a control variable the interaction of this industry measure with the measure of skilled labor abundance used in the Heckscher-Ohlin skilled labor interaction.

positive and statistically significant in explaining U.S. imports and offshoring shares.

Column (1) of Table 5.7 reports the results of adding the seven institutional interactions *one at a time* to a simple OLS regression of the log of U.S. imports from a given country in a given sector on sectoral and country-year fixed effects and the two Heckscher-Ohlin interactions. All the coefficients in the table are beta coefficients. Due to data availability, some specifications include fewer observations than others, but these differences are small (the number of observations ranges from 180,653 to 196,584). As is clear from the results in column (1), all seven institutional interactions appear with the expected sign, are sizeable in magnitude and are statistically significant at the extremely low significant levels. More precisely, better rule of law increases exports to the United States disproportionately less in sectors that are less dependent on formal contract enforcement. Furthermore, higher financial development increases exports to the United States disproportionately more in sectors with higher external capital dependence or lower asset tangibility, while more flexible labor markets foster exports to the United States disproportionately more in sectors with high sales volatility.

In column (2) I re-run these seven specifications but applying the Wright and Nunn-Trefler corrections to U.S. imports in an attempt to restrict the analysis to intermediate input purchases by U.S.-based firms. This leads to a loss of about 35 percent of observations associated with U.S. imports of final goods, and remember that it also modifies U.S. imports differentially across sectors and countries. Despite these modifications, the results in column (2) are quite comparable to those in column (1) and are suggestive of the importance of the seven institutional interactions for the global sourcing decisions of U.S. firms. In the remainder of the table, the analysis is restricted to these Wright and Nunn-Trefler corrected U.S. imports.

In column (3), I follow Chor (2010) in including the seven institutional interaction terms in the *same* specification. This leads to a noticeable reduction of the partial effect of each of these interactions, but with the exception of the Rajan-Zingales interaction, all of the other key explanatory variables remain significant.

A natural concern with the results in column (3) is that the included interaction terms simply capture the effect of alternative interaction effects that are omitted from the specification. For instance, one might worry that the interaction of the contract intensity variables and rule of law simply captures the fact that richer countries (which typically have a better rule of law) tend to specialize in relatively complex goods (which typically are recorded as being contract-intensive) for reasons distinct from contractual considerations. A commonly used way to deal with this concern is to include interactions of all seven industry-level institutional variables with a measure of overall development, such as GDP per capita. In column (4), I report

TABLE 5.7 Contractual Determinants of U.S. Offshoring Shares

Dep. Var.: ln $\left(\frac{Imp}{Imp+Ship.-Exp}\right)$	(1)	(2)	(3)	(4)	(5)
Nunn × Rule	-0.139**	-0.175**	-0.051**	-0.152**	-0.134**
	(0.012)	(0.014)	(0.019)	(0.033)	(0.033)
Levchenko × Rule	-0.165**	-0.166**	-0.123**	-0.076**	-0.087**
	(0.009)	(0.010)	(0.013)	(0.026)	(0.026)
Costinot × Rule	-0.242**	-0.178**	-0.038[+]	-0.015	-0.019
	(0.014)	(0.018)	(0.021)	(0.031)	(0.032)
BJRS × Rule	-0.270**	-0.178**	-0.118**	-0.053	-0.048
	(0.016)	(0.022)	(0.025)	(0.045)	(0.045)
Rajan-Zingales × Credit/GDP	0.309**	0.272**	0.059	-0.200*	0.041
	(0.025)	(0.029)	(0.037)	(0.096)	(0.044)
Braun × Credit/GDP	-0.392**	-0.400**	-0.185**	-0.187**	-0.169**
	(0.030)	(0.035)	(0.047)	(0.054)	(0.053)
Firm Volatility × Labor Flexibility	0.123**	0.119**	0.076**	0.100**	0.101**
	(0.025)	(0.028)	(0.029)	(0.029)	(0.029)
Sample Restrictions	$\Upsilon_O > 0$	W+NT[+]	W+NT[+]	W+NT[+]	W+NT[+]
Ctr/Year & Ind Fixed Effects	Yes	Yes	Yes	Yes	Yes
Interactions with GDP pc	No	No	No	Yes	No
Industry Effects × GDP pc	No	No	No	No	Yes
Observations	≃ 190,000	≃ 125,000	120,034	120,034	120,034
R-squared	≃ 0.610	≃ 0.607	0.622	0.623	0.637

Standard errors clustered at the country/ind. level. [+], [*], [**] denote 10 , 5 , 1% significance.

the results associated with that specification. The impact of that robustness test on the estimates is more significant. On the plus side, the Nunn, Levchenko, Braun, and Cuñat-Melitz interactions retain their expected sign as well as their economic and statistical significance. The Costinot and Bernard et al. interaction terms also continue to have the expected sign, but are now indistinguishable from zero. More puzzlingly, the addition of these GDP per capita interactions now reverses the sign of the Rajan-Zingales interaction, thus indicating that better financial development is associated with higher exports in sectors with low external dependence.

Finally, in column (5) I perform an even more stringent robustness test by incorporating interactions of GDP per capita with sectoral dummies (as advocated by Nunn and Trefler, 2013a). This is motivated by the same concerns as in column (4), but the wide set of interactions allows the level of development to affect U.S. intermediate input imports in each individual sector differentially in an unrestricted way. The results of this test are very similar to those in column (4), except that the Rajan and Zingales interaction term recovers its expected sign (though not in a statistically significant fashion).

Overall, the results in Table 5.7 indicate that even when restricting attention to the cross-country and cross-industry determinants of U.S. imports of intermediate inputs, we find similar results to those obtained in previous contributions studying the institutional determinants of comparative advantage. This fact enhances our confidence in the use of very similar specifications with the goal of testing our global sourcing model, a task to which we turn next.

Back to the Test of the Multi-Country Sourcing Model

We now return to the specification in (5.13) and (5.14) motivated by our global sourcing model. In order to transition to a precise estimating equation, I first let the vector Z_{ijzv} comprise again an interaction $k_v K_j$ of capital intensity and capital relative abundance of the exporting country and an analogous interaction $s_v S_j$ based on skilled-labor intensity and skilled-labor relative abundance data (see the Data Appendix for more details). Second, I proxy for trade frictions τ_{ijv} with measures of freight costs and tariffs analogous to those used in the cross-industry regressions above, but with those variables being computed at the country and sectoral levels with U.S. import data. Finally, I assume that the function Γ in (5.11) is linear in its interactions, so we can succinctly write the empirical specification as follows:

$$\ln \chi_{jv} = \alpha_v + \alpha_j + \beta_1 k_v K_j + \beta_2 s_v S_j + \gamma_1 freight_{jv} + \gamma_2 tariff_{jv}$$

$$+ \delta_1 \rho_v \mu_j + \delta_2 \sigma_v \mu_j + \delta_3 \epsilon_v \mu_j + \delta_4 \eta_v \mu_j + \delta_5 \eta_v \phi_j + \varepsilon_{jv}. \quad (5.15)$$

As mentioned earlier, in constructing the institutional interactions, I proxy ρ_v, σ_v, and ϵ_v in the same manner as in the cross-industry tests above, while μ_j and ϕ_j correspond to the rule of law and the log private credit over GDP ratio of the exporting country, respectively. Headquarter intensity η_v is measured as the first principal component from a factor analysis of the buyer versions of R&D, equipment capital, and skill intensity variables. I have dropped the subscript i referring to the importing country because in the results below, i is always the United States. Notice also that because the denominator of χ_{ijv} in (5.10) is common for all exporting countries j, one can simply replace the dependent variable $\ln \chi_{jv}$ with the logarithm of U.S. imports from country j in sector v, which is the same dependent variable included in the results in Table 5.7.

In light of the global sourcing model, one would expect the coefficients β_1, $\beta_2, \delta_2, \delta_3$ and δ_5 to be positive, and the coefficients γ_1, γ_2, and δ_1 to be negative. The model instead does not provide an unambiguous prediction for the sign of δ_4 (though it suggests that this interaction should affect trade flows, which motivates its inclusion).

The first column of Table 5.8 reports the results of estimating equation (5.15) without the institutional interactions, but with the trade costs variables, which were missing in Table 5.7. Both Heckscher-Ohlin interactions affect U.S. imports in a positive and significant way, with the effect being particularly highly significant for the case of the skilled labor interaction. Freight costs and tariffs in turn have a negative effect on U.S. imports, with the former effect being significant at the 1 percent level and the latter at the 10 percent level. In column (2) of Table 5.8, I re-run the same specification, but this time attempting to restrict the sample to U.S. imports of intermediate inputs by U.S.-based firms by applying the Wright and Nunn-Trefler corrections. The effect on the coefficients is rather modest, except for the effect of tariffs, which is now notably larger in absolute terms and statistically significant at the 5 percent level.

I next experiment with the inclusion of the five interactions motivated by our model to the specification in column (2). I first do so in column (3) by introducing these interactions *one at a time*, so even though all coefficients appear in the same column, it should be understood that these are obtained by running five separate regressions.[22] Interestingly, each of the five institutional interactions appears to be highly significant and with a sign consistent

---

[22] This also explains why the Heckscher-Ohlin and trade cost coefficients are not reported in column (3). These omitted coefficients and their standard errors vary slightly across specifications, but they are very close in levels and statistical significance to those reported in column (2), except that the positive and significant effect of the physical capital Heckscher-Ohlin interaction is not robust to the inclusion of the interactions involving headquarter intensity.

TABLE 5.8 Testing the Global Sourcing Model

Dep. Var.: $\ln\left(\frac{Imp}{Imp+Ship.-Exp}\right)$	(1)	(2)	(3)	(4)	(5)	(6)
K Intensity × K Abund.	0.120*	0.151*		0.380**	0.357**	0.469
	(0.058)	(0.069)		(0.078)	(0.081)	(0.294)
Skill Inten × Skill Abund	0.435**	0.467**		0.252**	0.251**	0.118*
	(0.028)	(0.031)		(0.034)	(0.038)	(0.046)
Freight Costs	-0.102**	-0.085**		-0.089**	-0.089**	-0.089**
	(0.018)	(0.010)		(0.010)	(0.010)	(0.010)
Tariffs	-0.015+	-0.023*		-0.018+	-0.018+	-0.015+
	(0.008)	(0.011)		(0.010)	(0.011)	(0.009)
Input Substit. × Rule			-0.037**	-0.009	-0.026+	-0.012
			(0.009)	(0.009)	(0.016)	(0.016)
Demand Elasticity × Rule			0.026**	0.027**	0.001	-0.002
			(0.008)	(0.008)	(0.012)	(0.016)
Nunn Specificity × Rule			0.189**	0.164**	0.255	0.224**
			(0.015)	(0.016)	(0.161)	(0.030)
Headq. Inten. × Rule			0.093**	0.050**	0.050**	0.047**
			(0.010)	(0.012)	(0.013)	(0.012)
Headq. Int. × Credit/GDP			0.074**	0.045**	0.044**	0.045**
			(0.007)	(0.009)	(0.012)	(0.012)
Sample Restrictions	$\Upsilon_O > 0$	W+NT+	W+NT+	W+NT+	W+NT+	W+NT+
Ctr/Year & Ind Fixed Eff	Yes	Yes	Yes	Yes	Yes	Yes
Interactions with GDP	No	No	No	No	Yes	No
Industry Effects × GDP	No	No	No	No	No	Yes
Observations	188,187	128,482	≃ 127,999	126,068	126,068	126,068
R-squared	0.601	0.619	≃ 0.621	0.624	0.624	0.641

Standard errors clustered at the country/ind. level. +, *, ** denote 10,5, 1% significance.

with the theory. More specifically, better rule of law appears to foster U.S. imports disproportionately in sectors with lower input substitutability, higher buyer elasticities of demand, higher input specificity, and higher headquarter intensity. Furthermore, higher levels of financial development also have a differentially higher effect on U.S. imports in sectors with higher headquarter intensity.

In column (4), I present results in which the five institutional interactions are included in the *same* regression, together with the Heckscher-Ohlin interactions and the trade cost measures. Analogously to the results obtained when doing the same in Table 5.7, the partial effect of each of the independent variables on U.S. imports of inputs is lower than when included in isolation. Nevertheless, all coefficients retain their theoretically predicted sign and are highly significant, with the exception of the input elasticity times rule of law interaction ($\rho_v \times \mu_j$), which remains negative but is now statistically indistinguishable from zero.

Finally, in columns (5) and (6) I perform the same robustness tests as in columns (4) and (5) of Table 5.7 by first including interactions of the main industry-level institutional variables with GDP per capita, and later by controlling for a whole vector of interactions of sectoral dummies with GDP per capita. The inclusion of these controls reduces the statistical significance of some of the coefficients, most notably that of the interaction of the elasticity of demand with rule of law ($\sigma_v \times \mu_j$), but the results still provide broad support for the empirical validity of some of the key predictions of our global sourcing model.

I have also experimented with specifications that include all the institutional interactions from the previous literature in Table 5.7 with the new ones motivated by our global sourcing model. Consistently with the results above, the freight cost measure as well as the interactions of Nunn specificity with rule of law and headquarter intensity with financial development appear to be very robust and continue to affect U.S. input imports volumes with the expected sign and at high levels of statistical significance. We also generally find a negative and significant effect of tariffs on U.S. imports of intermediate inputs and a positive and significant effect of the interaction of headquarter intensity with rule of law. Conversely, the effects of the interactions of input substitutability and the elasticity of demand with rule of law are much less robust, particularly when adding interactions of industry variables or industry fixed effects with GDP per capita. Also consistently with Table 5.7, the Nunn, Levchenko, Braun, and Cuñat-Melitz interactions continue to be robust predictors of U.S. global sourcing decisions, retaining throughout their expected sign as well as their economic and statistical significance. These results can easily be replicated with the dataset and programs downloadable at http://scholar.harvard.edu/antras/books.

Concluding Remarks

Overall, it would be hard to argue that the results presented in this chapter provide resounding evidence supporting the empirical validity of the global sourcing model (and its various variants) developed in Chapter 4. Admittedly, some of the key predictions of the framework, such as its cross-industry implications for the determinants of offshoring shares, have been hard to validate with U.S. import data. Nevertheless, I have argued that this is in part due to the fact that these cross-industry specifications might be prone to serious econometric biases. When adopting a cleaner approach exploiting both the cross-country as well as the cross-industry variation in the data, while controlling for industry and country-year fixed effects, we have obtained much more favorable results for the model. For instance, controlling for standard Heckscher-Ohlin effects, U.S. firms appear to rely less on offshoring when trade costs (and particularly freight costs) are high. Variation in contract enforcement across countries also appears to be an important determinant of the observed variation in the propensity of U.S. firms to offshore, with the effect often being differentially higher precisely in those sectors in which the model predicts that the effects should be disproportionately higher.

A critical challenge in the empirical analyses performed in this chapter is that the key industry characteristics (specificity, input substitutability, demand elasticities, headquarter intensity, and so on) that shape the differential effect of contract enforcement on the profitability of offshoring across sectors are particularly hard to measure in the data. I have devoted significant space and effort to discussing the hurdles that one encounters when mapping these sectoral characteristics with available data. Similar challenges emerged in isolating the intermediate input component of U.S. imports. Although I have attempted to surpass these hurdles, I have obviously done so in imperfect ways, and this might explain some of the less favorable results I obtained when attempting to validate certain predictions of the model. This is obviously a favorable interpretation of the few negative results obtained above, but future research with newer data sources and more ingenious empirical strategies will ultimately verify or falsify that the contractual determinants of offshoring highlighted in this book are indeed a central feature of the global sourcing decisions of firms.

PART III

Internalization

6

The Transaction-Cost Approach

In the last two chapters, we have studied how imperfect contract enforcement across countries shapes the global sourcing decisions of firms. The models in those chapters have illustrated how, other things equal, a particularly weak institutional environment will act as a deterrent for foreign firms seeking offshoring opportunities in a particular country. Furthermore, we have studied which type of product and industry characteristics tend to be associated with a disproportionately deleterious effect of weak contracting on the profitability of offshoring.

As argued in Chapter 1, choosing the locations from which a firm sources its inputs is just one of the many organizational decisions that firms need to make when designing their global production strategies. In this chapter and the next, I will turn attention to a second key organizational decision of firms, namely the extent of control that firms choose to exert over the production of the different parts and components in their value chain. In many circumstances, ownership of the input producer's physical assets is the key method to enhance such control. For this reason, this decision is often dubbed *internalization*, since equity ownership amounts to bringing the production of intermediate inputs inside firm boundaries. When such internalization occurs across borders, the investing entity becomes a multinational firm and any flow of physical goods between related parties constitutes intrafirm international trade.[1]

At the risk of oversimplifying the global organizational decisions of firms, it may be useful to represent these decisions in terms of choosing a cell in the following two-by-two matrix, in which the rows denote different location

---

[1] The internalization decision is key in John Dunning's (1981) celebrated *OLI* or "ecletic" theory of the multinational firm, where OLI is an acronym for Ownership, Location, and Internalization. Put succinctly, the emergence of the multinational firm is explained by an Ownership advantage stemming from firm-specific assets that allow firms to compete in unfamiliar environments, a Location advantage that makes it efficient to exploit the firm assets in production facilities in multiple countries, and an Internalization advantage that makes the within-firm exploitation of assets dominate exploitation at arm's length.

decisions (domestic or foreign sourcing), while the columns are associated with distinct internalization choices

	Internal Procurement	**External Procurement**
Domestic Sourcing	Domestic Integration	Domestic Outsourcing
Foreign Sourcing	Foreign Integration	Foreign Outsourcing

Note that when the location decision is associated with foreign sourcing, internalization will be associated with foreign direct investment and intrafirm international trade in physical goods, while in the case of foreign outsourcing, any exchange of goods will also be recorded in international trade statistics, but it will constitute non-related-party trade.

Why do firms find it optimal to carry out certain production stages within firm boundaries while conducting others at arm's length? Beginning with the seminal work of Coase (1937), the leading approach to answering this question posits that activities take place within or across firm boundaries depending on which of these organizational modes leads to the minimization of transaction costs. Furthermore, it is widely accepted that transaction costs stem, to a large degree, from contractual incompleteness. Indeed, firm boundaries would be indeterminate and irrelevant in a world in which transactions were governed by comprehensive contracts that specify (in an enforceable way) the course of action to be taken in *any* possible contingency that the contracting parties may encounter. In such a case, formal contracting would leave no room for residual rights of control to matter for economic decisions.

The main unifying theme of the theoretical literature on (multinational) firm boundaries is thus the departure from the classical assumption of complete or perfect contracting. Nevertheless, different theories of internalization emphasize different types of contractual frictions and they also adopt different approaches with regard to how the internalization of transactions affects these frictions. In this Part III of the book, I will restrict the analysis to what I consider to be the two leading approaches to the analysis of the internalization decision. On the one hand, the so-called *Transaction-Cost Theory* focuses on describing the type of contractual frictions that naturally emerge in arm's-length transactions when contracts are incomplete, but tends to be much less precise about the source of transaction costs in internalized transactions. On the other hand, the *Property-Rights Theory* assumes that the contractual sources of transaction costs are not too distinct in internal versus external transactions, and instead places at the center stage the study of how the allocation of ownership rights over physical assets shapes the size of transaction costs under different organizational modes.

The transaction-cost theory, which draws inspiration from Coase (1937) but is mostly associated with the work of Williamson (1971, 1975, 1985), has arguably been the leading paradigm in the analysis of the internalization decision in international environments. In line with the theory, it is typically perceived that vertical (or lateral) integration is an effective way for firms to deal with situations of contractual incompleteness in international transactions, in which it may be hard to provide incentives to subcontracted producers.

To give a particular example, consider Boeing's organizational decisions in recent years as it was struggling to complete the production phase of the new 787 Dreamliner. According to Boeing's website, the 787 "Development Team" encompasses fifty suppliers located in ten countries and the involvement of foreign suppliers is not anecdotal as it accounts for close to 70 percent of the aircraft's parts (Newhouse, 2007, p. 29).[2] The repeated delays experienced during the production phase, which ran more than three years behind schedule, have been ascribed in part to the fact that multiple suppliers did not stand by their contractual obligations.[3] Boeing responded to these delays by partially reorganizing their sourcing model and bringing some of the problematic upstream production stages within their firm boundaries. For example, during 2008 and 2009, Boeing successively acquired operations from Vought Aircraft Industries, a company that was producing the rear sections of the Dreamliner's fuselage but that had been identified as a problematic supplier. One of those acquisitions entailed forming a 50-50 joint venture with a subsidiary of Italy's Alenia Aeronautica, another key supplier for Boeing, from which it procures the horizontal stabilizer and the center fuselage for the Dreamliner, and with which it has also struggled in past years.

The experience of Boeing illustrates that firms often design the ownership structure along their value chain in a way that attempts to minimize frictions resulting from suppliers not honoring their contractual commitments. As argued by the property-rights theory, however, vertical integration is not always a panacea to deal with those situations; the problem of getting procurement incentives right does not simply disappear when firms source inputs internally. In fact, it is not uncommon for firms to fail to get their own divisions to produce what they want at low cost, thereby leading to externalization of certain production processes and foreign direct *divestment* in international environments. One example of such an externalization is

---

[2] The full list of suppliers, as of June 2014, can be found at http://www.boeing.com/commercial/787family/dev_team.html.

[3] See http://www.bloomberg.com/apps/news?pid=newsarchive&sid=aF6uWvMb9C08 for a more complete account.

provided by Sony Corporation, which in 2010 decided to sell a 90 percent stake in its LCD TV assembly plant in Nitra, Slovakia, to Taiwanese electronics parts maker Hon Hai Precision Industry (which operates under the trade name Foxconn). As admitted by Sony, the decision was motivated by a desire to cut fixed costs and turn around their loss-making TV operations, and had been preceded a year earlier by a similar divestment in its production plant in Tijuana, Mexico.[4]

In the next two chapters, I will review in greater detail the theoretical underpinnings of these two mainstream theories of the firm, and will then show how to apply them to the study of the global ownership decisions of multinational firms. In the process, I will derive a series of testable implications that distinguish these two approaches and that will guide the empirical analysis carried out in Chapter 8.

The Transaction-Cost Approach: A Non-Technical Overview

The late Ronald Coase was the father of transaction-cost economics, and his 1937 article in *Economica* marks the birth of this field of study in economics. His paper can be interpreted as a reaction to the neoclassical approach to the optimal size of firms, which was being developed at that time. To put things in historical perspective, Viner's 1932 celebrated paper on cost and supply curves had appeared only five years earlier. The neoclassical approach was technological in nature and treated the optimal scale of operation as being determined by a firm's profit-maximization problem given a cost function obtained by choosing inputs in a cost-minimizing fashion.

Coase (1937) instead argued that there are substantial transaction costs associated with running the economic system, and that firms emerge precisely when certain transactions can be undertaken with less transaction costs inside the firm than through the market mechanism. Or, in his own words: "The main reason why it is profitable to establish a firm would seem to be that there is a cost of using the price mechanism" (1937, p. 390). In his article, Coase mentions a few transaction-cost disadvantages of market transactions, including the costs of negotiating and concluding a separate contract for each exchange transaction and the costs of specifying all possible contingencies in a long-term contract. Coase also proposed certain factors that might limit the size of the firm, such as decreasing returns to the entrepreneur function or an increasing supply price of some factors, but his treatment of the costs of integration was closest in spirit to the one used by neoclassical approach to rationalize upward sloping marginal cost curves.

---

[4] For more details, see http://www.reuters.com/article/2010/03/31/sony-honhai-idUSTOE62U08020100331 and http://www.pcworld.com/article/171181/article.html.

Coase's view of the firm did not instantly become part of mainstream economics. It was criticized for its vagueness and was dubbed tautological. What kind of empirical evidence would be supportive of Coase's theory? How could the theory be refuted? Between 1940 and 1970, the literature focused instead on exploring technological theories of the firm.

Oliver Williamson brought transaction-cost considerations back into the spotlight by developing much more explicit theories of the inefficiencies of market transactions, thus making the transaction-cost approach operational. His theory, as laid out in his classic 1985 book *The Economic Institutions of Capitalism*, is based on three concepts: (1) bounded rationality, (2) opportunism, and (3) asset specificity.

Williamson appeals to *bounded rationality* to provide a foundation for the incompleteness of contracts. In particular, in a complex and unpredictable world, boundedly rational agents will be unable to plan ahead for all the contingencies that may arise. Furthermore, even when contingencies are foreseen, it may be hard for contracting parties to negotiate about these plans because of limited capability of describing these possible states. Finally, even when parties can plan and negotiate these contingencies, it may be hard for a third party to verify them and enforce the contract. As a result, formal contracts will tend to be incomplete and will tend to be renewed or renegotiated as the future unfolds.

By *opportunism*, Williamson means that economic actors are "self-interest seeking with guile" (1985, p. 47). The fact that agents are opportunistic is a necessary condition for the incompleteness of contracts to lead to inefficiencies. If agents could credibly pledge at the outset to execute the contract efficiently, then although the contract would have gaps, renegotiation would always occur in a joint profit maximizing manner.

Finally, Williamson points out that certain assets or investments are *relationship-specific*, in the sense that the value of these assets or investments is higher inside a particular relationship than outside of it. This is important because it implies that, at the renegotiation stage, parties cannot costlessly switch to alternative trading partners and are partially locked in a bilateral relationship. This is what Williamson calls the "*fundamental transformation*" from an ex-ante competitive situation to one of bilateral monopoly.

Williamson then shows how the combination of contract incompleteness, opportunism, and specificities gives rise to inefficiencies which can be interpreted as equilibrium transaction costs. In his own work, Williamson primarily emphasized ex-post inefficiencies related to haggling (i.e., parties spending resources in order to improve their bargaining position), which could lead to inefficient terminations or executions of contracts. Subsequent work, beginning with the important contribution of Klein, Crawford, and Alchian (1978), has largely focused on ex-ante or hold-up inefficiencies associated with the suboptimal provision of relationship-specific investments.

By now, the reader should have a sneaking suspicion that Williamson's notion of transaction-cost inefficiencies, particularly in their ex-ante form, appears to be closely related to the type of contractual inefficiencies described in Chapter 4 of this book. I will indeed confirm such a connection very shortly.

A key limitation of the transaction-cost approach, even in its most refined versions developed by Williamson, is that it does not have an awful lot to say about the nature of transaction costs associated with intrafirm transactions. In Williamson's view, contract incompleteness, opportunism, and relationship specificity are irrelevant within firm boundaries because decisions within firms are taken by fiat, so agents would not bother to spend time and resources haggling over profits. Instead, Williamson appealed to a broad notion of *governance costs* to justify the limits to firm size.

Despite the vagueness in its description of the costs of internalization, Williamson's careful description of the sources of transaction costs in market transactions provided an operational theory that could be mapped to particular observable economic variables, such as measures of contractual complexity or relationship specificity. It is thus not surprising that a rich empirical literature on the determinants of the internalization decision emerged in the 1980s, shortly after Williamson's seminal work. The key papers in this literature are surveyed in Lafontaine and Slade (2007). Some of these empirical contributions relate to internalization decisions by multinational firms in open-economy environments, so I will return to them in Chapter 8.

A Transaction-Cost Model of Multinational Firm Boundaries

As many readers will have recognized, there is a clear connection between the informal description of the transaction-cost approach to the theory of the firm above and the model of global sourcing with contractual frictions developed in Chapter 4. In particular, in that chapter I illustrated how the combination of imperfect contracting, bargaining by self-interested parties, and the existence of relationship-specific investments led to production inefficiencies that would, other things equal, reduce the profitability of global sourcing. An important distinctive feature of the model in Chapter 4 is that it emphasized weak contract enforcement – rather than bounded rationality – as the cause for the lack of complete contracting. As we shall explore in Chapter 8, this will be of some relevance when choosing the variables used to proxy for the key objects in the model. A second, perhaps less crucial distinguishing aspect of the models in Chapter 4 is that they focused attention on ex-ante, hold-up inefficiencies (as in Klein et al. 1978), rather than on ex-post inefficiencies which featured prominently in Williamson's work.

There is, however, one fundamental dimension in which in Chapters 4 and 5 I departed from the transaction-cost approach. More specifically, both when discussing the models and when taking them to the data, I made no distinction between within-firm and across-firm sourcing decisions. The model introduced two agents—a final-good producer F and a manufacturing plant manager M, both with a zero reservation utility, but I was not explicit about whether or not the manufacturing plant was vertically integrated. In other words, I did not specify whether M was an employee of F or an independent subcontractor. In the empirical analysis, I studied the implications of the model for the share of imported inputs coming from different markets, regardless of whether those imports were transacted within or across firm boundaries.

The transaction-cost theory argues, however, that the production inefficiencies identified in Chapter 4 should apply only to market transactions, and not to those conducted within firm boundaries. In choosing whether or not to own upstream producers, firms trade off these contractual inefficiencies against the higher *governance costs* associated with intrafirm procurement.

Let us now turn to a more formal exposition of a transaction-cost model of multinational firm boundaries. In line with the two-by-two matrix introduced at the beginning of this chapter, I will first consider a simple two-country model along the lines of the benchmark global-sourcing model in Chapter 4. A continuum of heterogeneous final-good producing firms based in a rich North combine locally produced headquarter services with manufacturing components that can be produced domestically or in a foreign location, which is referred to as South. Offshoring lowers the marginal cost of production of Northern firms but entails disproportionately high fixed costs, and thus some final-good producers optimally opt out of procuring inputs abroad. I continue to index the location choice by a subscript $\ell = D$ or $\ell = O$, for Domestic sourcing and Offshoring, respectively. Final-good production and headquarter services provision are overviewed by agent F in the North, while manufacturing production is controlled by agent M in the location where manufacturing takes place.

The main novelty in the framework is that I will now incorporate a decision as to whether M is an employee of F or the manager of an unaffiliated subcontractor. I will assume that the models developed in Chapter 4 capture accurately the type of contractual difficulties encountered in market transactions, and as a result the profit functions associated with domestic outsourcing and foreign outsourcing correspond to those derived in that chapter (more on this below). Conversely, when F internalizes its provision of manufacturing components, it can make all relevant decisions by fiat and thus can choose all investment levels in a profit-maximizing manner regardless of the contracting environment. I capture the notion of governance costs by assuming that the marginal cost of input provision is multiplied by a factor $\lambda > 1$ when M is

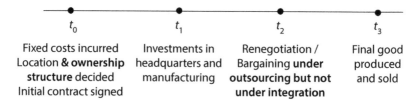

Figure 6.1 Timing of Events

integrated by F. Furthermore, I shall assume that the fixed costs of production are also higher under an integrated structure than under a non-integrated one.

Figure 6.1 depicts the timing of events in the model. This is analogous to Figure 4.1 in Chapter 4, but it includes (in bold) the new actions or assumptions associated with the modeling of the internalization decision. Notice that F is still allowed to demand an ex-ante transfer from potential M agents for their participation in production and that the key contractual difference between integration and outsourcing is that renegotiation and bargaining only occur under the latter, while under the former, F's authority dictates M's abidance by whatever was stipulated in the initial contract.

I will index the internationalization decision by a second subscript $k = V$ or $k = O$, to refer to **V**ertical integration and **O**utsourcing, respectively. In sum, agent F will choose from one of four potential organizational modes, $(\ell, k) \in \{DO, DV, OO, OV\}$, associated with domestic outsourcing, domestic vertical integration, offshore outsourcing, and offshore vertical integration (or vertical FDI). Assuming that the fixed costs of offshoring are higher than those associated with domestic sourcing regardless of the ownership structure, we have that the ranking of fixed costs satisfies

$$f_{OV} > f_{OO} > f_{DV} > f_{DO}. \tag{6.1}$$

This is the same ranking of fixed costs adopted by Antràs and Helpman (2004, 2008), but I will discuss below the robustness of the theoretical predictions to alternative rankings of fixed costs.

Let us now discuss the equilibrium profitability of the different organizational forms available to the Northern final-good producer. In the case of vertical integration, F's authority and the existence of unrestricted lump-sum transfers ensures that these profit flows will be given by

$$\pi_{DV}(\varphi) = (w_N)^{1-\sigma} B \varphi^{\sigma-1} \lambda^{1-\sigma} - w_N f_{DV} \tag{6.2}$$

under domestic integration, and by

$$\pi_{OV}(\varphi) = \left((w_N)^{\eta}(\tau w_S)^{1-\eta}\right)^{1-\sigma} B \lambda^{1-\sigma} \varphi^{\sigma-1} - w_N f_{OV} \tag{6.3}$$

under offshore integration, where, you recall, the market demand term B is defined as

$$B = \frac{1}{\sigma} \left(\frac{\sigma}{(\sigma - 1) P} \right)^{1-\sigma} \beta (w_N L_N + w_S L_S).$$

Importantly, these profit flows apply to all the variants of the global sourcing model studied in Chapter 4 which considered the inclusion of generalized bargaining power, constraints on ex-ante transfers, variable degrees of relationship specificity, partial contractibility, multiple suppliers, and a sequential production process.[5]

The profitability of domestic outsourcing and offshore outsourcing will instead vary with changes in the contracting and economic environments, but as in Chapter 4 we can write these profit levels succinctly as

$$\pi_{DO}(\varphi) = (w_N)^{1-\sigma} B\Gamma_{DO}\varphi^{\sigma-1} - w_N f_{DO} \tag{6.4}$$

and

$$\pi_{OO}(\varphi) = \left((w_N)^{\eta} (\tau w_S)^{1-\eta} \right)^{1-\sigma} B\Gamma_{OO}\varphi^{\sigma-1} - w_N f_{OO}, \tag{6.5}$$

where $\Gamma_{DO} \leq 1$ and $\Gamma_{OO} \leq 1$ denote the contractual efficiency associated with domestic and offshore outsourcing, respectively. The determination of these terms was developed in detail in Chapter 4, so I will not repeat it here. Below, however, I will review some of the key insights that were obtained in Chapter 4 when studying the dependence of Γ_{DO} and Γ_{OO} on the deep parameters of the model.

Equilibrium Sorting

With the profit functions (6.2) through (6.5) in hand, we can now study the optimal organization of production, as summarized by the choice of location $\ell \in \{D, O\}$ and of ownership $k \in \{V, O\}$. As a first step, I will describe how, depending on their core productivity parameter φ, firms self-select into different organizational modes. In order to build intuition and focus on the key objects that will be taken to the data in Chapter 8, I will begin by considering a benchmark case in which contracting is complete when sourcing domestically, which implies that $\Gamma_{DO} = 1$ in equation (6.4). An immediate implication of this assumption is that $\pi_{DO}(\varphi) > \pi_{VO}(\varphi)$ for all φ,

---

[5] In Chapter 4, I rationalized the existence of limitations on ex-ante transfers to potential misbehavior on the part of suppliers. Under the assumptions of the transaction-cost theory, such misbehavior can be avoided through the use of authority, and thus it is natural to focus on the case in which they have no impact on the profitability of sourcing.

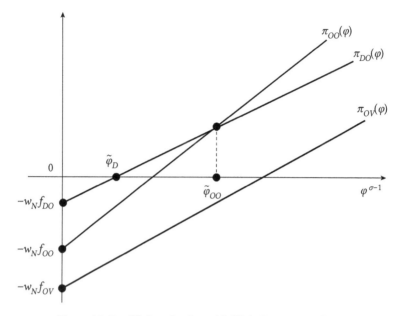

Figure 6.2 Equilibrium Sorting with High Governance Costs

and thus domestic integration is a dominated strategy in this scenario and can be safely ignored for the time being. We will later introduce versions of the model with a well-defined choice between domestic integration and outsourcing. This simplifying assumption is, however, not too unrealistic when focusing on the U.S. case, for which Atalay, Hortacsu, and Syverson (2013) have shown that within-firm shipments of physical goods account for a very small share of overall shipments of U.S. establishments.

The remaining three profit functions are all linearly increasing in $\varphi^{\sigma-1}$ with a slope that is inversely related to governance costs λ in the foreign integration case and positively related to the index of contractual efficiency Γ_{OO} in the offshore outsourcing case. Figure 6.2 depicts these profit functions whenever governance costs are disproportionately high, so that foreign direct investment is a strictly dominated strategy since it entails high fixed and variable costs. In the figure, it is also implicitly assumed that wage differences across countries are high relative to the contractual inefficiencies of offshore outsourcing, so that the most productive firms in an industry find the latter strategy to be the profit-maximizing one. The sorting pattern is thus analogous to that discussed in Chapter 4, but with offshoring taking the specific form of subcontracting.

In Figure 6.3, I depict instead the case in which, for reasons that I will review shortly, the contractual efficiency of foreign outsourcing is very low,

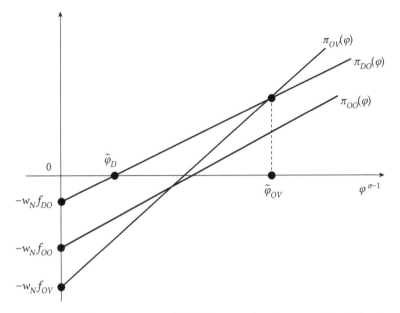

Figure 6.3 Equilibrium Sorting with High Outsourcing Contractual Inefficiencies

and no firm finds it optimal to use this strategy when sourcing inputs abroad. As shown in the figure, this does not rule out the possibility that some relatively productive firms will still find it optimal to offshore in the South, but those transactions will unavoidably happen within firm boundaries. Naturally, for this to be the case, it is necessary for governance costs λ to be sufficiently low relative to wage differences across countries.[6]

Finally, in Figure 6.4, I illustrate the most interesting case in which wage differences are large relative to both arm's-length transaction costs and governance costs. In such a case, one can easily construct equilibria of the type depicted in the figure, with a positive measure of active firms adopting each of the three candidate organizational forms. The least productive active firms make use of domestic outsourcing, the most productive firms engage in vertical foreign direct investment (offshore integration), while firms with intermediate levels of productivity opt for foreign outsourcing.

It may seem that the model generates a plethora of possible types of equilibria, with small changes in the parameters leading to large changes in the nature of the equilibrium. Fortunately, however, this is not the case. First, it is important to emphasize a key robust prediction emerging from

[6] To avoid describing a taxonomy of cases, I ignore situations in which wage differences are low relative to both governance costs and contractual inefficiencies associated with market transactions. In those cases, all active firms would simply resort to domestic sourcing.

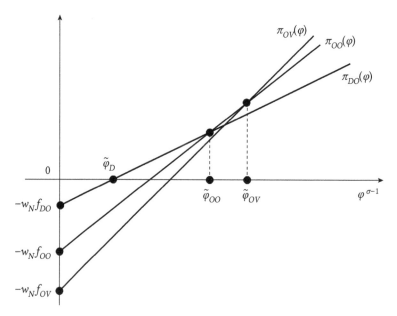

Figure 6.4 Equilibrium Sorting with Low Contractual Inefficiencies and Governance Costs

the sorting patterns depicted in Figures 6.2, 6.3, and 6.4; namely, when foreign outsourcing and foreign integration coexist within an industry (so the share of intrafirm trade is strictly between 0 and 1), it is necessarily the case that firms integrating foreign suppliers are more productive than those choosing subcontracting. Thus, the model predicts a similar type of performance premia for multinationals (relative to firms resorting to foreign outsourcing) as the one observed in the data and documented in Chapter 2 for exporters (relative to non-exporters) and for offshoring firms (relative to firms sourcing domestically).

A second reason not to be dismayed by the different cases illustrated in Figures 6.2, 6.3, and 6.4 is that although small changes in parameters might lead to the disappearance of a certain type of organizational form from the industry equilibrium, it is necessarily the case that this particular organizational form accounted for a very small fraction of the sourcing activity in the industry. Put differently, and as I am about to show formally, the relative prevalence of the different organizational forms within an industry varies smoothly with the parameters of the model.

Relative Prevalence and Intrafirm Trade Shares

We are now ready to aggregate the decisions of the various firms in a sector and study the determinants of the relative importance of different organizational forms—domestic sourcing, foreign outsourcing, foreign integration—in a particular industry. As in Chapters 2, 4, and 5, I measure the relative prevalence of an organizational form by the relative magnitude of intermediate input purchases under that organizational form. In principle, one could aggregate arm's-length and intrafirm foreign input purchases and use the framework above to revisit the determinants of the share of *imported* manufacturing inputs over total manufacturing input purchases in a particular industry. I will not do so here because the results of such an exercise deliver results essentially identical to those derived in Chapter 4 and tested in Chapter 5. Instead, I will focus on describing the determinants of the relative prevalence of intrafirm versus arm's-length foreign sourcing decisions, as measured by the share of intrafirm intermediate input imports over total imported inputs. As explained in Chapter 1 and described in more detail in Chapter 8, this is an object we can attempt to measure with available data, so it seems natural to focus on it.

In order to trace the implications of our transaction-cost model for input purchases, one needs again to take a stance on how these inputs are priced in market transactions. As in Chapter 4, I follow the agnostic approach of assuming that foreign inputs are priced such that these input expenditures constitute the same multiple $(1 - \eta)(\sigma - 1)$ of operating profits as in the case of foreign intrafirm input purchases. Under this assumption, the share Sh_{i-f} of intrafirm imported inputs over the total imported input purchases is given by

$$Sh_{i-f} = \frac{\lambda^{1-\sigma} \int_{\tilde{\varphi}_{OV}}^{\infty} \varphi^{\sigma-1} dG(\varphi)}{\Gamma_{OO} \int_{\tilde{\varphi}_{OO}}^{\tilde{\varphi}_{OV}} \varphi^{\sigma-1} dG(\varphi) + \lambda^{1-\sigma} \int_{\tilde{\varphi}_{OV}}^{\infty} \varphi^{\sigma-1} dG(\varphi)}, \qquad (6.6)$$

where $\tilde{\varphi}_{OO}$ is such that

$$\frac{(w_N)^{\sigma} (f_{OO} - f_{DO})}{B \left[\left(\frac{w_N}{\tau w_S} \right)^{(1-\eta)(\sigma-1)} \Gamma_{OO} - 1 \right]} = (\tilde{\varphi}_{OO})^{\sigma-1}, \qquad (6.7)$$

and $\tilde{\varphi}_{OV}$ is such that

$$\frac{(w_N)^{\sigma} (f_{OV} - f_{OO})}{\left(\frac{w_N}{\tau w_S} \right)^{(1-\eta)(\sigma-1)} B \left[\lambda^{1-\sigma} - \Gamma_{OO} \right]} = (\tilde{\varphi}_{OV})^{\sigma-1}. \qquad (6.8)$$

For some firms to potentially find foreign outsourcing more profitable than domestic sourcing, we need to assume that $\Gamma_{OO} > (w_N/\tau w_S)^{-(1-\eta)(\sigma-1)}$, while for some firms to possibly prefer foreign insourcing to foreign outsourcing, it is also necessary that $\lambda^{1-\sigma} > \Gamma_{OO}$. Note that these two conditions guarantee that both $\tilde{\varphi}_{OO}$ and $\tilde{\varphi}_{OV}$ are positive, but they are *not* sufficient to guarantee that $\tilde{\varphi}_{OV} > \tilde{\varphi}_{OO}$ or that the share of intrafirm trade in (6.6) falls strictly between 0 and 1 (more on this below). For the time being we shall sidestep this issue and assume that we are in an industry equilibrium in which all organizational forms are chosen by a positive measure of firms, as depicted in Figure 6.4.

Inspection of equations (6.6), (6.7), and (6.8) reveals that, holding constant the market demand level B, a decrease in governance costs (lower λ) decreases the threshold productivity level $\tilde{\varphi}_{OV}$, while leaving $\tilde{\varphi}_{OO}$ unchanged. As a result, it appears that the share of intrafirm trade tends to be higher in lower governance cost industries. On the other hand, a higher foreign outsourcing contractual efficiency Γ_{OO} increases $\tilde{\varphi}_{OV}$ and reduces $\tilde{\varphi}_{OO}$, thereby tending to reduce Sh_{i-f}. These predictions should be treated with caution, however, because these parameter changes will affect the residual demand level B as well.

In order to obtain sharper comparative statics, we next turn to the case in which the distribution of core productivity φ is Pareto with shape parameter $\kappa > \sigma - 1$, as in previous chapters. Such a parameterization is also necessary to tease out the effects of lower trade costs, lower Southern wages, or lower headquarter intensity η, which are all associated with lower levels of both $\tilde{\varphi}_{OO}$ and $\tilde{\varphi}_{OV}$. Assuming a Pareto distribution of productivity, equations (6.6), (6.7), and (6.8) can be reduced to

$$Sh_{i-f} = \frac{\lambda^{1-\sigma}}{\Gamma_{OO}\left[\left(\frac{\tilde{\varphi}_{OV}}{\tilde{\varphi}_{OO}}\right)^{\kappa-\sigma-1} - 1\right] + \lambda^{1-\sigma}} \tag{6.9}$$

where

$$\frac{\tilde{\varphi}_{OV}}{\tilde{\varphi}_{OO}} = \left[\frac{f_{OV} - f_{OO}}{f_{OO} - f_{DO}} \times \frac{\Gamma_{OO} - (w_N/\tau w_S)^{-(1-\eta)(\sigma-1)}}{\lambda^{1-\sigma} - \Gamma_{OO}}\right]^{1/(\sigma-1)}. \tag{6.10}$$

Note that the share of intrafirm imported inputs is now only a function of parameters and the ratio of thresholds $\tilde{\varphi}_{OV}/\tilde{\varphi}_{OO}$, which itself is independent of the residual demand level B.

These features greatly simplify the characterization of Sh_{i-f}. First, it is now clear that lower governance costs λ or lower foreign outsourcing contractual efficiency Γ_{OO} are associated with a higher share of intrafirm imports, which are intuitive results. It is also apparent and obvious that lower fixed costs of foreign integration f_{OV} or higher fixed costs of offshore outsourcing f_{OO} will also tend to increase the share of intrafirm trade. Less trivially, equations (6.9) and (6.10) also reveal that the share of intrafirm imported inputs is decreasing in the term $(w_N/\tau w_S)^{(1-\eta)(\sigma-1)}$ and is thus increasing in headquarter intensity η, trade costs, and Southern labor costs. The extensive margin of offshoring is key for understanding these effects. Intuitively, decreases in these parameters lead firms that were sourcing domestically to select into offshoring, but as observed in Figure 6.4, these new foreign input purchases necessarily occur at arm's length, hence decreasing the relative prevalence of intrafirm imports in overall imports. For the same reason, the share Sh_{i-f} is also decreasing in the fixed costs of domestic sourcing f_{DO}. Finally, and in analogy to our results in Chapters 2 and 4, the fact that firms engaged in foreign integration are more productive than those engaged in offshore outsourcing translates into a positive effect of productivity dispersion (a lower κ) on the share of intrafirm trade.

I have focused so far on equilibria of the type depicted in Figure 6.4 in which all organizational forms are chosen by a positive measure of firms. It should be clear, however, that if λ becomes larger and larger, not only will the share of intrafirm trade decline, but if eventually $\lambda^{1-\sigma}$ becomes lower than Γ_{OO}, then no firm will find it optimal to engage in foreign integration and the share of intrafirm trade will be 0 regardless of the particular value of λ. Similarly, if Γ_{OO} becomes lower and lower, the share of intrafirm trade rises monotonically until Γ_{OO} exceeds a threshold level $\tilde{\Gamma}_{OO}$ at which $Sh_{i-f} = 1$ regardless of the particular value of $\Gamma_{OO} > \tilde{\Gamma}_{OO}$.[7]

Determinants of Foreign Outsourcing Efficiency

The result that the relative prevalence of intrafirm imported input purchases is increasing in the transaction costs associated with offshore outsourcing is intuitive but of little use in guiding an empirical analysis of the determinants of the relative prevalence of foreign integration in the data. Fortunately, in Chapter 4 we discussed at length the determination of arm's-length contractual efficiency Γ_{OO} (referred to as Γ_O in that chapter) in several types of environments featuring generalized bargaining power, constraints on ex-ante transfers, variable degrees of relationship specificity, partial contractibility, multiple supplier, and a sequential production process. As summarized in Table 5.5, for instance, remember that Γ_{OO} is decreasing in the elasticity of demand σ, the level of financial constraints $(1 - \phi)$, and the degree of input relationship specificity ϵ, while it is increasing in the level of Southern contractibility μ_S and input substitutability ρ. The effect of headquarter intensity η on the level of transaction costs is instead generally ambiguous.

When combining these comparative statics with those discussed above regarding the effect of Γ_{OO} and other parameters on Sh_{i-f} in equation (6.9), we can conclude that the share of intrafirm imports is shaped by the various

---

[7] The threshold value is given by $\tilde{\Gamma}_{OO} = \varpi\lambda^{1-\sigma} + (1 - \varpi)(w_N/\tau w_S)^{-(1-\eta)(\sigma-1)}$ where $\varpi = (f_{OO} - f_{DO}) / (f_{OV} - f_{DO})$.

"deep" parameters of our global sourcing models in the following manner:

$$Sh_{i-f} = Sh_{i-f}\left(\underset{-}{\lambda}, \underset{-}{w_N/w_S}, \underset{+}{\tau}, \underset{-}{\kappa}, \underset{-}{\phi}, \underset{-}{\mu_S}, \underset{+}{\epsilon}, \underset{-}{\rho}, \underset{?}{\sigma}, \underset{?}{\eta}\right). \qquad (6.11)$$

I will defer until Chapter 8 a discussion of the implementation of an empirical test of these predictions, but a general insight obtained in transaction-cost models of global sourcing is that the same type of parameters that in Chapter 4 were associated with *high* offshoring shares (e.g., a high w_N/w_S, ϕ, μ_S, or ρ, and a low τ or ϵ) will now tend to be associated with *low* intrafirm trade shares.[8] Similarly, as I will further elaborate in Chapter 8, the same type of interactions of industry and country characteristics that we demonstrated in Chapters 4 and 5 to affect positively the efficiency of offshore outsourcing, are now expected to exert a negative effect on intrafirm trade shares.

Downstreamness and Integration

As shown throughout this book, in the various versions of the global sourcing model, it is relatively easy to transition from the individual firm-level organizational decisions to predictions for the share of intrafirm imported inputs at the sectoral level. Unfortunately, the variant of the model with sequential production is a bit more difficult to handle because it yields predictions for the differential incentives to integrate different production stages by firms in the sector under study. As shown by Antràs and Chor (2013), a natural way to deal with this complication is to aggregate the decisions of all firms in all sectors related to the optimal sourcing of the individual stages of production. To give a specific example, the idea is to aggregate the decisions of all firms buying a specific input, say rubber, and then study the extent to which those purchases are internalized.

In the presence of fixed costs of outsourcing and integration at the input level, Antràs and Chor (2013) then show that the model can be aggregated to deliver implications for the relative prevalence of integration of a particular input as a function of the position (i.e., downstreamness) of that input in the value chain. Furthermore, under the plausible assumption that the input-specific costs of integration are higher than those under outsourcing, the model delivers the implication that more productive firms will tend to integrate a larger share of the inputs they use in production, and that the share

---

[8] The overall effect of σ is nevertheless ambiguous because the negative effect of σ on Γ_{OO} is counterbalanced by its negative effect on $\lambda^{1-\sigma}$, as well as by the direct effects working via the terms in σ in (6.9) and (6.10).

of firms integrating a particular stage is weakly increasing in the dispersion of productivity across the buyers of that input.

How does the downstreamness of an input affect the incentives of firms to integrate that input in the transaction-cost model? In order to answer this question, one can refer back to Chapter 4, where we discussed the choice between domestic sourcing and offshoring whenever the main contractual difference between these two modes was in their associated level of contractibility. There we argued that (contractually insecure) foreign sourcing is particularly appealing in downstream stages in the sequential complements case, but particularly unappealing in those same downstream stages in the sequential substitutes case. In a similar vein, in the Theoretical Appendix (section A.3), I develop a sequential model of production with a transaction-cost determination of firm boundaries. More specifically, under outsourcing, production and contracting decisions are as described in Chapter 4. Instead, under integration, governance costs inflate marginal costs by a factor $\lambda > 1$, but supplier investment levels can be set to maximize the full incremental contribution $\Delta R(v)$ in (4.29) rather than $(1 - \beta_O)\,\Delta R(v)$, and the final-good producer captures all surplus from the relationship.

As shown in the Theoretical Appendix, this sequential model delivers the prediction that downstreamness should have a negative effect on foreign integration relative to offshore outsourcing whenever inputs are sequential complements, while it should have a positive effect on foreign integration when inputs are sequential substitutes. Intuitively, in the sequential complements case, it is particularly important to eliminate (via integration) the contractual inefficiencies of upstream investments because of the positive trickle-down effect of high investments in those early stages. Conversely, in the sequential substitutes case, high values of upstream stages are now relatively detrimental, so internalization is least advantageous in those early stages.

Contractual Frictions in Domestic Sourcing

In our analysis we have so far simplified matters by assuming complete contracting in domestic input purchases, which made domestic integration a dominated strategy for firms. It should be clear, however, that when contracts are also incomplete in domestic transactions (so $\Gamma_{DO} < 1$), and both governance costs and wage differences are small, it may be the case that a subset of firms finds domestic integration optimal. Given our assumption on the ranking of fixed costs in equation (6.1), any equilibrium in which all four possible organization forms (domestic outsourcing, domestic integration, offshore outsourcing, and offshore integration) are chosen by a positive measure of firms must satisfy the sorting depicted in Figure 6.5. This sorting

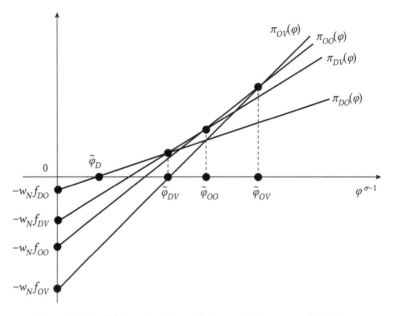

Figure 6.5 Equilibrium Sorting with Domestic Contractual Frictions

pattern is analogous to that in Figure 6.4 but notice that domestic integration emerges as the most appealing option for a set of firms with productivity levels above those of firms choosing domestic outsourcing, but below those of firms choosing offshore outsourcing.

Following the approach in Antràs and Helpman (2004, 2008), one could use this variant of the model to study the determinants of the share of intrafirm input purchases in both domestic as well as offshore purchases. I will, however, continue to focus on the implications of the framework for the share of *offshore* input purchases that are transacted within firm boundaries. Assuming a Pareto distribution of productivity, this share continues to be given by equation (6.9), but the ratio $\tilde{\varphi}_{OV}/\tilde{\varphi}_{OO}$ is now slightly modified to

$$\frac{\tilde{\varphi}_{OV}}{\tilde{\varphi}_{OO}} = \left[\frac{f_{OV} - f_{OO}}{f_{OO} - f_{DV}} \times \frac{\Gamma_{OO} - \lambda^{1-\sigma} (w_N/\tau w_S)^{-(1-\eta)(\sigma-1)}}{\lambda^{1-\sigma} - \Gamma_{OO}} \right]^{1/(\sigma-1)}.$$

The only two differences relative to equation (6.10) are that f_{DV} replaces f_{DO} and there is an additional term $\lambda^{1-\sigma}$ in the numerator of the second term. These modifications have little bearing on the comparative statics discussed above and, in particular, those related to the effect of the "deep" parameters in (6.11) remain unaltered.

When governance costs λ or the fixed costs of domestic integration are sufficiently large, it may be the case that no firm in the industry finds it optimal to vertically integrate domestic suppliers of inputs, and the equilibrium sorting pattern in the industry will be as in Figure 6.4 above. Notice, however, that domestic outsourcing now entails positive transaction costs captured by a contractual efficiency level $\Gamma_{OD} < 1$. In such a case, the ratio of thresholds $\tilde{\varphi}_{OV}/\tilde{\varphi}_{OO}$ in (6.10) now includes an additional term Γ_{OD} in the numerator of the second term:

$$\frac{\tilde{\varphi}_{OV}}{\tilde{\varphi}_{OO}} = \left[\frac{f_{OV} - f_{OO}}{f_{OO} - f_{DO}} \times \frac{\Gamma_{OO} - \Gamma_{OD}(w_N/\tau w_S)^{-(1-\eta)(\sigma-1)}}{\lambda^{1-\sigma} - \Gamma_{OO}}\right]^{1/(\sigma-1)}. \tag{6.12}$$

As shown in Chapter 5, however, and summarized in particular in Table 5.5, the deep parameters of the model affect the term Γ_{OO} and the ratio Γ_{OO}/Γ_{OD} in the same exact fashion, and thus the comparative statics emerging from this equilibrium will again coincide with the predicted signs summarized in (6.11).

Alternative Ranking of Fixed Costs

Up to this point, we have computed intrafirm trade shares under the assumption that the ranking of fixed costs is given by the inequalities in (6.1). Indeed, I believe it is natural to assume that (i) fixing the ownership structure, offshoring is associated with higher fixed costs than domestic sourcing; and (ii) fixing the location of input production, vertical integration is associated with higher fixed costs than outsourcing. It is less clear, however, that the fixed costs of offshore outsourcing are necessarily higher than those of domestic integration. One may wonder how our results would change if instead one assumed that the ranking of fixed costs was as follows:

$$f_{OV} > f_{DV} > f_{OO} > f_{DO}.$$

Notice that in such a case, the only type of equilibria in which all organizational modes are chosen by some firms in the industry is of the type depicted in Figure 6.6. As is clear from the graph, the most productive firms continue to engage in foreign integration and intrafirm trade, while the least productive active firms make use of domestic outsourcing. The main novel feature of this equilibrium is that firms engaging in domestic integration now feature higher productivity levels than those outsourcing abroad. How important is this distinction for the comparative statics discussed above?

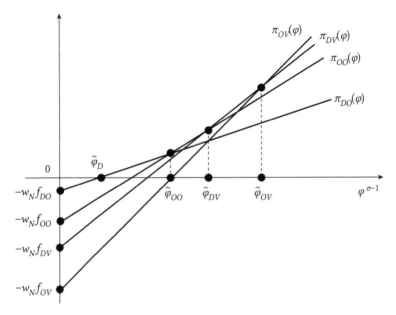

Figure 6.6 Equilibrium Sorting with an Alternative Ranking of Fixed Costs

In this new type of equilibrium, the share Sh_{i-f} of intrafirm imported inputs over the total imported input purchases is now given by

$$Sh_{i-f} = \frac{\lambda^{1-\sigma} \int_{\tilde{\varphi}_{OV}}^{\infty} \varphi^{\sigma-1} dG(\varphi)}{\Gamma_{OO} \int_{\tilde{\varphi}_{OO}}^{\tilde{\varphi}_{DV}} \varphi^{\sigma-1} dG(\varphi) + \lambda^{1-\sigma} \int_{\tilde{\varphi}_{OV}}^{\infty} \varphi^{\sigma-1} dG(\varphi)},$$

where you may notice that, relative to the formula for the share in (6.6), the upper limit of the first integral of the denominator is now $\tilde{\varphi}_{DV}$ rather than $\tilde{\varphi}_{OV}$. The definitions of the thresholds $\tilde{\varphi}_{OO}$ and $\tilde{\varphi}_{OV}$ are also different from those under the previous sorting in Figure 6.5. Despite these differences, in the Theoretical Appendix I show that, when firm productivity φ is drawn from a Pareto distribution, this variant of the model continues to deliver the *exact* same comparative statics as those summarized in (6.11). Conversely, the results in the property-rights model developed in the next chapter will prove to be a bit more sensitive to the assumed ranking of fixed costs across organizational forms, so with that in mind, in Chapter 8 I will study which ranking is most consistent with available empirical evidence.

An Overview of Other Applications of the Transaction-Cost Approach

The transaction-cost model of the internalization decision of multinational firms I have developed above does not originate in any specific paper in the literature. Nevertheless, it borrows heavily from previous work in this area and thus it is pertinent to briefly outline other contributions to the transaction-cost literature in international trade. My goal is not to offer an encyclopedic overview of the literature but rather to highlight some key aspects of the international organization of production that have been studied in the literature but from which I have abstracted in my discussion above.

An early application of the transaction-cost approach to international economics is offered by Ethier (1986). In his seminal paper, Ethier argues that the main difference between transacting within the boundaries of multinational firms and transacting at arm's length is that, in the latter case, headquarters cannot offer quality-contingent contracts to downstream producers or distributors (rather than the upstream suppliers in the models developed above). As a result, headquarters cannot always devise a contract that ensures ex-post efficiency and extracts all surplus from their contracting partners. In those situations, the headquarters may be better off integrating the downstream producer. Interestingly, Ethier (1986) finds that integration is more attractive when differences in production costs across countries are small, which resonates with our result above that the share of intrafirm trade is lower the farther is $w_N/\tau w_S$ from one.[9]

The work of Grossman and Helpman (2002) is much more closely related to the transaction-cost model developed above. In fact, their framework is an important source of inspiration for the benchmark global sourcing model studied in this book. Grossman and Helpman (2002) offer an alternative general-equilibrium framework that also emphasizes a tradeoff between hold-up inefficiencies and governance costs. In their framework, suppliers undertake relationship-specific investments that enhance the value of a good sold by a final-good producer. Their framework is simpler as they focused on a closed-economy model with no producer heterogeneity and with no headquarter investments (or $\eta = 0$ in the model above). The Grossman and Helpman (2002) setup was later extended by the authors to open-economy environments with cross-country variation in the degree of contractibility of inputs in Grossman and Helpman (2003, 2005).

It is important to emphasize that the Grossman and Helpman framework is richer than the one developed in this book as it includes search frictions

---

[9] In subsequent work, Ethier and Markusen (1996) further explored the role of contractual frictions, trade costs and scale economies in shaping the horizontal integration decisions of multinational firms.

and an endogenous choice of the customization of inputs. More specifically, in our transaction-cost model, we have assumed that when a firm chooses outsourcing instead of integration, it can simply post a contract and pick an operator M from the set of firms applying to fulfill the order. Grossman and Helpman (2002) instead assume that the matching between stand-alone F agents and M operators is random and depends on the relative mass of each type of agents looking for matches. Furthermore, once a match is formed, agents are not allowed to exchange transfers prior to production. Other things equal, it is clear that these features will tend to reduce the attractiveness of outsourcing vis-à-vis integration, even holding constant supplier investments. Intuitively, search frictions and the lack of transfers inhibit the ability of final-good producers to fully capture the rents generated in production relative to a situation in which they can make take-it-or-leave-it offers to a perfectly elastic supply of M operators. Search frictions can generate much more subtle and interesting results when allowing the matching function governing the search process to feature increasing returns to scale. In such a case, Grossman and Helpman (2002) show that there may exist multiple equilibria with different organizational forms (or industry systems) applying in ex-ante identical countries or industries. Furthermore, the likelihood of an equilibrium with outsourcing is enhanced by an expansion in the market size, which increases the efficiency of matching in the presence of increasing returns to scale in the matching function.

Another distinguishing feature of the Grossman and Helpman (2002, 2003, 2005) papers is that they incorporate an organizational decision related to the degree to which suppliers customize their intermediate products to their intended buyers. This is related to the parameter ϵ in our global sourcing model, but Grossman and Helpman study the endogenous determination of such level of specificity by trading off the productivity gains associated with a higher level of customization with the increased contractual frictions associated with these. In that respect, their framework shares features with those in Qiu and Spencer (2002) and Chen and Feenstra (2008) (see also Spencer, 2005).

The papers by Grossman and Helpman were actually preceded by a noteworthy paper by McLaren (2000), who also developed a framework that allowed for interdependencies in the organizational decisions of firms within an industry. Rather than introducing search/congestion externalities of the type in the Grossman and Helpman frameworks, McLaren (2000) focused on the implications of market thickness for the ex-post division of surplus between F and M agents. In his framework, the thicker is the market for inputs, the larger is the ex-post payoff obtained by M producers since they are in a better position to find an alternative buyer for their customized inputs. Thicker downstream markets thereby alleviate hold-up inefficiencies. Crucially, however, the thickness of the market for inputs depends in turn on the extent to which final-good producers rely on outsourcing versus integration in their procurement decisions, since only firms engaged in outsourcing populate that market. McLaren (2000) demonstrates that this setup too generates the possibility of multiple equilibria and shows that trade opening, by thickening the market for inputs, may lead to a worldwide move toward more disintegrated industrial systems, thus increasing world welfare and leading to gains from trade quite different from those emphasized in traditional trade theory.

The vast majority of applications of the transaction-cost approach in the international trade literature have modeled the transaction costs emanating from incomplete contracts as taking the form of ex-ante inefficiencies associated with the suboptimal provision of relationship-specific investments. As noted earlier, Williamson's own work, particularly Williamson (1975), instead emphasized the role of ex-post inefficiencies related to the inefficient termination or execution of contracts. For instance, in an uncertain environment, parties might need to adapt to ex-post situations that were not foreseen in an initial (incomplete) contract. In those situations, transaction-cost theory would posit that adaptation can be carried out more efficiently within firm boundaries than at arm's length due to the useful role of authority in reducing the scope for opportunism and costly renegotiation. Costinot, Oldenski, and Rauch (2011) develop a simple theory of multinational firm boundaries based on these ideas and show, theoretically as well as empirically, that the propensity to integrate foreign suppliers is lower in more routine sectors.

7
The Property-Rights Approach

The transaction-cost theory of firm boundaries reviewed in the last chapter has fundamentally enhanced our understanding of the sources and nature of inefficiencies that arise when transacting via the market mechanism. The pioneering work of Ronald Coase and its operationalization in the writings of Oliver Williamson spun a successful empirical agenda on the determinants of the internalization decision of firms.

At the same time that this empirical research agenda was flourishing, theorists began questioning some of the basic tenets of the transaction-cost approach. The most notable criticism of the theory was that, even if one bought the notion that the transaction-cost literature had correctly identified the costs of transacting via the market, there still remained the issue of what exactly were the benefits of the market mechanism. In other words, if market transactions are plagued by contract incompleteness, opportunistic behavior and inefficient haggling over prices, why do firms use the market at all? Why is world production not carried out within the boundaries of one huge multinational firm that circumvents the need to use contracts to provide incentives to producers to carry out relationship-specific investments?

Naturally, these are not questions that Coase or Williamson ignored in their writings.[1] To obtain a nontrivial tradeoff in internalization decisions, transaction-cost models typically appeal to some vague notion of "governance costs," but these governance costs are treated as exogenous parameters unrelated to the sources of transaction costs in market transactions. Sometimes these costs are associated with a limited span of control by managers, but this still leaves the theory open to the criticism that, in the absence of contracting and incentive concerns, the firm could always hire more and more managers to expand its scale indefinitely.

Of course, in the real world, the challenge of incentivizing the agents involved in a production process does not disappear when those agents become employees of the firm. The example of the recent divestures of

---

[1] For instance, Coase (1937, p. 394) writes: "A pertinent question to ask would appear to be [...], why, if by organising one can eliminate certain costs and in fact reduce the cost of production, are there any market transactions at all? Why is not all production carried on by one big firm?"

Sony Corporation mentioned at the beginning of Chapter 6 illustrates the fact that firms often come to the (painful) realization that certain parts of the production process can be done more efficiently by external subcontractors than by internal divisions. And in many instances, the reason for the poor performance of employees is associated with the lack of high-powered incentives.

The remainder of this chapter will be centered on the study of the Property-Rights Theory of the firm, which arguably constitutes the most compelling and influential theory of the firm explaining in a unified framework *both* the benefits as well as the costs of vertical integration.

The Property-Rights Approach: A Non-Technical Overview

The property-rights theory of the firm, as first exposited in Grossman and Hart (1986), and further developed in Hart and Moore (1990) and Hart (1995), begins by arguing that it is not satisfactory to assume that the contractual frictions that plague the relationship between two non-integrated firms will simply disappear when these firms become an integrated entity. After all, intrafirm transactions are not secured by all-encompassing contracts, and there is no reason to assume that relationship specificity will be any lower in integrated relationships than in non-integrated ones. For these reasons, opportunistic behavior and incentive provision are arguably just as important in within-firm transactions as they are in market transactions.

If one accepts the notion that within-firm transactions typically entail transaction costs and that the source of these transaction costs is not too distinct from those in market transactions, then a natural question is: what then defines the boundaries of the firm? To answer this question, Grossman and Hart (1986) resort to the legal definition of ownership. From a legal perspective, integration is associated with the ownership (via acquisition or creation) of non-human assets, such as machines, buildings, inventories, patents, copyrights, etc.

The central idea of the property-rights approach is that internalization matters because ownership of non-human assets is a source of power when contracts are incomplete. More specifically, when parties encounter contingencies that were not foreseen in an initial contract, the owner of these assets naturally holds *residual* rights of control, and he or she can decide on the use of these assets that maximizes his payoff at the possible expense of that of the integrated party. For instance, the owner can insist or impose certain courses of action (such as production ramp-ups) that might be good for him or her but less appealing to the integrated party.

The seminal paper by Grossman and Hart (1986) shows that, in the presence of relationship-specific investments, these ideas lead to a theory of the boundaries of the firm in which both the benefits and the costs of integration are endogenous. In particular, vertical integration entails endogenous (transactions) costs because it reduces the incentives of the integrated firm to make investments that are partially specific to the integrating firm, and that this underinvestment lowers the overall surplus of the relationship.

The property-rights theory of the firm has featured prominently in the international trade literature on multinational firm boundaries, beginning with the first chapter of my Ph.D. thesis, published as Antràs (2003). I will next develop a variant of that model that is closely connected to the global sourcing model with heterogeneous firms we have worked with in the last chapter as well as in Chapters 2 and 4. This framework is closely related to those in Antràs and Helpman (2004, 2008), though we shall discuss richer variants of the model than the simpler models in those papers.

A Property-Rights Model of Multinational Firm Boundaries

Let us then go back to our two-country model of global sourcing. I will continue to assume that the source of contractual inefficiencies in market transactions is well captured by the models in Chapter 4. As a result the profitabilities of domestic outsourcing and offshore outsourcing are still represented by the profit flows $\pi_{DO}(\varphi)$ and $\pi_{OO}(\varphi)$ in equations (6.4) and (6.5), which for convenience I reproduce here

$$\pi_{DO}(\varphi) = (w_N)^{1-\sigma} B\Gamma_{DO}\varphi^{\sigma-1} - w_N f_{DO};$$
$$\pi_{OO}(\varphi) = \left((w_N)^{\eta}(\tau w_S)^{1-\eta}\right)^{1-\sigma} B\Gamma_{OO}\varphi^{\sigma-1} - w_N f_{OO}. \tag{7.1}$$

In these equations, Γ_{DO} and Γ_{OO} summarize the level of contractual efficiency associated with domestic and international arm's-length sourcing purchases and they are themselves a function of the primitive parameters of the various variants of the model, as derived in Chapter 4 and reviewed in Chapter 6. For the time being, and to keep matters simple, I will assume that the contracts governing domestic transactions are complete, so that $\Gamma_{DO} = 1$, while contracts governing international sourcing transactions are totally incomplete. I will also assume that there is only one supplier, that investments are fully relationship-specific, that bargaining power is symmetric, and that there are no constraints on ex-ante transfers. This effectively brings us back to what I referred to as the "Basic" model in Chapter 4, in which you recall that

$$\Gamma_{OO} = (\sigma + 1)\left(\frac{1}{2}\right)^{\sigma} < 1 \text{ for } \sigma > 1. \tag{7.2}$$

The key innovation in this property-rights framework is that I will now assume that integrated transactions also entail transaction costs. Following Grossman and Hart (1986) and Hart and Moore (1990), the source of these costs is related to the fact that intrafirm transactions are also governed by incomplete contracts.[2] In particular, I shall assume that when F decides its mode of organization at t_0, it anticipates playing an analogous game with a manufacturing operator M regardless of whether the operator is an employee of F or an independent contractor. Both the "outsourcing" and "integration" branches of the game feature an ex-ante contracting stage t_0, an investment stage t_1, and an ex-post bargaining stage t_2. The only difference between the two branches of the game is at t_2, where the outside options available to F and M will now be a function of the ownership decision at t_0.

How does the ownership structure decision shape the outside options at t_2? Remember that in the outsourcing branch of the game we have assumed that in the absence of an agreement at t_2, F was left with a zero payoff (since it could not create output without an input m and there was no time to find an alternative M that could provide an input). Similarly, M's investment was also fully customized to F, and thus M's outside option was zero as well.

In the case of integration, the above formulation of the outside options is unrealistic. It seems natural to assume instead that H will hold property rights over the input m produced by M, and thus F has the ability to fire a stubborn operator M that is refusing to agree on a transfer price, while still being able to capture part, say a fraction $\delta < 1$, of the revenue generated by combining h and m. The fact that δ is assumed to be lower than one reflects the intuitive idea that F cannot use the input m as effectively as it can with the cooperation of its producer, i.e., M.

In the ex-post bargaining at t_2, each party will capture its outside option plus an equal share of the ex-post gains from trade. Denote by β_k the share of revenue accruing to F at t_2 under organizational form $k = V, O$. Given our assumptions, we have

$$\beta_V \equiv \frac{1}{2}(1 + \delta) > \frac{1}{2} \equiv \beta_O, \tag{7.3}$$

which captures the key property-rights idea that F holds more *power* under integration than under outsourcing.

Because the degree of contractibility or relationship specificity and the other contractual aspects of the model are common in the outsourcing and integration branches of the game, the equilibrium under integration is

---

[2] As discussed below, our framework could easily accommodate variation in contractibility *across* organizational forms, but we will refrain from doing so in the spirit of the property-rights approach.

identical to the one under outsourcing but with $\beta_V = (1 + \delta)/2$ replacing $\beta_O = 1/2$ throughout. We can then refer back to the generalized Nash bargaining variant of the global sourcing model in Chapter 4, and more specifically to equation (4.14), to conclude that the profitability of foreign integration will be given by

$$\pi_{OV}(\varphi) = \left((w_N)^\eta (\tau w_S)^{1-\eta}\right)^{1-\sigma} B\Gamma_{OV}\varphi^{\sigma-1} - w_N f_{OV}, \tag{7.4}$$

where

$$\Gamma_{OV} = (\sigma - (\sigma - 1)(\beta_V\eta + (1 - \beta_V)(1 - \eta))) \left(\beta_V^\eta (1 - \beta_V)^{1-\eta}\right)^{\sigma-1}. \tag{7.5}$$

Given our assumption of complete contracting in domestic transactions, ownership of physical assets is immaterial for the profitability of domestic integration, and $\Gamma_{DV} = 1$. Furthermore, since Γ_{DO} is also equal to 1 while the fixed costs of sourcing are larger for domestic integration than for domestic outsourcing, we necessarily have that $\pi_{DO}(\varphi) > \pi_{DV}(\varphi)$ for all φ and no firm in the industry integrates domestic suppliers. When discussing the empirical implementation of the model in Chapter 8, I will re-introduce contractual frictions in domestic transactions and consider equilibria with some firms engaged in domestic integration.

The Choice between Offshore Outsourcing and Foreign Integration

To build intuition, let us first consider the choice between offshore out-sourcing and foreign integration. This amounts to comparing the profit flows in (7.1) and (7.4). These two profit flows only differ in the fixed costs and transaction costs associated with these strategies. We shall continue to assume that fixed costs of foreign integration are higher than those of offshore outsourcing ($f_{OV} > f_{OO}$). A key aspect of the property-rights model is the extent to which contractual efficiency is higher in integrated versus non-integrated transactions, as summarized in the relative size of Γ_{OV} and Γ_{OO}. In fact, as we shall demonstrate later in this chapter and again in Chapter 8, the ratio Γ_{OV}/Γ_{OO} is a central determinant of the share of intrafirm trade.

In our basic model with one input, totally incomplete contracting in international transactions, no financial constraints, and full relationship specificity, this ratio is given by:

$$\frac{\Gamma_{OV}}{\Gamma_{OO}} = \frac{\sigma - (\sigma - 1)(\beta_V\eta + (1 - \beta_V)(1 - \eta))}{\sigma - (\sigma - 1)(\beta_O\eta + (1 - \beta_O)(1 - \eta))} \left(\frac{\beta_V}{\beta_O}\right)^{\eta(\sigma-1)} \left(\frac{1 - \beta_V}{1 - \beta_O}\right)^{(1-\eta)(\sigma-1)}. \tag{7.6}$$

Under symmetric Nash bargaining, β_V and β_O are given in equation (7.3). Even with generalized Nash bargaining, the ratio Γ_{OV}/Γ_{OO} would still continue to be given by (7.6), but with

$$\beta_V = \beta + (1 - \beta)\,\delta > \beta = \beta_O,$$

where β is the primitive bargaining power of F.

In Chapter 8, when studying the properties of the level of contractual efficiency Γ_{OO}, we showed that whether increases or decreases in the bargaining power of the final-good producer increased or decreased, this term crucially depended on the level of headquarter intensity η. This naturally implies that whether the ratio Γ_{OV}/Γ_{OO} is higher or lower than one will also depend on the value of η. Indeed, it is easily verified that $\Gamma_{OV} > \Gamma_{OO}$ when $\eta \to 1$, while $\Gamma_{OV} < \Gamma_{OO}$ when $\eta \to 0$.[3] In other words, for sufficiently high level of headquarter intensity, the transaction costs of using the market mechanism are higher than those of transacting within firm boundaries, just as is assumed in the transaction-cost theory. When η is sufficiently low, however, the converse is true and the contractual efficiency of outsourcing is actually higher than that of integration.

We can provide a sharper characterization of this result by noting that for any $\beta_V > \beta_O$, the ratio Γ_{OV}/Γ_{OO} is necessarily increasing in η (see the Theoretical Appendix for a proof). This in turn implies that there exists a unique threshold headquarter intensity $\hat{\eta}$ such that, if the fixed costs of these two organization forms were to be identical, the profitability of foreign integration would be higher than that of offshore outsourcing for $\eta > \hat{\eta}$ and lower for $\eta < \hat{\eta}$. This result, which corresponds to Proposition 1 in Antràs (2003), resonates with one of the central results in the property-rights theory: with incomplete contracting, ownership rights of assets should be allocated to parties undertaking noncontractible investments that contribute disproportionately to the value of the relationship. The relative importance of the operator M's investment is captured in (7.6) by the elasticity of output with respect to that agent's investment, i.e., $1 - \eta$, and thus the lower is η, the higher the need for F to give away ownership rights to M by engaging in outsourcing.

As suggested by Antràs and Helpman (2004, 2008), another pedagogically useful way to characterize the optimal choice of ownership structure is to consider the hypothetical case in which F could freely choose β from the continuum of values in $[0, 1]$, rather than choosing from the pair (β_V, β_O).

---

[3] Note, in particular, that $(\sigma - (\sigma - 1)\,x)\,x^{\sigma-1}$ is increasing in x for $x \in (0, 1)$.

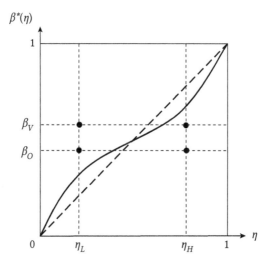

Figure 7.1 Optimal Bargaining Share

Formally, this amounts to solving the problem

$$\max_{\beta_k \in [0,1]} \quad \beta_k R(h_k, m_k) - w_N h_k - w_N f_{Ok} - s_k$$

$$\text{s.t.} \quad s_k + (1 - \beta_k) R(h_k, m_k) - \tau w_S m_k \geq 0$$

$$h_k = \arg\max_h \{\beta_k R(h, m_k) - w_N h\} \tag{7.7}$$

$$m_k = \arg\max_m \{(1 - \beta_k) R(h_k, m) - \tau w_S m\},$$

where remember that the revenue function $R(h_k, m_k)$ is given in (4.20). This problem can in turn be reduced to

$$\max_{\beta_k \in [0,1]} \Gamma(\beta) = (\sigma - (\sigma - 1)(\beta \eta + (1 - \beta)(1 - \eta)))(\beta^\eta (1 - \beta)^{1-\eta})^{\sigma-1}.$$

As already mentioned in Chapter 4, the value β^* that minimizes transaction costs (or maximizes $\Gamma(\beta)$) is given by

$$\frac{\beta^*}{1 - \beta^*} = \sqrt{\frac{\eta}{1 - \eta} \frac{\sigma - (\sigma - 1)(1 - \eta)}{\sigma - (\sigma - 1)\eta}}, \tag{7.8}$$

and is an increasing function of η. This function is plotted in Figure 7.1 together with two potential values of β_V and β_O. As is clear from the graph, when η is low, β_O is closer to the optimal β^* than β_V is, but the converse is true when η is high.

Equilibrium Sorting in the Property-Rights Model

Having provided a primer on the choice between different organizational forms, let us now turn to a more formal exposition of the sorting of different firms into different organizational forms depending on their productivity level φ. Formally, we seek to characterize the optimal organizational form $(\ell, k) \in \{DO, DV, OO, OV\}$ that solves $\max \pi_{\ell k}(\varphi)$. For the time being, we shall do so under the maintained assumption that $\Gamma_{DO} = \Gamma_{DV} = 1$ and thus domestic integration is a dominated strategy.

A first obvious observation in light of our above discussion of the choice between offshore outsourcing and integration is that whenever headquarter intensity η is sufficiently low, foreign integration will also be a dominated strategy. More specifically, we have shown above that for η below a certain threshold level, outsourcing features higher contractual efficiency (i.e., $\Gamma_{OV} < \Gamma_{OO}$), which coupled with the higher fixed costs of integration, necessarily implies that $\pi_{OV}(\varphi) < \pi_{OO}(\varphi)$ for all φ. When foreign integration is a dominated strategy, the sorting of firms into organizational forms is analogous to that in Figure 6.2, with the most productive firms engaging in foreign outsourcing, and the least productive firms (among the active ones) relying on domestic outsourcing.

For higher levels of headquarter intensity η, richer sorting patterns can emerge. In particular, the effective marginal cost is now lower under integration than under outsourcing ($\Gamma_{OV} > \Gamma_{OO}$), but outsourcing continues to be a strategy associated with lower fixed costs, and thus a subgroup of relatively unproductive firms might continue to prefer outsourcing over integration. For certain parameter configurations, one can then construct an industry equilibrium in which three organizational forms—domestic outsourcing, foreign outsourcing, and foreign integration—coexist in equilibrium, as depicted in Figure 6.4 in Chapter 6, and reproduced in Figure 7.2. In such an equilibrium, firms with productivity $\varphi^{\sigma-1}$ below $\tilde{\varphi}_D$ do not produce, those with $\varphi^{\sigma-1} \in (\tilde{\varphi}_D, \tilde{\varphi}_{OO})$ outsource domestically, those with $\varphi^{\sigma-1} \in (\tilde{\varphi}_{OO}, \tilde{\varphi}_{OV})$ outsource abroad, and those with $\varphi^{\sigma-1} > \tilde{\varphi}_{OV}$ integrate abroad, i.e., they engage in foreign direct investment.

Naturally, for certain configuration of parameter values, it may be the case that no firm finds it optimal to outsource abroad, in which case the sorting pattern is as depicted in Figure 6.3 in Chapter 6. Note, however, that in any equilibrium in which different organizational forms coexist, their ranking by productivity will not be affected. In particular, in any industry with a share of intrafirm trade strictly between 0 and 1, it is necessarily the case that firms offshoring within firm boundaries are more productive than firms offshoring at arm's length.

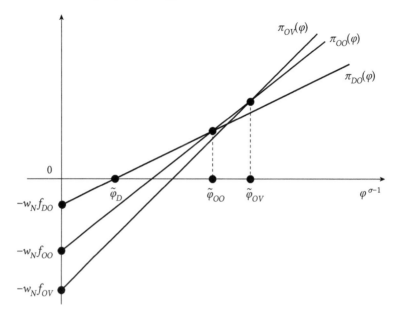

Figure 7.2 Equilibrium Sorting with High Headquarter Intensity

Implications for the Share of Intrafirm Trade

We next use the model to aggregate all firms' decisions within an industry to characterize the relative prevalence of different organizational forms within a sector or industry. As in the case of the transaction-cost model developed earlier in this chapter, I will restrict the analysis to computing the relative prevalence of offshore outsourcing and foreign integration, as measured by the share of intrafirm input imports over total input imports. I will also focus on equilibria with a positive measure of firms relying on domestic outsourcing, offshore outsourcing, and offshore integration.

Following the same steps as in the derivation of equation (6.9), one finds that whenever φ is distributed according to a Pareto distribution, this share is given by

$$Sh_{i-f} = \frac{\Gamma_{OV}/\Gamma_{OO}}{\left[\left(\frac{\tilde{\varphi}_{OV}}{\tilde{\varphi}_{OO}}\right)^{\kappa-\sigma-1} - 1\right] + \Gamma_{OV}/\Gamma_{OO}} \tag{7.9}$$

where

$$\frac{\tilde{\varphi}_{OV}}{\tilde{\varphi}_{OO}} = \left[\frac{f_{OV} - f_{OO}}{f_{OO} - f_{DO}} \times \frac{1 - (w_N/\tau w_S)^{-(1-\eta)(\sigma-1)}/\Gamma_{OO}}{\Gamma_{OV}/\Gamma_{OO} - 1} \right]^{1/(\sigma-1)}. \qquad (7.10)$$

In order to derive these equations, I have assumed again that foreign inputs are priced such that these input expenditures constitute the same multiple $(1 - \eta)(\sigma - 1)$ of operating profits under all organizational forms. This is a restrictive assumption, but note that it does not impose that transfer prices within firms are identical to those under offshore outsourcing. It would be interesting to trace the implications of this framework for the transfer pricing practices of multinational firms, but I will not attempt to do so here.[4]

Equations (7.9) and (7.10) can be used to formally study the determinants of the share of intrafirm trade. Notice first that, holding constant the indices of contractual efficiency Γ_{OV} and Γ_{OO}, the share of intrafirm imports Sh_{i-f} is decreasing in κ (since $\tilde{\varphi}_{OV} > \tilde{\varphi}_{OO}$) and in the term $(w_N/\tau w_S)^{-(1-\eta)(\sigma-1)}$. Because Γ_{OV} and Γ_{OO} in equations (7.2) and (7.5) are in turn independent of κ and $w_N/\tau w_S$, we can conclude that the share of intrafirm imports is increasing in productivity dispersion, trade costs, and Southern labor costs. These effects are identical to those I derived in the transaction-cost model, and the mechanisms behind these effects are also the exact same ones. The productivity dispersion effect relies on the sorting pattern by which firms that integrate abroad are more productive than those that outsource abroad, while the effect of trade costs and wage difference stems from the fact that the extensive margin of offshoring affects outsourcing disproportionately.

In our basic transaction-cost model with one input, symmetric Nash bargaining, and totally incomplete contracts, we also concluded from the effect of the term $(w_N/\tau w_S)^{-(1-\eta)(\sigma-1)}$ that the share of intrafirm trade is also predicted to increase in the level of headquarter intensity η. This is because governance costs λ and the contractual efficiency of outsourcing $\Gamma_{OO} = (\sigma + 1)/2^\sigma$ were both independent of η. In the present property-rights model, matters are a bit more complex because Γ_{OV} in (7.5) does depend on the value of η. Nevertheless, we showed above that for any $\beta_V > \beta_O$, the ratio Γ_{OV}/Γ_{OO} is increasing in η. As a result, the share of intrafirm imports is positively correlated with η for reasons *distinct* from those in the transaction-cost model. These distinct effects are in turn of two types. First, there is an extensive margin effect related to firms selecting into foreign direct investment when η is high, and second, there is an intensive margin effect associated with the relatively higher contractual efficiency (and thus firm's size) of integration relative to outsourcing whenever η is high.

---

[4] For recent work on transfer pricing and multinational firm organizational decisions, see Keuschnigg and Devereux (2013) and Bauer and Langenmayr (2013).

Extensions of the Basic Model

In order to guide the empirical analysis in Chapter 8, I next turn to studying more general environments that relax some of the strong assumptions of our basic model. This will serve to expand the range of predicted determinants of the share of intrafirm trade and compare those predicted effects to those derived in the transaction-cost model in Chapter 6.

When generalizing that transaction-cost model, we were able to simply invoke the results in Chapter 4 regarding the determinants of the offshore contractual efficiency Γ_{OO}, or the results in Chapter 5 (and the Theoretical Appendix) regarding the determinants of the ratio Γ_{OO}/Γ_{DO}. The reason for this is that the costs of integration were captured by a "governance-costs" term that was assumed independent of the determinants of the contractual efficiency of outsourcing. As I have shown above, however, in the property-rights model, the same parameters that shape the efficiency of offshore outsourcing also affect the efficiency of foreign direct investment (i.e., offshore integration). And, more specifically, we have seen that the share of intrafirm trade is not only affected negatively by Γ_{OO}, as in the transaction-cost model, but it is also positively affected by the ratio Γ_{OV}/Γ_{OO}.

In order to simplify the exposition, in the remainder of this chapter I will focus attention on the effect of different primitive parameters of our global sourcing model on this ratio Γ_{OV}/Γ_{OO}, capturing the relative marginal-cost efficiency of integration versus outsourcing. When motivating the empirical specifications in Chapter 8, I will reconsider how this ratio Γ_{OV}/Γ_{OO}, together with the level of Γ_{OO}, shape the share of intrafirm trade in a multi-industry and multi-country environment. For pedagogical reasons, I will also abstract for now from contractual frictions in domestic sourcing and will also stick to the benchmark ranking of fixed costs $f_{OV} > f_{OO} > f_{DV} > f_{DO}$. In the next chapter, when discussing the empirical implementation of the model, I will relax these assumptions in a similar way as I did when presenting the transaction-cost global sourcing model in Chapter 6.

To save space, all proofs of the theoretical results discussed below are relegated to the Theoretical Appendix.

Generalized Bargaining and General Functional Forms

I begin the discussion of extensions of the framework with the case in which the primitive bargaining power of F agents is different than 1/2 and is given by some general value $\beta \in (0, 1)$. As already mentioned, this has little impact on the ratio Γ_{OV}/Γ_{OO}, which continues to be given by expression (7.6) but now with $\beta_V = \beta + (1 - \beta)\delta > \beta = \beta_O$. I also anticipated above (and offer a formal proof in the Theoretical Appendix) that for any $\beta \in (0, 1)$—and not just $\beta = 1/2$—this ratio Γ_{OV}/Γ_{OO} is increasing in the level of headquarter intensity η.[5]

Although the positive effect of headquarter intensity on the efficiency of integration relative to outsourcing is robust to the specification of the bargaining process, one might wonder whether it is driven by the very special functional forms of the model. To investigate this, in Antràs (2014) I solved the above problem (7.7) for a general revenue function $R(h_k, m_k)$, rather than the Cobb-Douglas function in equation (4.20). In such a case, the profit maximizing division of surplus β^* is characterized by

$$\frac{\beta^*}{1 - \beta^*} = \frac{\eta_{R,h} \cdot \xi_{h,\beta}}{\eta_{R,m} \cdot \left(-\xi_{m,\beta}\right)}, \tag{7.11}$$

where $\eta_{R,j} \equiv jR_j/R$ is the elasticity of surplus to investments in input $j = h, m$, and $\xi_{j,\beta} \equiv \frac{dj}{d\beta}\frac{\beta}{j}$ is the elasticity of investment in j to changes in the distribution of surplus β. In words, the (hypothetical) optimal share of revenue allocated to an agent is again increasing in the elasticity of revenue with respect to that agent's investment and in the elasticity of that agent's investment with respect to changes in the distribution of surplus.

This characterization is intuitive but it is expressed in terms of investment elasticities $\xi_{h,\beta}$ and $\xi_{m,\beta}$ that are themselves functions of subtle features of the revenue function (see Antràs, 2014, for details). It can be shown, however, that whenever the revenue function is homogeneous of degree $\alpha \in (0, 1)$ in h and m, equation (7.11) can be expressed as:

$$\frac{\beta^*}{1 - \beta^*} = \sqrt{\frac{\eta_{R,h}}{\eta_{R,m}} \frac{\alpha\left(1 - \eta_{R,m}\right) + (1 - \alpha)\left(\sigma_{h,m} - 1\right)\eta_{R,m}}{\alpha\left(1 - \eta_{R,h}\right) + (1 - \alpha)\left(\sigma_{h,m} - 1\right)\eta_{R,h}}}, \tag{7.12}$$

where $\eta_{R,h}$ and $\eta_{R,m}$ again denote the revenue elasticities of headquarter services and components, respectively, and $\sigma_{h,m}$ is the elasticity of substitution between headquarter services h and the input m in revenue. Simple differentiation then confirms that for any constant $\sigma_{h,m} > 0$, β^* continues to be increasing in $\eta_{R,h}$ and decreasing in $\eta_{R,m}$, and as a result it continues to be efficient to allocate residual rights of control and thus "power" to the party whose investment has a relatively larger impact on surplus. In other words, the prediction of the model that integration is more attractive in headquarter-intensive sectors than in component-intensive sectors appears robust.[6]

---

[5] This ratio is also a function of the elasticity of demand σ, but such dependence is complex and depends in nontrivial ways on the values of β and δ.

[6] Under which circumstances will the revenue function be homogeneous of degree $\alpha \in (0, 1)$ in h and m? This would be the case, for instance, if the inverse demand faced by the

Financial Constraints

I next consider the extension of the model discussed in Chapter 4 featuring constraints on the exchange of ex-ante lump-sum transfers between F and M. More specifically, the only new assumption is that M agents can pledge to external financiers in their domestic economy at most a share ϕ of the net income they receive from transacting with F. As a result, their ex-ante transfer to F can be no larger than a fraction ϕ of their ex-post surplus, which is given by $\phi\left[(1 - \beta_k)\,p\,(q(\varphi))\,q(\varphi) - \tau w_S m(\varphi)\right]$ under organizational form $k = \{V, O\}$. Solving the problem (7.7) with this additional financial constraint, one finds that the ratio Γ_{OV}/Γ_{OO} is now given by

$$\frac{\Gamma_{OV}}{\Gamma_{OO}} = \frac{\beta_V\,(\sigma - (\sigma - 1)\eta) + \phi\,(1 - \beta_V)\,(\sigma - (\sigma - 1)(1 - \eta))}{\beta_O\,(\sigma - (\sigma - 1)\eta) + \phi\,(1 - \beta_O)\,(\sigma - (\sigma - 1)(1 - \eta))}$$

$$\times \left(\frac{\beta_V}{\beta_O}\right)^{\eta(\sigma-1)} \left(\frac{1 - \beta_V}{1 - \beta_O}\right)^{(1-\eta)(\sigma-1)}. \tag{7.13}$$

It is straightforward to verify that this ratio is decreasing in ϕ. Hence, as in our transaction-cost model, the relative profitability of foreign integration vis-à-vis foreign outsourcing is particularly large whenever suppliers face tighter financial constraints. Intuitively, and although a low ϕ also reduces the efficiency of intrafirm offshoring, the share of ex-post surplus by M agents is higher under outsourcing than integration, and thus it is natural that financial constraints disproportionately affect F's profits under outsourcing.

In the Theoretical Appendix, I also show that the ratio Γ_{OV}/Γ_{OO} continues to be increasing in η. This is the combination of two effects. On the one hand, the standard role of headquarter intensity in the property-rights theory continues to be operative here, and on the other hand, the larger is η, the larger is the loss of rents for F of tight financial constraints, and thus again the bigger the incentive to integrate suppliers.

Partial Contractibility

Consider now the variant of the model with partial contractibility in international transactions in which the degree of contractibility is allowed to vary across inputs and countries, along the lines of the modeling in Antràs and Helpman (2008). In Chapter 4, we discussed their framework in some detail

---

final-good producer is homogeneous of degree $\alpha_r - 1 < 0$ in output—as with the type of CES preferences assumed throughout the book—and the production function combining h and m is *any* homogenenous function of degree $\alpha_q \in (0, 1]$. In such a case, we would have $\alpha = \alpha_r \alpha_q$.

and derived the equilibrium profitability of offshoring under symmetric Nash bargaining with zero outside options (so ex-post surplus is shared equally between agents). As shown in section A.2 of the Theoretical Appendix, one can follow the approach in Antràs and Helpman (2008) to obtain a formula for the level of contractual efficiency for *any* ex-post division of revenue (β_h, β_m). Applying this formula to the cases (i) $\beta_h = \beta_V$, $\beta_m = 1 - \beta_V$, and (ii) $\beta_h = \beta_O$, $\beta_m = 1 - \beta_O$, one can then express the ratio Γ_{OV}/Γ_{OO} as a function of these bargaining shares, headquarter intensity, and the degree of contractibility of headquarter services μ_{hS} and manufacturing μ_{mS} under offshoring:

$$
\frac{\Gamma_{OV}}{\Gamma_{OO}} = \left(\frac{\sigma - (\sigma - 1)(\beta_V \eta (1 - \mu_{hS}) + (1 - \beta_V)(1 - \eta)(1 - \mu_{mS}))}{\sigma - (\sigma - 1)(\beta_O \eta (1 - \mu_{hS}) + (1 - \beta_O)(1 - \eta)(1 - \mu_{mS}))} \right)^{\sigma - (\sigma - 1)\mu_S}
$$

$$
\times \left(\frac{\beta_V}{\beta_O} \right)^{\eta(1 - \mu_{hS})(\sigma - 1)} \left(\frac{1 - \beta_V}{1 - \beta_O} \right)^{(1-\eta)(1 - \mu_{mS})(\sigma - 1)}. \tag{7.14}
$$

Consistently with the spirit of the property-rights theory, I assume that the space of contracts available to agents within and across firm transactions is the same, so the levels of contractibility μ_{hS} and μ_{mS} are common across organizational forms. This framework could, however, flexibly accommodate differences in contractibility depending on the ownership structure.

As shown in the Theoretical Appendix, the ratio Γ_{OV}/Γ_{OO} is monotonically increasing in η and μ_{mS}, and monotonically decreasing in μ_{hS}. The rationale for the positive effect of headquarter intensity is analogous to that in the benchmark model and illustrates again the robustness of this result.

The opposite effects of μ_{mS} and μ_{hS} on the attractiveness of integration relative to outsourcing are more novel and interesting. As opposed to our previous transaction-cost model in which *any* type of increase in contractibility enhanced the relative profitability of outsourcing, in our property-rights model the relative degree of contractibility of different production processes plays a central role in the integration decision. While improvements in the contractibility of headquarter services in international transactions (a higher μ_h) continue to increase the relative profitability of outsourcing, improvements in the contractibility of offshore manufacturing have the opposite effect. The key behind the latter result is that, in the property-rights theory, the integration decision is crucially shaped by the relative intensity (or importance) of the *noncontractible* investments carried out by each agent. Fixing the level of headquarter intensity η and the contractibility of headquarter services μ_h, increases in μ_m necessarily reduce the relative importance of the *noncontractible* investments carried out by M, and as a result the benefits of arm's-length contracting are reduced relative to their costs.

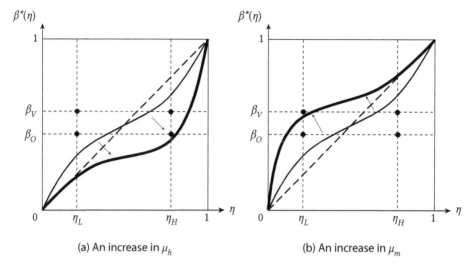

(a) An increase in μ_h (b) An increase in μ_m

Figure 7.3 Optimal Bargaining Share with Partial Contractibility

Another way to illustrate this result is by reviewing the determination of the (hypothetical) optimal ex-post division of surplus that would lead to investment levels that maximize ex-ante surplus. In our Benchmark model, this led to equation (7.8), which was depicted in Figure 7.1. In the current extension of the model with partial contractibility, equation (7.8) is slightly modified to

$$\frac{\beta^*}{1-\beta^*} = \sqrt{\frac{(1-\mu_h)\,\eta}{(1-\mu_m)\,(1-\eta)}\,\frac{\sigma - (\sigma-1)\,(1-\mu_m)\,(1-\eta)}{\sigma - (\sigma-1)\,(1-\mu_h)\,\eta}}. \qquad (7.15)$$

Note that this expression collapses back to (7.8) when $\mu_h = \mu_m = 0$, and the relative intensity of noncontractible investments carried out by F and M again equals η and $1 - \eta$ rather than $(1 - \mu_h)\eta$ and $(1 - \mu_m)(1 - \eta)$. Figure 7.3 depicts the effect of changes in different types of contractibility on this optimal β^*. In the left panel, an increase in μ_h reduces β^* and makes it more likely that outsourcing is the optimal organizational form. Conversely, in the right panel, an increase in μ_m increases β^* and expands the range of parameter values for which integration is the optimal organizational form.

In the Theoretical Appendix, I also study how the effect of changes in contractibility on the ratio Γ_{OV}/Γ_{OO} depends on other characteristics of production. First, I show that high levels of headquarter intensity tend to magnify the negative effect of μ_h and attenuate the positive effect of μ_m on Γ_{OV}/Γ_{OO}. Thus, the model predicts a positive cross-partial effect of headquarter intensity and contractibility on the relative attractiveness of integration, regardless of the source of increased contractibility. Second,

I show that low levels of the elasticity of demand σ attenuate the effect of μ_h and μ_m on Γ_{OV}/Γ_{OO}, which suggest that the sign of cross-partial derivative of Γ_{OV}/Γ_{OO} with respect to σ and the level of contractibility will depend crucially on the source of increased contractibility. The cross-partial derivative is positive in the case of μ_m but negative in the case of μ_h.

Partial Relationship Specificity

Let us next consider the extension of the model with partial relationship specificity sketched in Chapter 4. Remember that a secondary market for inputs was introduced, where each input could potentially command a price equal to a share $1 - \epsilon$ of the value of the marginal product of this input when combined with the headquarter services of the intended (primary) buyer F. A large value of ϵ was thus associated with a high degree of customization or relationship specificity. In Chapter 4 we showed that, given an organizational form, the equilibrium of this extension of the model was isomorphic to that of the full relationship-specificity Benchmark model, but with the share of ex-post revenue accruing to each agent given by $\beta_h = \beta_m = 1 - \epsilon/2$ rather than $\beta_h = \beta_m = 1/2$. Naturally, the lower is ϵ, the lower the inefficiencies arising from incomplete contracting. Although we did not do so in Chapter 4, it is straightforward to extend this result to the case of generalized Nash bargaining. In such a case, the equilibrium is isomorphic to one with full relationship specificity but with F capturing a share $1 - (1 - \beta)\epsilon$ of revenue and M capturing a share $1 - \beta\epsilon$.[7]

Adapting this modeling of partial specificity to within-firm transactions raises some difficult issues. As readers may recall, the higher *perceived* share of revenue accruing to agents reflected their expectation that their ex-ante investments would pay off in a secondary market for the components they produce. Nevertheless, our rationalization of the higher bargaining share of F agents in related-party transactions invoked the notion that F would hold property rights over the fruits of M's investments (i.e., the manufacturing input), and thus it becomes less clear that M would be able to access that secondary market. It seems clear, however, that some of the investments incurred by M agents will not be fully embodied in manufacturing inputs, and thus their outside options are likely to remain positive even under integration.

Rather than attempting to fully specify how specificity and firm boundaries interact with each other, consider the case in which equilibrium behavior in intrafirm transactions is isomorphic to that of our benchmark model with full

---

[7] Note that $1 - (1 - \beta)\epsilon + 1 - \beta\epsilon = 2 - \epsilon > 1$ for $\epsilon < 1$. To be clear, in the bargaining, F and M obtain shares of the ex-post gains from trade that add up to exactly one, but their investment behavior is *as if* they captured shares of revenue that strictly exceed one.

relationship specificity but with F capturing a share $1 - (1 - \beta_V)\,\epsilon$ of revenue and M capturing a share $1 - \beta_V\epsilon$, where $\beta_V > \beta_O = 0$. Needless to say, this is a stark assumption to make, but it is not worth devoting too much space to fleshing out a potential microfoundation for this specification, since the results I am about to discuss are not entirely general or robust to begin with.

Applying the general formula in Antràs and Helpman (2008) (see section A.2 of the Theoretical Appendix), one can then express the ratio Γ_{OV}/Γ_{OO} as follows:

$$\frac{\Gamma_{OV}}{\Gamma_{OO}} = \left(\frac{\sigma - (\sigma - 1)\left((1 - (1 - \beta_V)\,\epsilon)\,\omega_h + (1 - \beta_V\epsilon)\,\omega_m\right)}{\sigma - (\sigma - 1)\left((1 - (1 - \beta_O)\,\epsilon)\,\omega_h + (1 - \beta_O\epsilon)\,\omega_m\right)}\right)^{\sigma(1-\omega_h-\omega_m)}$$

$$\times \left(\frac{1 - (1 - \beta_V)\,\epsilon}{1 - (1 - \beta_O)\,\epsilon}\right)^{\sigma\omega_h} \left(\frac{1 - \beta_V\epsilon}{1 - \beta_O\epsilon}\right)^{\sigma\omega_m}, \qquad (7.16)$$

where $\omega_h = (\sigma - 1)\eta\,(1 - \mu_{hS})/\sigma$ and $\omega_m = (\sigma - 1)(1 - \eta)\,(1 - \mu_{mS})/\sigma$. When studying this ratio, we cannot simply invoke the comparative static results in Antràs and Helpman (2008) regarding this ratio because F and M's bargaining shares do not add up to one.[8] In fact, a first disappointing result is that it is no longer necessarily the case that Γ_{OV}/Γ_{OO} is increasing in η and μ_{mS}, and decreasing in μ_{hS} for any values of β_O, β_V, or ϵ. Furthermore, when studying the effects of ϵ on this ratio, we find this effect to be ambiguous.

As I show in more detail in the Theoretical Appendix, one can make a bit more progress with this extension by assuming that the degree of relationship specificity is different for different inputs. Let us denote these specificity levels by ϵ_h and ϵ_m for headquarter services and manufacturing, respectively. In such a case, the expression (7.16) needs to be modified by replacing $(1 - (1 - \beta_k)\epsilon)$ with $(1 - (1 - \beta_k)\,\epsilon_h)$ and $(1 - \beta_k\epsilon)$ with $1 - \beta_k\epsilon_m$ for $k = V, O$. When studying this more general ratio Γ_{OV}/Γ_{OO}, one finds that it generally increases in ϵ_h and decreases in ϵ_m. The result is not fully general, however, as one can find numerical examples in which such dependence is non-monotonic for all possible parameter values, particularly when bargaining shares β_O and β_V are extremely high or low. But in the Theoretical Appendix, I show formally that when $\beta_O = 1/2$, the negative effect of ϵ_m on the ratio Γ_{OV}/Γ_{OO} holds unambiguously. Similarly, I show that when $\beta_V = 1/2$ (and thus $\beta_O = (1/2 - \delta)/(1 - \delta)$), the positive effect of ϵ_h on the ratio Γ_{OV}/Γ_{OO} is also unambiguous.[9]

---

[8] As mentioned in Chapter 4, the positive effect of μ_{hS} and μ_{mS} on Γ_{OO} holds for *any* (β_h, β_m). Their results regarding the ratio Γ_{OV}/Γ_{OO} instead use the fact that $\beta_h = 1 - \beta_m$.

[9] Numerical simulations also indicate that the effect of changes in specificity levels ϵ_h and ϵ_m tend to be magnified when the levels of contractibility are low, an intuitive result. Yet, again these results do not hold for *all* possible values of parameters.

Multiple Inputs and Multilateral Contracting

Up to now, we have focused on variants of our property-rights model in which only one manufacturing input was necessary for production and contracting was only bilateral in nature. I next turn to the variant of the model with multiple inputs and suppliers presented in Chapter 4, which in turn built on tools developed by Acemoglu, Antràs, and Helpman (2007). Remember from our analysis in that chapter that a key parameter shaping the contractual efficiency of offshoring was ρ, which in equation (4.25) governed the degree of substitutability across inputs. When $\rho \to 1$, these inputs become perfect substitutes, while when $\rho \to 0$, they are all essential in production. Adopting the Shapley value as the solution concept for the multilateral contracting between F and the different suppliers, we showed in Chapter 4 that the final-good producer ended with a share of surplus $\sigma\rho / ((\sigma - 1)(1 - \eta) + \sigma\rho)$ and the set of suppliers jointly captured the remaining share $(\sigma - 1)(1 - \eta) / ((\sigma - 1)(1 - \eta) + \sigma\rho)$. Nevertheless, in the Nash equilibrium of the investment stage t_1, the relevant payoff of each supplier held constant the investment of other suppliers, and this led to novel effects relative to the one-supplier model. More specifically, the payoff for supplier $M(v)$ was given by

$$P_m(v) = \frac{(\sigma - 1)(1 - \eta)}{(\sigma - 1)(1 - \eta) + \sigma\rho} R(\varphi) \left(\frac{m_n(v)}{m_n(-v)} \right)^\rho, \qquad (7.17)$$

and thus ρ—rather than $(\sigma - 1)(1 - \eta)/\sigma$—governed the elasticity of each supplier's payoff to its investment level. An implication of this result is that the equilibrium profitability of offshoring in the model was identical to that of our single-supplier benchmark model but with $\beta_h = \beta_m = \rho\sigma / ((\sigma - 1)(1 - \eta) + \sigma\rho)$.

In our specification of the model in Chapter 4, we assumed that in the ex-post bargaining, each supplier could withhold the services from the noncontractible manufacturing activities in production. In that sense, it is natural to interpret that solution as corresponding to one in which all suppliers are subcontractors. How would the integration of suppliers affect the ex-post negotiations between the firm and its suppliers?

For simplicity, consider the polar case in which all suppliers are integrated by F.[10] Assume that in such a case, suppliers cannot withhold the full value of their marginal contribution to revenue (given in equation (4.26)), but only a

---

[10] As recently shown by Schwarz and Suedekum (2014), this is not without loss of generality, as hybrid sourcing, where some suppliers are vertically integrated while the others remain independent, might emerge in equilibrium even with our symmetry assumptions on technology and contracting. See also Du, Lu, and Tao (2009), and Van Biesebroeck and Zhang (2014) for alternative frameworks with hybrid sourcing strategies.

share $1 - \delta$ of it, as in our benchmark model above.[11] Following analogous derivations to those in Chapter 4, this results in t_1 payoffs for suppliers equal to

$$P_{mV}(v) = \frac{(1 - \delta)(\sigma - 1)(1 - \eta)}{(\sigma - 1)(1 - \eta) + \sigma\rho} R(\varphi) \left(\frac{m_n(v)}{m_n(-v)} \right)^{\rho}. \tag{7.18}$$

Remembering that, in equilibrium, $m_n(v) = m_n$ for all v, note that F is left with a share $(\sigma\rho + (\sigma - 1)(1 - \eta)\delta) / ((\sigma - 1)(1 - \eta) + \sigma\rho)$ of revenue. In the spirit of the property-rights theory, vertical integration enhances the bargaining power of F agents (and the more so the larger is δ), while reducing that of suppliers.

As in the case of outsourcing, one can also easily verify that the equilibrium of this multi-agent model turns out to be isomorphic to that of a single-supplier model with an appropriately redefined bargaining share β_m. Under integration, this equivalent bargaining share is given by

$$\beta_m = (1 - \delta) \rho\sigma / ((\sigma - 1)(1 - \eta) + \sigma\rho).$$

With this equivalent representation in hand, it is a simple matter of applying the general formula in Antràs and Helpman (2008) (see equation (A.10) in the Theoretical Appendix) to express the ratio Γ_{OV}/Γ_{OO} as

$$\frac{\Gamma_{OV}}{\Gamma_{OO}} = \left(1 - \frac{(\sigma - 1)(1 - \eta)\delta\omega_h - \sigma\rho\delta\omega_m}{(\sigma - 1)(1 - \eta) + \sigma\rho(1 - \omega_h - \omega_m)} \right)^{\sigma(1 - \omega_h - \omega_m)}$$

$$\times \left(1 + \frac{(\sigma - 1)(1 - \eta)\delta}{\sigma\rho} \right)^{\sigma\omega_h} (1 - \delta)^{\sigma\omega_m}, \tag{7.19}$$

where $\omega_h = (\sigma - 1)\eta(1 - \mu_{hS})/\sigma$ and $\omega_m = (\sigma - 1)(1 - \eta)(1 - \mu_{mS})/\sigma$. In the Theoretical Appendix, I show that Γ_{OV}/Γ_{OO} in (7.19) is increasing in ω_h and decreasing in ω_m, which immediately implies that this same ratio is decreasing in headquarter contractibility μ_h and increasing in manufacturing contractibility μ_m, just as in the model with a single supplier. This result does not imply, however, that the ratio Γ_{OV}/Γ_{OO} is necessarily increasing in headquarter intensity η, since this parameter enters the formula (7.19) independently of how it shapes ω_h and ω_m. In fact, it is not difficult to generate numerical examples in which the ratio is decreasing in η for a certain range of η. This is in turn related to the fact that headquarter intensity shapes

---

[11] Acemoglu, Antràs, and Helpman (2007) consider an alternative formulation in which suppliers withhold a share $1 - \delta$ of their intermediate input (rather than of their contribution). This generates analogous predictions for how input substitutability shapes the integration decision, but the proofs are much more cumbersome in that case.

the effective primitive bargaining power of agents and as η increases, the effective bargaining power of suppliers is reduced, and other things equal, the attractiveness of further reducing their bargaining power by integrating them is also reduced.

The main new result that emerges from the modeling of multiple suppliers is the role of input substitutability, as captured by ρ, in shaping the integration decisions of final-good producers. We showed in Chapter 4 that the contractual efficiency of outsourcing is higher, the more substitutable inputs are in the sense that $\partial\Gamma_{OO}/\partial\rho > 0$. Although a higher ρ also enhances the contractual efficiency of foreign integration, such an effect is less pronounced for integration than for outsourcing. More precisely, in the Theoretical Appendix, I show that there exists a unique threshold $\hat{\rho} > 0$ such that for all $\rho < \hat{\rho}$, the contractual efficiency of foreign integration is higher $\Gamma_{OV} > \Gamma_{OO}$, while the converse is true for $\rho \geq \hat{\rho}$ (i.e., $\Gamma_{OV} < \Gamma_{OO}$).[12] In sum, the incentives to integrate suppliers are higher the more complementary are inputs in production.

The intuition behind this result is as follows. When there is a high degree of technological complementarity across inputs, the ex-post payoff of F under outsourcing tends to be relatively low (note, in particular, that F's payoff under outsourcing is 0 when $\rho \to 0$) and the choice of headquarter services is particularly distorted. In such cases, vertical integration is particularly attractive because it helps restore the incentives of F to provide these headquarter services. Conversely, when ρ is high, suppliers face a particularly acute hold-up problem since their inputs are highly substitutable with each other; in those situations, strengthening the bargaining power of suppliers via an outsourcing contract constitutes the profit-maximizing organizational mode.

Sequential Production

I finally study the variant of the model in Antràs and Chor (2013), in which the production process is sequential in nature and the relationship-specific investments made by suppliers in upstream stages can affect the incentives of parties involved in later downstream stages. In Chapter 4, I already discussed that if final-good producers were able to choose the profit-maximizing division $\beta(v)$ of the surplus generated at every stage $v \in [0, 1]$, they would set it equal to

$$\frac{\partial\beta^*(v)}{\partial v} = \frac{1 - \sigma\rho/\sigma}{\sigma\rho - 1} v^{\frac{-\sigma\rho(\sigma-1)}{(\sigma\rho-1)\sigma}}. \tag{7.20}$$

[12] When this threshold $\hat{\rho}$ is higher than one, then $\Gamma_{OV}/\Gamma_{OO} > 1$ for all $\rho \in (0, 1]$.

From this it followed that when $\sigma > \sigma_\rho$, the final-good producer would have an incentive to retain a higher share of the surplus in downstream stages than in upstream stages, while the converse is true when $\sigma < \sigma_\rho$. The reason for this is that in the former case, supplier investments are sequential complements, and thus high upstream values of $\beta(v)$ would be particularly costly since they would reduce the incentives to invest not only of these early suppliers but also of all suppliers downstream. Conversely, when $\sigma < \sigma_\rho$, supplier investments are sequential substitutes.

How does this result relate to the relative incentives to integrate suppliers along the value chain? To answer this question, consider the case in which, instead of freely choosing $\beta^*(v)$ from the set $[0, 1]$, final-good producers are constrained to choosing between two potential values, β_V and β_O with $\beta_V > \beta_O$. It is clear from equation (7.20) that when inputs are sequential complements (i.e., $\sigma > \sigma_\rho$), the firm will choose to forgo control rights over upstream suppliers in order to incentivize their investment effort, since this generates positive spillovers on the investment decisions to be made by downstream suppliers. Conversely, when investments are sequential substitutes (i.e., $\sigma < \sigma_\rho$), if any suppliers are integrated at all, it will necessarily be those producing in upstream stages.

Antràs and Chor (2013) formalize this intuitive result by showing that in the complements case ($\sigma > \sigma_\rho$), there exists a unique $v_C^* \in (0, 1]$, such that: (i) all production stages $v \in [0, v_C^*)$ are outsourced; and (ii) all stages $v \in [v_C^*, 1]$ are integrated within firm boundaries. Conversely, in the substitutes case ($\sigma < \sigma_\rho$), there exists a unique $v_S^* \in (0, 1]$, such that: (i) all production stages $v \in [0, v_S^*)$ are integrated within firm boundaries; and (ii) all stages $v \in [v_S^*, 1]$ are outsourced.

As readers may recall from Chapter 6, these results resonate with those of the transaction-cost model, but the predictions of that model were actually the opposite ones. In that model, upstream integration was particularly beneficial in the sequential complements case, and downstream integration was particularly attractive in the sequential substitutes case. We shall return to this distinction in Chapter 8.

So far, I have discussed the case with no investments in headquarter services and unconstrained ex-ante transfers between F and its suppliers. As shown in Antràs and Chor (2013), in this scenario, whenever $\sigma > \sigma_\rho$, $\beta^*(v) < 0$ for all v and thus F finds it optimal to choose outsourcing along the *whole* value chain. Or, in terms of our previous formalization of the result, $v_C^* = 1$. Nevertheless, one can show that integration and outsourcing can again coexist along the value chain regardless of the relative size of σ and σ_ρ whenever F cannot extract all surplus from suppliers via ex-ante lump-sum transfer or whenever the model includes headquarter service provision (see Antràs and Chor, 2013, for details). Interestingly, in those cases, Antràs and Chor (2013) show that the range of integrated stages (downstream stages in the complements case, upstream stages in substitutes case) is necessarily increasing in the level of headquarter intensity and decreasing in the degree of input substitutability, in line with the results obtained in the variants of the model with simultaneous investments.

To summarize, the main novel prediction that emerges from this extension of the model is that the position of an input in the value chain constitutes a new determinant of the extent to which a production process is integrated or not. Furthermore, such dependence is crucially determined by the size of the elasticity of demand faced by the final-good producer relative to the elasticity of substitution of inputs in production. Interestingly, in the transaction-cost model in Chapter 6, the effect of downstreamness also interacted with the relative size of these elasticities, but the prediction of that model for that interaction was diametrically opposite to the one delivered by the property-rights theory.

Other Applications and Extensions

I have so far focused on studying various extensions of a benchmark property-rights model with heterogeneous firms. This model is most closely related to my joint work with Elhanan Helpman, particularly Antràs and Helpman (2004, 2008). In some of the extensions, I have borrowed from other work of mine, such as from Acemoglu, Antràs, and Helpman (2007), Antràs and Chor (2013), or Antràs (2014). As I hope to convince the reader in the next chapter, I view this framework as a very useful toolbox to motivate cross-sectoral and cross-country studies of the intrafirm component of trade.

The general-equilibrium characteristics of this framework are, however, restrictive. The fact that the model features an outside sector that pins down factor costs regardless of the contractual aspects that shape the equilibrium in the differentiated-good sector might be of particular concern. Likewise, the above framework imposes stark Ricardian assumptions on technology that immediately pin down the location of headquarter service provision.

In Antràs (2003), the first paper I wrote on this topic, I considered instead a general-equilibrium model of trade with two sectors subject to contractual frictions, each producing a continuum of differentiated varieties. As in our benchmark model, manufacturing varieties are produced combining head-quarter services provided by F and manufacturing services provided by M under a Cobb-Douglas technology. It is further assumed that headquarter services are produced with capital, while manufacturing production uses only labor. This is the key assumption of the paper, as it introduces a positive correlation between the abstract concept of headquarter intensity and an observable variable, namely capital intensity.[13] Sectors differ in the intensity with which these inputs (or factors) are combined, while countries differ in their relative abundance of physical capital. To simplify the complexities inherent in the general equilibrium of such a model, I assumed that countries differ *only* in their relative factor endowments. In particular, I ruled intermediate trade costs and differences in contract incompleteness across countries, and also assumed that the fixed costs of sourcing are independent of ownership structure and feature the same factor intensity as variable costs (i.e., they combine h and m under the same Cobb-Douglas aggregator as these enter the firm's production function). Finally, I assumed that headquarter and manufacturing services were nontradable, but that the physical output embodying these services was perfectly tradable.

The combination of these assumptions made the equilibrium particularly easy to characterize because the ownership structure and location decisions could be treated independently from each other. In particular, from our results above, the ownership structure decision is such that, *worldwide*, F agents choose to integrate their suppliers if headquarter (i.e., capital) intensity is above a given threshold $\hat{\eta}$. Meanwhile, the location decision boils down to choosing the location of input production that minimizes the marginal cost of provision of inputs, which, for common contractual frictions, reduced to minimizing a Cobb-Douglas function of factor prices. The framework thus achieves a separation of an ownership decision à la Grossman-Hart-Moore, with a location decision familiar from the new trade theory model in Helpman and Krugman (1985). Still, these forces interact with each other in shaping bilateral trade across countries as well as its intrafirm component. As I showed in the paper, the model predicts a cross-industry positive correlation between the share of intrafirm imports in total imports and capital intensity in production, and a cross-country positive correlation between the share of intrafirm imports in total imports and the aggregate capital-labor ratio of the exporting country (as labor-abundant countries tend to export small amounts of capital-intensive goods).[14]

The insights of the property-rights theory have also been applied to dynamic, general-equilibrium models of international trade with the goal of understanding how ownership decisions vary along the life cycle of a product or input. Antràs (2005), for instance, develops a model in which the incomplete nature of contracts governing international transactions limits the

---

[13] In the paper, I justified this assumption on empirical grounds, arguing that cost-sharing practices of multinational firms in their relations with independent subcontractors tend to be associated with physical capital investments rather than with labor input choices.

[14] Our benchmark model of global sourcing could also generate the latter result under the plausible scenario that relative wage differences w_N / w_S are increasing in aggregate capital-labor ratio differences, and are thus not pinned down by Ricardian differences in the outside sector.

extent to which the production process can be fragmented across borders, thereby generating the emergence of Vernon-type product cycles, with new goods being initially manufactured in North (where product development takes place), and only later (when the goods are mature) is manufacturing carried out in South. Antràs (2005) also draws the boundaries of multinational firms and shows that the model gives rise to a new version of the product cycle in which, consistently with empirical evidence, manufacturing is shifted to the South first within firm boundaries, and only at a later stage to independent firms in the South.

Above, I have discussed the effect of financial constraints on the relative contractual efficiency of foreign integration and outsourcing. That discussion builds on Antràs (2014), which in turn is inspired by the work of Carluccio and Fally (2011) and Basco (2013). Both of these papers develop open-economy models in which, consistently with our results above, multinationals are more likely to integrate suppliers located in countries with poor financial institutions. Furthermore, both papers predict that the effect of financial development should be especially large when trade involves complex goods, and both provide independent empirical evidence supporting this prediction.

As emphasized by Legros and Newman (2010), in the presence of financial constraints, equilibrium firm boundaries will also depend on the relative ex-ante bargaining power of each party and their ability to exchange lump-sum transfers. This idea has been fruitfully applied in open-economy environments by Conconi, Legros, and Newman (2012), who show that vertical integration should be relatively more prevalent in industries in which (relative) prices are high, perhaps due to import-protecting trade policies. Intuitively, in their setup, which builds on Hart and Holmstrom (2010) and Legros and Newman (2013), ownership decisions are not ex-ante optimal, but instead trade off the pecuniary benefits of coordinating production achieved under integration and the managers' private benefits of operating in their preferred ways associated with non-integration. Consequently, the higher the industry price, the higher are the monetary benefits of integration and thus the more attractive this option is. Alfaro, Conconi, Fadinger, and Newman (2014) provide evidence of a positive association between import tariffs and domestic integration decisions. Díez (2014) finds similar evidence in a cross-section of U.S. industries when looking at intrafirm trade flows, but interprets the result in light of the Antràs and Helpman (2004, 2008) models which, as mentioned above, also predict a positive effect of imports tariffs on foreign integration.

Throughout this chapter, I have restricted attention to reviewing papers that adopt variants of the property-rights approach to drawing firm boundaries in open-economy environments. In the presence of incomplete contracts, another important organizational decision of firms concerns the allocation of decision rights among employees. In particular, in the presence of noncontractible effort decisions by workers, managers face a tradeoff between granting decision rights to workers or keeping these to themselves. The former option has the benefit of providing workers with "initiative," which may lead to higher effort, but delegation may result in decisions that are not necessarily optimal from the point of view of the manager. Avoiding delegation (i.e., exerting "authority") tends to inhibit the initiative of workers but entails more control over the course of production. This tradeoff was first formalized by Aghion and Tirole (1997) and has been applied to general-equilibrium frameworks by Marin and Verdier (2003, 2008, 2009, 2012) and Puga and Trefler (2002, 2010).

8

Internalization: Empirical Evidence

In the last two chapters, I have reviewed two of the leading theories of the boundaries of the firm and I have shown how to embed them into our benchmark model of global sourcing with heterogeneous firms. In this last chapter of the book, I will describe how these internalization theories can be taken to the data. The empirical literature on this topic is still budding and has yet to provide fully convincing empirical tests of these models. Several well-crafted papers have offered different pieces of evidence that are consistent with one or more of those models, but the power of such tests remains fairly low, as I will try to explain below. The goal of this chapter is thus not only to overview and replicate past work, but to try to highlight some of its limitations and suggest avenues for future research in this area.

In great measure, the current limitations of the empirical literature on multinational firm boundaries are due to the fact that empirically testing internalization theories poses at least two important challenges. First, data on the integration decisions of firms are not readily available, and thus researchers are often left to test these theories with specific industry- or product-level data. Second, the predictions from these models are associated with subtle features of the environment (such as the relative value of the marginal return to non-contractible, relationship-specific investments) that, by their own nature, are generally unobservable in the data (see Whinston, 2003).

As already explained in Chapter 1, the first limitation is not specific to the study of *international* internalization decisions. There are very few comprehensive datasets that allow researchers to measure the extent to which firms control the different agents involved in their production processes. Indeed, the pioneering empirical literature in the 1980s that implemented tests of the transaction-cost theory relied on records of the integration decisions of a handful of firms in quite specific industries. For instance, Monteverde and Teece (1982) employed data for 133 components purchased by two U.S. automakers (General Motors and Ford). Masten (1984) focused on a single firm in the aerospace industry that procured a large number (1,887 to be precise) of inputs. The classical studies of Joskow (1985, 1987) studied the ownership and contractual relationships between U.S. coal suppliers and electric utilities.

Even the more recent studies testing alternative theories of the boundaries of the firm have relied on rather peculiar sectors, such as Baker and Hubbard's (2003) or Gil's (2007) studies of the trucking and movie industry, respectively. This approach has also pervaded the international business literature, where the transaction-cost theory has been frequently tested using a small sample of specific internalization decisions of multinational firms in certain industries and countries.[1]

The second limitation of the empirical literature on firm boundaries, namely the limited ability of researchers to proxy for the key objects in those theories, has also been a recurrent concern when assessing the literature on integration decisions. Product complexity, contractual incompleteness, and relationship specificity might have a precise definition in economic models, but they are much harder to gauge in the data. Admittedly, the existing contributions to the empirical literature on multinational firm boundaries have not made much progress in addressing this second measurement hurdle.

With regard to the first challenge on data availability, however, an advantage of researchers in the international trade field is that customs offices keep a detailed record of the exchange of goods crossing political borders. To give a precise example, while it would be hard to imagine that a researcher would gain access to information on each domestic input purchase of General Motors, the U.S. Bureau of Customs and Border Protection keeps a record of each international trade transaction involving a U.S.-based firm, including all of General Motors's *imported* input purchases. Furthermore, each U.S. import transaction includes various pieces of information, such as the identity of the foreign entity exporting goods into the United States and whether that entity is related (in an ownership sense) to the U.S. buyer. In sum, the U.S. customs data contain rich information on the integration decisions of *every* U.S. firm with regard to its foreign suppliers of components.

Gaining access to these type of firm-level data is not a simple matter, however.[2] In practice, most researchers (including myself) need to rely on product-level data that aggregate the purchases of that particular product by firms and consumers in the importing country. Crucially, for some countries, these product-level data also contain information on the extent to which these aggregated import transactions are transacted between related parties or non-related parties. In this chapter, I will make extensive use of the

---

[1] For instance, Davidson and McFetridge (1984) studied 1,376 internal and arm's-length transactions involving high-technology products carried out by 32 U.S.-based multinational enterprises between 1945 and 1975. See also Mansfield, Romeo, and Wagner (1979); Mansfield and Romeo (1980); and Kogut and Zander (1993) for related contributions.

[2] In the U.S. case, one needs to first obtain security clearance and then have a project approved by the U.S. Census data administrators. Most young researchers in the field first access the U.S. Census and Customs data by serving as research assistants to other researchers with approved projects using those data.

U.S. Related-Party Trade database collected by the U.S. Bureau of Customs and Border Protection and managed by the U.S. Census Bureau. This dataset is publicly available from the U.S. census website (http://sasweb. ssd.census.gov/relatedparty/) and provides information on related and non-related-party U.S. imports and exports at the six-digit Harmonized System (HS) classification (which consists of over 5,000 categories) and at the origin/destination country level. This is exactly the same dataset I used in the empirical tests of the global sourcing model performed in Chapter 5, except that I will now be exploiting the related-party information in the data.[3]

The remainder of this chapter is structured as follows. I will first review some key features and limitations of the U.S. Related-Party Trade database, and will discuss how it can be used to construct tests of the transaction-cost and property-rights theories of multinational firm boundaries. In the process, I will illustrate how one can extend these models to multi-country environments to better exploit the variation in the intrafirm trade share both across products and countries. Toward the end of the chapter, I will briefly describe alternative data sources that have been and are being used to shed light on the internalization decisions of multinational firms. When doing so, I will put particular emphasis on the availability of firm-level datasets (with different levels of representativeness) that contain detailed information on the sourcing strategies of *firms* in different countries. I will conclude the chapter by offering some thoughts on future avenues for empirical research in the area.

The U.S. Related-Party Trade Database

Because the U.S. Related-Party Trade database will feature prominently in this chapter, it is important to devote some space to discussing its main advantages and disadvantages. To some extent, this discussion will reiterate some arguments that were already presented in Chapters 1 and 5, but it is worth repeating them here.

Several features of the U.S. Related-Party Trade database make it particularly attractive to empirical researchers. First, the database is publicly available and easily downloadable from the U.S. Census website. Second, the data are of high quality and are not subject to sampling error, since (i) several quality assurance procedures are performed, and (ii) the data offer a *complete* picture of the sourcing transactions of U.S. firms. Third, there is a large

---

[3] The U.S. Related-Party Trade database is in fact available at the more disaggregated six-digit Harmonized System (HS) industrial classification. This dataset is not freely downloadable but can be purchased from the U.S. Census at a fee. Although I have not used these richer data in the tests performed in this book, I have made it available for download at http://scholar.harvard.edu/antras/books.

amount of variation in the data: the share of U.S. intrafirm imports over total U.S. imports is very large (close to 50%), but varies widely across products and origin countries. (In Chapter 1, I documented this variation through various figures.) Fourth, by including information on *all* industrial sectors, rather than a single sector, these data make it easier to spot certain *fundamental* factors that appear to shape whether or not international transactions are internalized independently of the sector one studies. This is particularly relevant because the models I have developed in this book are highly stylized, and do not aspire to capture the precise workings of any specific sector. A fifth advantage of using these comprehensive datasets is that, by covering a wide range of sectors, countries, and time periods, they offer the potential to exploit exogenous changes in sector characteristics (due perhaps to technological change) or in institutional characteristics of exporting or importing countries (due, for instance, to institutional reforms) to better identify some of the effects predicted by the theories. I will speculate on this last potential use of these data at the end of this chapter.

Let us next turn to some of the limitations of using the U.S. Related-Party Trade database. These largely overlap with the limitations described in Chapter 5, when I used this same database to study the global location decisions of U.S. firms. First, there is an obvious tension in using aggregated product-level data to test the validity of theories of firm boundaries. Second, the data are reported based on the sector or industry category of the good being transacted and do not contain information on the sector that is purchasing the good. Third, the dataset does not distinguish between imports of intermediate inputs and imports of finished products. Fourth, in related-party transactions, the data do not typically report which firm is owned by whom, that is, whether integration is backward or forward, and whether trade occurs within U.S.-based or foreign-based multinationals. Fifth, the data provide no information on the extent to which parties are related with each other, such as, for instance, an equity share of the parent company in the affiliate. A sixth and final concern is that U.S. data can only capture those sourcing decisions that entail goods being shipped back to U.S. headquarters or affiliates, while in practice some large firms ship parts and components across foreign locations (within and across firm boundaries) and then only ship back to the United States fully assembled products (as is the case of the iPad 3 discussed in Chapter 1).

I will defer addressing the second, third, and fourth limitations until I present the empirical tests below, but let me briefly consider the other three concerns upfront. With regard to the first limitation, it is important to point out that, as in the case of the tests performed in Chapter 5, the specifications considered below are derived from the models by aggregating the individual producers' ownership decisions into product-level intrafirm trade shares. Thus, *product*-level data are used to test *product*-level predictions.

This is not to say, of course, that firm-level data would not be enormously useful in testing these models, as emphasized later in the chapter. The fifth concern regarding the lack of information on equity shares is particularly worrisome given that the threshold equity stake of 6 percent for recording a transaction as involving related parties is very low. As already mentioned in Chapter 1, however, extracts from the confidential foreign direct investment dataset collected by the Bureau of Economic Analysis indicate that well over 90 percent of intrafirm trade appears to involve majority-owned affiliates. The sixth and final limitation concerning global value chains implies that U.S. intrafirm imports generally underrepresent the involvement of U.S. multinational firms in global production networks. This is indeed a reason for concern, but it is not obvious how this phenomenon biases the results of empirical studies using these data. An active literature in international trade is attempting to shed light on global value chains through the use of the recently constructed World Input Output tables (see Timmer, Erumban, Los, Stehrer, and de Vries, 2014, for a review). Unfortunately, this data source is too aggregated to adequately complement the other sources of data used in this book, and they contain no information on the extent to which global value chains exchange goods within or across firm boundaries.

Cross-Industry Tests: Model Predictions

Having discussed the pros and cons of the U.S. intrafirm trade data, let us now put them to work. I will begin by implementing empirical tests of some cross-industry implications of the two-country transaction-cost and property-rights models developed in Chapters 6 and 7. Because I do not have information on the extent to which U.S. firms source domestic inputs within firm boundaries or at arm's length, I will focus on the predictions of these models for the share of overall foreign input purchases that are imported within firm boundaries. Furthermore, I will largely concentrate on the case in which contractual frictions in domestic transactions are relatively small, and we can ignore domestic integration as an equilibrium sourcing mode. I do so for three reasons. First, because it seems a sensible assumption to make when the domestic economy is the United States, which has a legal system that ensures a high degree of contract enforcement. Second, because the findings of Atalay, Hortacsu, and Syverson (2013) suggest that intrafirm shipments of physical goods indeed account for a very small share of overall domestic shipments of U.S. establishments. And third, because ruling out domestic integration will significantly simplify our overview of the empirical predictions emanating from the models. In any event, toward the end of the chapter, I will discuss the implications of re-introducing domestic integration into the framework.

From the results in Chapters 6 and 7, a succinct way to express the share of overall foreign input purchases that are imported within firm boundaries is

$$Sh_{i-f} = \frac{\Psi_{OV}/\Gamma_{OO}}{\left[\left(\frac{\tilde{\varphi}_{OV}}{\tilde{\varphi}_{OO}}\right)^{\kappa-\sigma-1} - 1\right] + \Psi_{OV}/\Gamma_{OO}} \tag{8.1}$$

where

$$\frac{\tilde{\varphi}_{OV}}{\tilde{\varphi}_{OO}} = \left[\frac{f_{OV} - f_{OO}}{f_{OO} - f_{DO}} \times \frac{1 - (w_N/\tau w_S)^{-(1-\eta)(\sigma-1)} \Gamma_{DO}/\Gamma_{OO}}{\Psi_{OV}/\Gamma_{OO} - 1}\right]^{1/(\sigma-1)}, \tag{8.2}$$

and

$$\Psi_{OV} = \begin{cases} \lambda^{1-\sigma} & \text{in the Transaction-Cost Model;} \\ \Gamma_{OV} & \text{in the Property-Rights Model.} \end{cases} \tag{8.3}$$

More specifically, in the transaction-cost model, this corresponds to equations (6.9) and (6.12), while in the property-rights model, it follows from equation (7.9) and a variation of equation (7.10) incorporating domestic contractual frictions (i.e., with an extra term $\Gamma_{DO} < 1$). Equations (8.1), (8.2), and (8.3) are useful in highlighting both the common and distinct predictions of the transaction-cost and property-rights models. It is worth fleshing out these predictions one last time before discussing the evidence.

Let us begin with the common predictions. Note first that, in both models, we have that the share of intrafirm imports is decreasing in κ and $w_N/\tau w_S$, and increasing in Γ_{DO}/Γ_{OO}. This is because these terms are tightly related to the sorting pattern of firms by productivity into sourcing modes, according to which firms engaged in intrafirm trade are more productive than those conducting offshore outsourcing. On the one hand, this sorting pattern implies that $\tilde{\varphi}_{OV} > \tilde{\varphi}_{OO}$, and this delivers the negative effect of κ (or positive effect of productivity and size dispersion) on the share of intrafirm trade in (8.1). The intuition behind this result is identical to that of any model with heterogeneous firms and a Pareto distribution of productivity, as described in Chapters 2 and 4. On the other hand, the equilibrium sorting pattern also implies that when the effective marginal cost of foreign sourcing decreases (either because trade costs fall, wage differences increase, or relative offshore contractual frictions decrease), some firms are led to select into offshoring, but these firms necessarily do so via offshore outsourcing, thus reducing the intrafirm trade share. To fix ideas, I will refer to this mechanism as the *selection into offshoring* channel, and it is captured by the terms $(w_N/\tau w_S)^{-(1-\eta)(\sigma-1)}$ and Γ_{DO}/Γ_{OO} in equation (8.2).

Leaving aside these common features, the key distinction between the two models resides in the ratio Ψ_{OV}/Γ_{OO}, which captures the relative

TABLE 8.1 Effect of Parameters on Ψ_{OV}/Γ_{OO} and Γ_{DO}/Γ_{OO}

Transaction-Cost Model	σ	η	ϕ	μ_{hS}	μ_{mS}	ϵ_h	ϵ_m	ρ
Ψ_{OV}/Γ_{OO}	Ambiguous	Ambiguous	−	−	−	+	+	−
Γ_{DO}/Γ_{OO}	+	Ambiguous	−	−	−	+	+	−
Property-Rights Model	σ	η	ϕ	μ_{hS}	μ_{mS}	ϵ_h	ϵ_m	ρ
Ψ_{OV}/Γ_{OO}	Ambiguous	+	−	−	+	+	−	−
Γ_{DO}/Γ_{OO}	+	Ambiguous	−	−	−	+	+	−

organizational efficiency of intrafirm and outsource offshoring. This ratio is important because it governs (i) the selection of firms into intrafirm trade, and (ii) the relative demand for inputs by firms integrating and outsourcing abroad.[4] In the transaction-cost model, the numerator Ψ_{OV} is a function of exogenously given governance costs λ, i.e., $\Psi_{OV} = \lambda^{1-\sigma}$. Instead, in the property-rights model, Ψ_{OV} is shaped by the determinants of the contractual efficiency of intrafirm foreign sourcing Γ_{OV}, and the share of intrafirm trade depends on the relative contractual efficiency of foreign integration and outsourcing. As I have discussed in detail in Chapters 4, 6, and 7, Γ_{OV} and Γ_{OO} can be mapped to several primitive features of the models, such as the level of headquarter intensity, the degree of contractual incompleteness and relationship specificity, demand and input substitution elasticities, and so on.

In order to empirically test and discriminate across these two models, a crucial question is then how are the ratios $\lambda^{1-\sigma}/\Gamma_{OO}$ and Γ_{OV}/Γ_{OO} shaped by these deep parameters of the model? In Table 8.1, I provide a summary of some of the key comparative statics I discussed in Chapters 6 and 7. For completeness, I also include comparative statics related to the *selection-into-offshoring* ratio Γ_{DO}/Γ_{OO}, which was discussed at length in the empirical tests in Chapter 5, and which is common for both models.

Table 8.1 indicates that both models have identical qualitative implications for the following five parameters: the elasticity of demand σ, the level of financial contractibility ϕ, the degree of contractibility μ_{hS} and of relationship-specificity ϵ_h of headquarter services, and the elasticity of substitution across inputs ρ. Thus, empirically testing these predictions is useful for validating or rejecting the two models, but *not* for discriminating among them.

A first difference between the two models is in the role of headquarter intensity in shaping the ratio Ψ_{OV}/Γ_{OO}. While in the transaction-cost model, such dependence was generally ambiguous and depended in subtle ways on the environment, in the property-rights model the predicted sign is

---

[4] The first effect is captured by the term Ψ_{OV}/Γ_{OO} in (8.2), while the second one corresponds to the terms Ψ_{OV}/Γ_{OO} in (8.1).

unambiguously and robustly positive.[5] When it comes to assessing the overall effect of headquarter intensity on the share of intrafirm trade Sh_{i-f}, one cannot forget however its effect via the selection into offshoring channel. This selection effect can in turn be broken down into two components. On the one hand, there is the direct effect of a higher η in equation (8.2), which reduces the relevance of cross-country wage differences for profits, thereby hindering selection into offshoring and increasing Sh_{i-f} on that account. On the other hand, there also exists an effect of η via the term Γ_{DO}/Γ_{OO} governing relative offshore contractual frictions; as indicated in Table 8.1, such an effect is generally ambiguous. Where do all these different effects leave us? A cautious way to summarize the above discussion is that one could interpret a positive dependence of the share of intrafirm trade on headquarter intensity as (weak) supportive evidence for the property-rights model, but without such a dependence necessarily leading one to reject the validity of the transaction-cost model.

A second key difference between the two models relates to the effects of μ_{mS} and ϵ_m on the ratio Ψ_{OV}/Γ_{OO}. As discussed in Chapter 6, in the transaction-cost model, any increase in contractibility or decrease in relationship specificity of manufacturing inputs tends to reduce the relative profitability of integration. Instead, we have seen in Chapter 7 that in the property-rights model, increases in μ_{mS} or reductions in ϵ_m actually tend to *increase* the relative efficiency of vertical integration. The presence of the selection into offshoring channel again complicates matters, because these same changes in the parameters also increase the relative efficiency of offshore outsourcing relative to domestic outsourcing, thereby leading to a decrease in the share of intrafirm trade on that account. Nevertheless, I would argue that evidence of a positive effect of input contractibility on the share of intrafirm trade or evidence of a negative effect of input specificity on this same share can be interpreted as supporting the property-rights model over the transaction-cost one.

Cross-Industry Tests: Data and Benchmark Results

Let us next turn to the empirical implementation of these tests. The general strategy I will follow here is very simple. I will attempt to find valid empirical proxies for the key parameters in Table 8.1 and see how they shape the share of intrafirm imports, as measured using the U.S. Related-Party Trade database. I will begin by using the raw six-digit NAICS dataset, which is available for

---

[5] To be precise, in Chapter 7, we encountered one violation of this result, under certain parameter values, when dealing with the extension with relationship specificity and generalized Nash bargaining.

TABLE 8.2 The Ten Industries with the Lowest and Highest Intrafirm Trade Shares

10 with Lowest Intrafirm Trade Shares		10 with Highest Intrafirm Trade Shares	
.012	Guided missile & space vehicle ma.	.794	Pharmaceutical preparation manuf.
.022	Motor home manuf.	.797	Computer storage device manuf.
.026	Manufactured mobile home manuf.	.799	Other aluminum rolling and drawing
.037	Rubber & plastics footwear manuf.	.805	Medicinal and botanical manuf.
.038	Other footwear manuf.	.807	Electronic capacitor manuf.
.039	Cut stone & stone product manuf.	.814	Asphalt shingle/coating materials ma.
.043	Canvas and related product mills	.844	Irradiation apparatus manuf.
.053	Infants' cut and sew apparel manuf.	.854	Photographic film & chemical manuf.
.053	Poultry processing	.945	Heavy-duty truck manuf.
.058	Women's footwear manuf.	.949	Automobile manuf.

Source: U.S. Census Related-Party Trade Dataset, 2000–11

390 manufacturing industries and 12 years. Although this should lead to a total of 4,680 observations, the volume of total U.S. imports is zero for 29 of those observations. Thus the share of intrafirm trade, defined as the ratio of related-party imports to the sum of related and non-related imports, is only available for 4,651 industry-year observations.[6] It would be more satisfactory to have a richer econometric model that jointly attempted to explain the existence of positive import volumes as well as their breakup into intrafirm and arm's-length imports, but I will not attempt to do so in this book. I do not think that this should be a huge matter of concern in regressions using industry-year level data, but I admit that it may be less immaterial in the specifications developed below which exploit the source-country variation in the U.S. Related-Party Trade database, which contains many observations with zero trade flows.

Before diving into the econometrics, the left panel of Table 8.2 reports the ten industries with the lowest average intrafirm import share Sh_{i-f} over the period 2000–11. The right panel of this same table lists the ten industries with the highest intrafirm import share over the same period. The set of industries in the right panel generally appear to involve more complex production

---

[6] As noted in Chapter 1, a very small share of the volume of imports is categorized as "nonreported." Defining the share of intrafirm imports as the ratio of related-party imports to total imports makes virtually no difference for the results presented in this chapter.

processes than those in the left panel, but there are important exceptions, such as the presence of "Guided missiles and space vehicles manufacturing" in the left panel or of "Asphalt shingle and coating materials manufacturing" in the right panel. Inspection of the table also raises the key concern that many of the sectors in the list appear to produce almost exclusively final goods. As in Chapter 5, we will work to refine our sample to restrict the analysis to imports of intermediate inputs.

Leaving these caveats aside for the time being, Table 8.3 presents a set of benchmark regressions in which the share of intrafirm imports is correlated with various industry-level variables. The specifications and variables used in the estimation are almost identical to those in Table 5.2 in Chapter 5, except that the dependent variable is now the intrafirm import share rather than the offshoring share.

The first three columns of Table 8.3 focus on the role of headquarter intensity in shaping intrafirm trade shares. I begin by proxying headquarter intensity with standard measures of R&D, skill, and physical capital intensity of U.S. manufacturing firms. These variables were discussed in Chapter 5 and interested readers can consult the Data Appendix for details. The use of physical capital intensity to proxy for headquarter intensity can be motivated by referring to my own work in Antràs (2003). Remember that in that framework, I assumed that the investments provided by headquarters were more physical-capital intensive than those provided by suppliers. Furthermore, I assumed that all investments were noncontractible and fully relationship-specific and thus the model generated a positive correlation between *unobservable* headquarter intensity and observable physical capital intensity. The assumptions needed to make that connection are strong, so I will work on relaxing them below.

The first column of Table 8.3 documents a positive correlation between the three benchmark measures of headquarter intensity and the share of intrafirm trade. R&D and physical capital intensity appear to be particularly important in shaping this share. Both of these coefficients are highly statistically significant and the magnitude of the coefficients is large. The table shows beta coefficients, and thus an increase of one standard deviation in R&D intensity or physical capital intensity increases the share of intrafirm trade by 0.385 or 0.274, respectively. The effect of skill intensity is significant at the 10 percent confidence level, but its magnitude is much smaller. In Antràs (2014), I provide scatter plots of the partial correlations between the share of intrafirm imports and each of these measures of headquarter intensity and demonstrate that they are not driven by a few outliers.

Early papers using intrafirm trade data to shed light on the empirical determinants of multinational firm boundaries have typically interpreted correlations of the type shown in column (1) as providing support for the property-rights theory. This interpretation is explicit, for instance, in Antràs

TABLE 8.3 Determinants of U.S. Intrafirm Trade Shares

Dep. Var. $\frac{Intrafirm\ Imp}{Total\ Imports}$	(1)	(2)	(3)	(4)	(5)	(6)
Log(R&D/Sales)	0.385**	0.361**	0.328**	0.301**	0.085**	0.337**
	(0.047)	(0.046)	(0.052)	(0.048)	(0.015)	(0.057)
Log(Skilled/Unskilled)	0.091$^+$	0.097*	0.192**	0.061	0.006	−0.146*
	(0.051)	(0.049)	(0.064)	(0.055)	(0.015)	(0.074)
Log(Capital/Labor)	0.274**					
	(0.042)					
Log(Capital Struct/Labor)		−0.256**	0.007	−0.253**	−0.060**	−0.126$^+$
		(0.076)	(0.069)	(0.078)	(0.023)	(0.074)
Log(Capital Equip/Labor)		0.529**		0.554**	0.106**	0.303**
		(0.073)		(0.076)	(0.022)	(0.082)
Log(Autos/Labor)			−0.250**			
			(0.050)			
Log(Computer/Labor)			−0.012			
			(0.049)			
Log(Other Eq./Labor)			0.290**			
			(0.066)			
Freight Costs				−0.173**	−0.104**	−0.076*
				(0.055)	(0.014)	(0.038)
Tariffs				0.007	−0.010*	−0.049
				(0.028)	(0.004)	(0.041)
Productivity Dispersion				−0.019	−0.013	−0.059
				(0.050)	(0.016)	(0.055)
Elasticity of Demand				0.036	−0.021$^+$	0.136$^+$
				(0.060)	(0.011)	(0.073)
Weighting	None	None	None	None	None	Imports
Fixed Effects	Year	Year	Year	Year	Ctr/Year	Ctr/Year
Observations	4,651	4,651	4,651	4,651	312,884	312,884
R-squared	0.312	0.343	0.344	0.369	0.170	0.585

Standard errors clustered at the industry level. $^+$, *, ** denote 10, 5, 1% significance.

(2003), Yeaple (2006), and Nunn and Trefler (2008). There are, however, various reasons why one should be cautious in interpreting the results in that manner. First, the statistical power of these tests is low; as mentioned before, these positive correlations are consistent with the property-rights theory but they are not necessarily inconsistent with alternative theories of firm boundaries, such as the transaction-cost theory. Second, U.S. physical capital, skill, and R&D intensity measures are imperfect proxies for headquarter intensity as they only capture imperfectly the relative importance of the non-contractible, relationship-specific investments carried out by headquarters and their suppliers. Nunn and Trefler (2013b) point out, for instance, that standard measures of capital intensity embody several investments that are fairly easy to contract on or that are not particularly relationship-specific. If the property-rights theory is correct, one would then expect investments in specialized equipment to be much more relevant for the integration decision than investments in structures or in non-specialized equipment (such as automobiles or computers), which tend to lose little value when not used in the intended production process.

In columns (2) and (3) of Table 8.3, I explore these ideas and confirm the empirical findings of Nunn and Trefler (2013b) when using disaggregated measures of capital intensity. More specifically, in column (2) of Table 8.3, I find that the positive effect of physical capital on the share of intrafirm trade is concentrated in equipment capital, while structures actually have a negative and significant effect on integration. A further decomposition using data from the Annual Survey of Manufactures (see the Data Appendix) reveals that the effect of equipment capital intensity is *not* driven by expenditures on computers and data processing equipment or on automobiles and trucks, which would be problematic for the theory. In fact, the effect of expenditures on automobiles and trucks appears to have a statistically significant *negative* effect on the share of intrafirm trade, a result that is tempting to map to the negative effect of higher headquarter service contractibility (or lower headquarter services relationship specificity) on the integration decision predicted by both the transaction-cost and property-rights models. The scatter plots provided in Antràs (2014) confirm again that these partial correlations are not driven by a handful of outliers.

The fourth column of Table 8.3 reverts back to the specification with capital equipment being a composite category but incorporates proxies for (i) freight costs and U.S. tariffs to capture trade frictions τ; (ii) a measure of within-industry productivity dispersion $1/\kappa$; and (iii) a proxy for the elasticity of demand σ. The sources of these variables are Peter Schott's website, the World Integrated Trade Solution (WITS) database, Nunn and Trefler (2008), and Broda and Weinstein (2006), respectively, as documented in Chapter 5 and the Data Appendix.[7] The reason for including these variables in our first set of results is that they are predicted to shape the share of intrafirm imports even in the Benchmark versions of the transaction-cost and property-rights models, featuring totally incomplete contracts, full relationship specificity, and bilateral contracting with a single supplier.

Of these four additional variables, only freight costs appear to have predictive power for the intrafirm trade share, but the sign of this dependence is the opposite of what the theories would predict. The selection into offshoring mechanism would tend to associate higher freight costs with fewer firms offshoring and higher intrafirm import shares, yet the coefficient on this variable is negative, highly significant, and sizable in economic terms.

---

[7] As in the case of Chapter 5, the entire dataset and Stata program codes used in the empirical analysis in this chapter are available for download at http://scholar.harvard.edu/antras/books.

Coupled with the negative (though statistically insignificant) effect of productivity dispersion, this result casts doubt on the empirical validity of the sorting pattern underlying the models of multinational firm boundaries developed in Chapters 6 and 7. We will return to this issue toward the end of the chapter, when discussing studies using firm-level data on intrafirm versus arm's-length global sourcing decisions of firms.

Columns (5) and (6) of Table 8.3 exploit the full cross-sectoral *and* cross-country variation of the intrafirm import data. I first compute sectoral intrafirm trade shares at the exporter-country level, by computing the ratio of related-party imports to the sum of related- and non-related-party imports from a particular country *j*. By including source-country-year fixed effects into the regressions, I continue to exploit purely cross-product variation, but this specification better isolates the effect of sectoral-level characteristics by controlling for unobservable country characteristics that might shape both the types of products the U.S. imports from those countries as well as whether those transactions are internalized or not. Because at the country-industry level there are many more observations with zero import volumes than in the purely cross-sectoral data, the number of observations in columns (5) and (6) falls very short of the potential 1,085,760 observations corresponding to 390 sectors, 232 countries, and 12 years of data. In particular, only 312,884 of those observations feature positive imports for the sum of related and non-related import values. This number is extremely close to the number of observations in column (6) of Table 5.2 in which we restricted the sample of offshoring shares to those featuring a positive value, with the small discrepancy being explained by a few observations in which only import flows with non-reported relatedness are positive.

The only difference between columns (5) and (6) is that in the latter column I follow Antràs and Chor (2013) in weighting each data point by the value of total imports for that industry-country-year. This is motivated by possible measurement error introduced into the intrafirm trade share by the presence of trade flows whose related-party status was not reported to the U.S. Census Bureau, an issue of particular concern for observations with small trade volumes. Indeed, the raw correlation between the share of "unreported" trade and the log of total imports is negative and very large (−0.52). Notice also that the weighted regression features a substantially higher R-squared (0.585) than the unweighted one (0.170).

The qualitative nature of the results in columns (5) and (6) is similar to that in the regressions with the aggregated cross-industry data. High levels of R&D and equipment capital intensity continue to be associated with significantly higher intrafirm trade shares, though the effects are quantitatively smaller when not weighting the observations in column (5). The troublesome negative effect of freight costs on the intrafirm trade share also appears to be robust to the use of the country-level related-party information, though its statistical significance is greatly reduced by weighting observations by import volumes. Furthermore, in column (5) I now also find that U.S. tariffs have a statistically negative effect on intrafirm trade shares, though this effect is no longer significant in the weighted regression in column (6).[8] Finally, the effect of skill intensity appears significantly negative in column (6), suggesting perhaps that this variable is not an appropriate proxy for headquarter intensity.

Cross-Industry Tests: Refined Benchmark Tests

As pointed out in Chapter 5 and again earlier in this chapter, there exist at least six serious limitations associated with using U.S. import data to construct a measure of the relative propensity to integrate foreign suppliers. Earlier, I elaborated on the first, fifth, and sixth concerns, so I can now focus on the second, third, and fourth ones. Fortunately, there is a close parallel in the way that I address these concerns here and how I dealt with them in Chapter 5, so I can swiftly work through them.

Remember that our second concern with product-level U.S. import data is that they do not identify the industry or sector purchasing the imported goods. Consistent with the bulk of the literature, the industry-level controls in Table 8.2 corresponded to data on the industry of the product being imported. This seems justified when studying the effect of freight costs and tariffs, but it is clearly invalid when exploring the role of the final-good producer's elasticity of demand σ. Furthermore, using this approach when constructing measures of headquarter intensity is only consistent with models of multinational firm boundaries under restrictive assumptions.[9] As argued in Chapter 5, a more satisfactory approach is to construct measures of headquarter intensity and demand elasticities of the average industry *buying* those inputs using information from Input-Output tables, as first proposed by Antràs and Chor (2013). Although one could similarly advocate the construction of a buyer version of our productivity dispersion measure, I have argued in Chapter 5 that this methodology cannot be suitably applied to measures of dispersion.

As in Chapter 5, building buyer versions of some variables leads me to switch from the NAICS six-digit industry classification (at which the raw data

---

[8] It should be noted that this result contrasts with that obtained by Díez (2014), who using similar data instead finds a positive association between the prevalence of intrafirm trade and U.S. tariffs. He also finds a negative correlation between U.S. intrafirm imports and foreign tariffs and shows that it can be reconciled with a variant of the Antràs and Helpman (2004) framework.

[9] For the case of capital intensity, it can be justified in Antràs's (2003) framework due to the unrealistic assumption that factors of production are internationally immobile so the headquarter's capital investments are undertaken in the location of the supplier division or firm and embodied in the imported good.

are reported) to 2002 Input-Output industry codes (IO2002). The number of sectors in the sample is thus reduced to 253 for a total of 3,036 observations. Column (1) of Table 8.4 reports results analogous to those in column (4) of Table 8.3, but with the IO2002 classification instead of NAICS classification. The change in industry classification leads to relatively small changes in the qualitative and even quantitative nature of the results. Relative to column (4) in Table 8.3, skill intensity now has a positive and significant effect on the intrafirm import share, while the effect of capital structures now appears to be positive (when before it was negative). Still, as the next few specifications will demonstrate, these two effects are not robust to further refinements of the sample. A more robust result that is already visible in column (1) of Table 8.4 is the fact that not only freight costs but also U.S. tariffs now appear to be significantly negatively correlated with the intrafirm trade share.

Buyer versions of the elasticity of demand and of the proxies for headquarter intensity are introduced in column (2) of Table 8.4. There are three main consequences of this change in these independent variables. First, the positive effects of skill intensity and capital structures disappears, consistently with our NAICS results in Table 8.3. Second, the magnitude of the positive coefficients on R&D and capital equipment intensity increases markedly. Third, the positive effects of productivity dispersion and of the elasticity of demand become significant at standard confidence levels. Both of these effects are consistent with the predictions of both the transaction-cost and property-rights models, though as mentioned before, these theories do not ensure an unambiguously positive effect of the elasticity of demand.

In column (3) of Table 8.4 I tackle what I earlier identified to be the third limitation of U.S. product-level import data, namely the fact that it conflates intermediate input and finished goods imports. Although the models developed above are not inconsistent with headquarters importing fully assembled goods from abroad, it is important to attempt to purge finished products from the data for at least two reasons. First, the models developed in this book emphasize input transactions and thus, at the very least, one should check that the results continue to hold when focusing on those type of transactions. Second, I would guess that a significant share of finished goods entering the United States are imported by wholesalers and retailers, and these types of firms are not represented in the industry-level manufacturing database that I am using to construct the buyer versions of headquarter intensity and the elasticity of demand.

As in Chapter 5, I adopt the methodology developed by Wright (2014) in order to attempt to isolate intrafirm and arm's-length imports of intermediate inputs. This methodology was briefly discussed in Chapter 5 and it is reviewed in detail in the Data Appendix, so I will not elaborate on it here. I will simply note that this correction lead us to drop thirty-nine industries that exclusively produce final goods, but it also modifies different sectors

TABLE 8.4 Refined Determinants of U.S. Intrafirm Trade Shares

Dep. Var. $\frac{Intrafirm\ Imp}{Total\ Imports}$	(1)	(2)	(3)	(4)	(5)	(6)
Log(R&D/Sales)	0.164**	0.222**	0.240**	0.251**	0.052**	0.246**
	(0.058)	(0.064)	(0.072)	(0.072)	(0.017)	(0.068)
Log(Skilled/Unskilled)	0.174*	0.009	0.036	0.025	−0.031	−0.182
	(0.072)	(0.081)	(0.082)	(0.082)	(0.023)	(0.113)
Log(Capital Struct/Labor)	0.199**	−0.105	−0.027	−0.031	−0.013	−0.032
	(0.066)	(0.105)	(0.121)	(0.121)	(0.038)	(0.089)
Log(Capital Equip/Labor)	0.144**	0.392**	0.232*	0.235*	0.071*	0.149⁺
	(0.046)	(0.099)	(0.117)	(0.118)	(0.032)	(0.077)
Seller Freight Costs	−0.231**	−0.221**	−0.254**	−0.240**	−0.131**	−0.081
	(0.069)	(0.075)	(0.089)	(0.087)	(0.020)	(0.068)
Seller Tariffs	−0.076*	−0.070**	−0.104**	−0.102**	−0.022**	−0.079⁺
	(0.031)	(0.025)	(0.021)	(0.021)	(0.006)	(0.044)
Seller Dispersion	0.039	0.120⁺	0.043	0.046	0.035⁺	0.060
	(0.077)	(0.073)	(0.081)	(0.082)	(0.018)	(0.038)
Elasticity of Demand	0.105	0.163*	0.186*	0.184*	−0.011	0.085**
	(0.078)	(0.065)	(0.080)	(0.081)	(0.011)	(0.025)
Sample Restrictions	None	None	W	W+NT	W+NT	W+NT
Weighting	None	None	None	None	None	Imports
Fixed Effects	Year	Year	Year	Year	Ctr/Year	Ctr/Year
Buyer vs. Seller Controls	Seller	Buyer	Buyer	Buyer	Buyer	Buyer
Observations	3,036	3,036	2,480	2,478	148,947	148,947
R-squared	0.348	0.359	0.322	0.313	0.194	0.526

Standard errors clustered at the industry level. ⁺, *, ** denote 10, 5, 1% significance.

differentially because the discount factor applied to the data is constructed starting with highly disaggregated (i.e., HS ten-digit) product and country-level import data. The intrafirm import share will be reduced in sectors in which, relative to arm's-length imports, related-party imports originate from countries that tend to export finished goods to the United States, as deduced from the disaggregated product-level data. In practice, however, these smooth adjustments are small and the correlation between the Wright-adjusted intrafirm trade shares and the raw ones is very high (0.919). Hence, the largest effect of the Wright adjustment on the intrafirm trade shares used in the regressions stems from dropping the thirty-nine industries from the sample.[10] Comparing columns (2) and (3) of Table 8.4, it is clear, however, that this sample correction only has a minor effect on the estimates, with the main result being that the effect of productivity ceases to be statistically significant at standard confidence levels.

[10] The number of observations in column (3) drops by more than $39 \times 12 = 468$ because for 88 additional industry-year observations, the Wright adjustments sets *total* intermediate input imports to zero.

TABLE 8.5 The Ten Input Industries with the Lowest and Highest *Corrected* Intrafirm Trade Shares

10 with Lowest Intrafirm Trade Shares		10 with Highest Intrafirm Trade Shares	
.019	Footwear manufacturing	.734	Tire manufacturing
.047	Cut stone and stone product manuf.	.737	Travel trailer and camper manuf.
.058	Other leather manufacturing	.750	Electro-medical & -therapeutic appl. ma.
.063	Primary smelting/refining copper ma.	.765	Pharmaceutical preparation manuf.
.066	Institutional furniture manuf.	.797	Computer storage device manuf.
.078	Prefabricated wood building manuf.	.800	Automobile manufacturing
.080	Fiber, yarn, and thread mills manuf.	.809	Lighting fixture manufacturing
.084	Household & institutional furniture man.	.832	Asphalt shingle/coating materials manuf.
.094	Seafood product preparation	.845	Irradiation apparatus manuf.
.112	Paper bag & treated paper manuf.	.901	Heavy duty truck manuf.

Source: U.S. Census Related-Party Dataset plus a sample adjustment based on Wright (2014)

The fourth concern we raised regarding the use of the U.S. Related-Party database was that it did not distinguish between trade within U.S. multinationals (which might map better to backwards integration) and trade within foreign multinationals operating in the United States (which perhaps better reflects forward integration). With that in mind, in column (4) of Table 8.4, I follow Nunn and Trefler (2013b) in checking the robustness of the results to a restricted sample that better fits the spirit of our global sourcing model. In particular, I drop from the sample those U.S. imports originating from five countries (Iceland, Italy, Finland, Liechtenstein, and Switzerland) for which shipments from foreign headquarters to their U.S. affiliates are likely to be predominant, relative to shipments to U.S. parents from their foreign affiliates in those countries. More details on how these countries are identified and on robustness to alternative sets of dropped countries are available in Chapter 5 and in the Data Appendix. The results of implementing this sample restriction are shown in column (4) of Table 8.4, and it is evident that the impact on the estimates is very modest.

Although the Wright and Nunn-Trefler sample corrections have not produced a sizeable impact on the estimated coefficients, I still view these adjustments to be worth performing given the nature of the models that are being taken to the data. Furthermore, in order to illustrate their significance, in Table 8.5 I report the ten sectors with the lowest and highest

Wright- and Nunn-Trefler-corrected intrafirm import shares averaged over the period 2000–11. Comparing these rankings with those in Table 8.2, it is encouraging to see that some of the problematic sectors in Table 5.1 (such as "Guided missiles and space vehicles manufacturing") are no longer listed. It is also interesting to note that these adjustments have a nontrivial effect on certain intrafirm import shares, such as the case of the "Automobile manufacturing" sector, whose intrafirm import share drops from 0.949 to 0.800.

In the last two columns of Table 8.4, I exploit the full variation of the intrafirm trade data across both products and countries, while applying the Wright and Nunn-Trefler corrections to trade flows. The specifications include country-year fixed effects, so the variation being exploited is again cross-sectoral, but I am now controlling for time-varying unobserved country characteristics. Columns (5) and (6) only differ in that, in the latter specification, I weight observation by the total volume of U.S. imports to alleviate measurement error concerns. This last set of estimates in column (6) is broadly consistent, both qualitatively as well as quantitatively, with the aggregated cross-industry specification in column (4). An important difference is that the magnitude of the negative effect of the two trade costs variables is greatly reduced, and the coefficient on freight costs in particular is no longer significant. Similarly, the effect of productivity dispersion is positive but is only significant at the 12 percent level.

Cross-Industry Tests: The Role of Contracting

So far, I have focused on an empirical analysis of the predictions of the Benchmark transaction-cost and property-rights models developed in Chapters 6 and 7. The robust positive effect of R&D and equipment capital intensity we have documented is often interpreted as providing support for the property-rights model, since η is a key determinant of the optimal allocation of ownership rights in that model. Still, when working with product-level data that aggregates the individual decisions of firms, the share of intrafirm imports is also shaped by the selection into offshoring effect, which in both types of models tends to generate a positive correlation between intrafirm import shares and measures of headquarter intensity.

I will next explore more elaborate tests that exploit some of the novel predictions that emerged when studying the various extensions of these benchmark models. More specifically, in the next two tables, I will build on the insights in Chapters 6 and 7—and summarized in Table 8.1— and incorporate into the specifications in Table 8.4 proxies for financial constraints (ϕ), contractibility (μ_{hS}, μ_{mS}), relationship specificity (ϵ_h, ϵ_m), input substitutability ρ, and downstreamness.

TABLE 8.6 Contractual Determinants of U.S. Intrafirm Trade Shares

Dep. Var. $\frac{IntrafirmImp}{TotalImports}$	(1)	(2)	(3)	(4)	(5)	(6)
Financial Dependence	0.186*	0.028	0.206**	0.182*	0.029	0.196**
	(0.087)	(0.019)	(0.045)	(0.088)	(0.019)	(0.041)
Asset Tangibility	−0.124	−0.015	−0.256**			
	(0.078)	(0.019)	(0.062)			
Nunn Contractibility	−0.084	−0.012	−0.166*	−0.073	0.000	−0.121⁺
	(0.070)	(0.019)	(0.070)	(0.076)	(0.021)	(0.073)
Levchenko Contractibility	−0.124⁺	−0.054**	−0.176**			
	(0.073)	(0.019)	(0.055)			
Costinot Contractibility	−0.131⁺	−0.001	−0.131*			
	(0.071)	(0.018)	(0.063)			
BJRS Contractibility	−0.191*	−0.056**	−0.085⁺			
	(0.078)	(0.021)	(0.046)			
Specificity	0.044	0.020	0.180*	0.006	0.017	0.055
	(0.070)	(0.019)	(0.074)	(0.074)	(0.021)	(0.067)
Input Substitutability	−0.014	−0.016	−0.078⁺	−0.000	−0.014	−0.014
	(0.042)	(0.017)	(0.047)	(0.043)	(0.017)	(0.028)
Sample Restrictions	W+NT	W+NT	W+NT	W+NT	W+NT	W+NT
Fixed Effects	Year	Ctr/Year	Ctr/Year	Year	Ctr/Year	Ctr/Year
Weighting	None	None	Imports	None	None	Imports
Observations	2,478	148,947	148,947	2,478	148,947	148,947
R-squared	≃0.322	≃0.194	≃0.548	0.336	0.195	0.582

Standard errors clustered at the industry level. ⁺, *, ** denote 10, 5, 1% significance.

As a first step, in Table 8.6, I present results of specifications analogous to those in Table 8.4, but that include eight new regressors: two proxies for the importance of financial constraints in a given sector, four related to the degree of contractibility, one measure capturing the relationship specificity of investments, and a final one related to the degree of input substitutability in production. These variables are the same ones included in Table 5.6 of Chapter 5, so I refer the reader to that chapter (and to the Data Appendix) for a discussion of the underlying sources. All of these variables are constructed based solely on information of the product being imported into the United States, so the proxies for contractibility and relationship specificity are more closely related to the parameters μ_{mS} and ϵ_m, respectively, than to μ_{hS} and ϵ_h.

In the first three columns of Table 8.6, I report the results of introducing these eight variables *one at a time* into the Wright- and Nunn-Trefler-corrected regressions in columns (4), (5), and (6) of Table 8.4. Although eight coefficients appear on each column, it should be understood that these coefficients are obtained by running eight separate regressions. To save space, I do not report the coefficients on the variables already included in Table 8.4, but these coefficients are only modestly affected by the inclusion of these eight new variables.[11]

These first three columns of the table provide broad support for the notion that larger financial frictions (i.e., higher financial dependence or lower asset tangibility) are associated with higher intrafirm trade shares, with the size and statistical significance of these results being particularly high when exploiting the cross-country dimension of the data while weighting observations by total import volumes. Similarly, all four measures of product contractibility are negatively associated with the extent to which foreign input purchases are internalized, and again the magnitude and statistical significance of these effects is highest when introducing these measures into our preferred weighted specification with country-industry-year data. Finally, the evidence points toward a positive effect of specificity and a negative effect of input substitutability on intrafirm import shares, though these coefficients are generally insignificant except for the case of our preferred specification in column (3).

In the last three columns of Table 8.6, I run regressions analogous to those in columns (1), (2), and (3), but in which a single proxy for financial constraints, a single proxy for contractibility, and the proxies for specificity and input substitutability are all included *in the same* specification. As in Table 5.6 of Chapter 5, in those columns I select Rajan and Zingales's financial dependence measure and Nunn's measure of contractibility because they are particularly popular in the literature. As is clear from the table, the simultaneous inclusion of these variables reduces the impact of each of them individually, but the sign of these effects is the same as in columns (1), (2), and (3), and the effects of financial dependence and Nunn contractibility continue to be statistically significant in the final preferred specification in column (6).

If one refers back to Table 8.1, one will quickly verify that the signs of the coefficients in Table 8.6 exactly correspond to the predictions of the transaction-cost model. We cannot, however, invoke these results to discard the property-rights model because, if the selection into offshoring effect is powerful enough, these same patterns could be generated by that model (see Table 8.1).

Discriminating between Models

Is there then any hope in discriminating between the property-rights and transaction-cost theories of multinational firm boundaries? In Table 8.7,

---

[11] The whole set of regression coefficients can be obtained by accessing the data and programs available online at http://scholar.harvard.edu/antras/books.

TABLE 8.7 Further Contractual Determinants of U.S. Intrafirm Trade Shares

Dep. Var. $\frac{IntrafirmImp}{TotalImports}$	(1)	(2)	(3)	(4)	(5)	(6)
Downstreamness x High σ	0.291⁺	0.330**	0.296⁺	0.344**	0.291*	0.321**
	(0.150)	(0.060)	(0.150)	(0.058)	(0.148)	(0.052)
Downstreamness x Low σ	−0.159	0.099	−0.155	0.100	−0.165	0.040
	(0.138)	(0.078)	(0.139)	(0.077)	(0.137)	(0.074)
Seller Nunn Contractibility	−0.059	−0.026	−0.027	0.138	−0.046	0.033
	(0.068)	(0.057)	(0.092)	(0.085)	(0.070)	(0.053)
Buyer Nunn Contractibility			−0.051	-0.185*		
			(0.096)	(0.075)		
Seller Nunn Specificity	−0.015	−0.011	−0.028	−0.038	−0.090	-0.176**
	(0.078)	(0.061)	(0.083)	(0.064)	(0.092)	(0.068)
Buyer Nunn Specificity					0.124	0.284**
					(0.116)	(0.060)
Sample Restrictions	W+NT	W+NT	W+NT	W+NT	W+NT	W+NT
Fixed Effects	Year	Ctr/Year	Year	Ctr/Year	Year	Ctr/Year
Weighting	None	Imports	None	Imports	None	Imports
Observations	2,478	148,947	2,478	148,947	2,478	148,947
R-squared	0.357	0.614	0.358	0.620	0.362	0.632

Standard errors clustered at the industry level. ⁺, *, ** denote 10, 5, 1% significance.

I experiment with two alternative ways to do so. First, I exploit the rich but diametrically opposite implications of both models for the effect of downstreamness on the integration decision. As readers may recall, we showed in Chapter 6 that, in the transaction-cost model, downstreamness had a negative effect on integration whenever inputs are sequential complements, while it had a positive effect on integration when inputs are sequential substitutes. Instead, in the property-rights model of Chapter 7, the opposite is true: downstreamness has a positive effect on integration in the sequential complements case, while it has a negative effect on integration in the sequential substitutes case.

Which of these two predictions is most consistent with available data? In order to answer this question, one needs to first take a stance on (i) how to measure downstreamness, and (ii) how to proxy for whether the integration decision corresponds to the sequential complements or sequential substitutes case. In the first two columns of Table 8.7, I make progress on these fronts by building on the approach in Antràs and Chor (2013). First, they define the downstreamness of the product being imported into the United States as a weighted index of the average position in the value chain at which an industry's output is used (i.e., as final consumption, as direct input to other industries, as direct input to industries serving as direct inputs to other industries, and so on), with the weights being given by the ratio of the use of that industry's output in that position relative to the total output of that industry.[12] Second, in order to distinguish between the cases of sequential complements and substitutes, they use the U.S. import demand elasticities estimated by Broda and Weinstein (2006) and data on U.S. Input-Output Tables to compute a weighted average of the demand elasticity faced by the *average* buyer of the product being imported into the United States. The idea is that for sufficiently high values of this average demand elasticity, one can be relatively confident that input substitutability is lower than the demand elasticity, with the converse being true for sufficiently low values of this average demand elasticity.

In column (1) of Table 8.7, I include two interactions of downstreamness with dummy variables for high and low σ sectors into the cross-industry specification of column (4) of Table 8.6. The "High-σ" dummy variable takes a value of 1 if the average buying industry of the imported product sector features a Broda-Weinstein demand elasticity above the median one in the sample, while the "Low-σ" dummy variable takes a value of 1 when a product's average buyer demand elasticity is below the median one. In column (2) of Table 8.7, I add these same interactions to the weighted specification with cross-country and cross-industry specification in column (6) of Table 8.6.[13] As is clear from the results in these two tables, there is robust evidence of a differentially more positive effect of downstreamness on integration in high-σ sectors (i.e., in the complements case) than in low-σ sectors. This is consistent with the property-rights model, but inconsistent with the transaction-cost model. In fact, in column (1), the signs of these coefficients are exactly as predicted by the property-rights model and opposite to those implied by the transaction-cost model, though the coefficient on the second interaction is not statistically different from zero.

Antràs and Chor (2013) show that this differential positive effect of downstreamness on integration in high-σ sectors is robust to alternative measures of downstreamness and various specifications. Furthermore, when looking at the effect for different quintiles of the distribution of σ, the positive effect is consistently concentrated in the highest quintiles of σ, while the effect is often negative in the lowest quintiles of σ. The differential effect is also apparent even without controlling for other factors, as illustrated in Figure 8.1. In the figure, for the subset of industries with above-median average buyer demand elasticities (labeled as "Complements"), the average 2005 U.S. intrafirm import share increases as we move from the lowest tercile of *DownMeasure* to the highest. When considering those industries facing

---

[12] This measure was developed independently by Fally (2012), and its properties were further studied in Antràs, Chor, Fally, and Hillberry (2012). More details on this measure are available in the Data Appendix.

[13] In both columns, I also add a dummy variable for whether the average buying industry σ is above the median one, to be able to better interpret the interaction coefficients.

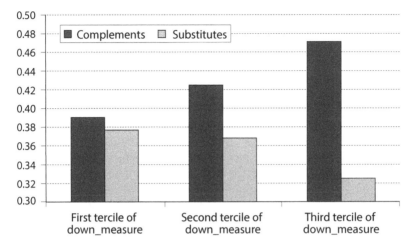

Figure 8.1 Downstreamness and the Share of Intrafirm Trade

below-median average buyer demand elasticities (labeled as "Substitutes"), the pattern is exactly reversed, with the intrafirm import share steadily declining across terciles of downstreamness. These patterns exactly line up with those predicted by the property-rights model of global sourcing, while they contradict those predicted by the transaction-cost model.

A second promising way to discriminate between the property-rights theory and the transaction-cost one consists of exploiting the implications of these theories for the effect of contractibility and relationship specificity on the share of intrafirm trade. Remember, in particular, that in the property-rights model, the effect of these variables on the prevalence of integration depends crucially on the extent to which contractual incompleteness stems from noncontractibilities or specificities in the inputs controlled by the final-good producer or by his or her suppliers. If production processes in certain sectors are particularly noncontractible or feature high specificities because of the nature of the investments carried out by headquarters, then the theory would predict that the share of intrafirm trade should be negatively affected by the level of these sectors' contractibility and positively affected by specificity. Conversely, if the source of noncontractibilities or specificity stem from the nature of the supplier's activities, the theory may instead predict a positive correlation between the share of intrafirm trade and contractibility and a negative correlation with specificity.[14] The latter results would be hard to reconcile with transaction-cost theories of multinational firm boundaries.

---

[14] The qualifier "may" in the previous sentence is necessary because via the selection into offshoring mechanism, improvements in manufacturing input contractibility may reduce the share of intrafirm trade on that account.

Although the property-rights theory generates sharp predictions for how the source of noncontractibilities or specificity affects the share of intrafirm trade, a natural challenge for empirical work is finding appropriate proxies for these different types of noncontractibilities and specificity. In the last four columns of Table 8.7, I experiment with a simple approach to attempt to separate those effects. In particular, I argued above that because the Nunn measure of contractibility is based solely on the product being imported, it seems natural to relate it to the parameters μ_{mS} in the model. In columns (3) and (4), I add a measure of the contractibility of the average sector buying the good entering the United States (as inferred from Input-Output tables) to the specifications in columns (1) and (2), respectively. I interpret that average buyer contractibility as reflecting the contractibility of headquarter services, i.e., the parameter μ_{hS}. Adding this variable to the cross-industry specification in column (1) of Table 8.7 has little effect on the estimates, but when doing the same to our preferred weighted specification in column (2), notice that the sign of the coefficient on seller contractibility (i.e., μ_{mS}) becomes positive and is very close to being significant at the 10 percent level, while the sign of the coefficient on buyer contractibility (i.e., μ_{hS}) is negative and significant at the 5 percent level. These patterns are precisely those predicted by the property-rights model.

In columns (5) and (6), I repeat the same exercise, but this time focusing on our measure of specificity. The results in this case are even more supportive of the property-rights model. Buyer and seller specificity shape the intrafirm trade share in opposite directions in both specifications. Buyer specificity is positively associated with integration, but the opposite is true for the case of seller specificity, a result that is not easily reconcilable with transaction-cost models, but that is predicted by the property-rights theory (at least under a wide range of parameter values). Furthermore, in our preferred weighted regression in column (6), both coefficients are highly statistically significant.

Limitations and Alternative Approaches

The empirical results presented so far in this chapter are broadly supportive of some of the key features of the internalization models presented in Chapters 6 and 7. The property-rights model, in particular, seems to fare especially well in the data. We have found robust evidence of a positive effect of headquarter intensity on the share of intrafirm trade, particularly when attempting to isolate the relative intensity of the noncontractible and relationship-specific investments carried out by suppliers. Furthermore, the evidence also points to a positive effect of productivity dispersion and financial constraints on the integration decision, and to a negative effect of input substitutability on this share, although the statistical significance of these effects has generally been found to be weaker. Finally, the differential effect of downstreamness on high-versus low-σ sectors, as well as the contrasting role of buyer versus seller measures of contractibility and relationship specificity on the integration decision, have provided sharper evidence permitting a discrimination between the property-rights and transaction-cost theories.

As encouraging as these results might appear to be for the property-rights theory, there are various reasons for taking them with a grain of salt. At a broad level, it is clear that the independent variables used in the empirical analysis are only imperfect proxies for the key primitive parameters shaping the internalization decisions of firms in the models. For instance, the results in columns (4) and (6) are highly suggestive of the opposite effects of μ_{hS} and μ_{mS} and of ϵ_h and ϵ_m on the integration decision, but they fall short of tightly identifying those effects. A specific reason to treat these results on contractibility with caution is that the buyer and seller versions of the contractibility and specificity variables are highly correlated with each other; the correlation between the buyer and seller (Nunn) contractibility and specificity measures are 0.834 and 0.814, respectively.[15]

A second reason to remain skeptical about the empirical validity of the property-rights model is the fact that we have found fairly robust evidence of some effects that run counter to some of the key predictions of the model, at least in their benchmark versions. Most notably, freight costs and U.S. tariffs appear to be negatively correlated with intrafirm import shares, with these effects being statistically significant at standard confidence levels, except in our weighted specifications exploiting both the cross-country and cross-industry data (consistently with the results reported in Table 8.4). Remember that this negative effect of trade barriers is inconsistent with the predictions of both models, at least under the derived equilibrium sorting pattern of firms by productivity into organizational forms. A key question, however, is whether this equilibrium sorting pattern is consistent with available firm-level evidence. I will return to this issue below.

A third concern with the tests performed so far is that, even if one is persuaded with the way I have proxied for the key parameters in the models, it would be hard to claim that these tests convincingly *identify* the role of these parameters in shaping the internalization decisions of firms. One might worry, for instance, that I have omitted certain sectoral characteristics that are crucial for integration and that may be correlated with the industry variables included in the regressions above. Readers might recall that, in Chapter 5, I alluded to a similar reasoning when justifying the poor performance of contractual variables in explaining the cross-sectional variation in

---

[15] This is due in turn to the disproportionate weight of the diagonal (within-industry) elements in the Input-Output tables.

offshoring shares. This in turn led me to explore alternative approaches that exploited the idea that industry characteristics should have a differential effect on the propensity of firms to offshore from particular countries, depending on characteristics of these countries.

I will next apply a similar strategy to regressions explaining the intrafirm trade share, but before doing so it is important to emphasize two points. First, although I remain worried about omitted variable biases, I believe that this concern is greatly reduced in regressions explaining the intrafirm import share relative to regressions explaining offshoring shares. The reason for this is that it is much easier to envision omitted factors that shape differentially domestic versus foreign input purchases than omitted factors that are relevant for the relative propensity to import inputs from abroad within or across firm boundaries. To substantiate that claim, simply notice that the R-squared obtained in the cross-industry regressions in Table 8.6 or 8.7 are more than twice as large as those obtained in the analogous Table 5.6 in Chapter 5. Similarly, the R-squared of the weighted regressions using cross-industry and cross-country data are very large (reaching 0.632 in column (6) of Table 8.7) and are more than three times as large as the highest R-squared in the offshoring share regressions in Table 5.6.

A second point worth highlighting is that, as I will soon review, the property-rights model of Chapter 7 does not offer particularly sharp predictions for how the interaction of country and industry characteristics should shape intrafirm trade shares. Hence, although exploring alternative strategies is worthwhile, it is less clear in the current context that they will be as useful as they were in Chapter 5 in empirically validating or rejecting the theoretical models developed in this book.

As in the case of Chapter 5, before turning to these richer tests, I briefly describe how to extend the transaction-cost and property-rights models to a multi-country environment in order to provide a semi-structural interpretation of the tests to be performed below.

Internalization Theories in a Multi-Country World

Let us then return to the multi-country framework first introduced toward the end of Chapter 2 and further expanded to include contractual frictions in Chapter 5. As in the analysis in Chapter 5, I simplify matters by focusing on a version of the model in which each final-good producer procures only one input (as in the two-country model) and in which the firm-level extensive margin of offshoring is not operative.

Remember that in our multi-country global sourcing model, final-good producers learned the productivity with which they could source inputs from any given country $j \in \mathcal{J}$ only after paying the fixed cost f_{ij} of sourcing from that country j. I then defined the global sourcing strategy $\mathcal{J}_i(\varphi) \subseteq \mathcal{J}$ of a firm with productivity φ as the set of countries in which a firm from country i with productivity φ had paid the associated fixed costs of offshoring f_{ij}. A simple way to extend the framework to incorporate a choice between intrafirm and arm's-length sourcing is to redefine the global sourcing strategy as choosing a set $\tilde{\mathcal{J}}_i(\varphi) \subseteq \mathcal{J} \times K$, where $K = \{V, O\}$ is an indicator function capturing whether input provision is vertically integrated (V) or outsourced (O). Simply stated, the firm not only decides whether or not to invest in being able to source from any country $j \in \mathcal{J}$, but also chooses whether its intermediate input purchases should come from an integrated affiliate in j, from an arm's-length supplier in j, or from both of them. In a general version of the model, the fixed costs associated with these different options would be allowed to vary and a natural counterpart of our assumption in the two-country model would be to assume that $f_{ijV} > f_{ijO}$. This would lead relatively larger firms to be more likely to select into intrafirm trade, and might also explain (when allowing for multiple inputs) why firms often buy inputs from foreign countries both within and across firm boundaries.

As mentioned before, however, I will simplify matters by shutting down these selection effects and assume that the fixed costs of sourcing f_{ijV} and f_{ijO} are small enough such that all firms from i find it profitable to incur these costs and draw a productivity parameter $1/a_{mjk}$ from each country $j \in \mathcal{J}$ and for each organizational form $k \in \{V, O\}$. I will further assume that although the values of $1/a_{mjV}$ and $1/a_{mjO}$ are firm-specific, they are drawn *independently* from each other (and also independently from the draws in other countries) from a Fréchet distribution:

$$Pr(a_{mj} \geq a) = e^{-T_j a^\theta}, \quad \text{with } T_j > 0 \text{ and } \theta > \sigma - 1.$$

These are obviously strong and unrealistic assumptions, but attempting to relax them here would lead me too far astray.

Given this setup, it is then a simple matter to follow closely the steps in Chapter 5 to verify that the share of all intermediate inputs purchased by firms in i that originate from country $j \in \mathcal{J}$ and are transacted under the ownership structure $k \in \{V, O\}$ is given by

$$\chi_{ijk} = \frac{T_j \left(\tau_{ij} w_j \Psi_{ijk}^{1/(1-\eta)(1-\sigma)} \right)^{-\theta}}{\sum_{l \in \mathcal{J}} \sum_{k' \in \{V, O\}} T_l \left(\tau_{il} w_l \Psi_{ilk'}^{1/(1-\eta)(1-\sigma)} \right)^{-\theta}} \quad \text{for } j \in \mathcal{J} \text{ and } k \in \{V, O\}$$

where Ψ_{ijk} summarizes the transaction-cost efficiency of sourcing from j under organizational form k. The value of Ψ_{ijk} under outsourcing, i.e., Ψ_{ijO}, captures the contractual efficiency with which firms from i can outsource from country j. In our simpler two-country model, this corresponds to the terms Γ_{DO} and Γ_{OO} for domestic and offshore outsourcing in both the property-rights and transaction-cost models. On the other hand, the determination of Ψ_{ijV} is distinct in the two models. In the transaction-cost model, we simply have $\Psi_{ijV} = \lambda^{1-\sigma}$, where $\lambda > 1$ captures the governance costs of running an integrated structure. This parameter λ could easily be allowed to vary across country-pairs. In the property-rights model, Ψ_{ijV} corresponds to the contractual efficiency of vertical integration, which in the two-country model we denoted by Γ_{DV} and Γ_{OV} in domestic and offshore sourcing relationships.

With our additional recurring assumption that, regardless of ownership structure, input purchases are priced such that they constitute the same multiple of operating profits in all countries and under all organizational forms, we can then conclude that when looking at the intermediate input imports from any country j, the share of those imports that is transacted within firm boundaries is simply given by

$$Sh_{i-f} = \frac{\left(\Psi_{ijV}/\Psi_{ijO}\right)^{\theta/(1-\eta)(\sigma-1)}}{1 + \left(\Psi_{ijV}/\Psi_{ijO}\right)^{\theta/(1-\eta)(\sigma-1)}}. \tag{8.4}$$

Hence, the share of intrafirm imports at the origin-country level is crucially shaped by the ratio Ψ_{ijV}/Ψ_{ijO}, which was thoroughly studied in Chapters 6 and 7. Obviously, equation (8.4) is much simpler than our earlier equations (8.1), (8.2), and (8.3). Notice, in particular, that it is not a function of wage rates or trade frictions, and that it only depends on two indices of efficiency corresponding to integration and outsourcing in a particular sourcing country j, rather than on indices in multiples countries, including the home one. Naturally, the reason for this simplicity is that we have ignored the extensive margin of firms and this, of course, is not a virtue of this variant of the model, but rather a limitation. For this reason, in some of the specifications below, I will include some variables (in particular, freight costs and tariffs) that would almost surely affect the intrafirm import share if we allowed firms to face a nontrivial choice regarding whether or not to invest in being able to source inputs from a given country within or across firm boundaries (or both).

Empirical Implementation of the Multi-Country Model

Leaving aside these important caveats, I will next leverage the extremely simple form of (8.4) to motivate an empirical specification that studies the effect of interactions of industry and country characteristics on the propensity of firms to engage in intrafirm trade. With that in mind, I first note that if instead of focusing on the intrafirm import share Sh_{i-f}, I instead compute the ratio of intrafirm imports to arm's-length imports, equation (8.4) becomes log-linear. Reintroducing input subscripts v and taking logs, we can then express (8.4) as:

$$\ln\left(M_{ijv}^{if}/M_{ijv}^{nif}\right) = \frac{\theta}{(1-\eta_v)(\sigma_v-1)}\ln\left(\Psi_{ijVv}/\Psi_{ijOv}\right) + \varepsilon_{ijv}, \qquad (8.5)$$

where ε_{ijv} is an error term assumed to satisfy all the necessary orthogonality conditions. Obviously the ratio Ψ_{ijVv}/Ψ_{ijOv} is not something we observe in the data, but one can follow the guidance of the models developed in Chapters 6 and 7—as summarized in Table 8.1—to write this ratio as a function of empirical proxies of the deep parameters of those models.

A tricky issue in making that mapping is deciding whether certain parameters of the model are (i) industry-specific but common across countries, (ii) country-specific but common across industries, or (iii) industry- and country-specific. In Chapter 5, I argued that on conceptual grounds and also due to data limitations, it was natural to treat the elasticity of demand σ, headquarter intensity η, relationship-specificity ϵ, and input substitutability ρ as deep industry parameters unaffected by the particular country from which U.S. firms source. Conversely, I treated the degree of financial constraints ϕ and contractibility μ as either an industry characteristic (in Table 5.6), a country characteristic (in Table 5.8), or an interaction of a sector-specific component and a country-pair-specific component (in Table 5.7). Maintaining these assumptions, we can then express equation (8.4) in a general form as

$$\ln\left(M_{ijv}^{if}/M_{ijv}^{nif}\right) = \frac{\theta}{(1-\eta_v)(\sigma_v-1)}\Phi\left(\sigma_v,\eta_v,\epsilon_v,\rho_v,\mu_v,\phi_v,\mu_{ij},\phi_{ij}\right) + \varepsilon_{ijv}. \qquad (8.6)$$

Note that this equation is closely related to our regressions above using both cross-product and cross-country variation. More specifically, suppose that the country-year fixed effects included in those specifications appropriately controlled for the terms μ_{ij} and ϕ_{ij} (and any other unobserved country-specific determinant of integration). In such a case, one could indeed invoke (8.6) when claiming to estimate the partial effect of the industry-specific variables $\sigma_v,\eta_v,\epsilon_v,\rho_v,\mu_v$, and ϕ_v on the ratio $M_{ijv}^{if}/M_{ijv}^{nif}$, a ratio that is tightly related to the intrafirm import share.[16]

Unfortunately, it is pretty clear from the formulae for the ratio Ψ_{ijVv}/Ψ_{ijOv} derived in Chapters 6 and 7 that the effects of country-level variables and industry-level variables interact with each other, and thus demeaning

---

[16] A key difference relative to the previous regressions is that trade barriers and final-good producers' productivity dispersion play no role in equation (8.6). This is of course because selection effects have been neutralized in the multi-country model.

intrafirm trade shares or $\ln(M_{ijv}^{if}/M_{ijv}^{nif})$ within countries (and years) will not absorb the effects of these country-level variables. This is precisely the same reasoning we used in Chapter 5 to motivate the inclusion of both country-year *and* industry fixed effects when explaining the level of offshoring. We shall now follow a similar approach in empirical specifications attempting to explain the relative prevalence of intrafirm transactions in offshoring.

Before diving back into the empirics, there is one more issue worth discussing. One might wonder, in particular, why in light of equation (8.6) I have focused above on linear specifications in which the share of intrafirm imports—rather than $\ln(M_{ijv}^{if}/M_{ijv}^{nif})$—was the dependent variable. It should be stressed, however, that in order to reach the simple specification (8.6), I have had to shut down selection effects, which in our two-country model were essential for generating certain comparative static results, such as those related to trade barriers τ or productivity dispersion κ on the intrafirm trade shares. These selection effects are key features of the data. In the raw NAICS data, of the total 1,085,760 product-country-year observations, only 313,152 (28.8%) feature positive import volumes, and of those only 189,340 (17.4%) feature positive intrafirm imports. Furthermore, for another 13,816 (1.27%) observations, intrafirm imports are positive, but non-related-party imports are not. Thus, in regressions in which the left-hand-side variable is $\ln(M_{ijv}^{if}/M_{ijv}^{nif})$, a significant share of observations in which the intrafirm trade share is not strictly between zero and one will be discarded. This is why I have chosen to present results explaining the *level* of the intrafirm import share up to this point in the chapter. And it is precisely for this reason that the results to be presented below explaining $\ln(M_{ijv}^{if}/M_{ijv}^{nif})$ should be treated with caution, in the same way that I argued that one should take the results with the logarithm of imports as a dependent variable in Chapter 5 with a grain of salt.[17]

Results of the Difference-in-Difference Specifications

As in Chapter 5, I will now explore specifications including industry and country fixed effects as well as interactions of industry and country characteristics. In particular, I express (8.6) as

$$\ln\left(M_{USjv}^{if}/M_{USjv}^{nif}\right) = \alpha_v + \alpha_j + \beta \mathbf{Z}_j \mathbf{z}_v + \varepsilon_{jv}, \tag{8.7}$$

[17] I have also experimented with log-linear regressions in which the share of intrafirm imports is the dependent variable in the regressions in Tables 8.8 and 8.9, and the results I obtained were very similar. Nevertheless, the regressions with $\ln(M_{i-f}/M_{ni-f})$ as dependent variable featured a higher R-squared.

TABLE 8.8 Contractual Determinants of U.S. Intrafirm Trade Shares

Dep. Var.: $\ln(M^{if}_{USjv}/M^{nif}_{USjv})$	(1)	(2)	(3)	(4)	(5)
K Intensity × K Abund.	0.019		−0.215	−0.205	−3.518**
	(0.183)		(0.213)	(0.257)	(0.708)
Skill Inten × Skill Abund	−0.344*		−0.426+	−0.207	0.203
	(0.175)		(0.230)	(0.265)	(0.322)
Nunn × Rule		0.134*	0.068	−0.044	−0.098
		(0.067)	(0.066)	(0.118)	(0.103)
Levchenko × Rule		0.060+	0.057	0.064	0.027
		(0.032)	(0.035)	(0.070)	(0.059)
Costinot × Rule		−0.046	−0.184*	−0.341*	−0.294*
		(0.071)	(0.075)	(0.144)	(0.146)
BJRS × Rule		0.083	0.159*	0.137	0.069
		(0.079)	(0.066)	(0.125)	(0.123)
Rajan-Zingales × Credit/GDP		0.102*	0.302+	0.874**	0.238
		(0.145)	(0.167)	(0.288)	(0.152)
Braun × Credit/GDP		0.220	0.290+	0.318*	0.301*
		(0.154)	(0.156)	(0.152)	(0.131)
Firm Volatility × Labor Flexibility		−0.275+	−0.374*	−0.332+	−0.344**
		(0.154)	(0.171)	(−0.188)	(0.161)
Sample Restrictions	W+NT+	W+NT+	W+NT+	W+NT+	W+NT+
Ctr/Year & Ind Fixed Effects	Yes	Yes	Yes	Yes	Yes
Interactions with GDP pc	No	No	No	Yes	No
Industry Effects × GDP pc	No	No	No	No	Yes
Observations	89,669	≃88,000	84,738	77,307	77,307
R-squared	0.732	≃0.73	0.738	0.745	0.769

Standard errors clustered at the country/ind. level. +, *, ** denote 10, 5, 1% significance.

where $\mathbf{Z}_j$ and $\mathbf{z}_v$ are vectors of source-country and industry variables, while α_v and α_j are industry and country-year fixed effects (as in Chapter 5, I omit time subscripts for simplicity).

I begin in Table 8.8 by including the same set of interaction terms as in Table 5.7 of Chapter 5. Again, the inclusion of these variables is not motivated on theoretical terms (at least not based on the models developed in this book), but rather because they have featured prominently in the recent literature on trade and institutions. More specifically, Table 8.8 includes nine interaction terms: two Heckscher-Ohlin interactions related to physical capital and skilled labor intensity and relative abundance, four interactions of industry-level contractual "intensity" and country-level contractual enforcement, two interactions of financial "dependence" and financial development, and a final interaction capturing the differential role of rigid labor markets across sectors. I refer the reader to Chapter 5 and to the Data Appendix for more details on the source of these variables.

In column (1) of Table 8.8, I begin by presenting a bare-bones specification that includes only the two Heckscher-Ohlin interactions, which as pointed out in Chapter 5 had a positive and significant effect on the propensity of U.S. firms to offshore. The table indicates a positive but negligible effect of the physical capital interaction, but a negative and significant effect of the skilled labor interaction. The latter result suggests a lower propensity to integrate skill-intensive production processes in relatively skill-abundant countries. In the remaining columns of Table 8.8, I introduce the seven "institutional" interaction terms, first one at a time in column (2), and then jointly in the remaining columns. All columns use the Wright and Nunn-Trefler corrected data and the last three columns only differ in the set of additional controls included in the regression. As in Table 5.7, column (3) includes no additional controls (other than the industry and country-year fixed effects), column (4) includes interactions of the seven institutional industry variables with GDP per capita, and column (5) includes interactions of sector dummies with GDP per capita. These different specifications were rationalized in Chapter 5 and the same arguments apply to the current context.

Because the specifications in this table are not motivated by any of the models developed above, one should not infer too much from the results to be discussed. It should be noted, however, that to the extent that the included institutional interactions capture different sources of transaction costs, one would expect based on the transaction-cost theory that the sign of the coefficient of these interactions should now be the opposite of the one obtained in Chapter 5. Intuitively, if intrafirm trade circumvents all contractual inefficiencies, any contracting-related interaction term that positively predicts the overall level of offshoring should now necessarily reduce the share of this offshoring conducted within firm boundaries. Judged by this criterion, how well does the transaction-cost model fare against the evidence?

Consider first the interactions related to contract enforcement. In Table 5.7 we found robust evidence of a negative effect of these interactions on U.S. intermediate input imports. In other words, the positive effect of source country contract enforcement on U.S. firms' input purchases was lower, the more contractible inputs are. Based on the transaction-cost model, one would thus expect these same interactions to have a positive effect on intrafirm import shares. Although the effect of the Nunn and Levchenko contracting interactions is positive and significant when introduced alone in column (2), their significance disappears in the columns that include all interactions simultaneously. Furthermore, the only interaction term whose significance survives is the Costinot interaction, but it does so with the same negative sign obtained in Table 5.7.

On a more positive note, Table 8.8 indicates that the Braun and Cuñat-Melitz interactions do appear to shape intrafirm import shares with the opposite sign with which they affected overall offshoring levels. That is, those results indicate that an improvement in source-country financial or labor-market institutions will tend to disproportionately decrease the propensity of U.S. firms to internalize transactions in sectors with hard access to finance and in sectors with higher needs for labor reallocations across firms. Finally, it is worth pointing out that the effect of the Heckscher-Ohlin interactions appear to be negative in most specifications, but their size and significance differs dramatically across specifications, as reflected for instance in the implausibly large negative coefficient on the physical capital interaction in column (5).

In Table 8.9, I turn to a specification that is more closely related to the global sourcing models in Chapters 6 and 7. In the same manner that Table 8.8 basically replicated the results of Table 5.7 but with a different dependent variable, in Table 8.9 I build closely on the specification of Table 5.8. In particular, the specification is again equation (8.7) but the vector of interaction terms now includes: (i) the two Heckscher-Ohlin interactions mentioned above; (ii) measures of freight costs and U.S. tariffs that vary across both sectors and countries; and (iii) five institutional interactions inspired by the global sourcing models. All but one of the latter institutional regressors constitute interactions of the source-country level of contract enforcement μ_j (as proxied by their rule-of-law index) with empirical proxies for some of the key "industry" parameters of the model: input substitutability (ρ_v), demand elasticity (σ_v), specificity (ϵ_v), and headquarter intensity (η_v). The last interaction is the product of headquarter intensity η_v and financial development ϕ_{ij}. The data sources are the same as those detailed in Chapter 5 (see the Data Appendix), where recall the headquarter intensity η_v is measured as the first principal component from a factor analysis of the buyer versions of R&D, equipment capital, and skill intensity variables.

Before discussing the empirical results, let us briefly review what the two models of internalization developed in this book would predict for the sign of these different interactions terms. For reasons discussed at length in previous chapters and also reviewed earlier in this chapter, both the transaction-cost and property-rights model would predict a positive effect of trade barriers (freight costs, U.S. tariffs) on the intrafirm trade share. Remember that the selection into offshoring channel was key for these effects, so it is not too surprising that trade barriers do not feature in our multi-country specification in (8.6). Still, I believe it is sensible to include these in the empirical specifications. As in our previous results in this chapter, Table 8.9 will demonstrate that these proxies for trade barriers appear to have a negative effect on the intrafirm import share, a finding that is hard to reconcile with the benchmark sorting pattern assumed in the models.

The empirical relevance of the selection into offshoring channel also justifies the inclusion of the two Heckscher-Ohlin interactions. More precisely, if we were to close the models in such a way that the relative wage costs were affected by relative factor endowments, we would typically obtain that the relative wage w^N/w^S would be lower, the more abundant is the source country in physical capital and skilled labor. As a result, we would expect the intrafirm trade share to be higher for inputs originating in more capital- and skill-abundant countries, with the effect being disproportionate for less headquarter-intensive sectors. In sum, a more realistic general equilibrium version of our models would predict a negative sign on the two Heckscher-Ohlin interactions. This is consistent with the results in Table 8.8, although we have seen that those coefficients are not particularly stable. The coefficients on these interactions in Table 8.9 are very similar in magnitude to those in Table 8.8, so I do not report them to save space (interested readers can inspect the dataset and programs downloadable at http://scholar.harvard.edu/antras/books).

We are then left with the five interaction terms capturing institutional factors. What are the predicted signs for these interactions predicted by the models in Chapters 6 and 7? To answer this question for the case of the transaction-cost model, it suffices to refer to the predictions of the model for the arm's-length component of U.S. intermediate input imports, and then simply invert the sign of those predictions. Building on equation (5.14), we can write this in succinct form as

$$\ln\left(M_{USjv}^{if}/M_{USjv}^{nif}\right) = \Phi_{TC}\left(\underset{+}{\mu_{ij} \times \rho_v}, \underset{-}{\mu_{ij} \times \sigma_v}, \underset{-}{\mu_{ij} \times \epsilon_v}, \underset{\text{ambiguous}}{\mu_{ij} \times \eta_v}, \underset{-}{\phi_{ij} \times \eta_v}\right).$$

(8.8)

For the case of the property-rights model, deriving sharp predictions for the effects of these interactions on the intrafirm import share proves to be much more challenging. In the Theoretical Appendix, I discuss in more detail these comparative statics. The bottom line, however, is that although in some cases the numerical examples appear to point toward a particular sign for these effects, it is often possible to construct numerical examples in which the opposite sign applies for a region of the parameter space. The analytical results derived in the Appendix can be summarized as follows:

$$\ln\left(M_{USjv}^{if}/M_{USjv}^{nif}\right) = \Phi_{PR}\left(\underset{\text{ambiguous}}{\mu_{ij} \times \rho_v}, \underset{\text{ambiguous}}{\mu_{ij} \times \sigma_v}, \underset{\text{ambiguous}}{\mu_{ij} \times \epsilon_v}, \underset{-}{\mu_{ij} \times \eta_v}, \underset{\text{ambiguous}}{\phi_{ij} \times \eta_v}\right),$$

(8.9)

implying that only the interactions $\mu_{ij} \times \eta_v$ has an unambiguous predicted sign. It should be noted, however, that in most numerical examples, I have found the interaction $\mu_{ij} \times \rho_v$ to affect the intrafirm trade share negatively, while the interaction of $\mu_{ij} \times \sigma_v$ can be shown to affect integration negatively when contract enforcement in country j affects only the contractibility of headquarter services, but positively when it affects only the contractibility of manufacturing production (see the Theoretical Appendix).

Comparing the predicted signs in (8.8) and (8.9), it should be clear that it will be extremely difficult to discriminate between the two theories based on this difference-in-difference approach. In particular, for none of the interactions I have experimented with can one state that the effect of that interaction on the relative propensity to integrate is unambiguously of opposite sign in the two theories. Hence, even if one finds robust evidence for some of the predictions of one of the models, this same evidence cannot possibly be used to refute the other theory. In sum, for the goal of discriminating across models, I view the type of cross-industry results in Tables 8.6 and especially 8.7 as being much more useful.

With these caveats in mind, let us then turn to Table 8.9 to study how these different interaction terms affect the relative prevalence of intrafirm imports in the data. Column (1) implements the same specification as in column (1) of Table 8.8, but now expanded to include measures of freight costs and U.S. tariffs (the Heckscher-Ohlin interactions are not reported to save space). As anticipated before, and consistently with our findings throughout this chapter, both of the coefficients on trade barriers are negative and significant, which constitutes a challenge for the models.

In column (2), I introduce the five interactions motivated by our model, *one at a time*, though for compactness I report all five coefficients in a single column. Note that the sign of the coefficients is consistent with the predictions of the transaction-cost model for four of the five coefficients, with the exception being $\phi_{ij} \times \eta_v$, whose effect is positive though indistinguishable from zero. Nevertheless, only two of these five interaction terms appear to have a statistically significant effect on $\ln (M_{USjv}^{if}/M_{USjv}^{nif})$.

In the last three columns of Table 8.9, I present results in which the five institutional interactions are included in the *same* regression, together with the Heckscher-Ohlin interactions and the trade cost measures. The three columns differ in that column (4) includes interactions between the industry-level institutional variables and GDP per capita, while column (5) includes a whole vector of interactions of sectoral dummies with GDP per capita.

The results in column (3) are very similar to those in column (2). Although now *all* the coefficients on the institutional interactions are consistent with the transaction-cost model, it continues to be the case that only two of them are significant at the 5 percent confidence level. The inclusion of interactions with GDP per capita in column (5) has a bigger impact on the coefficients, particularly on the interaction of specificity and the rule of law, which changes dramatically from being negative and significant at the 5% level to being positive, large in magnitude and significant at the 10% level. Controlling for interactions of sectoral dummies and GDP per capita in column (6) also affects the estimates in a sizable manner. The coefficient on freight costs is no longer significant, while only U.S. tariffs and the interaction of headquarter intensity with the rule of law remain statistically significant at standard levels.

TABLE 8.9 Testing the Transaction-Cost and Property-Rights Models

Dep. Var.: $\ln(M^{if}_{USjv}/M^{nif}_{USjv})$	(1)	(2)	(3)	(4)	(5)
Freight Costs	−0.201**		−0.162**	−0.142**	−0.086
	(0.058)		(0.059)	(0.055)	(0.059)
Tariffs	−0.156*		−0.197**	−0.185**	−0.168**
	(0.067)		(0.059)	(0.055)	(0.048)
Input Substit. × Rule		0.036	0.033	0.073	0.057
		(0.028)	(0.024)	(0.048)	(0.048)
Demand Elasticity × Rule		−0.062**	−0.062**	−0.109*	−0.060
		(0.012)	(0.012)	(0.043)	(0.073)
Nunn Specificity × Rule		−0.196**	−0.150*	1.697+	−0.005
		(0.063)	(0.060)	(0.906)	(0.115)
Headquarter Intensity × Rule		0.015	−0.006	0.069	0.105*
		(0.030)	(0.027)	(0.053)	(0.051)
Headquarter Intensity × Credit/GDP		0.018	−0.003	−0.004	−0.007
		(0.042)	(0.050)	(0.044)	(0.041)
Sample Restrictions	W+NT+	W+NT+	W+NT+	W+NT+	W+NT+
Ctr/Year & Ind Fixed Eff	Yes	Yes	Yes	Yes	Yes
Interactions with GDP	No	No	No	Yes	No
Industry Effects × GDP	No	No	No	No	Yes
Observations	89,393	≃88,000	87,298	79,654	79,654
R-squared	0.737	≃ 0.74	0.744	0.749	0.770

Standard errors clustered at the country/ind. level. +, *, ** denote 10, 5, 1% significance.

The sign of both of these coefficients is, however, opposite to the one predicted by the property-rights model.

Overall, the difference-in-difference approach in Tables 8.8 and 8.9 has yielded much poorer results than the same approach applied to explaining offshoring shares in Chapter 5. It might be argued that part of the higher success in Chapter 5 is associated with the fact that the inclusion of country-year and industry fixed effects in those specifications still left a large share of the variation in U.S. intermediate input imports unexplained, while their inclusion in Tables 8.8 and 8.9 leaves less variation in the share of intrafirm imports to be explained. Indeed, the R-squared of a simple regression of $\ln(M^{if}_{USjv}/M^{nif}_{USjv})$ on country-year and industry fixed effects is 0.731, while the analogous R-squared in regressions with log U.S. offshoring shares as a dependent variable is 0.616. This might be a factor in justifying the higher statistical significance of the coefficients in the regressions in Chapter 5, but it cannot possibly explain the fact that our global sourcing model *correctly* predicted the sign of the coefficient on the institutional interactions.

The results in Table 8.9 are not only weak in statistical terms, but they do not generally support the qualitative predictions of the internalization models either, particularly in the case of the property-rights model. Nevertheless, as argued above, the property-rights model does not offer sharp predictions for how the interaction of country and industry characteristics should shape intrafirm trade shares. And even when some analytical results can be obtained, one needs to work sufficiently hard to derive them to worry that they might rely quite heavily on the chosen functional forms. For these reasons, I view the specification tests in Tables 8.3, 8.4, 8.6, and 8.7 with their own admitted limitations, as more transparent tests of the models of multinational firm boundaries.

Other Sources of Product-Level Data

So far, I have restricted attention to product-level tests employing intrafirm import data from the U.S. Related-Party Trade database. The focus on the U.S. data is partly justified by the fact that many of the key contributions to this literature conduct their analysis with that dataset. Recent examples include the work of Nunn and Trefler (2008, 2013b), Bernard, Jensen, Redding, and Schott (2010); Costinot, Oldenski, and Rauch (2011); and Díez (2014), while an early use of the same dataset can be found in Helleiner and Lavergne (1979).[18]

Even while maintaining the focus on U.S. trade flows, many researchers have constructed alternative measures of intrafirm trade by employing direct investment data from the U.S. Bureau of Economic Analysis, which can be downloaded from: http://www.bea.gov/iTable/index_MNC.cfm. Zeile (1997) and Ruhl (2013) provide insightful descriptions of this database, which essentially aggregates the intrafirm exports and imports of U.S. foreign affiliates and of U.S. affiliates of foreign companies. The BEA database has the advantage of providing more information on the extent to which the ownership link between importers and exporters is large enough to convey effective corporate control, in line with the models of internalization developed in previous chapters. Another useful feature of this dataset is that it allows one to distinguish between trade within U.S. multinationals from trade within foreign multinationals operating in the United States. As readers will recall, I made use of this aspect of the BEA data to refine my estimates above, in line with the approach in Nunn and Trefler (2013b). The main drawback of this data source is that it is not as comprehensive as the U.S. Related-Party database: It only covers a limited number of fairly aggregated sectors and is only recorded in a handful of benchmark years, forcing researchers to extrapolate from those years to create yearly series for U.S. intrafirm imports. Another limitation of the data is that the BEA records

---

[18] To be precise, Bernard et al. (2010) had access to the confidential firm-level U.S. census data on related-party trade, but their regression analysis was performed at the sectoral level.

intrafirm imports by U.S. affiliates of foreign parents as originating from the country of ownership (i.e., of the parent company) rather than from the country in which the shipment actually originated. Among others, this source of data has recently been used by Antràs (2003) and Yeaple (2006) to test the property-rights theory, though it had also been used by Lall (1978) and Siddharthan and Kumar (1990) to test the transaction-cost theory.

To the best of my knowledge, the United States is the only country that collects detailed customs-level trade statistics distinguishing trade between related parties (intrafirm trade) from trade between non-related parties (arm's-length trade). In that sense, the U.S. Related-Party Trade database is unique.[19] For other countries, one can use a similar methodology as is used with the BEA dataset to create measures of intrafirm trade based on survey information on the trade transactions of multinational firms and their affiliates. For example, the OECD Activities of Foreign Affiliates (AFA) database contains intrafirm data for nine countries (Canada, Israel, Italy, Japan, Netherlands, Poland, Slovenia, Sweden, and the United States), but coverage is far from complete, as described by Lanz and Miroudot (2011). Perhaps for this reason, this source of data has not been employed so far to shed light on the determinants of the internalization decisions of firms.

Some contributions to the empirical literature on multinational firm boundaries have used product-level export data from the Customs General Administration of the People's Republic of China. These data do not distinguish between intrafirm and arm's-length trade, but they do contain detailed information on whether the exporter is a foreign-owned plant or not. As such, the data are suitable for an analysis of the determinants of foreign ownership of suppliers in China, regardless of the identity of the buyers of their goods. A very interesting feature of the Chinese data is that not only do the data differentiate between ordinary trade and processing trade, but in addition processing trade is categorized under different types of customs regimes depending on whether the plant in China is in charge of importing inputs or that responsibility falls on a foreign producer. The former type is referred to as "import-and-assembly" while the latter is labeled "pure-assembly." Feenstra and Hanson (2005) and Fernandes and Tang (2010) exploit this feature of the data to test rich variants of the property-rights theory of multinational firm boundaries (see also Feenstra, 2011). More recently, Li (2013) has also employed the Chinese processing trade data to test a transaction-cost model of firm boundaries emphasizing the role of communications costs in hindering outsourcing transactions.

---

[19] It is hoped that this will change in the future as the United Nations Statistics Division has explicitly recommended the collection of intra-firm trade data in customs-based merchandise trade statistics (see United Nations, 2010).

Empirical Evidence Using Firm-Level Data

The transaction-cost and property-rights theories are theories of firm boundaries and thus *firm*-level data would appear to be the ideal laboratory to employ when testing these theories. To give a precise example, some of the comparative statics results derived in the transaction-cost and property-rights models in Chapters 6 and 7 were closely related to the equilibrium sorting pattern of firms by productivity into organizational forms. Is that sorting pattern consistent with available data? To answer this question one obviously needs to make use of firm-level data.

Unfortunately, firm-level data on the global sourcing decisions of firms are not readily available. Although most countries maintain census or survey data on the firms operating in their economy, there are many fewer datasets that provide sufficiently detailed information on the global sourcing practices of these firms, and more specifically on whether they import intermediate inputs within or across firm boundaries. I will next describe five firm-level datasets that have been used by researchers in recent years, while emphasizing both their main advantages and limitations and outlining some of the results that have been obtained when exploiting these data sources.

An early paper using firm-level data to shed light on the firm boundaries decisions of multinational firms is Tomiura (2007), who uses data from the Basic Survey of Commercial and Manufacturing Structure and Activity in Japan. The survey covers 118,300 Japanese manufacturing firms and is regarded as an accurate overall representation of the Japanese manufacturing sector. Unfortunately, the survey was carried out only in one year, 1998. The survey contains a variety of information on the operations of firms (sales, employment, capital expenditures, exports, foreign direct investment) and crucially also asks firms whether they "contract out manufacturing or processing tasks to other firms overseas." Hence, the survey can be used to explicitly distinguish firms that are engaged in foreign outsourcing versus those that are engaged in foreign direct investment. On the downside this Japanese dataset does not appear to contain information on the volume (i.e., the intensive margin) of foreign insourcing and outsourcing. Tomiura (2007) uses the dataset to show that, consistently with the equilibrium sorting of the transaction-cost and property-rights models (see for instance Figures 6.4 and 7.2), firms that are engaged in FDI and intrafirm trade are significantly more productive than firms that are engaged in foreign outsourcing, which in turn are more productive than firms sourcing domestically. An interesting feature of the data, which many other datasets have unveiled as well, is that most firms are neither "pure FDI" firms nor "pure outsourcing" firms, which is suggestive of the relevance of models in which firms follow hybrid global sourcing strategies (such as the model in Antràs and Chor, 2013).

A second line of papers, most notably Carluccio and Fally (2011); Defever and Toubal (2013); and Corcos, Irac, Mion, and Verdier (2013), have used French firm-level data from the EIIG (Échanges Internationaux Intra-Groupe).[20] The EIIG is a survey conducted in 1999 by the SESSI (Service des Études et des Statistiques Industrielles), which documents the extent to which firms import foreign inputs from related or non-related parties. Interestingly, the data identify those input purchases that are related to contract manufacturing (classified as "work based on plans"), and Defever and Toubal (2013) focus their analysis on these purchases because they better map to our global sourcing models. Another important feature of the EIIG survey is that it provides a firm-level breakup between intrafirm and arm's-length offshoring by source country and by four-digit HS input product codes. Thus, the data are similar in scope to the U.S. Related-Party Database, but they are at the firm level and also better capture the intermediate input component of imports. The main drawback of the dataset is its coverage. The survey includes only French firms that traded more than 1 million euros in 1999, and more importantly, it is restricted to firms that are owned by manufacturing groups that control at least 50 percent of the equity capital of an affiliate based outside France. Though not all firms responded to the survey, the 4,305 respondent firms represent more than 80 percent of total exports and imports of French multinationals in 1999. Still, the fact that only firms with at least one affiliate outside France were sampled raises serious concerns about sample selection biases. Corcos et al. (2013) acknowledge this problem and complement the dataset with data from the French Customs Office, documenting the universe of yearly imports and exports flows in 1999 at the firm, origin country, and product levels, hence allowing them to offer a more representative picture of the foreign outsourcing operations of French firms.[21]

The goals and scope of the papers using the EEIG dataset are somewhat different, but they all find supportive evidence of a positive correlation between headquarter intensity and the relative importance of intrafirm trade, with the measures of headquarter intensity in Corcos et al. (2013) being *firm-level* measures (namely, capital intensity, skill intensity and the ratio of value added over sales of the importing firm) based on the importer's operational data. Defever and Toubal (2013) and Corcos et al. (2013) instead find conflicting evidence regarding the relative productivity of firms engaged in foreign outsourcing and foreign integration. More specifically,

---

[20] This dataset has also been used recently by Carluccio and Bas (2014) to study the link between intrafirm trade and labor market institutions.

[21] The EEIG survey can in turn be matched with another SESSI database, the EAE (Enquête Annuelle Entreprise), which provides balance sheet data on manufacturing firms with at least 20 employees.

Defever and Toubal (2013) find that in the sample of French firms that own at least one affiliate abroad, firms engaging in foreign outsourcing are on average *more* productive than firms engaging in FDI. They rationalize this finding by appealing to the notion that for entities belonging to a multinational network, the fixed costs of procuring inputs from arm's-length suppliers external to the network are likely to be higher than the fixed costs of doing so from suppliers within the network. This reversal of the ranking of fixed costs relative to the one assumed in our models naturally leads to an analogous reversal in the equilibrium sorting pattern, with the average productivity of firms that engage in offshore outsourcing now being higher than that of firms engaging in offshore insourcing. Corcos et al. (2013) show, however, that when incorporating into the dataset the many firms in France that do not own affiliates abroad, the productivity advantage of FDI firms over foreign outsourcers predicted by our global sourcing models is restored (see, for instance, their Figure 1).

A third firm-level dataset available to test models of the boundaries of multinational firms is a panel dataset of Spanish manufacturing firms collected by the Fundación SEPI. The ESEE (Encuesta sobre Estrategias Empresariales) surveys approximately 2,000 Spanish firms with at least ten employees on a yearly basis since 1990. The ESEE provides information on the income and balance sheet statistics of firms, and also on a variety of firm-level organizational variables. A notable characteristic of the ESEE is its representativeness, which is ensured by the careful statistical criteria used in the initial year of the sample and the special attention that has been given to account for entry and exit of firms of different sizes in subsequent years.[22] For the purposes of testing global sourcing theories, a particularly relevant feature of the data is that they allow one to compute the overall spending on intermediate inputs by firms and their breakup into (i) domestic purchases from independent suppliers, (ii) domestic purchases from affiliated parties, (iii) imports from foreign independent suppliers, and (iv) imports from foreign affiliates. Hence, one can easily map some of the variables of the survey into the four key organizational forms emphasized by the models in Chapters 6 and 7. An important disadvantage of this Spanish dataset is that it only distinguishes between domestic and foreign input purchases, with the latter not being disaggregated by country of origin.

Using the ESEE dataset, Kohler and Smolka (2009, 2014) find that, conditional on the location of sourcing (domestic or foreign), firms that purchase inputs from integrated suppliers appear to be significantly more productive

---

[22] Details on the survey characteristics can be downloaded from the following website: http://www.fundacionsepi.es/esee/sp/presentacion.asp. The data are accessible for a relatively modest fee to any researcher regardless of nationality. Among others, it has been used in other contexts by Delgado, Fariñas, and Ruano (2002) and Guadalupe, Kuzmina, and Thomas (2012).

than those procuring inputs from arm's-length suppliers. This confirms the findings of Tomiura (2007) for Japan and of Corcos et al. (2013) for France, and further demonstrates that the superior performance of integrating firms holds also when focusing on domestic sourcing. This is consistent with the sorting pattern assumed in the models in Chapters 6 and 7. Conversely, Kohler and Smolka (2009) find mixed evidence regarding the relative productivity of firms outsourcing abroad and firms integrating in Spain.

Using the same data that Kohler and Smolka (2009) used, Figure 8.2 plots the distribution of (Olley-Pakes) total factor productivity of firms according to the organizational form they adopt when sourcing. The probability density functions in Figure 8.2 confirm that domestic outsourcers are (on average) the least productive firms, while foreign integrators are (on average) the most productive firms. More interestingly, it appears that the distribution of productivity of firms that engage in domestic integration is a shift to the right of that of firms that outsource abroad. This sorting pattern is inconsistent with the one assumed in the benchmark versions of the global sourcing models, but is in line with the alternative ranking of fixed costs $f_{OV} > f_{DV} > f_{OO} > f_{DO}$ we explored in Chapter 6. As discussed in that chapter, this alternative sorting pattern delivers the *exact* same comparative statics as our benchmark version of the transaction-cost model. In the Theoretical Appendix I show, perhaps surprisingly, that the same is not true in the property-rights model. In fact, through the lens of the property-rights model, the sorting pattern implied by Figure 8.2 may well help rationalize the robust negative effects of trade frictions on intrafirm trade shares unveiled in the empirical work developed earlier in this chapter. Intuitively, reductions in trade barriers not only lead firms that were sourcing domestically to select into outsourcing, but now also push the most productive among the domestic integrating firms to select into foreign integration. As a result, the predicted overall effect of reductions in trade barriers on the share of intrafirm imports can now well be negative, at least in the property-rights model. In the Theoretical Appendix, I show in addition that the overall effect of trade frictions is particularly likely to be negative when the contractual insecurity associated with offshoring stems largely from lower contractibility of input manufacturing.

One might worry that the sorting pattern unveiled in Figure 8.2 is specific to the Spanish data. The work of Federico (2010) suggests, however, that a similar sorting is observed when using firm-level data from Italy, this being the fourth of the five datasets I will review here. Federico (2010) uses firm-level data from the Survey on Italian Manufacturing Firms, conducted every three years by Mediocredito Capitalia (MCC). The MCC survey combines some of the virtues of the French EEIG and Spanish ESEE datasets. On the one hand, the survey provides information on the extent to which Italian firms make use of contract manufacturing, thus excluding the purchase of standardized

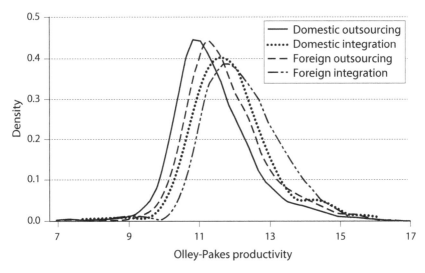

Figure 8.2 Organizational Sorting in Spain

inputs.[23] On the other hand, the data allow researchers to distinguish between four types of suppliers, corresponding to the same four organizational forms in the models and in the Spanish data. The main drawback of this dataset is that its coverage is far less complete than that of the other surveys described above, and severely undersamples small firms. Using these data, Federico (2010) finds a sorting pattern qualitatively similar to that in Figure 8.2, with firms with medium-low productivity choosing foreign outsourcing, and firms with medium-high productivity choosing domestic integration.

A fifth international firm-level dataset that has been used to shed light on the boundaries of multinational firms is the Dun & Bradstreet's WorldBase (DB) database. This massive dataset contains information on hundreds of thousands of establishments in more than 200 countries and territories. In contrast to the four surveys described above, the DB dataset does not contain comprehensive operational data related to these plants, but it does offer a comprehensive picture of firm boundaries across borders. In particular, the DB database contains detailed information on the location, ownership (e.g., its domestic or global parent), and industry classification of plants worldwide. Alfaro, Conconi, Fadinger, and Newman (2014) use these data to document a

---

[23] Contract manufacturing is defined as "a contract by which an entrepreneur engages itself on behalf of the buying company to carry out workings on semifinished products or raw materials, or to supply products or services to be incorporated or used in the buying company's economic activity or in the production of a complex good, in conformity with the buying company's projects, techniques, technologies, models or prototypes" (see Federico, 2010).

positive association between higher tariffs on final products (as measured by MFN tariffs at the four-digit SIC industry level for all WTO members) and an index of domestic vertical integration constructed using the ownership information in the DB database as well as input-output tables. Their empirical exercise exploits both cross-section and time-series variation in trade policy, but also considers China's entry into the WTO in 2001 as a quasi-natural experiment. The authors take these results as empirically validating the model of organizational design in Legros and Newman (2013) and Conconi, Legros, and Newman (2012).

Conclusions and the Road Ahead

The empirical evidence discussed in this chapter has offered broad support for some of the key predictions of the internalization models developed in Chapters 6 and 7. The property-rights model, in particular, has fared particularly well against the evidence. It would be premature, however, to interpret the evidence as being conclusive because, for the most part, the tests performed up to today have relatively low statistical power. In my view, successful testing of the theory will need to be based on one of the following three approaches.

A first possibility is to better exploit the large variation in the relative prevalence of integration retrievable from the U.S. Related-Party database or from some of the firm-level datasets described above. In particular, I believe that the cross-industry and cross-country specifications that I have experimented with earlier in this chapter are interesting and informative, but they cannot convincingly identify a causal effect of headquarter intensity or of product contractibility (even when appropriately measured) on the share of intrafirm imports. A potential avenue for future research is to use narrower slices of the data, perhaps (i) focusing on the patterns in a single industry, but exploiting exogenous changes in sector characteristics driven by technological or demand-driven shocks, in the spirit of Baker and Hubbard (2003); or perhaps (ii) performing analyses exploiting within-country variation stemming from changes in the institutional characteristics of countries, such as observable changes in the quality of institutions or in restrictions on foreign ownership in those countries.

A second approach would consist of using the available firm-level datasets to better identify the various channels via which contractual factors shape the intensive and extensive global sourcing decisions of firms. Many of the comparative static results described at length in Chapters 6 and 7 followed from a combination of selection channels and input demand channels. When working with product-level data, one can indeed only test the outcome of the balance of these effects. Nevertheless, firm-level datasets should in principle allow researchers to effectively separate these channels, which in turn could prove useful in better discriminating among available theories. Some aspects of the empirical analysis of Corcos et al. (2013) with the French EEIG dataset constitute a valuable first attempt along these lines, but more work is needed on this front. In a similar vein, there are surely many untapped sources of firm-level data on the global sourcing strategies of firms. For instance, the empirical studies of global sourcing in Fort (2014) and Antràs, Fort, and Tintelnot (2014) make use of a rich dataset that links the U.S. Census Bureau's 2007 Economic Censuses (EC), Longitudinal Business Database (LBD), and Import transaction database. The latter is the basis of the U.S. Related-Party database and thus contains information on whether firm-level import transactions are integrated or not. Another interesting aspect of the data, which Fort (2014) exploits in her empirical analysis, is that the data can be used to identify U.S. firms' decisions to contract for manufacturing services from domestic or foreign suppliers, which constitute a better match for the models developed in this book than overall input purchases.

A third fruitful area of future research would involve a more structural usage of available firm-level datasets. At present, little work has been devoted to structurally estimating the models I have discussed in this book. This is partly due to the stylized nature of these frameworks, and partly due to the under-utilization of this type of empirical techniques in the international trade field. An exception is the work of Antràs, Fort, and Tintelnot (2014), who structurally estimate a version of the multi-country global sourcing model developed in this book, but focusing on its complete-contracting version in Chapter 2. I would anticipate that future theoretical developments in this area will likely produce much richer frameworks of the internalization decisions of multinational firms. These frameworks should prove to be more amenable for structural work. Structural techniques of course have their own limitations, but their main appeal is that they open the door for a quantitative evaluation of the models. How do the organizational decisions of multinational firms shape firm-level performance? How do they affect labor markets, product markets, and social welfare? These are key questions that have so far not been sufficiently explored in the literature.

PART IV

Appendixes

A
Theoretical Appendix

The proofs of a few theoretical results in the main text of this book were only sketched or simply omitted to enhance the flow of text. In this Appendix, I provide the details of these proofs or refer the reader to the relevant papers where the proofs can be found.

A.1 Optimal Sourcing Strategy in the Multi-Country Global Sourcing Model in Chapter 2

In this appendix, I formally prove some statements related to the characterization of the optimal sourcing strategy in the multi-country global sourcing model in Chapter 2.

Remember that the problem of choosing an optimal sourcing strategy is given by

$$
\max_{\mathcal{J}_i(\varphi)} \pi_i\left(\varphi, \mathcal{J}_i\left(\varphi\right)\right) = (a_{hi}w_i)^{-\eta(\sigma-1)}\left(\gamma \sum_{k\in\mathcal{J}_i(\varphi)} T_k\left(\tau_{ik}w_k\right)^{-\theta}\right)^{(\sigma-1)(1-\eta)/\theta}
$$
$$
\times B\varphi^{\sigma-1} - w_i \sum_{k\in\mathcal{J}_i(\varphi)} f_{ik}.
$$

With a discrete number of locations, we can rewrite the problem as follows:

$$
\max_{I_1,I_2,...,I_J\in\{0,1\}^J} \pi_i\left(\varphi, I_1, I_2, ..., I_J\right) = \left(\sum_{k=1}^{J} I_k T_k\left(\tau_{ik}w_k\right)^{-\theta}\right)^{(\sigma-1)(1-\eta)/\theta} \widetilde{B}\varphi^{\sigma-1}
$$
$$
- w_i \sum_{k=1}^{J} I_k f_{ik}. \tag{A.1}
$$

where $\widetilde{B} = (a_{hi}w_i)^{-\eta(\sigma-1)}\gamma^{(\sigma-1)(1-\eta)}B$. The dummy variable I_j thus takes a value of 1 when $j \in \mathcal{J}_i(\varphi)$ and 0 otherwise.

The key thing to note is that, provided that $(\sigma-1)(1-\eta) > \theta$, the modified objective function in (A.1) features increasing differences in $\left(I_j, I_k\right)$ for $j, k \in \{1, ..., J\}$ such that $j \neq k$, and also features increasing differences in $\left(I_j, \varphi\right)$ for any $j \in \{1, ..., \mathcal{J}\}$. Invoking standard results in monotone comparative statics, we can then conclude that for $\varphi_1 \geq \varphi_0$, we must have $\left(I_1^*(\varphi_1), I_2^*(\varphi_1), ..., I_{\mathcal{J}}^*(\varphi_1)\right) \geq \left(I_1^*(\varphi_0), I_2^*(\varphi_0), ..., I_{\mathcal{J}}^*(\varphi_0)\right)$. Naturally, this rules out a situation in which $I_j^*(\varphi_1) = 0$ but $I_j^*(\varphi_0) = 1$, and thus we can conclude that $\mathcal{J}_i(\varphi_0) \subseteq \mathcal{J}_i(\varphi_1)$ for $\varphi_1 \geq \varphi_0$.

A.2 Comparative Statics of the Global Sourcing Model in Chapter 4

In this appendix, I will provide formal proofs for some comparative statics mentioned in Chapters 4 and 5. When a result has been proven in an existing paper, I will simply refer the reader to that paper.

DERIVATION OF A GENERAL FORMULA FOR THE OFFSHORING SHARE

In the first part of Chapter 5, I studied the determinants of the cross-section of offshoring shares. In Chapter 4, I derived a formula for this share but under the strong assumptions of complete contracting in the North, "totally" incomplete contracting in the South, a single input, and symmetric bargaining. In Chapter 5, I appealed to a general formula that applied to all the extensions of the two-country model developed in Chapter 4. Let me now provide more details on that derivation.

As explained in Chapter 4, the share of foreign input purchases in total input purchases typically depends on how these inputs are priced in the presence of incomplete contracting and renegotiation. Below, I stick to the assumption in the main text that the ratio of input expenditures to sale revenue is common for firms sourcing domestically and offshoring. As a result, the offshoring share is identical to the fraction of industry sales captured by firms offshoring intermediate inputs. With a constant price elasticity of demand $\sigma > 1$, firm revenues are in turn a multiple σ of operating profits. Operating profits are in turn equal to overall profits plus fixed costs, or

$$\pi_D(\varphi) + f_D w_N = (w_N)^{1-\sigma} B\Gamma_D \varphi^{\sigma-1}$$

$$\pi_O(\varphi) + f_O w_N = \left((w_N)^{\eta} (\tau w_S)^{1-\eta}\right)^{1-\sigma} B\Gamma_O \varphi^{\sigma-1}.$$

Assuming selection into offshoring, i.e., condition (2.21) in Chapter 2, we can define the thresholds $\tilde{\varphi}_O > \tilde{\varphi}_D$ satisfying $\pi_D(\tilde{\varphi}_D) = 0$ and $\pi_O(\tilde{\varphi}_O) = \pi_D(\tilde{\varphi}_O)$.

It is straightforward to verify that

$$\frac{\tilde{\varphi}_O}{\tilde{\varphi}_D} = \left[\frac{f_O/f_D - 1}{\frac{\Gamma_O}{\Gamma_D} \left(\frac{w_N}{\tau w_S} \right)^{(1-\eta)(\sigma-1)} - 1} \right]^{1/(\sigma-1)}. \tag{A.2}$$

The share of revenues (and of input purchases) accounted for by offshoring firms is then given by

$$\Upsilon_O = \frac{\int_{\tilde{\varphi}_O}^{\infty} \left((w_N)^{\eta} (\tau w_S)^{1-\eta} \right)^{1-\sigma} B \Gamma_O \varphi^{\sigma-1} dG(\varphi)}{\int_{\tilde{\varphi}_D}^{\infty} (w_N)^{1-\sigma} B \Gamma_D \varphi^{\sigma-1} dG(\varphi) + \int_{\tilde{\varphi}_O}^{\infty} \left((w_N)^{\eta} (\tau w_S)^{1-\eta} \right)^{1-\sigma} B \Gamma_O \varphi^{\sigma-1} dG(\varphi)}.$$

Assuming a Pareto distribution of productivity, i.e., $G(\varphi) = 1 - \left(\underline{\varphi}/\varphi \right)^{\kappa}$ for $\varphi \geq \underline{\varphi} > 0$, this expression further simplifies to

$$\Upsilon_O = \frac{\frac{\Gamma_O}{\Gamma_D} \left(\frac{w_N}{\tau w_S} \right)^{(1-\eta)(\sigma-1)}}{\left(\frac{\tilde{\varphi}_O}{\tilde{\varphi}_D} \right)^{\kappa-(\sigma-1)} - 1 + \frac{\Gamma_O}{\Gamma_D} \left(\frac{w_N}{\tau w_S} \right)^{(1-\eta)(\sigma-1)}},$$

where $\tilde{\varphi}_O/\tilde{\varphi}_D$ is given in (A.2). This corresponds to the general offshoring share equation (5.2) in Chapter 5. This formula is identical to the one applying in the complete-contracting case except for the term Γ_O/Γ_D.

With this expression in hand, we can next turn to the study of comparative statics in the different variants of the global sourcing model developed in Chapter 4. Below I will focus on how the different parameters of the model shape the ratio Γ_O/Γ_D, which differs across variants of the model. As argued in the main text, leaving aside this term Γ_O/Γ_D, the share Υ_O is increasing in w_N/w_S and σ, and decreasing in τ, f_O/f_D, κ, and η (these results are straightforward to prove by simple differentiation making use of $\kappa \geq \sigma - 1$).

SYMMETRIC NASH BARGAINING MODEL

Consider first the basic model with complete contracting in the North, "totally" incomplete contracting in the South, a single input, and symmetric bargaining. This implies $\Gamma_D = 1$ and thus (see eq. (4.10)

$$\frac{\Gamma_O}{\Gamma_D} = (\sigma + 1) \left(\frac{1}{2} \right)^{\sigma}.$$

But note that

$$\frac{\partial (\Gamma_O/\Gamma_D)}{\partial \sigma} = -\left(\frac{1}{2}\right)^{\sigma} ((1 + \sigma)\ln 2 - 1) < 0,$$

and thus the offshoring share is lower in higher elasticity sectors because of the effect of contractual frictions. This effect is of the opposite sign to the "standard" one operating in the complete-contracting case, and thus the overall effect of σ on the offshoring share Υ_O is ambiguous.

GENERALIZED NASH BARGAINING MODEL

Let us now turn to the basic model with generalized Nash bargaining. Again we have $\Gamma_D = 1$ and thus

$$\frac{\Gamma_O}{\Gamma_D} = \Gamma_\beta \equiv (\sigma - (\sigma - 1)(\beta\eta + (1 - \beta)(1 - \eta))) \left(\beta^\eta (1 - \beta)^{1-\eta}\right)^{\sigma-1},$$

as indicated by equation (4.14).

As mentioned in the main text, the effects of β and η on Γ_β are ambiguous and interact with each other. More specifically, we next show that Γ_β is decreasing in η when $\beta < 1/2$, while it is increasing in η when $\beta > 1/2$. To see this, first note that

$$\left.\frac{\partial \ln \Gamma_\beta}{\partial \eta}\right|_{\eta=0} = (\sigma - 1)\left(\frac{1 - 2\beta}{1 - \beta + \sigma\beta} + \ln\left(\frac{\beta}{1 - \beta}\right)\right)$$

and

$$\left.\frac{\partial \ln \Gamma_\beta}{\partial \eta}\right|_{\eta=1} = (\sigma - 1)\left(\frac{1 - 2\beta}{\sigma(1 - \beta) + \beta} + \ln\left(\frac{\beta}{1 - \beta}\right)\right).$$

It is not hard to show that each of these two expressions is negative for $\beta < 1/2$ and positive for $\beta > 1/2$. In particular, one can use $1 - x + \ln x \leq 0$ and $\ln 1/x - (1 - x) \geq 0$, with $x = \beta/(1 - \beta)$ to rewrite these expressions in a way that makes this obvious by inspection.[1] Next, notice that

$$\frac{\partial^2 \ln \Gamma_\beta}{\partial \eta^2} = -\frac{(\sigma - 1)^2 (1 - 2\beta)^2}{(\sigma - (\sigma - 1)(\beta\eta + (1 - \beta)(1 - \eta)))^2} < 0.$$

[1] For completeness, note that $\frac{1-2\beta}{1-\beta+\sigma\beta} + \ln\left(\frac{\beta}{1-\beta}\right) = (2\beta - 1)\frac{\sigma\beta}{(1-\beta)(1-\beta+\sigma\beta)} + \left(1 - \frac{\beta}{1-\beta}\right) +$ $\ln\left(\frac{\beta}{1-\beta}\right) = (2\beta - 1)\frac{(\sigma-2)\beta+1}{\beta((\sigma-1)\beta+1)} + \ln\left(\frac{\beta}{1-\beta}\right) - \left(1 - \frac{1-\beta}{\beta}\right)$ and $\frac{1-2\beta}{\sigma(1-\beta)+\beta} + \ln\left(\frac{\beta}{1-\beta}\right) = (2\beta - 1)$ $\frac{\sigma-1-(\sigma-2)\beta}{(1-\beta)(\sigma+\beta-\sigma\beta)} + \left(1 - \frac{\beta}{1-\beta}\right) + \ln\left(\frac{\beta}{1-\beta}\right) = \sigma(2\beta - 1)\frac{1-\beta}{\beta(\sigma+\beta-\sigma\beta)} + \ln\left(\frac{\beta}{1-\beta}\right) - \left(1 - \frac{1-\beta}{\beta}\right).$

In sum, we have that when $\beta < 1/2$, $\partial \ln \Gamma_\beta / \partial \eta < 0$ when evaluated at $\eta = 0$, while for $\beta > 1/2$, $\partial \Gamma_\beta / \partial \eta > 0$ when evaluated at $\eta = 1$. Together with the concavity of Γ_β, we can then conclude that $(\partial \ln \Gamma_\beta / \partial \eta)(\beta - 1/2) \geq 0$ for all η, with strict inequality for $\beta \neq 1/2$. The practical relevance of this result is that it complicates the overall comparative static of the offshoring share Υ_O with respect to η (remember that under complete contracting, Υ_O is unambiguously decreasing in η).

We next consider how the ambiguous effect of changes in β interacts with η. I begin by noting that simple differentiation delivers

$$\frac{\partial \ln(\Gamma_O/\Gamma_D)}{\partial \beta} = (\sigma - 1) \frac{\eta(1 - \eta) + \sigma \eta^2 - ((\sigma - 1)\eta + 1) 2\eta\beta + \sigma(2\eta - 1)\beta^2}{\beta(1 - \beta)(\sigma - (\sigma - 1)(\beta\eta + (1 - \beta)(1 - \eta)))}$$

and

$$\frac{\partial^2 \ln(\Gamma_O/\Gamma_D)}{\partial \beta^2} = -(\sigma - 1)^2 \left(\frac{(2\eta - 1)^2}{(\sigma - (\sigma - 1)(\beta\eta + (1 - \beta)(1 - \eta)))^2} \right.$$
$$\left. + \frac{\eta(1 - \beta) + \beta(\beta - \eta)}{(\sigma - 1)\beta^2(1 - \beta)^2} \right) < 0.$$

Thus, Γ_O/Γ_D is maximized for the value(s) of β that solve the quadratic equation in the numerator of $\partial \ln(\Gamma_O/\Gamma_D)/\partial \beta$. It turns out that there is only one solution β^* of this quadratic equation satisfying $\beta^* \in [0, 1]$. Rearranging this solution, we find equation (4.15) in Chapter 4, which makes it clear that β^* is increasing in η.

Consider finally how the elasticity of demand affects the ratio Γ_O/Γ_D. Simple (though tedious) differentiation confirms first that

$$\frac{\partial^2 (\ln(\Gamma_O/\Gamma_D))}{\partial \sigma^2} = -\frac{(\beta + \eta - 2\beta\eta)^2}{(\sigma - (\sigma - 1)(\beta\eta + (1 - \beta)(1 - \eta)))^2} < 0.$$

Hence $\partial \ln(\Gamma_O/\Gamma_D)/\partial \sigma$ is bounded above by the value of this derivative when evaluated at the lowest possible value of σ, namely $\sigma = 1$. But note that

$$\left. \frac{\partial \ln(\Gamma_O/\Gamma_D)}{\partial \sigma} \right|_{\sigma=1} = \beta + \eta - 2\beta\eta + \ln\left(\beta^\eta(1 - \beta)^{1-\eta}\right).$$

To evaluate this expression, notice that it increases in η when $\beta > 1/2$, while it decreases in η when $\beta < 1/2$.[2] Furthermore, the expression equals $\beta + \ln(1 - \beta) \leq 0$ when $\eta = 0$, $1 - \beta + \ln(\beta) \leq 0$ when $\eta = 1$, and $\frac{1}{2} + \ln\left(\frac{1}{2}\right) < 0$ when $\beta = 1/2$. We can thus conclude that $\partial \ln(\Gamma_O/\Gamma_D)/\partial \sigma < 0$ for $\sigma > 1$.

---

[2] This in turn can be shown again by applying the inequalities $1 - x + \ln x \leq 0$ and $\ln 1/x - (1 - x) \geq 0$ with $x = \beta/(1 - \beta)$, and decomposing $1 - 2\beta + \ln \frac{\beta}{1-\beta} = \beta \frac{2\beta - 1}{1 - \beta} + 1 - \frac{\beta}{1-\beta} + \ln \frac{\beta}{1-\beta} = (2\beta - 1)\frac{1-\beta}{\beta} - \left(1 - \frac{1-\beta}{\beta}\right) + \ln \frac{\beta}{1-\beta}$.

LIMITATIONS ON EX-ANTE TRANSFERS: FINANCIAL CONSTRAINTS

Remember that the case in which M cannot transfer to F ex ante more than a share ϕ of his or her ex-post rents delivered

$$\frac{\Gamma_O}{\Gamma_D} = \Gamma_\phi \equiv (\sigma + \phi - (\sigma - 1)(1 - \phi)\eta)\left(\frac{1}{2}\right)^\sigma,$$

since again we assumed $\Gamma_D = 1$. It is obvious from this expression that Γ_ϕ increases in ϕ and η, and these effects interact in a positive manner, or $\partial^2\Gamma_\phi/(\partial\phi\partial\eta) > 0$. The positive effect of η on Γ_ϕ again renders ambiguous the overall effect of headquarter intensity on the offshoring share Υ_O (with complete contracting, Υ_O is unambiguously decreasing in η).

Consider next the effect of the demand elasticity σ. Straightforward differentiation delivers

$$\frac{\partial \ln \Gamma_\phi}{\partial \sigma} = \frac{(1 - \eta + \phi\eta)}{(\sigma + \phi - (\sigma - 1)(1 - \phi)\eta)} - \ln 2,$$

as well as $\partial^2 \ln \Gamma_\phi/\partial\sigma^2 < 0$. It is then straightforward to show that for a sufficiently high σ, we necessarily have $\partial \ln \Gamma_\phi/\partial\sigma < 0$. In fact, the weak condition $\sigma + \phi > (\ln 2)^{-1} = 1.4427$ is sufficient for this inequality to hold, regardless of the value of η.

PARTIAL CONTRACTIBILITY

In the extension of the model with partial contractibility in both countries, I alluded to the results in Antràs and Helpman (2008) to motivate the following expressions for the index of contracting distortions under domestic sourcing and offshoring:

$$\Gamma_D = \left(\frac{\sigma}{\sigma - (\sigma - 1)(1 - \mu_N)} + 1\right)^{\sigma-(\sigma-1)(1-\mu_N)}\left(\frac{1}{2}\right)^\sigma; \qquad (A.3)$$

$$\Gamma_O = \left(\frac{\sigma}{\sigma - (\sigma - 1)(1 - \mu_S)} + 1\right)^{\sigma-(\sigma-1)(1-\mu_S)}\left(\frac{1}{2}\right)^\sigma, \qquad (A.4)$$

where

$$\mu_N \equiv \eta\mu_{hN} + (1 - \eta)\mu_{mN};$$
$$\mu_S \equiv \eta\mu_{hS} + (1 - \eta)\mu_{mS}.$$

In fact, these expressions are a special case of those that apply in the framework in Antràs and Helpman (2008). Because I will be referring to these more general results repeatedly in the derivations below, it might be useful to sketch here the steps that lead to that more general formula.

With that in mind, consider the following generalization of the problem in (4.19) after substitution of the participation constraint pinning down the ex-ante transfer:

$$\max_{h_c, h_n, m_c, m_n} \quad R - w_N \left(\mu_{hj} h_c + \left(1 - \mu_{hj} \right) h_n \right) - c_j \left(\mu_{mj} m_c + \left(1 - \mu_{mj} \right) m_n \right)$$

$$\text{s.t.} \quad h_n = \arg\max_h \{ \beta_h R - w_N \left(1 - \mu_{hj} \right) h_n \}$$

$$m_n = \arg\max_m \{ \beta_m R - c_j \left(1 - \mu_{mj} \right) m_n \}, \tag{A.5}$$

where revenue is given by

$$R = B^{1/\sigma} \sigma (\sigma - 1)^{-(\sigma-1)/\sigma} \varphi^{(\sigma-1)/\sigma}$$

$$\times \left(\frac{(h_c)^{\mu_{hj}} (h_n)^{1-\mu_{hj}}}{\eta} \right)^{(\sigma-1)\eta/\sigma} \left(\frac{(m_c)^{\mu_{mj}} (m_n)^{1-\mu_{mj}}}{1 - \eta} \right)^{(\sigma-1)(1-\eta)/\sigma}, \tag{A.6}$$

and where $c_j = w_N$ when $j = N$ and $c_j = \tau w_S$ when $j = S$. The problem above thus covers the cases of symmetric and generalized Nash bargaining, but it also encompasses environments with partial relationship specificity in which F and M only bargain over a fraction of revenue ex post, and thus $\beta_h + \beta_m < 1$. And, as discussed below, this formulation will also prove useful in the characterization of the equilibrium under multiple suppliers.

In order to derive the formula for profits associated with this more general problem, notice first that from the two constraints of the problem, we have

$$h_n = \frac{\beta_h (\sigma - 1) \eta}{\sigma w_N} R$$

$$m_n = \frac{\beta_m (\sigma - 1) (1 - \eta)}{\sigma w_j} R.$$

Plugging these expressions into (A.6) delivers

$$R = \left(B^{1/\sigma} \sigma (\sigma - 1)^{-(\sigma-1)/\sigma} \varphi^{(\sigma-1)/\sigma} \right)^{\frac{\sigma}{\sigma-(\sigma-1)\left(1-\mu_j\right)}} \left(\frac{h_c}{\eta} \right)^{\frac{(\sigma-1)\eta\mu_{hj}}{\sigma-(\sigma-1)\left(1-\mu_j\right)}}$$

$$\times \left(\frac{m_c}{1 - \eta} \right)^{\frac{(\sigma-1)(1-\eta)\mu_{mj}}{\sigma-(\sigma-1)\left(1-\mu_j\right)}} \left(\frac{\beta_h (\sigma - 1)}{\sigma w_N} \right)^{\frac{(\sigma-1)\eta\left(1-\mu_{hj}\right)}{\sigma-(\sigma-1)\left(1-\mu_j\right)}}$$

$$\times \left(\frac{\beta_m (\sigma - 1)}{\sigma w_j} \right)^{\frac{(\sigma-1)(1-\eta)\left(1-\mu_{mj}\right)}{\sigma-(\sigma-1)\left(1-\mu_j\right)}}. \tag{A.7}$$

Given the Cobb-Douglas structure, we can then characterize the choice of contractible investments as satisfying

$$h_c = \frac{(\sigma-1)\eta\left(1 - \frac{(\sigma-1)}{\sigma}\left(\beta_h\eta\left(1-\mu_{hj}\right) + \beta_m\left(1-\eta\right)\left(1-\mu_{mj}\right)\right)\right)}{\left(\sigma - (\sigma-1)\left(1-\mu_j\right)\right)w_N} R \quad (A.8)$$

$$m_c = \frac{(\sigma-1)(1-\eta)\left(1 - \frac{(\sigma-1)}{\sigma}\left(\beta_h\eta\left(1-\mu_{hj}\right) + \beta_m\left(1-\eta\right)\left(1-\mu_{mj}\right)\right)\right)}{\left(\sigma - (\sigma-1)\left(1-\mu_j\right)\right)w_j} R. \quad (A.9)$$

As a result, operating profits are given by

$$\left(\frac{\sigma - (\sigma-1)\left(\beta_h\eta\left(1-\mu_{hj}\right) + \beta_m\left(1-\eta\right)\left(1-\mu_{mj}\right)\right)}{\sigma - (\sigma-1)\left(1-\mu_j\right)}\right)\frac{R}{\sigma},$$

where R can be solved by plugging the above expressions (A.8) and (A.9) into (A.7). This delivers, after some manipulations

$$R = \sigma B\left((w_N)^{\eta}\left(w_j\right)^{1-\eta}\right)^{1-\sigma}\varphi^{\sigma-1}\left(\beta_h\right)^{(\sigma-1)\eta(1-\mu_{hj})}\left(\beta_m\right)^{(\sigma-1)(1-\eta)(1-\mu_{mj})}$$

$$\times\left(\frac{\sigma - (\sigma-1)\left(\beta_h\eta\left(1-\mu_{hj}\right) + \beta_m\left(1-\eta\right)\left(1-\mu_{mj}\right)\right)}{\sigma - (\sigma-1)\left(1-\mu_j\right)}\right)^{(\sigma-1)\mu_j},$$

and thus

$$\pi_D(\varphi) + f_D w_N = (w_N)^{1-\sigma} B\Gamma_D\varphi^{\sigma-1}$$

$$\pi_O(\varphi) + f_O w_N = \left((w_N)^{\eta}(\tau w_S)^{1-\eta}\right)^{1-\sigma} B\Gamma_O\varphi^{\sigma-1},$$

where

$$\Gamma_\ell = \left(\frac{\sigma - (\sigma-1)\left(\beta_h\eta\left(1-\mu_{hj}\right) + \beta_m\left(1-\eta\right)\left(1-\mu_{mj}\right)\right)}{\sigma - (\sigma-1)\left(1-\mu_j\right)}\right)^{\sigma-(\sigma-1)(1-\mu_j)}$$

$$\times\left(\beta_h\right)^{(\sigma-1)\eta(1-\mu_{hj})}\left(\beta_m\right)^{(\sigma-1)(1-\eta)(1-\mu_{mj})} \quad (A.10)$$

captures the contractual frictions associated with the sourcing options $\ell = D$ and $\ell = O$, which entail manufacturing in country $j = N$ and country $j = S$, respectively. Setting $\beta_h = \beta_m = 1/2$, it is straightforward to verify that equation (A.10) reduces to equations (A.3) and (A.4) above.

Having derived these equations, we can next turn to discussing some key comparative statics. Below, I will focus on an analysis of the general formula (A.10), with the understanding that the results obtained below also apply to the particular case with $\beta_h = \beta_m = 1/2$. Consider first the effect of the indices of contractibility μ_{hj} and μ_{mj}, and their weighted average μ_j. As shown in Antràs and Helpman (2008) (see the proof of their Proposition 1), Γ_ℓ is necessarily non-decreasing in each of these parameters. The proof in that paper is rather cumbersome, so it may be worth offering a much simpler proof here. Consider the case of an increase in μ_{hj} (the derivations associated with a change in μ_{mj} are analogous). Taking logs of (A.10), differentiating and rearranging terms, we can write

$$\frac{\partial \ln \Gamma_\ell}{\partial \mu_{hj}} = \eta \, (\sigma - 1) \, (- \ln \mathcal{Q} - (1 - \mathcal{Q}) - \ln \beta_h - (1 - \beta_h)) + \mathcal{W}, \qquad (A.11)$$

where

$$\mathcal{Q} = \frac{\sigma - (\sigma - 1) \left(1 - \mu_j\right)}{\sigma - (\sigma - 1) \left(\beta_h \eta \left(1 - \mu_{hj}\right) + \beta_m \left(1 - \eta\right) \left(1 - \mu_{mj}\right)\right)}$$

and

$$\mathcal{W} = \eta \, (\sigma - 1)^2 \, (1 - \beta_h) \frac{(1 - \eta) \left(1 - \mu_{mj}\right) (1 - \beta_m) + \eta \left(1 - \mu_{hj}\right) (1 - \beta_h)}{\sigma - (\sigma - 1) \left(\beta_h \eta \left(1 - \mu_{hj}\right) + \beta_m \left(1 - \eta\right) \left(1 - \mu_{mj}\right)\right)}.$$

It is clear that the second term $\mathcal{W}$ in (A.11) is positive, while the first one is non-negative as well because $- \ln x - (1 - x) \leq 0$ for all x. Thus, $\partial \ln \Gamma_\ell / \partial \mu_{hj} \geq 0$.

It is also clear from inspection of equation (A.10) that, as stated in the main text, the effect of improvements in contractibility interacts with the headquarter intensity of production depending on the source of these changes in contractibility. Increases in μ_{hj} will be particularly beneficial when η is high, while the converse is true for μ_{mj}. For the same reason, and as in the model with totally incomplete contracting and generalized Nash bargaining, the effect of changes in headquarter intensity on Γ_ℓ is ambiguous.

Let us now turn to the effect of the elasticity of demand σ on Γ_ℓ. Tedious differentiation of Γ_ℓ delivers

$$\frac{\partial^2 \ln \Gamma_\ell}{\partial \sigma^2} = - \frac{(1 - \mu - \eta \, (1 - \mu_h) \, \beta_h - (1 - \eta) \, (1 - \mu_m) \, \beta_m)^2}{(1 - \mu + \sigma \mu) \, (\sigma - (\sigma - 1) \, (\beta_h \eta \, (1 - \mu_h) + \beta_m \, (1 - \eta) \, (1 - \mu_m)))^2} < 0$$

and

$$\frac{\partial \ln \Gamma}{\partial \sigma} \bigg|_{\sigma = 1} = 1 - \mu + \eta \, (1 - \mu_h) \, (\ln \beta_h - \beta_h) + (1 - \eta) \, (1 - \mu_m) \, (\ln \beta_m - \beta_m) \leq 0.$$

To prove the negative sign in the second equation, note that this expression is maximized when $\beta_h = \beta_m = 1$, and at that level $\partial \ln \Gamma / \partial \sigma|_{\sigma=1} = 1 - \mu - \eta \, (1 - \mu_h) - (1 - \eta) \, (1 - \mu_m) = 0$. In light of these results, we can conclude that

$\partial \ln \Gamma / \partial \sigma < 0$ for all $\sigma > 1$, and thus contractual frictions are again aggravated by high demand elasticities in this variant of the model.

We next show how the effects of contractibility and the elasticity of demand interact with each other. In particular, differentiating $\partial \ln \Gamma_\ell / \partial \mu_{hj}$ in (A.11) with respect to σ, we find:

$$\frac{\partial^2 \ln \Gamma_\ell}{\partial \mu_{hj} \partial \sigma} = \frac{1}{(\sigma - 1)} \frac{\partial \ln \Gamma_\ell}{\partial \mu_{hj}} + \eta (\sigma - 1) \frac{\partial (-\ln \mathcal{Q} - (1 - \mathcal{Q}))}{\partial \sigma} + \frac{\partial \mathcal{W}}{\partial \sigma}.$$

We have established before that the first term is non-negative. Differentiating the second and third terms, we find

$$\frac{\partial \left(\ln \mathcal{Q}^{-1} - 1 + \mathcal{Q} \right)}{\partial \sigma} = \frac{(\sigma - 1) \left(\frac{(1-\eta)(1-\mu_m)(1-\beta_m)+\eta(1-\mu_h)(1-\beta_h)}{\sigma-(\sigma-1)(\beta_h\eta(1-\mu_h)+\beta_m(1-\eta)(1-\mu_m))} \right)^2}{(\sigma - (\sigma - 1) (1 - \eta \mu_h - (1 - \eta) \mu_m))}$$

and

$$\frac{\partial \mathcal{W}}{\partial \sigma} = (1 - \beta_h) \frac{(1 - \eta) (1 - \mu_m) (1 - \beta_m) + \eta (1 - \mu_h) (1 - \beta_h)}{(\sigma - (\sigma - 1) (\beta_h \eta (1 - \mu_h) + \beta_m (1 - \eta) (1 - \mu_m)))^2},$$

and thus these terms are non-negative as well. In sum, we can conclude that $\frac{\partial^2 \ln \Gamma_\ell}{\partial \mu_{hj} \partial \sigma} \geq 0$, as stated in the main text. Notice that the result is *not* particular to the special case $\beta_h = \beta_m = 1/2$, nor does it require $\beta_h + \beta_m = 1$. It is worth pointing out that it is important that we are considering the partial derivative of the logarithm of Γ_ℓ. Computing $\frac{\partial^2 \Gamma_\ell}{\partial \mu_{hj} \partial \sigma}$, we find that this expression may take negative values for some parameter values. This justifies the use of logarithms of import flows in certain empirical specifications in Chapter 5, as discussed in the main text.

I have thus far focused on providing formal proofs of the results mentioned in Chapter 4, which are key for interpreting the cross-country, cross-industry results in the second part of Chapter 5. The first part of that chapter focuses on studying the determinants of the offshoring share Υ_O, which in turn depend on the ratio Γ_O / Γ_D:

$$\frac{\Gamma_O}{\Gamma_D} = \frac{\left(\frac{\sigma-(\sigma-1)(\beta_h\eta(1-\mu_{hS})+\beta_m(1-\eta)(1-\mu_{mS}))}{\sigma-(\sigma-1)(1-\mu_S)} \right)^{\sigma-(\sigma-1)(1-\mu_S)}}{\left(\frac{\sigma-(\sigma-1)(\beta_h\eta(1-\mu_{hN})+\beta_m(1-\eta)(1-\mu_{mN}))}{\sigma-(\sigma-1)(1-\mu_N)} \right)^{\sigma-(\sigma-1)(1-\mu_N)}}$$
$$\times (\beta_h)^{(\sigma-1)\eta(\mu_{hN}-\mu_{hS})} (\beta_m)^{(\sigma-1)(1-\eta)(\mu_{mN}-\mu_{mS})}.$$

From the results above, it is immediate that Γ_O / Γ_D is increasing in μ_S and its components μ_{hS} and μ_{mS}, and decreasing in μ_N and its components μ_{hN} and μ_{mN}. Less trivially, we can also use the results above to show that

Γ_O/Γ_D is decreasing in the elasticity of demand σ provided that contract enforcement is higher in domestic transactions vis-a-vis offshoring transactions. In particular, notice that

$$\frac{\partial \ln (\Gamma_O/\Gamma_D)}{\partial \sigma} = \frac{\partial \ln (\Gamma_O)}{\partial \sigma} - \frac{\partial \ln (\Gamma_D)}{\partial \sigma},$$

and provided that $\mu_{hN} \geq \mu_{hS}$ and $\mu_{mN} \geq \mu_{mS}$, we can appeal to the above results $\frac{\partial^2 \ln \Gamma_\ell}{\partial \mu_{hj} \partial \sigma} \geq 0$ and $\frac{\partial^2 \ln \Gamma_\ell}{\partial \mu_{mj} \partial \sigma} \geq 0$ to conclude that $\partial \ln (\Gamma_O/\Gamma_D)/\partial \sigma \leq 0$.

Finally, it is important to emphasize that our results above do not suggest that offshoring shares will be higher for more "contractible" goods. To see this, suppose that contractibility in the South is always a fraction $\delta < 1$ of the one in the North, so we can write $\mu_{hS}/\mu_{hN} = \mu_{mS}/\mu_{mN} = \delta$. For the special case, $\beta_h = \beta_m = 1/2$, we then have

$$\frac{\Gamma_O}{\Gamma_D} = \frac{\left(\frac{\sigma}{\sigma-(\sigma-1)(1-\delta\mu_N)} + 1\right)^{\sigma-(\sigma-1)(1-\delta\mu_N)}}{\left(\frac{\sigma}{\sigma-(\sigma-1)(1-\mu_N)} + 1\right)^{\sigma-(\sigma-1)(1-\mu_N)}}.$$

Increases in μ_N can then be interpreted as overall increases in the contractibility of goods, since they affect their contractibility proportionately, regardless of the country where production takes place. It is not hard to confirm, however, that the effect of μ_N on the expression above is non-monotonic. For instance, if one sets $\sigma = 10$ and $\delta = 0.9$, Γ_O/Γ_D is lower when $\mu_N = 0.7$ than when either $\mu_N = 0.5$ or $\mu_N = 0.9$.

RELATIONSHIP SPECIFICITY

As discussed in the main text, this is a special case of the more general Antràs-Helpman (2008) framework with $\beta_h = \beta_m = 1 - \epsilon/2$, with $\epsilon \in [0, 1]$. The results derived above for the case of partial contractibility thus continue to apply. Improvements in contractibility are associated with larger values of Γ_ℓ, the elasticity of demand σ affects Γ_ℓ negatively, and the positive "interaction" effect $\partial \left(\partial \ln \Gamma_\ell/\partial \mu_j\right)/\partial \sigma > 0$ continue to apply. Similarly, we have that the offshoring share is negatively impacted by the elasticity of demand σ on account of the term Γ_O/Γ_D (remember though that there is a positive counterbalancing effect that applies even in the complete-contracting case).

Let us then focus on the new comparative statics that emerge when introducing relationship specificity. Consider first the direct effect of the specificity parameter ϵ. Simple differentiation of (4.24) delivers

$$\frac{\partial \ln \Gamma_\ell \left(\mu_j, \epsilon\right)}{\partial \epsilon} = -\frac{\sigma \epsilon (\sigma - 1) \left(1 - \mu_j\right)}{(2 - \epsilon) \left(2 \left(1 - \mu_j\right) + (2 - \epsilon) \sigma \mu_j + \left(\sigma - 1 + \mu_j\right) \epsilon\right)} < 0$$

and

$$\frac{\partial^2 \ln \Gamma_\ell \left(\mu_j, \epsilon \right)}{\partial \epsilon \partial \mu_j} = \frac{2\sigma^2 \epsilon (\sigma - 1)}{(2 - \epsilon) \left(2 \left(1 - \mu_j \right) + (2 - \epsilon) \sigma \mu_j + \left(\sigma - 1 + \mu_j \right) \epsilon \right)^2} > 0,$$

as stated in the main text. Hence, profitability is decreasing in specificity, and improvements in contractibility are particularly profitability-enhancing at high levels of specificity. Furthermore, we can use the latter result to conclude that

$$\frac{\partial \ln \left(\Gamma_O / \Gamma_D \right)}{\partial \epsilon} = \frac{\partial \ln \left(\Gamma_O \right)}{\partial \epsilon} - \frac{\partial \ln \left(\Gamma_D \right)}{\partial \epsilon} \leq 0$$

for $\mu_{hN} \geq \mu_{hS}$ and $\mu_{mN} \geq \mu_{mS}$. In other words, whenever contract enforcement is higher in domestic transactions relative to offshore transactions, higher levels of specificity tend to be associated with lower offshoring shares Υ_O.

MULTIPLE INPUTS AND MULTILATERAL CONTRACTING

As mentioned in the main text, the equilibrium expressions of this variant of the model are analogous to those in Antràs and Helpman (2008) whenever $\beta_h = \beta_m = \sigma \rho / ((\sigma - 1)(1 - \eta) + \sigma \rho)$. Plugging these values into (A.10) delivers equation (4.28). Because (4.28) is a special case of (A.10), we can conclude once again that $\partial \Gamma_\ell \left(\mu_j, \rho \right) / \partial \mu_j \geq 0$. Furthermore, we can also appeal to previous results to establish that $\partial \Gamma_\ell \left(\mu_j, \rho \right) / \partial \sigma < 0$. This latter comparative static result would appear to be complicated by the fact that β_h and β_m are now a function of σ. But since $\Gamma_\ell \left(\mu_j, \rho \right)$ in (A.10) is increasing in β_h and β_m, and each of these two shares is decreasing in σ, we can again conclude that $\partial \Gamma_\ell \left(\mu_j, \rho, \beta_h (\sigma), \beta_m (\sigma) \right) / \partial \sigma < 0$. In addition, the cross-partial derivative $\partial \left(\partial \ln \Gamma_\ell \left(\mu_j, \rho \right) / \partial \mu_j \right) / \partial \sigma$ continues to be positive, despite the dependence of β_h and β_m on σ. To see this, we can just appeal to equation (A.11) and note that each of the terms in that expression is decreasing in β_h, which in turn decreases in σ. More precisely, we have that (i) $- \ln \mathcal{Q} - (1 - \mathcal{Q})$ is decreasing in $\mathcal{Q}$ whenever $\mathcal{Q} < 1$; (ii) $\mathcal{Q}$ is indeed lower than 1 and is increasing in β_h; (iii) $- \ln \beta_h - (1 - \beta_h)$ is decreasing in β_h for $\beta_h < 1$; and (iv) $\mathcal{W}$ is decreasing in β_h.

We can next turn to the effects of ρ which is the new parameter introduced in this variant of the model. Simple differentiation of equation (4.28) indicates

$$\frac{\partial \ln \Gamma_\ell \left(\mu_j, \rho \right)}{\partial \rho}$$

$$= \frac{(\sigma - 1)^3 (1 - \eta)^2 \left(1 - \mu_j \right)}{\rho (\rho \sigma + (\sigma - 1)(1 - \eta)) \left(\left(\sigma - (\sigma - 1) \left(1 - \mu_j \right) \right) \rho + (\sigma - 1)(1 - \eta) \right)} > 0$$

and

$$\frac{\partial^2 \ln \Gamma_\ell \left(\mu_j, \rho \right)}{\partial \rho \partial \mu_j} = -(\sigma - 1)^3 \frac{(1 - \eta)^2}{\rho \left(\left(\sigma - (\sigma - 1) \left(1 - \mu_j \right) \right) \rho + (\sigma - 1) (1 - \eta) \right)^2} < 0,$$

which are the two key novel comparative statics highlighted in the main text of that section. Again, this last cross-partial derivative is useful in deriving predictions for the offshoring share Υ_O since for $\mu_{hN} \geq \mu_{hS}$ and $\mu_{mN} \geq \mu_{mS}$, this result implies $\frac{\partial \ln(\Gamma_O / \Gamma_D)}{\partial \rho} = \frac{\partial \ln(\Gamma_O)}{\partial \rho} - \frac{\partial \ln(\Gamma_D)}{\partial \rho} \geq 0$. In sum, whenever contract enforcement is higher in domestic transactions relative to offshore transactions, higher degrees of input substitutability tend to be associated with higher offshoring shares Υ_O.

A.3 Derivation of Some Results in Chapter 6

INTRAFIRM TRADE SHARES WITH AN ALTERNATIVE RANKING OF FIXED COSTS

In Chapter 6, I computed intrafirm trade shares under the assumption that the ranking of fixed costs is given by $f_{OV} > f_{OO} > f_{DV} > f_{DO}$. This is a standard assumption in the literature (see for instance, Antràs and Helpman, 2004, 2008). Nevertheless, the evidence from Spain discussed in Chapter 8 suggests that perhaps a more empirically plausible ranking of fixed costs is as follows:

$$f_{OV} > f_{DV} > f_{OO} > f_{DO}.$$

In this appendix I study the robustness of the results to assuming this alternative ranking of fixed costs. As already mentioned in Chapter 6, the share Sh_{i-f} of intrafirm imported inputs over the total imported input purchases in this case is given by

$$Sh_{i-f} = \frac{\lambda^{1-\sigma} \int_{\tilde{\varphi}_{OV}}^{\infty} \varphi^{\sigma-1} dG(\varphi)}{\Gamma_{OO} \int_{\tilde{\varphi}_{OO}}^{\tilde{\varphi}_{DV}} \varphi^{\sigma-1} dG(\varphi) + \lambda^{1-\sigma} \int_{\tilde{\varphi}_{OV}}^{\infty} \varphi^{\sigma-1} dG(\varphi)},$$

which, assuming a Pareto distribution of productivity with shape parameter $\kappa > \sigma - 1$, reduces to

$$Sh_{i-f} = \frac{\lambda^{1-\sigma}}{\Gamma_{OO} \left[\left(\frac{\tilde{\varphi}_{OV}}{\tilde{\varphi}_{OO}} \right)^{\kappa-\sigma-1} - \left(\frac{\tilde{\varphi}_{OV}}{\tilde{\varphi}_{DV}} \right)^{\kappa-\sigma-1} \right] + \lambda^{1-\sigma}}.$$

Given the sorting in Figure 6.6, the key ratios of thresholds in the above equation satisfy:

$$\frac{\tilde{\varphi}_{OV}}{\tilde{\varphi}_{OO}} = \left[\frac{f_{OV} - f_{DV}}{f_{OO} - f_{DO}} \times \frac{\Gamma_{OO}}{\lambda^{1-\sigma}} \times \frac{1 - (w_N/\tau w_S)^{-(1-\eta)(\sigma-1)}\Gamma_{DO}/\Gamma_{OO}}{1 - (w_N/\tau w_S)^{-(1-\eta)(\sigma-1)}}\right]^{1/(\sigma-1)};$$

$$\frac{\tilde{\varphi}_{OV}}{\tilde{\varphi}_{DV}} = \left[\frac{f_{OV} - f_{DV}}{f_{DV} - f_{OO}} \times \frac{\lambda^{1-\sigma}(w_N/\tau w_S)^{-(1-\eta)(\sigma-1)} - \Gamma_{OO}}{\lambda^{1-\sigma} - \lambda^{1-\sigma}(w_N/\tau w_S)^{-(1-\eta)(\sigma-1)}}\right]^{1/(\sigma-1)}.$$

Notice that $\tilde{\varphi}_{OV}/\tilde{\varphi}_{OO}$ increases in Γ_{OO} and λ, and decreases in Γ_{DO}/Γ_{OO} and $(w_N/\tau w_S)^{-(1-\eta)(\sigma-1)}$ (for the natural case in which $\Gamma_{OO} < \Gamma_{DO}$). Conversely, $\tilde{\varphi}_{OV}/\tilde{\varphi}_{DV}$ decreases in Γ_{OO} and λ, and increases in $(w_N/\tau w_S)^{-(1-\eta)(\sigma-1)}$. We can thus conclude that Sh_{i-f} necessarily decreases in Γ_{OO} and λ, and increases in $(w_N/\tau w_S)^{-(1-\eta)(\sigma-1)}$ and Γ_{DO}/Γ_{OO}.

Invoking the comparative statics derived for the transaction-cost model (see, for instance, Table 5.5) we can thus conclude that Sh_{i-f} is shaped by parameter values in the same manner as in the case with the fixed costs ranked according to $f_{OV} > f_{OO} > f_{DV} > f_{DO}$, and thus:

$$Sh_{i-f} = Sh_{i-f}\left(\underset{-}{\lambda}, \underset{-}{w_N/w_S}, \underset{+}{\tau}, \underset{-}{\kappa}, \underset{-}{\phi}, \underset{+}{\mu_S}, \underset{-}{\epsilon}, \underset{?}{\rho}, \underset{?}{\sigma}, \eta\right).$$

Let us next consider how the implications of the property-rights model are affected by this alternative ranking of fixed costs and implied sorting pattern consistent with the Spanish data. In such a case, the intrafirm trade share is given by

$$Sh_{i-f} = \frac{\Gamma_{OV}/\Gamma_{OO}}{\left[\left(\frac{\tilde{\varphi}_{OV}}{\tilde{\varphi}_{OO}}\right)^{\kappa-\sigma-1} - \left(\frac{\tilde{\varphi}_{OV}}{\tilde{\varphi}_{DV}}\right)^{\kappa-\sigma-1}\right] + \Gamma_{OV}/\Gamma_{OO}},$$

with

$$\frac{\tilde{\varphi}_{OV}}{\tilde{\varphi}_{OO}} = \left[\frac{f_{OV} - f_{DV}}{f_{OO} - f_{DO}} \times \frac{1 - (w_N/\tau w_S)^{-(1-\eta)(\sigma-1)}\Gamma_{DO}/\Gamma_{OO}}{\Gamma_{OV}/\Gamma_{OO} - (w_N/\tau w_S)^{-(1-\eta)(\sigma-1)}\Gamma_{DV}/\Gamma_{OO}}\right]^{1/(\sigma-1)};$$

$$\frac{\tilde{\varphi}_{OV}}{\tilde{\varphi}_{DV}} = \left[\frac{f_{OV} - f_{DV}}{f_{DV} - f_{OO}} \times \frac{(w_N/\tau w_S)^{-(1-\eta)(\sigma-1)}\Gamma_{DV}/\Gamma_{OO} - 1}{\Gamma_{OV}/\Gamma_{OO} - (w_N/\tau w_S)^{-(1-\eta)(\sigma-1)}\Gamma_{DV}/\Gamma_{OO}}\right]^{1/(\sigma-1)}.$$

It is clear that the intrafirm trade share thus continues to be increasing in the key ratio Γ_{OV}/Γ_{OO}. Furthermore, Sh_{i-f} continues to be increasing in Γ_{DO}/Γ_{OO}, reflecting a selection into offshore outsourcing effect.

An important novel feature of these equations is that they now also depend on the ratio Γ_{DV}/Γ_{OO}, and the overall dependence of the share of intrafirm trade on this term is ambiguous. Whenever $\Gamma_{OV} = \Gamma_{DV}$, the equations for $\tilde{\varphi}_{OV}/\tilde{\varphi}_{OO}$ and $\tilde{\varphi}_{OV}/\tilde{\varphi}_{DV}$ simplify significantly, and one can show that the intrafirm trade share continues to be increasing in Γ_{OV}/Γ_{OO} and Γ_{DO}/Γ_{OO} as in the case of our Benchmark model. Nevertheless, in the presence of differences in contractibility between domestic and foreign sourcing, we would expect that $\Gamma_{OV} < \Gamma_{DV}$, hence complicating matters.

Another point worth noting is that the overall effect of $(w_N/\tau w_S)^{-(1-\eta)(\sigma-1)}$ is no longer unambiguous because although $\tilde{\varphi}_{OV}/\tilde{\varphi}_{DV}$ is clearly increasing in this term, the effect of $(w_N/\tau w_S)^{-(1-\eta)(\sigma-1)}$ on $\tilde{\varphi}_{OV}/\tilde{\varphi}_{OO}$ crucially depends on the relative size of Γ_{OV}/Γ_{OO} and Γ_{DV}/Γ_{DO}. In particular, when $\Gamma_{OV}/\Gamma_{OO} < \Gamma_{DV}/\Gamma_{DO}$, we now have that $\tilde{\varphi}_{OV}/\tilde{\varphi}_{OO}$ is increasing in $(w_N/\tau w_S)^{-(1-\eta)(\sigma-1)}$, and thus through this mechanism, the intrafirm trade share might be negatively correlated with trade frictions τ, consistently with our regression results in Chapter 8. Conversely, when $\Gamma_{OV}/\Gamma_{OO} > \Gamma_{DV}/\Gamma_{DO}$, we revert to a scenario analogous to the transaction-cost model, in which $\tilde{\varphi}_{OV}/\tilde{\varphi}_{OO}$ is decreasing in $(w_N/\tau w_S)^{-(1-\eta)(\sigma-1)}$ and the overall effect of τ on the intrafirm trade share is necessarily positive. Which of the inequalities $\Gamma_{OV}/\Gamma_{OO} < \Gamma_{DV}/\Gamma_{DO}$ or $\Gamma_{OV}/\Gamma_{OO} > \Gamma_{DV}/\Gamma_{DO}$ is more reasonable? Building on the insights from our extension with partial contractibility, we can conclude that if the higher contractual insecurity of offshoring stems largely from lower contractibility of headquarter services, we will have that $\Gamma_{OV}/\Gamma_{OO} > \Gamma_{DV}/\Gamma_{DO}$. Conversely, when lower contractibility of input manufacturing is the key source of contractual insecurity in offshoring, we will instead have $\Gamma_{OV}/\Gamma_{OO} < \Gamma_{DV}/\Gamma_{DO}$.

In summary, with this alternative ranking of fixed costs, the comparative statics of the transaction-cost model are the same as with the Benchmark model sorting, while those of the property-rights model are now more complicated. This is due to the fact that the extensive margin of offshoring and foreign integration are shaped by the movements of several thresholds. Still the ratio Γ_{OV}/Γ_{OO} continues to be a key determinant of the intrafirm trade share. And the richer extensive margin effects imply that one cannot reject the property-rights model based on the negative effect of trade costs on that ratio estimated in Chapter 8.

DOWNSTREAMNESS AND INTEGRATION

In this section of the appendix, I provide some more details on the variant of the transaction-cost model in Chapter 6 with sequential production. The analysis is similar to the one in the property-rights model in Antràs and Chor (2013).

As in Chapter 4, I focus on the case in which production does not use headquarter services and offshore outsourcing is associated with totally incomplete contracts. As also discussed in Chapter 4, the contractual efficiency of offshore outsourcing, given unconstrained ex-ante transfers and bargaining share $\beta(v)$ for each state v, is given by equation (4.30), which I reproduce here:

$$\Gamma_\ell\left(\{\beta(v)\}_{v=0}^1\right) = \frac{(\sigma-1)}{(\sigma_\rho-1)} \left(\frac{\sigma_\rho}{\sigma}\right)^{\frac{\sigma-\sigma_\rho}{\sigma_\rho-1}} \int_0^1 \{\left(\frac{\sigma_\rho}{1-\beta(v)} - (\sigma_\rho-1)\right)$$

$$\times (1-\beta(v))^{\sigma_\rho} \left[\int_0^v (1-\beta(u))^{\sigma_\rho-1} du\right]^{\frac{\sigma-\sigma_\rho}{\sigma_\rho-1}} \}dv. \qquad \text{(A.12)}$$

Also, as in Chapter 4, one can then solve for the optimal path of bargaining shares $\beta^*(v)$ and see how it relates to v as a function of the other parameters of the model. The main lessons we obtained in that chapter are that when $\sigma > \sigma_\rho$, $\beta^*(v)$ is increasing in v, while when $\sigma < \sigma_\rho$, $\beta^*(v)$ is decreasing in v.

As discussed in Chapter 7, Antràs and Chor (2013) consider a situation where the firm cannot freely choose any arbitrary $\beta(v)$ at any stage v, but rather has to decide whether or not to integrate the different suppliers, with integration being associated with a higher bargaining share (β_V) than outsourcing (β_O). Their results are explained in Chapter 7 and their derivations can be obtained from their paper and their Supplementary Appendix.

Consider instead a transaction-cost version of the model in which integration is not associated with higher bargaining power in the same contracting environment, but is rather associated with the ability to circumvent contracting and bargaining at the expense of some "governance costs." More specifically, assume that when a supplier is owned by the final-good producer, the firm has the authority to force the supplier to choose a level of investment at stage v that maximizes its incremental contribution to revenue minus the (inflated) cost of investment provision. More formally, I assume that, under integration, $m(v)$ is set to maximize $\Delta R(v) - \lambda c_j m(v)$ rather than $(1-\beta_O)\Delta R(v) - c_j m(v)$, where $\Delta R(v)$ is given in equation (4.29). Thus, integration resolves the hold-up problem at stage v but it is associated with higher governance costs (since $\lambda > 1$).

The key question is then: in which type of stages is it crucial to resolve the hold-up problem? Our results on the optimal bargaining shares $\beta^*(v)$ suggest that resolving the hold-up problem via integration is particularly beneficial in upstream stages for $\sigma > \sigma_\rho$, and in downstream stages for $\sigma < \sigma_\rho$. In other words, downstreamness should have a negative effect on foreign integration relative to offshore outsourcing whenever inputs are sequential complements ($\sigma > \sigma_\rho$), while it should have a positive effect on foreign integration when inputs are sequential substitutes ($\sigma < \sigma_\rho$).

This result can be formalized along the lines of the proof of Proposition 2 in Antràs and Chor (2013). Take the case $\sigma > \sigma_\rho$, and suppose there exists a stage $\tilde{v} \in (0, 1)$ and a positive constant $\varepsilon > 0$ such that stages in $(\tilde{v} - \varepsilon, \tilde{v})$ are outsourced, while stages in $(\tilde{v}, \tilde{v} + \varepsilon)$ are integrated. This situation would provide a counterexample of our claim that only the most upstream stages can possibly be integrated. We shall then show that this counterexample leads to a contradiction. Let the firm profits associated with this scenario be denoted by Π_1. On the other hand, consider an alternative organizational mode which instead integrates the stages in $(\tilde{v} - \varepsilon, \tilde{v})$ and outsources the stages in $(\tilde{v}, \tilde{v} + \varepsilon)$, while retaining the same organizational decision for all other stages. Let profits from this alternative be Π_2. Both of these profit flows are naturally proportional to the indices of contractual efficiency Γ_ℓ associated with each of these scenarios.

Using the expression for Γ_ℓ in (A.12), one can then show that, up to a positive multiplicative constant:

$$\Pi_1 - \Pi_2 \propto \int_{\tilde{v}-\varepsilon}^{\tilde{v}} \left(1 - \frac{(\sigma_\rho - 1)}{\sigma_\rho}(1 - \beta_O)\right)(1 - \beta_O)^{\sigma_\rho - 1}$$

$$\times \left[B + \varepsilon\lambda^{1-\sigma_\rho} + (j - \tilde{v})(1 - \beta_O)^{\sigma_\rho - 1}\right]^{\frac{\sigma - \sigma_\rho}{\sigma_\rho - 1}} dj$$

$$+ \int_{\tilde{v}}^{\tilde{v}+\varepsilon} \frac{1}{\sigma_\rho}\lambda^{1-\sigma_\rho}\left[B + (j - \tilde{v} + \varepsilon)\lambda^{1-\sigma_\rho}\right]^{\frac{\sigma - \sigma_\rho}{\sigma_\rho - 1}} dj$$

$$- \int_{\tilde{v}-\varepsilon}^{\tilde{v}} \frac{1}{\sigma_\rho}\lambda^{1-\sigma_\rho}\left[B + \varepsilon(1 - \beta_O)^{\sigma_\rho - 1} + (j - \tilde{v})\lambda^{1-\sigma_\rho}\right]^{\frac{\sigma - \sigma_\rho}{\sigma_\rho - 1}} dj$$

$$- \int_{\tilde{v}}^{\tilde{v}+\varepsilon} \left(1 - \frac{(\sigma_\rho - 1)}{\sigma_\rho}(1 - \beta_O)\right)(1 - \beta_O)^{\sigma_\rho - 1}$$

$$\times \left[B + (j - \tilde{v} + \varepsilon)(1 - \beta_O)^{\sigma_\rho - 1}\right]^{\frac{\sigma - \sigma_\rho}{\sigma_\rho - 1}} dj.$$

where we define $B \equiv \int_0^{\tilde{v}-\varepsilon} \lambda^{1-\sigma_\rho} dk$ (since those upstream stages are integrated given that $1 - \beta^*(0) \to +\infty$). That the difference in profits depends only on profits in the interval $(\tilde{v} - \varepsilon, \tilde{v} + \varepsilon)$ and is not affected by decisions downstream follows from the fact that we have chosen the width ε to be common for both sub-intervals. Evaluating the integrals above with respect to j and simplifying, we obtain after some tedious algebra:

$$\Pi_1 - \Pi_2 \propto \beta_O \frac{\sigma_\rho - 1}{\sigma_\rho} \left[\left(B + \varepsilon\lambda^{1-\sigma_\rho}\right)^{\frac{\sigma - \sigma_\rho}{\sigma_\rho - 1}} + \left(B + \varepsilon(1 - \beta_O)^{\sigma_\rho - 1}\right)^{\frac{\sigma - \sigma_\rho}{\sigma_\rho - 1}}\right.$$

$$\left. - \left(B + \varepsilon\lambda^{1-\sigma_\rho} + \varepsilon(1 - \beta_O)^{\sigma_\rho - 1}\right)^{\frac{\sigma - \sigma_\rho}{\sigma_\rho - 1}} - B^{\frac{\sigma - \sigma_\rho}{\sigma_\rho - 1}}\right].$$

To show a contradiction, i.e., $\Pi_1 - \Pi_2 < 0$, it thus suffices to show that the expression in square parentheses is negative. To see this, consider the function

$f(y) = y^{\frac{\sigma-\sigma_\rho}{\sigma_\rho-1}}$. Simple differentiation will show that for $y, a > 0$ and $b \geq 0$, $f(y + a + b) - f(y + b)$ is an increasing function in b when $\sigma > \sigma_\rho$. Hence, $(y + a + b)^{\frac{\sigma-\sigma_\rho}{\sigma_\rho-1}} - (y + b)^{\frac{\sigma-\sigma_\rho}{\sigma_\rho-1}} > (y + a)^{\frac{\sigma-\sigma_\rho}{\sigma_\rho-1}} - (y)^{\frac{\sigma-\sigma_\rho}{\sigma_\rho-1}}$. Setting $y = B$, $a = \varepsilon(1 - \beta_O)^{\sigma_\rho-1}$ and $b = \varepsilon\lambda^{1-\sigma_\rho}$, it follows that the last term in square brackets is negative and that $\Pi_1 - \Pi_2 < 0$. This yields the desired contradiction as profits can be strictly increased by switching to the organizational mode that yields profits Π_2. The proof that integration will occur in the most downstream stages whenever $\sigma < \sigma_\rho$ can be established using an analogous proof by contradiction.

A.4 The Determinants of the Ratio Γ_{OV}/Γ_{OO} in Chapter 7

BASIC MODEL

We will first prove that the ratio Γ_{OV}/Γ_{OO} in the basic model—see equation (7.6)—is monotonically increasing in η. To be able to apply this same proof to environments with partial contractibility, I begin by writing (7.6) in a slightly more general form:

$$\frac{\Gamma_{OV}}{\Gamma_{OO}} = \left(\frac{1 - \beta_V\omega_h - (1 - \beta_V)\omega_m}{1 - \beta_O\omega_h - (1 - \beta_O)\omega_m}\right)^{\sigma(1-\omega_h-\omega_m)} \left(\frac{\beta_V}{\beta_O}\right)^{\sigma\omega_h} \left(\frac{1 - \beta_V}{1 - \beta_O}\right)^{\sigma\omega_m}.$$

(A.13)

To obtain (7.6) from (A.13) one simply needs to set $\omega_h = (\sigma - 1)\eta/\sigma$ and $\omega_m = (\sigma - 1)(1 - \eta)/\sigma$.

I will next show that the ratio Γ_{OV}/Γ_{OO} in (A.13) is monotonically increasing in ω_h and monotonically decreasing in ω_m. It is clear that this will imply, in turn, that this ratio is increasing in η. The proof builds on, but greatly simplifies, the one in Antràs and Helpman (2008).

Let us start with the effect of ω_m. Straightforward differentiation of the log of the ratio Γ_{OV}/Γ_{OO} in (A.13) delivers

$$\frac{1}{\sigma}\frac{\partial\ln(\Gamma_{OV}/\Gamma_{OO})}{\partial\omega_m} = \ln\left(\frac{1 - \beta_V}{1 - \beta_O}\right) - \ln\left(\frac{1 - \beta_V\omega_h - (1 - \beta_V)\omega_m}{1 - \beta_O\omega_h - (1 - \beta_O)\omega_m}\right)$$
$$+ \frac{(1 - \omega_h)(1 - \omega_h - \omega_m)(\beta_V - \beta_O)}{(1 - \beta_O\omega_h - (1 - \beta_O)\omega_m)(1 - \beta_V\omega_h - (1 - \beta_V)\omega_m)}.$$

(A.14)

We next further differentiate with respect to β_O to obtain

$$\frac{1}{\sigma}\frac{\partial^2\ln(\Gamma_{OV}/\Gamma_{OO})}{\partial\omega_m\partial\beta_O} = (1 - \omega_h)\frac{\beta_O(1 - \omega_h) + \omega_h(1 - \beta_O)}{(1 - \beta_O)(1 - \beta_O\omega_h - (1 - \beta_O)\omega_m)^2} > 0.$$

Because $\beta_V \geq \beta_O$, the largest possible value that $\partial \ln (\Gamma_{OV}/\Gamma_{OO})/\partial \omega_m$ can take is when evaluated at $\beta_O = \beta_V$. But in such a case, we have that $\partial \ln (\Gamma_{OV}/\Gamma_{OO})/\partial \omega_m$ equals 0. It then follows that for any $\beta_O < \beta_V$, we must have $\partial \ln (\Gamma_{OV}/\Gamma_{OO})/\partial \omega_m < 0$. Hence, Γ_{OV}/Γ_{OO} is monotonically decreasing in ω_m.

The proof that $\partial \ln (\Gamma_{OV}/\Gamma_{OO})/\partial \omega_h > 0$ can be proved analogously. It suffices to note that letting $\beta_{mV} = 1 - \beta_V$ and $\beta_{mO} = 1 - \beta_O$, we can write (A.13) as

$$\frac{\Gamma_{OV}}{\Gamma_{OO}} = \left(\frac{1 - \beta_{mO}\omega_m - (1 - \beta_{mO})\,\omega_h}{1 - \beta_{mV}\omega_m - (1 - \beta_{mV})\,\omega_h} \right)^{-\sigma(1-\omega_h-\omega_m)}$$

$$\times \left(\frac{\beta_{mO}}{\beta_{mV}} \right)^{-\sigma\omega_m} \left(\frac{1 - \beta_{mO}}{1 - \beta_{mV}} \right)^{-\sigma\omega_h}.$$

Importantly, we now have $\beta_{mO} > \beta_{mV}$, and thus this expression is isomorphic to (A.13) above except for the negative exponents. We can thus conclude that if Γ_{OV}/Γ_{OO} is monotonically decreasing in ω_m, then it must be monotonically increasing in ω_h.

In the transaction-cost model we showed that Γ_{OO} was decreasing in the elasticity of demand σ, and thus on this account the relative attractiveness of integration was increasing in this parameter. In this property-rights model, the effect of σ on the ratio Γ_{OV}/Γ_{OO} is complex and depends non-monotonically on the other parameters of the model. Coupled with the various effects of σ on the other determinants of the share of intrafirm trade, the overall effect of this parameter is ambiguous.

Financial Constraints

We next turn to the model with financial constraints, in which the ratio Γ_{OV}/Γ_{OO} is given in equation (7.13). For reasons that will become clear, I rewrite this expression as

$$\frac{\Gamma_{OV}}{\Gamma_{OO}} = \left(\frac{\beta_V (1 - \omega_h) + \phi (1 - \beta_V)(1 - \omega_m)}{\beta_O (1 - \omega_h) + \phi (1 - \beta_O)(1 - \omega_m)} \right)^{\sigma(1-\omega_h-\omega_m)}$$

$$\times \left(\frac{\beta_V}{\beta_O} \right)^{\sigma\omega_h} \left(\frac{1 - \beta_V}{1 - \beta_O} \right)^{\sigma\omega_m}, \qquad \text{(A.15)}$$

where $\omega_h = (\sigma - 1)\,\eta/\sigma$ and $\omega_m = (\sigma - 1)(1 - \eta)/\sigma$.

We first demonstrate the claim in the main text that the incentive to integrate suppliers is higher, the tighter are financial constraints, in the sense that Γ_{OV}/Γ_{OO} is decreasing in ϕ. This follows from simple differentiation:

$$
\frac{1}{\sigma} \frac{\partial \ln(\Gamma_{OV}/\Gamma_{OO})}{\partial \phi}
$$

$$
= \frac{-(1-\omega_h)(1-\omega_m)(1-\omega_h-\omega_m)(\beta_V-\beta_O)}{(\beta_O(1-\omega_h)+\phi(1-\beta_O)(1-\omega_m))(\beta_V(1-\omega_h)+\phi(1-\beta_V)(1-\omega_m))} < 0.
$$

$$(A.16)$$

We now show that, even in the presence of financial constraints, the ratio $\ln(\Gamma_{OV}/\Gamma_{OO})$ continues to be monotonic in η. The proof is very closely related to the one developed above for the basic model. In particular, we first take logs and differentiate (7.13) to find

$$
\frac{1}{\sigma} \frac{\partial \ln(\Gamma_{OV}/\Gamma_{OO})}{\partial \omega_m} = \ln\left(\frac{1-\beta_V}{1-\beta_O}\right) - \ln\left(\frac{\beta_V(1-\omega_h)+\phi(1-\beta_V)(1-\omega_m)}{\beta_O(1-\omega_h)+\phi(1-\beta_O)(1-\omega_m)}\right)
$$

$$
+ \frac{\phi(1-\omega_h)(1-\omega_h-\omega_m)(\beta_V-\beta_O)}{(\beta_O(1-\omega_h)+\phi(1-\beta_O)(1-\omega_m))(\beta_V(1-\omega_h)+\phi(1-\beta_V)(1-\omega_m))},
$$

which again collapses to 0 when $\beta_O = \beta_V$. To complete the proof, it then suffices to note that

$$
\frac{1}{\sigma} \frac{\partial^2 \ln(\Gamma_{OV}/\Gamma_{OO})}{\partial \omega_m \partial \beta_O} = (1-\omega_h) \frac{\beta_O(1-\omega_h)+\phi\omega_h(1-\beta_O)}{(1-\beta_O)(\beta_O(1-\omega_h)+\phi(1-\beta_O)(1-\omega_m))^2} > 0,
$$

and thus $\partial \ln(\Gamma_{OV}/\Gamma_{OO})/\partial \omega_m < 0$ for any $\beta_O < \beta_V$. The proof that $\partial \ln(\Gamma_{OV}/\Gamma_{OO})/\partial \omega_h > 0$ is entirely analogous and is omitted to save space.

Next, we also note that straightforward differentiation of the expression for $\partial \ln(\Gamma_{OV}/\Gamma_{OO})/\partial \phi$ in (A.16) also demonstrates that

$$
\frac{\partial^2 \ln(\Gamma_{OV}/\Gamma_{OO})}{\partial \phi \partial \omega_h} > 0 \text{ and } \frac{\partial^2 \ln(\Gamma_{OV}/\Gamma_{OO})}{\partial \phi \partial \omega_m} > 0, \qquad (A.17)
$$

and thus the positive effect of financial constraints on the attractiveness of integration is lower, the higher are ω_h and ω_m.[3] These results imply that, unlike in our basic transaction-cost model, in our property-rights model it is no longer the case that an increase in improvement in the quality of financial contracting (higher ϕ) will have a differentially large positive effect on the profitability of outsourcing in production processes with high headquarter intensity (i.e., $\partial(\partial(\Gamma_{OV}/\Gamma_{OO})/\partial \phi)/\partial \eta < 0$). In particular, since η shapes ω_h and ω_m in opposite directions, it is not hard to find numerical examples in which $\partial(\partial(\Gamma_{OV}/\Gamma_{OO})/\partial \phi)/\partial \eta > 0$. Thus, our property-rights model does not

---

[3] More specifically, in each case, $\partial \ln(\Gamma_{OV}/\Gamma_{OO})/\partial \phi$ can be decomposed as the product of two ratios that are each increasing in ω_h or ω_m.

have clear predictions for the effects of interactions of empirical proxies for ϕ and η on the share of intrafirm trade.

PARTIAL CONTRACTIBILITY

Consider now the variant of the model with partial contractibility in international transactions, and let the degree of contractibility vary across inputs and countries. As mentioned in the main text, the ratio Γ_{OV}/Γ_{OO} in such a case is given by equation (7.14). But note that defining $\omega_h = (\sigma - 1)\eta (1 - \mu_{hS})/\sigma$ and $\omega_m = (\sigma - 1)(1 - \eta)(1 - \mu_{mS})/\sigma$, we can express (7.14) as

$$\frac{\Gamma_{OV}}{\Gamma_{OO}} = \left(\frac{1 - \beta_V \omega_h - (1 - \beta_V)\omega_m}{1 - \beta_O \omega_h - (1 - \beta_O)\omega_m}\right)^{\sigma(1 - \omega_h - \omega_m)} \left(\frac{\beta_V}{\beta_O}\right)^{\sigma \omega_h} \left(\frac{1 - \beta_V}{1 - \beta_O}\right)^{\sigma \omega_m}.$$

It should be clear that this expression is identical to equation (A.13), which we studied earlier in our discussion of the comparative statics in the Basic Model. We can thus refer to our earlier results to confirm that Γ_{OV}/Γ_{OO} is decreasing in the contractibility of headquarter services μ_{hS} and increasing in the contractibility of manufacturing μ_{mS}. It is also clear that the ratio Γ_{OV}/Γ_{OO} continues to be increasing in headquarter intensity η for *any* level of contractibility. Finally, from our previous analysis, we can also state that the effect of σ on the ratio Γ_{OV}/Γ_{OO} is ambiguous.

We next discuss how changes in the level of contractibility shape differentially the ratio Γ_{OV}/Γ_{OO} depending on other characteristics of production. A first result follows immediately from the definition of ω_h and ω_m. In particular, the negative effect of μ_{hS} on Γ_{OV}/Γ_{OO} is magnified by high levels of η, while the positive effect of μ_{mS} on Γ_{OV}/Γ_{OO} is decreasing in η. Or, more formally, $\partial(\partial \ln(\Gamma_{OV}/\Gamma_{OO})/\partial \mu_{hS})/\partial \eta < 0$ and $\partial(\partial \ln(\Gamma_{OV}/\Gamma_{OO})/\partial \mu_{mS})/\partial \eta < 0$. A second result follows from the same definitions of ω_h and ω_m, and the fact that the effects of contractibility are always enhanced by a large σ. In particular, note that in equation (A.13), contractibility shows up in the following terms: ω_h, ω_m, $\sigma \omega_h = (\sigma - 1)\eta(1 - \mu_{hS})$, $\sigma \omega_m = (\sigma - 1)(1 - \eta)(1 - \mu_{mS})$, and $\sigma(1 - \omega_h - \omega_m) = 1 + (\sigma - 1)\eta \mu_{hS} + (\sigma - 1)(1 - \eta)\mu_{mS}$. We can thus conclude that the effects of μ_{hS} and μ_{mS} are necessarily attenuated by a low σ, which implies that $\partial(\partial \ln(\Gamma_{OV}/\Gamma_{OO})/\partial \mu_{hS})/\partial \sigma < 0$ and $\partial(\partial \ln(\Gamma_{OV}/\Gamma_{OO})/\partial \mu_{mS})/\partial \sigma > 0$.

PARTIAL RELATIONSHIP SPECIFICITY

As argued in the main text, in the extension of the model with partial relationship specificity, it becomes harder to obtain sharp comparative statics. Let us consider one case in which we do find an analytical result. Suppose Nash bargaining is symmetric, so $\beta_O = 1/2$ and $\beta_V = (1 + \delta)/2$. Defining $\omega_h = (\sigma - 1)\eta(1 - \mu_{hS})/\sigma$ and $\omega_m = (\sigma - 1)(1 - \eta)(1 - \mu_{mS})/\sigma$, and allowing for a distinct specificity for headquarter services (ϵ_h) and for the manufacturing input (ϵ_m), we find that the ratio Γ_{OV}/Γ_{OO} in (7.16) can be expressed as:

$$\frac{\Gamma_{OV}}{\Gamma_{OO}} = \left(\frac{1 - \left(1 - \frac{1}{2}(1-\delta)\epsilon_h\right)\omega_h - \left(1 - \frac{1}{2}(1+\delta)\epsilon_m\right)\omega_m}{1 - \left(1 - \frac{1}{2}\epsilon_h\right)\omega_h - \left(1 - \frac{1}{2}\epsilon_m\right)\omega_m} \right)^{\sigma(1-\omega_h-\omega_m)}$$

$$\times \left(\frac{1 - \frac{1}{2}(1-\delta)\epsilon_h}{1 - \frac{1}{2}\epsilon_h} \right)^{\sigma\omega_h} \left(\frac{1 - \frac{1}{2}(1+\delta)\epsilon_m}{1 - \frac{1}{2}\epsilon_m} \right)^{\sigma\omega_m}.$$

Straightforward differentiation delivers

$$\frac{1}{\sigma}\frac{\partial \ln(\Gamma_{OV}/\Gamma_{OO})}{\partial \epsilon_h} = \frac{1}{2}\delta \frac{\omega_h}{\left(1 - \epsilon_h + \frac{1}{2}(1+\delta)\epsilon_h\right)\left(1 - \epsilon_h + \frac{1}{2}\epsilon_h\right)}$$

$$- \frac{1}{2}\delta \frac{\omega_h(1-\omega_h-\omega_m)(1-\omega_h-\omega_m+\epsilon_m\omega_m)}{\left[\begin{array}{c}\left(1 - \left(1 - \frac{1}{2}\epsilon_h\right)\omega_h - \left(1 - \frac{1}{2}\epsilon_m\right)\omega_m\right)\left(1 - \left(1 - \frac{1}{2}(1-\delta)\epsilon_h\right)\omega_h\right.\\ \left.- \left(1 - \frac{1}{2}(1+\delta)\epsilon_m\right)\omega_m\right)\end{array}\right]}.$$

It is clear that this derivative is increasing in ϵ_h, and thus it cannot be lower than when evaluated at $\epsilon_h = 0$. And in that case, we have

$$\frac{1}{\sigma}\frac{\partial \ln(\Gamma_{OV}/\Gamma_{OO})}{\partial \epsilon_h}\bigg|_{\epsilon_h=0}$$

$$= \frac{\frac{1}{8}\delta\omega_h\omega_m\epsilon_m(2\delta(1-\omega_h-\omega_m)+\omega_m\epsilon_m(1+\delta))}{\left(1 - \omega_h - \left(1 - \frac{1}{2}\epsilon_m\right)\omega_m\right)\left(1 - \omega_h - \left(1 - \frac{1}{2}(1+\delta)\epsilon_m\right)\omega_m\right)} > 0.$$

This confirms that the ratio Γ_{OV}/Γ_{OO} is increasing in ϵ_h whenever Nash bargaining is symmetric and $\beta_O = 1/2$. When departing from this symmetric Nash bargaining assumption, the derivative $\partial \ln(\Gamma_{OV}/\Gamma_{OO})/\partial \epsilon_h$ continues to be minimized at $\epsilon_h = 0$, but for a low value of β_O and β_V it may take a negative value at $\epsilon_h = 0$. More specifically, the key condition is $\beta_V\beta_O\epsilon_m\omega_m > (1 - \beta_O - \beta_V)(1 - \omega_h - \omega_m)$, which is satisfied for $\beta_O = 1/2$ and $\beta_V = (1+\delta)/2$ but not necessarily for sufficiently low values of these parameters.

Following analogous steps, it is also possible to show that the ratio Γ_{OV}/Γ_{OO} is typically decreasing in ϵ_m, with the effect of this parameter being unambiguously negative whenever $\beta_V = 1/2$, and thus $\beta_O = (1/2 - \delta)/(1 - \delta)$.

MULTIPLE INPUTS AND MULTILATERAL CONTRACTING

As argued in the main text, the equilibrium of the extension with multiple inputs and multilateral contracting is analogous to that in the model with just one F and M agents, but with bargaining powers β_{hO}, β_{mO}, β_{hV}, and

β_{mV} given by

$$\beta_{hO} = \beta_{mO} = \frac{\sigma\rho}{(\sigma - 1)(1 - \eta) + \sigma\rho}$$

$$\beta_{hV} = \frac{(\sigma - 1)(1 - \eta)\delta + \sigma\rho}{(\sigma - 1)(1 - \eta) + \sigma\rho} > \frac{\sigma\rho(1 - \delta)}{(\sigma - 1)(1 - \eta) + \sigma\rho} = \beta_{mV}.$$

We can then plug these values in a general formula analogous to (A.13) and given by

$$\frac{\Gamma_{OV}}{\Gamma_{OO}} = \left(\frac{1 - \beta_{hV}\omega_h - \beta_{mV}\omega_m}{1 - \beta_{hO}\omega_h - \beta_{mO}\omega_m}\right)^{\sigma(1 - \omega_h - \omega_m)} \left(\frac{\beta_{hV}}{\beta_{hO}}\right)^{\sigma\omega_h} \left(\frac{\beta_{mV}}{\beta_{mO}}\right)^{\sigma\omega_m},$$

where again $\omega_h = (\sigma - 1)\eta(1 - \mu_{hS})/\sigma$ and $\omega_m = (\sigma - 1)(1 - \eta)(1 - \mu_{mS})/\sigma$. As claimed in the main text, this substitution results, after some manipulations, in:

$$\frac{\Gamma_{OV}}{\Gamma_{OO}} = \left(1 - \frac{(\sigma - 1)(1 - \eta)\delta\omega_h - \sigma\rho\delta\omega_m}{(\sigma - 1)(1 - \eta) + \sigma\rho(1 - \omega_h - \omega_m)}\right)^{\sigma(1 - \omega_h - \omega_m)}$$

$$\times \left(1 + \frac{(\sigma - 1)(1 - \eta)\delta}{\sigma\rho}\right)^{\sigma\omega_h} (1 - \delta)^{\sigma\omega_m}. \tag{A.18}$$

We first prove that the ratio Γ_{OV}/Γ_{OV} in this expression continues to be increasing in ω_h and decreasing in ω_m. To see this, take logs of (A.18) and differentiate, to obtain:

$$\frac{1}{\sigma} \frac{\partial \ln(\Gamma_{OV}/\Gamma_{OO})}{\partial \omega_h} = -\ln\left(1 - \frac{(\sigma - 1)(1 - \eta)\delta\omega_h - \sigma\rho\delta\omega_m}{(\sigma - 1)(1 - \eta) + \sigma\rho(1 - \omega_h - \omega_m)}\right)$$

$$+ \ln\left(1 + \frac{(\sigma - 1)(1 - \eta)\delta}{\sigma\rho}\right)$$

$$- \frac{\delta((\sigma - 1)(1 - \eta) + \sigma\rho)((\sigma - 1)(1 - \eta) - \sigma\rho\omega_m)(1 - \omega_h - \omega_m)}{((\sigma - 1)(1 - \eta) + \sigma\rho(1 - \omega_h - \omega_m))^2 \left(1 - \frac{(\sigma-1)(1-\eta)\delta\omega_h - \sigma\rho\delta\omega_m}{(\sigma-1)(1-\eta) + \sigma\rho(1-\omega_h-\omega_m)}\right)},$$

where $(\sigma - 1)(1 - \eta) - \sigma\rho\omega_m = (\sigma - 1)(1 - \eta)(1 - \rho(1 - \mu_{mS})) > 0$. Next, notice that further differentiating with respect to δ, we find:

$$\frac{1}{\sigma} \frac{\partial \ln(\Gamma_{OV}/\Gamma_{OO})}{\partial \omega_h \partial \delta} = \frac{((\sigma - 1)(1 - \eta) + \sigma\rho)((\sigma - 1)(1 - \eta) - \sigma\rho\omega_m)}{((\sigma - 1)(1 - \eta) + \sigma\rho(1 - \omega_h - \omega_m))^2}$$

$$\times \frac{((\sigma - 1)(1 - \eta)(1 - \delta + \delta\omega_m) + \sigma\delta\rho\omega_m)}{((\sigma - 1)\delta(1 - \eta) + \sigma\rho)\left(1 - \frac{(\sigma-1)(1-\eta)\delta\omega_h - \sigma\rho\delta\omega_m}{(\sigma-1)(1-\eta) + \sigma\rho(1-\omega_h-\omega_m)}\right)^2} > 0.$$

It thus follows that $\partial \ln (\Gamma_{OV}/\Gamma_{OO})/\partial w_h$ cannot be lower than when evaluated at $\delta = 0$, at which it is clear from the above expression that this derivative is zero. In sum, we have $\partial \ln (\Gamma_{OV}/\Gamma_{OO})/\partial w_h > 0$ for all $\delta > 0$.

Next, differentiation delivers

$$\frac{1}{\sigma} \frac{\partial \ln (\Gamma_{OV}/\Gamma_{OO})}{\partial w_m} = -\ln \left(1 - \frac{(\sigma - 1)(1 - \eta)\, \delta w_h - \sigma \rho \delta w_m}{(\sigma - 1)(1 - \eta) + \sigma \rho (1 - w_h - w_m)} \right) + \ln (1 - \delta)$$

$$+ \frac{(1 - w_h - w_m)(1 - w_h)\, \sigma \delta \rho \left((\sigma - 1)(1 - \eta) + \sigma \rho \right)}{\left((\sigma - 1)(1 - \eta) + \sigma \rho (1 - w_h - w_m)\right)^2 \left(1 - \frac{(\sigma-1)(1-\eta)\delta w_h - \sigma\rho\delta w_m}{(\sigma-1)(1-\eta)+\sigma\rho(1-w_h-w_m)} \right)},$$

as well as

$$\frac{1}{\sigma} \frac{\partial \ln (\Gamma_{OV}/\Gamma_{OO})}{\partial w_m \partial \delta} = -\frac{(1 - w_h)\left((\sigma - 1)(1 - \eta) + \sigma \rho\right)}{\left((\sigma - 1)(1 - \eta) + \sigma \rho (1 - w_h - w_m)\right)^2}$$

$$\times \frac{\left((\sigma - 1)(1 - \eta)(1 - \delta w_h) + \sigma \delta \rho (1 - w_h)\right)}{(1 - \delta) \left(1 - \frac{(\sigma-1)(1-\eta)\delta w_h - \sigma\rho\delta w_m}{(\sigma-1)(1-\eta)+\sigma\rho(1-w_h-w_m)} \right)^2} < 0.$$

Thus, $\partial \ln (\Gamma_{OV}/\Gamma_{OO})/\partial w_m$ cannot be higher than when evaluated at $\delta = 0$, at which it is clear from the above expression that this derivative is zero. In sum, we have $\partial \ln (\Gamma_{OV}/\Gamma_{OO})/\partial w_m < 0$ for all $\delta > 0$.

The fact that Γ_{OV}/Γ_{OV} in (A.18) is increasing in w_h and decreasing in w_m immediately implies that this same ratio is decreasing in headquarter contractibility μ_h and increasing in manufacturing contractibility μ_m, just as in the model with a single supplier. As mentioned in the main text, however, this does not imply that the ratio Γ_{OV}/Γ_{OO} is necessarily increasing in headquarter intensity η, since this parameter enters the formula (A.18) independently of how it shapes w_h and w_m.

Next, we show that the ratio Γ_{OV}/Γ_{OO} can only be lower than one if the degree of input substitutability as governed by ρ is above a *unique* certain threshold $\hat{\rho} > 0$. When that threshold is higher than one, then $\Gamma_{OV}/\Gamma_{OO} > 1$ for all $\rho \in (0, 1]$. To show this, I begin by noting that when $\rho \to 0$, the ratio Γ_{OV}/Γ_{OO} in (A.18) clearly goes to $+\infty$, and thus the ratio is higher than one. When $\rho \to +\infty$, the ratio Γ_{OV}/Γ_{OO} goes to

$$\frac{\Gamma_{OV}}{\Gamma_{OO}} = \left(1 + \frac{\delta w_m}{1 - w_h - w_m} \right)^{\sigma(1 - w_h - w_m)} (1 - \delta)^{\sigma w_m} < 1,$$

where the inequality follows from the fact that the expression is decreasing in δ and equals 1 at $\delta = 0$. Hence, we have that $\Gamma_{OV}/\Gamma_{OO} > 1$ for sufficiently low ρ, and $\Gamma_{OV}/\Gamma_{OO} < 1$ for a high enough ρ. To demonstrate the existence of a unique threshold $\hat{\rho} > 0$ at which $\Gamma_{OV}/\Gamma_{OO} = 1$, we note that tedious differentiation delivers

$$\frac{1}{\sigma} \frac{\partial \ln (\Gamma_{OV}/\Gamma_{OO})}{\partial \rho} = \frac{\delta (\sigma - 1)(1 - \eta)}{((\sigma - 1)(1 - \eta) + \sigma\rho (1 - w_h - w_m))} \times$$

$$\left[\frac{(1 - w_h - w_m)\,\sigma\,(1 - w_h)(w_h + w_m)}{(\sigma - 1)(1 - \eta) + \sigma\rho (1 - w_h - w_m) - (\sigma - 1)(1 - \eta)\,\delta w_h + \sigma\rho\delta w_m} \right.$$

$$\left. - w_h \frac{(\sigma - 1)(1 - \eta) + \sigma\rho (1 - w_h - w_m)}{\sigma\rho^2 \left(1 + \frac{(\sigma-1)(1-\eta)\delta}{\sigma\rho} \right)} \right].$$

It can then be shown that the condition $\partial \ln (\Gamma_{OV}/\Gamma_{OO})/\partial \rho = 0$ can be expressed as a quadratic equation

$$\rho^2 + b\rho + c = 0,$$

in which

$$c = - \frac{w_h (\sigma - 1)^2 (1 - \eta)^2 (1 - \delta w_h)}{\sigma^2 w_m (1 - w_h - w_m)(1 - \delta w_h)} < 0.$$

The fact that c is negative implies, however, that there can only be one positive solution ($\rho > 0$) to this equation. Together with the limiting values $\lim_{\rho \to 0} (\Gamma_{OV}/\Gamma_{OO}) = +\infty$ and $\lim_{\rho \to +\infty} (\Gamma_{OV}/\Gamma_{OO}) < 1$, we can thus conclude that $\Gamma_{OV}/\Gamma_{OO} = 1$ for a unique value $\hat{\rho} > 0$.

It should be emphasized that this result does not imply that Γ_{OV}/Γ_{OO} is necessarily decreasing in ρ for all values of $\rho \in (0, 1)$. In fact, it is not difficult to construct examples in which Γ_{OV}/Γ_{OO} increases in ρ for a range of parameter values. For similar reasons, when studying the cross-partial derivative of $\ln (\Gamma_{OV}/\Gamma_{OO})$ with respect to ρ and the levels of contractibility μ_h and μ_m, one can generate numerical examples in which these derivatives take positive or negative numbers.

B
Data Appendix

In this Appendix, I provide more details on the data sources, refinements of the data, and some details on the estimation techniques associated with the empirical work in Chapters 5 and 8. The entire dataset and Stata program codes are available at http://scholar.harvard.edu/antras/books. I often refer to this url as the "book's website."

B.1 Raw U.S. Import and Export Data

The basis for the empirical work conducted in this book is the *U.S. Related-Party Trade* database collected by the U.S. Bureau of Customs and Border Protection and managed by the U.S. Census Bureau. This dataset can be downloaded from the following U.S. census website: http://sasweb.ssd.census.gov/relatedparty/. The data are available at different levels of industry aggregation, but the most disaggregated level available online is the six-digit North American Industry Classification System (NAICS). At the time of writing this appendix, the data are available for the period 2002–2012. In the empirical work I instead used data for the period 2000–2011. Data for 2000 and 2001 are available as part of the entire dataset on the book's website.

Throughout the data construction, non-manufacturing sectors were dropped. In addition, industries that are not reported in the Related-Party Trade data were also dropped. In the U.S. Related-Party Trade data, five manufacturing industries are reported at the five-digit NAICS: 31131X (Alumina and Aluminum Production and Processing), 31181X (Bread and Bakery Product Manufacturing), 31511X (Hosiery and Sock Mills), 33631X (Motor Vehicle Gasoline Engine and Engine Parts Manufacturing), and 33641X (Aerospace Product and Parts Manufacturing). This last industry 33641X is somewhat different from the rest. First, it is the only five-digit industry with zero import flows. Furthermore, it is the only one of these industries for which six-digit industries with the same initial five digits (in particular, 336411, 336412, 336413, 336414, 336415, and 336419) are reported in the dataset. For these reasons, this five-digit sector 33641X was dropped from the dataset. All other NAICS-level industry variables described below were also constructed for the four surviving synthetic five-digit industries.

The U.S. Related-Party Trade database reports imports and exports associated with each of 233 foreign countries. The data for South Sudan are, however, only available for 2011, so this country was dropped from the sample. The raw data were rectangularized by treating any missing values as zero import or export flows. Overall, we work with data for 390 industries, 232 countries, and 12 years, for a total of 1,085,760 observations.

The data define related-party import transactions involving parties "with various types of relationships including any person directly or indirectly, owning, controlling or holding power to vote, 6 percent of the outstanding voting stock or shares of any organization." On the other hand, a related-party export transaction is one "between a U.S. exporter and a foreign consignee, where either party owns, directly or indirectly, 10 percent or more of the other party." Although these ownership requirements are very low, I argued in Chapter 1 that BEA data suggest that intrafirm trade is generally associated with one of the entities having a controlling stake in the other entity. The dataset also contains data on non-related imports and exports, which involve parties that "have no affiliation with each other or who do not meet the relevant equity requirements" for related-party trade. Although in principle an indicator of whether or not a transaction involves related parties is required for *all* import or export transactions recorded by the U.S. Bureau of Customs and Border Protection, in practice that information is missing in some cases. The dataset labels those volumes of trade as "not reported."

Table B.1 presents descriptive statistics for the key variables in the U.S. Related-Party Trade database. A few features of the table are worth highlighting. First, related-party imports account for 51.6 percent of overall U.S. manufacturing imports over 2000–11, and for 31.8 percent of overall U.S. manufacturing exports. Second, the average (unweighted) related-party import and export shares are, however, much lower (23.8% for imports and 10.4% for exports). Third, the large number of zeros in the data implies that the number of observations with a well-defined intrafirm import share is less than one-third the total number of observations (i.e., country and six-digit NAICS combinations in the data). Conversely, on the export side, more than 50 percent of the observations feature positive exports and well-defined intrafirm export shares. Fourth, non-reported import transactions account for a negligible 0.04 percent of U.S. imports (that percentage goes up to 3.71% for exports, but I do not employ that export share in the empirical analyses in the book).

The U.S. Related-Party Trade database is also available at the finer six-digit Harmonized System (HS) industrial disaggregation. This dataset is not publicly available but can be purchased from the U.S. Census. Although I have not used it in the tests performed in this book, I have made it available for download at http://scholar.harvard.edu/antras/books. Over the period 2000–11, this more detailed dataset contains information on U.S. imports

Table B.1 Some Descriptive Statistics from the NAICS Related-Party Trade Database

Variable (in $ except shares)	Mean	Std. Dev	Min	Max	N
Total Imports	14,712,628	282,669,054	0	44,917,394,621	1,085,760
(a) Related-Party	7,587,177	220,242,612	0	44,134,184,241	1,085,760
(b) Non-related-Party	7,119,158	112,745,454	0	20,981,735,046	1,085,760
(c) Not Reported	6,294	567,136	0	269,396,613	1,085,760
(d) Related-Party Share a/(a+b)	0.2380	0.3265	0	1	312,884
Total Exports	8,594,996	113,419,707	0	19,996,871,796	1,085,760
(a) Related-Party	2,736,289	61,075,666	0	13,174,432,899	1,085,760
(b) Non-related-Party	5,539,536	67,292,534	0	14,757,989,972	1,085,760
(c) Not Reported	319,172	7,736,500	0	1,574,623,834	1,085,760
(d) Related-Party Share a/(a+b)	0.1039	0.2150	0	1	565,145

(related, non-related, and non-reported) for 5,705 products and for 238 countries and territories. Despite the fact that this finer disaggregation generates more than 16 million potential observations on U.S. imports, only for about 10 percent of these cases (1,572,949 to be precise) are U.S. imports positive. This in turn leads to an overall number of 1,568,711 intrafirm trade shares in the data, exceeding by a factor of five the 312,884 available shares when using the publicly available NAICS dataset.[1] Still, the mean and variance of intrafirm trade shares are very similar to those reported in Table B.1 for the six-digit NAICS data.

B.2 U.S. Import and Export Data at IO2002 Level

In many of the empirical tests presented in this book, offshoring is correlated with variables that, because of their nature and characteristics, can only be computed with Input-Output data (more on this below). For this reason, the natural industry classification to work with in those cases is the I-O commodity code classification. More specifically, I use the 2002 Input-Output industrial classification, or IO2002 for short.

Following Antràs and Chor (2013), the raw data in NAICS industry codes were mapped to six-digit IO2002 industries using a correspondence provided by the Bureau of Economic Analysis (BEA) as a supplement to the 2002 U.S. Input-Output Tables.[2] This concordance is a straightforward many-to-one mapping for the manufacturing industries (NAICS first digit = 3). Two industries required a separate treatment, as the NAICS data were at a coarser level of aggregation than could be mapped into six-digit IO2002 codes. A synthetic code 31131X was created to merge IO 311313 (Beet sugar manufacturing) and 31131A (Sugar cane mills and refining), while a separate code 33641X merged IO 336411, 336412, 336413, 336414, 33641A (all related to the manufacture of aircraft and related components). This approach is somewhat distinct from the one I used to handle these aircraft subsectors in the NAICS dataset, where I simply dropped 33641X rather than merging it into a single category with all other five-digit sectors starting with 33641. Because the NAICS sector 33641X features no U.S. imports, this small divergence should have little impact on the results. All other industry variables described below were also constructed for these two synthetic IO2002 codes 31131X and 33641X.

---

[1] For 4,238 observations, the data indicate positive imports that are entirely recorded as "Non-Reported." Because I define the share of intrafirm trade as related-party imports divided by the sum of related-party imports and non-related party imports, I cannot compute a well-defined intrafirm trade share in those cases.

[2] See, for instance, http://www.bea.gov/industry/xls/2002DetailedItemOutput.xls.

Overall, the IO2002 identifies U.S. imports and exports (related, non-related, and non-reported) for 253 sectors, 232 countries, and 12 years of data, for a total of 704,352 observations, of which again many are zeroes. Table B.2 provides some basic descriptive statistics from this related-party IO2002 trade data.

B.3 Isolating the Intermediate Input Component of U.S. Imports and Exports

In this section, I provide more details on the Wright (2014) methodology for isolating the intermediate input component of trade flows. The key input for this data correction is a list of End-Use industrial categories available from the U.S. Bureau of Economic Analysis. The BEA uses these end-use codes to allocate goods to their final use, within the National Income and Product Accounts. Importantly, U.S. imports and exports at the ten-digit Harmonized System level are similarly allocated to end-use codes. Foreign Trade Statistics distinguish six one-digit end-use categories: (0) Foods, feeds, and beverages; (1) Industrial supplies and materials; (2) Capital goods, except automobiles; (3) Automotive vehicles, parts and engines; (4) Consumer goods (nonfood), except auto; and (5) Other merchandise. Apart from these six principal end-use categories, the classification is further subdivided into about 140 broad commodity groupings. Wright (2014) advocates dropping all products with an end-use code equal to 0, 4, or 5, as well as a sub-set of the commodity groupings in the other three end-codes. The full list of dropped BEA commodity groupings can be found in table 7 of Wright (2014).

The practical implementation of this correction consists of four steps:

Step 1. We begin by mapping each ten-digit HS product to a BEA end-use code. In order to maximize such a mapping, we put together multiple years of concordance tables published by the Census Bureau. The Census website provides tables for recent years from 2008 to 2013. We also downloaded older tables for years from 1993 to 1997 from Jon Haveman's trade data website (http://goo.gl/5pyijB). Technically, import and export HS codes are administered by different federal agencies (Export codes, known as Schedule B, is administered by the Census, and import codes, known as Harmonized Tariff System (HTS), is administered by the U.S. International Trade Commissions (USITC)). As such, a complete mapping requires putting together concordance tables for both import codes and export codes. We first map each HS product to end-use code, using the most recent concordance table published in 2013, and move to the previous year's table, if the mapping is still incomplete.

TABLE B.2 Some Descriptive Statistics from the IO2002 Related-Party Trade Database

Variable (in $ except shares)	Mean	Std. Dev	Min	Max	N
Total Imports	22,679,545	376,502,066	0	44,917,395,456	704,352
(a) Related-Party	11,695,648	281,267,307	0	44,134,184,241	704,352
(b) Non-related-Party	10,974,196	166,941,030	0	20,981,735,046	704,352
(c) Not Reported	9,702	749,284	0	269,396,613	704,352
(d) Related-Party Share a/(a+b)	0.2438	0.3265	0	1	227,829
Total Exports	13,549,842	175,761,983	0	27,862,790,144	704,352
(a) Related-Party	4,259,789	86,715,148	0	13,174,432,899	704,352
(b) Non-related-party	8,797,599	103,436,155	0	15,297,237,562	704,352
(c) Not Reported	492,455	12,228,037	0	2,585,156,012	704,352
(d) Related-Party Share a/(a+b)	0.1068	0.2121	0	1	416,933

Step 2. We then use detailed ten-digit HS U.S. import and export data by foreign country for 2000–11 available from Peter Schott's website at Yale University and drop all ten-digit flows consisting of finished goods, as dictated by the concordance constructed in step 1. See Schott (2008) for more details on the ten-digit U.S. import and export data.

Step 3. Next, we aggregate the ten-digit HS U.S. import and export data back to the IO2002 level using a concordance between ten-digit HS codes and IO2002 codes available from the U.S. Bureau of Economic Analysis website at http://www.bea.gov/industry/xls/HSConcord.xls. We do so both for total flows as well as for only the intermediate input component of these flows (after dropping final goods). Comparing these two flows we obtain an IO2002-country-year specific "discount factor" by which overall imports and exports need to be multiplied to obtain intermediate input imports and exports.

Step 4. We then apply these discount factors to the Related-Party IO2002 trade data constructed based on the NAICS Related-Party trade data. Note that the applied discount factor varies across IO2002 codes, countries, and years, and is also distinct for imports and exports. When the discount factor is 0, this implies that particular IO2002-country-year observation does not contain any intermediate input flows. Whenever an IO2002 sector features zero aggregate imports of intermediate inputs in each year, we treat that sector as a final-good sector and drop it from the sample in all Wright-adjusted regressions. We also drop IO2002 sectors 325411 (Medicinal and botanical manufacturing) and 33299B (Arms, ordnance, and accessories) because they feature extremely low input import flows, and only for 2000 and 2001, and their recorded offshoring shares for those years are negative. Overall we entirely drop thirty-nine industries, which are listed in Table B.3.

Apart from these dropped sectors, many other industries feature small aggregate volumes of intermediate input flows, and many zero flows for imports from particular countries. Even though these observations are not dropped, their associated discount factor will be tiny or equal to zero (and in the latter case they will be dropped from log-linear specifications). Table B.4 presents basic descriptive statics comparing total and intermediate input U.S. imports and exports. The table indicates that, overall, intermediate input flows account for 53.1 percent of total U.S. imports and 67.8 percent of total U.S. exports. Although not reported in the table, one can also compute the share of intermediate inputs in related-party imports and exports. These turn out to be only marginally higher than for overall trade, equaling on aggregate for 54.4 percent of intrafirm imports and 68.4 percent of intrafirm exports.

Apart from this Wright (2014) correction, in some of the empirical tests in the book I follow Nunn and Trefler (2013*b*) in restricting the sample to the set of countries for which it is more plausible that U.S. intermediate

TABLE B.3 IO2002 Sectors Excluded from the Sample by the Wright (2014) Correction

311111	Dog and cat food manufacturing	314110	Carpet and rug mills
311119	Other animal food manufacturing	315100	Apparel knitting mills
311210	Flour milling and malt manuf.	315230	Women's and girls' cut & sew apparel
311230	Breakfast cereal manufacturing	321991	Manufactured mobile home manuf.
31131X	Sugar manufacturing	322291	Sanitary paper product manufacturing
311320	Chocolate & confectionery manuf	325411	Medicinal and botanical manufacturing
311340	Nonchocolate confectionery ma.	325620	Toilet preparation manufacturing
311410	Frozen food manufacturing	331314	Secondary smelting/alloying of alum.
311513	Cheese manufacturing	33299B	Arms, ordnance, and accessories
31151A	Fluid milk and butter manuf.	33461A	Software, audio, & video media reprod.
311520	Ice cream and frozen dessert ma.	335221	Household cooking appliances
311615	Poultry processing	335222	Household refrigerator & freezers
311820	Cookie, cracker, and pasta ma.	336213	Motor home manufacturing
311910	Snack food manufacturing	336991	Motorcycle, bicycle, & parts
311920	Coffee and tea manufacturing	336992	Military armored vehicle & tanks
311930	Flavoring syrup & concentrate ma.	337110	Wood kitchen cabinet & countertops
312110	Soft drink and ice manufacturing	337121	Upholstered household furniture
312120	Breweries	33721A	Office furniture manufacturing
312130	Wineries	337910	Mattress manufacturing
312140	Distilleries		

TABLE B.4 Descriptive Statistics Illustrating the Effects of the Wright (2014) Correction

Variable (in $)	Mean	Std. Dev	Min	Max	N
Total Imports	22,679,545	376,502,066	0	44,917,395,456	704,352
Wright-Adjusted Input Imports	12,042,991	216,171,921	0	44,206,174,208	704,352
Total Exports	13,549,842	175,761,983	0	27,862,790,144	704,352
Wright-Adjusted Input Exports	9,180,273	140,980,583	0	27,860,740,096	704,352

input purchases are associated with U.S. headquarters purchasing inputs from abroad (rather than foreign headquarters exporting inputs to U.S. suppliers). The details of this correction appear in the main text of Chapter 5, so I will not repeat them here. Quantitatively, this correction removes five countries from the sample, accounting for a mere 3.18 percent of U.S. imports. As mentioned in the main text, I have also experimented with a more extensive correction based on Nunn and Trefler (2013b) that drops eighteen countries accounting for 32.52 percent of U.S. imports. These corrected flows are available from the files in the book's website.

B.4 Computing Offshoring Shares

The construction of offshoring shares requires data not only on U.S. imports and exports, but also on U.S. domestic shipments. Ignoring the Wright adjustment for intermediate inputs, industry-level offshoring shares are simply computed as the ratio of U.S. imports to the sum of U.S. shipments plus U.S. imports minus U.S. exports in that sector. The analogous offshoring share for a given foreign country is computed as U.S. imports from that particular country divided by the same industry-level denominator, so the sum of country-industry-level offshoring shares corresponds to the aggregate industry-level offshoring share.

Data on U.S. shipments were obtained from the NBER-CES Manufacturing database for the period 2000–09 and from the Annual Survey of Manufacturing (ASM) for 2010 and 2011. Both of these data sources are available at the six-digit NAICS level, which facilitates their merging with the six-digit NAICS U.S. import and export data. The mapping between the trade data and the NBER-CES database is quite clean, but merging the ASM data required a series of small adjustments to deal with the fact that eighty-eight industries are reported at the more aggregated five-digit NAICS level in the ASM dataset. In order to minimize the loss of industry categories associated with adding those two last years of data, we imputed shipment values for all six-digit sectors available in the trade and NBER data for which only the more aggregated five-digit industry was available in the ASM data. This imputation was based on breaking up the 2010 and 2011 ASM total values of shipments at the five-digit level into six-digit values based on the relative weights of the different six-digit segments in the NBER-CES data over the period 2005–09.

As mentioned in Chapter 5, for a small percentage of industries and years the recorded value of total shipments falls short of the value of U.S. exports. This is true for years prior to 2009 so it is not explained by the adjustments described in the previous paragraph. These observations are typically dropped in the empirical tests in this book.

So far, I have described the construction of offshoring shares for the NAICS case and without any adjustment for intermediate input trade. In order to compute offshoring shares at the IO2002 level, we simply repeated the steps above but using as the basis U.S. imports and exports at the IO2002 level, as well as U.S. shipments at the same industry classification. The latter series was obtained by filtering the constructed NAICS shipment series described above through the same BEA concordance table used to transition from NAICS to IO2002 trade flows. Wright-adjusted offshoring shares were computed in an analogous manner based on Wright-adjusted U.S. imports, exports, and shipments. To isolate the intermediate input component of U.S. shipments, I applied a discount factor to overall shipments equal to the average of the import and export "Wright" discount factors applied to trade flows in that industry over the period 2000–11. Again, in some cases, the resulting value of input shipments fell short of the value of input exports, and these observations are dropped from most regressions.

This concludes our discussion of the construction of the main dependent variables in the empirical tests in the book. I now turn to describing the explanatory variables used in those tests.

B.5 Industry-Country-Level Covariates

Freight Costs. Sectoral and exporter-specific measures of freight costs associated with U.S. imports were downloaded from Peter Schott's website (see Schott, 2010, for further documentation). More specifically, freight costs are computed as the ratio of CIF imports to FOB imports for a given product and origin country for the period 2000–05. Although this variable varies year by year, to salvage observations for 2006 through 2011, we construct a time-invariant measure of freight costs equal to the average of the ratio of Cost Insurance and Freight (CIF) import volumes to Free On Board (FOB) import values for a given country and product over the period 2000–05. We then assign this average measure to all twelve observations associated with a given exporting country and sector. The data are originally available at the six-digit NAICS level but we also constructed them at the IO2002 level using the same BEA concordance table employed throughout the book.

U.S. Tariffs. U.S. tariffs corresponds to U.S. applied tariffs from the World Integrated Trade Solution (WITS) database maintained by the World Bank. We again construct a measure at the exporter-sector level based on the average of this variable over multiple years, and in this case we do so for 2000–10 given data availability. The data are originally available at the six-digit HS level. We used the concordance in Pierce and Schott (2009) to transition from six-digit HS codes to six-digit NAICS codes. To construct IO2002 tariff levels, we used the same BEA concordance from HS6 to IO2002 employed when applying the Wright intermediate input correction, as described in step 3 of section B.3 above.

B.6 Industry-Level Covariates

Trade Costs. Industry-level freight costs and tariffs were computed based on the industry-country series we have just described in section B.5 but averaging them over all exporting countries. In both the NAICS and IO2002 cases, data on freight costs and tariffs were missing for some industry codes. For those sectors, we imputed a value equal to the weighted freight costs and tariffs of the sectors with which the industry shared the same first four digits, or (if the value was still missing) the same first three digits, using industry shipment values as weights.

R&D Intensity. We build on Nunn and Trefler (2013*b*), who calculated R&D expenditures to total sales on an annual basis for the period 1998–2006 using the U.S. firms in the Bureau van Djik's Orbis dataset. Their original data are reported for IO1997 industries. To obtain IO2002 values, we follow Antràs and Chor (2013) and construct a crosswalk from IO1997 to IO2002 through the NAICS industry codes. More specifically, the R&D intensity for each IO2002 industry was calculated as the weighted average value of $\log(0.001 + R\&D/Sales)$ over that of its constituent IO1997 industries over the years 2000–2005, using the industry output values in the 1997 U.S. I-O Tables as weights. There remained thirteen IO2002 industries without R&D intensity values after the above procedure. A similar procedure to that described above for trade costs was used to obtain the R&D intensity for the remaining thirteen IO2002 codes (based on the R&D intensity of the IO2002 codes with which the industry shared the same first four or three digits). This yielded a complete series for R&D intensity of the "selling" sector. In many specifications we instead use a measure of the R&D intensity of the "average buyer" of an industrial good. This buyer version of the variable was computed as a weighted average of the R&D intensity of the industries that purchase the good in question (call it good v), with weights equal to these buying sectors' input purchase values of good v as reported in the 2002 U.S. I-O Tables. The construction of R&D intensity at the six-digit NAICS level was analogous, although in imputing values for missing observations we also made use of four-digit and three-digit measures of R&D intensity kindly provided by Heiwai Tang. Late in the production of this book, Davin Chor alerted me to the fact that, in the IO2002 dataset, there is one industry (IO334411, "Electron Tube Manufacturing"), with a huge ratio of R&D expenditures over sales. This ratio is equal to 660 and is a clear outlier relative to other sectors. It should thus be treated with caution. Fortunately, all the results presented in this book are virtually unaffected when excluding this industry from the analysis.

Capital and Skill Intensities. These were obtained from the NBER-CES Manufacturing Industry Database (Becker, Gray, and Marvakov, 2009). Skill intensity is the log of the number of non-production workers divided by total employment. Physical capital intensity is the log of the real capital stock per worker. Equipment capital intensity and plant capital intensity are respectively the log of the equipment and plant capital stock per worker. The NBER-CES data are originally available at the six-digit NAICS level, so matching them to the Related-Party Trade dataset only required minor adjustments related to trade data for five manufacturing industries being reported at the 5-digit NAICS (as explained in B.1 above). These industries were in turn mapped to IO2002 codes using the same procedure described in section B.2 above for the related-party trade data. For each factor intensity variable, a simple average of the annual values from 2000–05 was taken to obtain the seller industry measures. The factor intensities for the average buyer were then calculated using the same procedure as described for the average buyer R&D intensity.

Detailed Capital Equipment Intensities. In some specifications we report results that break capital equipment intensity into the separate effects of expenditures on (i) automobiles and trucks for highway use, (ii) computers and peripheral data processing equipment, and (iii) all other machinery and equipment computers. These were obtained from the Annual Survey of Manufactures (2002–2010) which reports the data at the six-digit NAICS level. As mentioned before when discussing data on shipments from 2010 and 2011 (which also originate in the ASM), for eighty-eight industries capital expenditures are reported at the more aggregated five-digit NAICS level. In order to impute those values to the six-digit sectors within each of these eighty-eight industries we followed the same approach as in the case for industry shipments, but using overall equipment expenditures from the NBER-CES dataset as weights. The final measures of auto, computer, and other equipment intensity were obtained by dividing these types of capital expenditures by the wage bill and taking logarithms. Values for these variables at the IO2002 level were obtained by filtering those variables through the BEA concordance described above, while "average buyer" versions of these variables were also computed using the same approach as with R&D intensity and capital and skill intensity.

Productivity Dispersion. As in Antràs and Chor (2013), we build on Nunn and Trefler (2008), who constructed dispersion for each HS6 code as the standard deviation of log exports for its HS10 sub-codes across U.S. port locations and destination countries in the year 2000, from U.S. Department of Commerce data. We associated the dispersion value of each HS6 code to each of its HS10 sub-codes. These were mapped into IO2002 industries using the IO-HS concordance, taking a trade-weighted average of the dispersion value over HS10 constituent codes; the weights used were the total value of U.S. imports for each HS10 code from 1989–2006, from Feenstra, Romalis, and Schott (2002). A similar procedure to that described above for trade costs and R&D intensity was used to obtain the dispersion measure for the remaining thirteen IO2002 codes. The construction of a productivity or size dispersion measure at the six-digit NAICS level was analogous to that of the R&D intensity and required using data from encompassing five- or four-digit sectors to impute values to industries that otherwise would have been left with missing values.

Demand Elasticities. U.S. demand elasticities at the IO2002 level were computed as in Antràs and Chor (2013). We begin with the U.S. import demand elasticities for HS10 products computed by Broda and Weinstein (2006). This was merged with a comprehensive list of HS10 codes from Pierce and Schott (2009). For each HS10 code missing an elasticity value, we assigned a value equal to the trade-weighted average elasticity of the available HS10 codes with which it shared the same first nine digits. This was done successively up to codes that shared the same first two digits, to fill in as many HS10 elasticities as possible. Using the IO-HS concordance provided by the BEA with the 2002 U.S. I-O Tables, we then took the trade-weighted average of the HS10 elasticities within each IO2002 category. At each stage, the weights used were the total value of U.S. imports by HS10 code from 1989–2006, calculated from Feenstra et al. (2002). U.S. demand elasticities at the six-digit NAICS level were computed in an analogous way based on the same HS10 elasticities but using the HS-NAICS concordance in Pierce and Schott (2009) to compute six-digit NAICS averages. In both cases, there remained industries without elasticity values after the above procedures. Values for these sectors were imputed following the same approach as for other variables above, using data from encompassing five- or four-digit sectors. Finally, in order to compute "average buyer" demand elasticities, we took a weighted average of the elasticities of industries that purchase the input in question, with weights equal to these input purchase values as reported in the 2002 U.S. I-O Tables. This is the same approach used to construct buyer versions of R&D, capital, and skill intensity.

Input Substitutability. We begin with the import demand elasticities estimated by Broda and Weinstein (2006), but this time we use their estimates at the SITC Revision 3 three-digit level (rather than ten-digit HS level). As documented in their paper (see in particular their footnote 22), these elasticities were estimated in part from the substitution seen across HS10 product codes that fall under each SITC three-digit heading. These estimates would contain information on the degree of substitution across inputs under the assumption that the constituent HS10 products in each SITC three-digit category are typically used together as inputs in production. The three-digit SITC elasticities were mapped into IO2002 codes by first assigning them to HS codes using the concordance in Feenstra et al. (2002) and then using the HS to IO concordance provided by the BEA.

Specificity. This measure is borrowed from Antràs and Chor (2013), who in turn build on Rauch (1999) and Nunn (2007). For each IO2002 industry, it is calculated as the fraction of HS10 constituent codes classified by Rauch (1999) as neither reference-priced nor traded on an organized exchange, under Rauch's "liberal" classification. The original Rauch classification was for SITC Rev. 2 products; these were associated with HS10 codes using a mapping derived from U.S. imports in Feenstra et al. (2002). A higher value of this share is interpreted as the industry producing more differentiated goods, which in an input setting we associate with specificity.

Contractibility. We experiment with four measures of contractibility at the IO2002 industrial level. "Nunn contractibility" was computed by Antràs and Chor (2013) from the 2002 U.S. I-O Tables following the methodology of Nunn (2007). We begin with the Rauch-Nunn sectoral measure of specificity above. For each IO2002 industry, we then calculate a weighted average specificity of the inputs used by that industry, where the weights correspond to each input's share in the overall input purchases of the industry in question. We took one minus this value as a measure of the Nunn contractibility of each IO2002 industry. Levchenko and Costinot contractibility were obtained from Chor (2010), who in turn built them following the methodology of Levchenko (2007) and Costinot (2009), respectively. These two measures were normalized so that higher levels imply higher contractibility or lower dependence on formal contract enforcement. In particular, Levchenko contractibility is computed as the Herfindahl index of intermediate input use—rather than minus the Herfindahl as in Levchenko (2007)—while Costinot contractibility is equal to the negative of the measure of complexity in Costinot (2009). Chor (2010) computed the Levchenko and Nunn measures at the 1987 Standard Industry Classification (SIC) level. We used a concordance from the U.S. census to map them into NAICS codes, and then the NAICS-IO2002 BEA concordance used for several measures above to obtain these variables at the IO2002 level.[3] Finally, BJRS contractibility corresponds to the measure of intermediation in Bernard, Jensen, Redding, and Schott (2010), who calculated this from U.S. establishment-level data as the weighted average of the wholesale employment share of firms in 1997, using the import share of each firm as weights. We use the IO2002 version of this variable constructed by Antràs and Chor (2013) (see their Data Appendix for more details).

We also compute "average buyer" contractibility for each of these four contractibility measures using the same procedure described for computing average buyer R&D, capital, and skill intensities.

Financial and Labor Contractibility. The Rajan and Zingales (1998) external dependence measure, the Braun (2002) asset tangibility measure, and the Cuñat and Melitz (2012) sales volatility measure are all borrowed from Chor (2010), who computed them at the 1987 SIC level. As with the Levchenko and Costinot contractibility variables discussed above, we used a concordance from the U.S. Census to map them into NAICS codes, and then the NAICS-IO2002 BEA concordance used for several measures above to obtain these variables at the IO2002 level.

Downstreamness. This variable is calculated based on data from the 2002 U.S. I-O Tables, as described in Antràs and Chor (2013). It corresponds to a weighted index of the average position in the value chain at which an industry's output is used (i.e., as final consumption, as direct input to other industries, as direct input to industries serving as direct inputs to other industries, and so on), with the weights being given by the ratio of the use of that industry's output in that position relative to the total output of that industry. I next provide some more specific details on this measure for the interested reader. To build intuition, recall the basic input-output identity:

$$Y_i = F_i + Z_i,$$

where Y_i is total output in industry i, F_i is the output of i that goes toward final consumption and investment ("final use"), and Z_i is the use of i's output as inputs to other industries (or its "total use" as an input). In a world with N industries, this identity can be expanded as follows:

$$Y_i = F_i + \underbrace{\sum_{j=1}^{N} d_{ij} F_j}_{\text{direct use of } i \text{ as input}} + \underbrace{\sum_{j=1}^{N}\sum_{k=1}^{N} d_{ik} d_{kj} F_j + \sum_{j=1}^{N}\sum_{k=1}^{N}\sum_{l=1}^{N} d_{il} d_{lk} d_{kj} F_j + \cdots,}_{\text{indirect use of } i \text{ as input}}$$

(B.1)

---

[3] See http://www.census.gov/eos/www/naics/concordances/concordances.html.

where d_{ij} for a pair of industries (i, j), $1 \leq i, j \leq N$, is the amount of i used as an input in producing one dollar worth of industry j's output. Building on this identity, Antràs and Chor (2013) suggest computing the (weighted) average position of an industry's output in the value chain, by multiplying each of the terms in (B.1) by their distance from final use plus one and dividing by Y_i:

$$U_i = 1 \cdot \frac{F_i}{Y_i} + 2 \cdot \frac{\sum_{j=1}^{N} d_{ij} F_j}{Y_i}$$

$$+ 3 \cdot \frac{\sum_{j=1}^{N} \sum_{k=1}^{N} d_{ik} d_{kj} F_j}{Y_i}$$

$$+ 4 \cdot \frac{\sum_{j=1}^{N} \sum_{k=1}^{N} \sum_{l=1}^{N} d_{il} d_{lk} d_{kj} F_j}{Y_i} + \dots \qquad (B.2)$$

It is clear that $U_i \geq 1$ and that larger values are associated with relatively higher levels of upstreamness of industry i's use. Although computing (B.2) might appear to require computing an infinite power series, notice that provided that $d_{ij} < 1$ for all (i, j) (a natural assumption), the numerator of the above measure equals the i-th element of the $N \times 1$ matrix $[I - D]^{-2} F$, where D is an $N \times N$ matrix whose (i, j)-th element is d_{ij} and F is a column matrix with F_i in row i.[4] In order to obtain a measure of downstreamness (rather than upstreamness), Antràs and Chor (2013) simply take the reciprocal of U_i, which necessarily lies in the interval $[0, 1]$. Antràs, Chor, Fally, and Hillberry (2012) discuss additional appealing features of this downstreamness measure.

B.7 Country-Level Covariates

Relative Factor Abundance. Physical capital abundance corresponds to the log of the physical capital per worker averaged over 2000–2005. Physical capital was constructed by Davin Chor based on investment data from the Penn World Tables (version 7.1) using the perpetual inventory method. Skill abundance is measured as the average years of schooling at all levels (primary, secondary, and tertiary) averaged over 2000 and 2005 based on the Barro and Lee (2013) dataset.

Rule of Law. Country rule of law is obtained from the Worldwide Governance Indicators (see also Kaufmann, Kraay, and Mastruzzi, 2010). The annual index ranges from -2.5 to 2.5 and it was averaged over the period 2000–05.

---

[4] Because $Y = [I - D]^{-1} F$, this numerator also equals the i-th element of the $N \times 1$ matrix $[I - D]^{-1} Y$, where Y is a column matrix with Y_i in row i.

Financial Development. Computed as private credit provided by banking sector is measured as the percentage of GDP, averaged over 2000–05, based on data from the World Bank's World Development Indicators.

Labor Market Flexibility. This corresponds to the countrylabor market flexibility index for the year 2004 used by Cuñat and Melitz (2012). It was originally constructed by the World Bank building on the work of Botero, Djankov, La Porta, Lopez-de Silanes, and Shleifer (2004).

GDP per capita. Computed as the log of Real GDP per capita in constant 2005 dollars from the Penn World Tables (version 7.1), averaged over the period 2000–05.

Bibliography

Acemoglu, D., Antràs, P., and Helpman, E. (2007). "Contracts and Technology Adoption," *American Economic Review* **97**(3), 916–943.

Aghion, P., Dewatripont, M., and Rey, P. (1994). "Renegotiation Design with Unverifiable Information," *Econometrica* **62**(2), 257.

Aghion, P. and Tirole, J. (1997). "Formal and Real Authority in Organizations," *Journal of Political Economy* **105**(1), 1–29.

Ahn, J. (2011). A Theory of Domestic and International Trade Finance, IMF Working Paper 11/262, International Monetary Fund.

Albornoz, F., Calvo Pardo, H. F., Corcos, G., and Ornelas, E. (2012). "Sequential Exporting," *Journal of International Economics* **88**(1), 17–31.

Alfaro, L., Conconi, P., Fadinger, H., and Newman, A. F. (2014). "Do Prices Determine Vertical Integration?" *National Bureau of Economic Research Working Paper Series* **No. 16118**.

Amiti, M. and Davis, D. R. (2012). "Trade, Firms, and Wages: Theory and Evidence," *Review of Economic Studies* **79**(1), 1–36.

Amiti, M. and Weinstein, D. E. (2011). "Exports and Financial Shocks," *Quarterly Journal of Economics* **126**(4), 1841–1877.

Anderson, J. E. and Marcouiller, D. (2002). "Insecurity and the Pattern of Trade: An Empirical Investigation," *Review of Economics and Statistics* **84**(2), 342–352.

Anderson, J. E. and Marcouiller, D. (2005). "Anarchy and Autarky: Endogenous Predation as a Barrier to Trade," *International Economic Review* **46**(1), 189–213.

Anderson, J. E. and van Wincoop, E. (2003). "Gravity with Gravitas: A Solution to the Border Puzzle," *American Economic Review* **93**(1), 170–192.

Antràs, P. (2003). "Firms, Contracts, and Trade Structure," *Quarterly Journal of Economics* **118**(4), 1375–1418.

Antràs, P. (2005). "Incomplete Contracts and the Product Cycle," *American Economic Review* **95**(4), 1054–1073.

Antràs, P. (2014). "Grossman–Hart (1986) Goes Global: Incomplete Contracts, Property Rights, and the International Organization of Production," *Journal of Law, Economics, and Organization* **30**(suppl 1), i118–i175.

Antràs, P. and Chor, D. (2013). "Organizing the Global Value Chain," *Econometrica* **81**(6), 2127–2204.

Antràs, P., Chor, D., Fally, T., and Hillberry, R. (2012). "Measuring the Upstreamness of Production and Trade Flows," *American Economic Review* **102**(3), 412–416.

Antràs, P. and Costinot, A. (2011). "Intermediated Trade," *Quarterly Journal of Economics* **126**(3), 1319–1374.

Antràs, P. and Foley, F. (forthcoming). "Poultry in Motion: A Study of International Trade Finance Practices", *Journal of Political Economy* **123**(4),

Antràs, P., Fort, T. C., and Tintelnot, F. (2014). "The Margins of Global Sourcing: Theory and Evidence from U.S. Firms." NBER Working Paper 20772. Work in Progress.

Antràs, P., Garicano, L., and Rossi-Hansberg, E. (2006). "Offshoring in a Knowledge Economy," *Quarterly Journal of Economics* **121**(1), 31–77.

Antràs, P., and Helpman, E. (2004). "Global Sourcing," *Journal of Political Economy* **112**(3), 552–580.

Antràs, P. and Helpman, E. (2008). "Contractual Frictions and Global Sourcing," in *The Organization of Firms in a Global Economy*, Cambridge, MA: Harvard University Press.

Antràs, P. and Rossi-Hansberg, E. (2009). "Organizations and Trade," *Annual Review of Economics* **1**(1), 43–64.

Antràs, P. and Staiger, R. W. (2012*a*). "Offshoring and the Role of Trade Agreements," *American Economic Review* **102**(7), 3140–3183.

Antràs, P. and Staiger, R. W. (2012*b*). "Trade Agreements and the Nature of Price Determination," *American Economic Review* **102**(3), 470–476.

Antràs, P. and Yeaple, S. (2013), "Multinational Firms and International Trade Structure," in *Handbook of International Economics*, Vol. 4. Amsterdam: Elsevier.

Araujo, L. F., Mion, G., and Ornelas, E. (2012), Institutions and Export Dynamics, Technical report, London School of Economics Working Paper.

Arkolakis, C., Costinot, A., and Rodríguez-Clare, A. (2012). "New Trade Models, Same Old Gains?" *American Economic Review* **102**(1), 94–130.

Arkolakis, C., Demidova, S., Klenow, P. J., and Rodríguez-Clare, A. (2008). "Endogenous Variety and the Gains from Trade," *American Economic Review* **98**(2), 444–450.

Atalay, E., Hortacsu, A., and Syverson, C. (2013). "Vertical Integration and Input Flows." Mimeo, University of Chicago.

Aumann, R. J. and Shapley, L. S. (1974). *Values of Non-Atomic Games*, Princeton, NJ: Princeton University Press.

Bagwell, K. and Staiger, R. W. (1999), "An Economic Theory of GATT," *American Economic Review* **89**(1), 215–248.

Bagwell, K. and Staiger, R. W. (2001). "Domestic Policies, National Sovereignty, and International Economic Institutions," *Quarterly Journal of Economics* **116**(2), 519–562.

Baker, G. P. and Hubbard, T. N. (2003). "Make Versus Buy in Trucking: Asset Ownership, Job Design, and Information," *American Economic Review* **93**(3), 551–572.

Baldwin, R. E. and Forslid, R. (2010). "Trade Liberalization with Heterogeneous Firms," *Review of Development Economics* **14**(2), 161–176.

Bardhan, P., Mookherjee, D., and Tsumagari, M. (2013). "Middlemen Margins and Globalization," *American Economic Journals: Micro* **5** (4), 81–119.

Barro, R. J. and Lee, J. W. (2013). "A New Dataset of Educational Attainment in the World, 1950–2010," *Journal of Development Economics* **104**, 184–198.

Basco, S. (2013). "Financial Development and the Product Cycle," *Journal of Economic Behavior & Organization* **94**, 295–313.

Bauer, C. J. and Langenmayr, D. (2013). "Sorting into Outsourcing: Are Profits Taxed at a Gorilla's Arm's Length?" *Journal of International Economics* **90**(2), 326–336.

Becker, R. A., Gray, W. B., and Marvakov, J. (2009). *NBER-CES manufacturing industry database*, National Bureau of Economic Research.

Behar, A. and Freund, C. (2011). "Factory Europe? Brainier but not Brawnier," Unpublished Manuscript.

Berkowitz, D., Moenius, J., and Pistor, K. (2006). "Trade, Law, and Product Complexity," *Review of Economics and Statistics* **88**(2), 363–373.

Bernard, A. B., Eaton, J., Jensen, J. B., and Kortum, S. (2003). "Plants and Productivity in International Trade," *American Economic Review* **93**(4), 1268–1290.

Bernard, A. B., Jensen, J. B., Redding, S. J., and Schott, P. K. (2007). "Firms in International Trade," *Journal of Economic Perspectives* **21**(3), 105–130.

Bernard, A. B., Jensen, J. B., Redding, S. J., and Schott, P. K. (2009). "The Margins of U.S. Trade," *American Economic Review* **99**(2), 487–493.

Bernard, A. B., Jensen, J. B., Redding, S. J., and Schott, P. K. (2010). "Intrafirm Trade and Product Contractibility," *American Economic Review* **100**(2), 444–48.

Bernard, A. B., Jensen, J. B., Redding, S. J., and Schott, P. K. (2012). "The Empirics of Firm Heterogeneity and International Trade," *Annual Review of Economics* **4**(1), 283–313.

Bernard, A. B., Jensen, J. B., and Schott, P. K. (2009). "Importers, Exporters, and Multinationals: A Portrait of Firms in the U.S. that Trade Goods", in T. Dunne, J. B. Jensen, and M. J. Roberts, eds. *Producer Dynamics: New Evidence from Micro Data*, NBER.

Bhagwati, J. and Ramaswami, V. K. (1963). "Domestic Distortions, Tariffs and the Theory of Optimum Subsidy," *Journal of Political Economy* **71**(1), 44–50.

Blaum, J., Lelarge, C., and Peters, M. (2013). "Non-Homothetic Import Demand: Firm Productivity and Quality Bias," Unpublished paper.

Botero, J. C., Djankov, S., La Porta, R. L., Lopez-de Silanes, F., and Shleifer, A. (2004). "The Regulation of Labor," *Quarterly Journal of Economics* **119**(4), 1339–1382.

Braun, M. (2002). "Financial Contractibility and Assets' Hardness: Industrial Composition and Growth." Mimeo, Harvard University.

Bresnahan, T. and Levin, J. (2012), "Vertical Integration and Market Structure," in *The Handbook of Organizational Economics*, Princeton, NJ: Princeton University Press.

Broda, C. and Weinstein, D. E. (2006). "Globalization and the Gains from Variety," *Quarterly Journal of Economics* **121**(2), 541–585.

Campa, J. M. and Goldberg, L. S. (1997). "The Evolving External Orientation of Manufacturing: A Profile of Four Countries," *Federal Reserve Bank of New York Economic Policy Review* **3**, 53–81.

Carluccio, J. and Bas, M. (forthcoming). "The Impact of Worker Bargaining Power on the Organization of Global Firms," *Journal of International Economics.*

Carluccio, J. and Fally, T. (2011). "Global Sourcing under Imperfect Capital Markets," *Review of Economics and Statistics* **94**(3), 740–763.

Chaney, T. (2008). "Distorted Gravity: The Intensive and Extensive Margins of International Trade," *American Economic Review* **98**(4), 1707–1721.

Chen, H., Kondratowicz, M., and Yi, K.-M. (2005). "Vertical Specialization and Three Facts about U.S. International Trade," *North American Journal of Economics and Finance* **16**(1), 35–59.

Chen, Y. and Feenstra, R. C. (2008). "Buyer Investment, Export Variety and Intrafirm Trade," *European Economic Review* **52**(8), 1313–1337.

Chor, D. (2010). "Unpacking Sources of Comparative Advantage: A Quantitative Approach," *Journal of International Economics* **82**(2), 152–167.

Clermont, K. M. and Eisenberg, T. (2007). "Xenophilia or Xenophobia in U.S. Courts? Before and After 9/11," *Journal of Empirical Legal Studies* **4**(2), 441–464.

Coase, R. H. (1937). "The Nature of the Firm," *Economica* **4**(16), 386–405.

Conconi, P., Legros, P., and Newman, A. F. (2012). "Trade Liberalization and Organizational Change," *Journal of International Economics* **86**(2), 197–208.

Corcos, G., Irac, D. M., Mion, G., and Verdier, T. (2013). "The Determinants of Intrafirm Trade: Evidence from French Firms," *Review of Economics and Statistics* **95**(3), 825–838.

Costinot, A. (2009). "On the Origins of Comparative Advantage," *Journal of International Economics* **77**(2), 255–264.

Costinot, A., Oldenski, L., and Rauch, J. (2011). "Adaptation and the Boundary of Multinational Firms," *Review of Economics and Statistics* **93**(1), 298–308.

Costinot, A. and Rodríguez-Clare, A. (2013), "Trade Theory with Numbers: Quantifying the Consequences of Globalization", in *Handbook of International Economics*, Amsterdam: Elsevier.

Cuñat, A. and Melitz, M. J. (2012). "Volatility, Labor Market Flexibility, and the Pattern of Comparative Advantage," *Journal of the European Economic Association* **10**(2), 225–254.

Davidson, W. H. and McFetridge, D. G. (1984). "International Technology Transactions and the Theory of the Firm," *Journal of Industrial Economics* **32**(3), 253–264.

Davis, D. R. and Weinstein, D. E. (2001). "An Account of Global Factor Trade," *American Economic Review* **91**(5), 1423–1453.

Deardorff, A. V. (2001). "Fragmentation in Simple Trade Models," *North American Journal of Economics and Finance* **12**(2), 121–137.

Defever, F. and Toubal, F. (2013). "Productivity, Relationship-Specific Inputs and the Sourcing Modes of Multinationals," *Journal of Economic Behavior & Organization* **94**, 345–357.

Delgado, M. A., Fariñas, J. C., and Ruano, S. (2002). "Firm Productivity and Export Markets: A Non-parametric Approach," *Journal of International Economics* **57**(2), 397–422.

Demidova, S. and Rodríguez-Clare, A. (2009). "Trade Policy under Firm-level Heterogeneity in a Small Economy," *Journal of International Economics* **78**(1), 100–112.

Demidova, S. and Rodríguez-Clare, A. (2013). "The Simple Analytics of the Melitz Model in a Small Economy," *Journal of International Economics* **90**(2), 266–272.

Díez, F. J. (2014). "The Asymmetric Effects of Tariffs on Intra-firm Trade and Offshoring Decisions," *Journal of International Economics* **93**(1), 76–91.

Dixit, A. K. and Stiglitz, J. E. (1977). "Monopolistic Competition and Optimum Product Diversity," *American Economic Review* **67**(3), 297–308.

Djankov, S., La Porta, R., Lopez-De-Silanes, F., and Shleifer, A. (2003). "Courts," *Quarterly Journal of Economics* **118**(2), 453–517.

Du, J., Lu, Y., and Tao, Z. (2009). "Bi-sourcing in the Global Economy," *Journal of International Economics* **77**(2), 215–222.

Dunning, J. H. (1981), *International Production and the Multinational Enterprise*, Crows Nest, Australia: Allen & Unwin.

Eaton, J. and Kortum, S. (2002). "Technology, Geography, and Trade," *Econometrica* **70**(5), 1741–1779.

Eaton, J., Kortum, S., and Kramarz, F. (2011). "An Anatomy of International Trade: Evidence from French Firms," *Econometrica* **79**(5), 1453–1498.

Ethier, W. J. (1986). "The Multinational Firm," *Quarterly Journal of Economics* **101**(4), 805–833.

Ethier, W. J. (2001). "Dixit-Stiglitz, Trade and Growth," in S. Brakman and B. J. Heijdra, eds., *The Monopolistic Competition Revolution in Retrospect*, Cambridge, UK: Cambridge University Press.

Ethier, W. J. and Markusen, J. R. (1996). "Multinational Firms, Technology Diffusion and Trade," *Journal of International Economics* **41**(1–2), 1–28.

Fally, T. (2012). *Production Staging: Measurement and Facts*. Mimeo, University of Colorado.

Federico, S. (2010). "Outsourcing versus Integration at Home or Abroad and Firm Heterogeneity," *Empirica* **37**(1), 47–63.

Feenstra, R. C. (1998). "Integration of Trade and Disintegration of Production in the Global Economy," *Journal of Economic Perspectives* **12**(4), 31–50.

Feenstra, R. C. (2011), *Offshoring to China: The Local and Global Impacts of Processing Trade*. University of International Business and Economics, Beijing.

Feenstra, R. C. and Hanson, G. H. (1996*a*), "Foreign Investment, Outsourcing and Relative Wages, in R. Feenstra, G. Grossman, and D. Irwin, eds., *The Political Economy of Trade Policy: Papers in Honor of Jagdish Bhagwati*, Cambridge, MA: MIT Press.

Feenstra, R. C. and Hanson, G. H. (1996*b*). "Globalization, Outsourcing, and Wage Inequality," *American Economic Review* **86**, 240–245.

Feenstra, R. C. and Hanson, G. H. (2005). "Ownership and Control in Outsourcing to China: Estimating the Property-Rights Theory of the Firm," *Quarterly Journal of Economics* **120**(2), 729–761.

Feenstra, R. C., Romalis, J., and Schott, P. K. (2002). U.S. Imports, Exports, and Tariff Data, 1989–2001, Working Paper 9387, National Bureau of Economic Research.

Felbermayr, G., Jung, B., and Larch, M. (2013). "Optimal Tariffs, Retaliation, and the Welfare Loss from Tariff Wars in the Melitz Model," *Journal of International Economics* **89**(1), 13–25.

Fernandes, A. and Tang, H. (2010). "The Determinants of Vertical Integration in Export Processing: Theory and Evidence from China," *SSRN eLibrary*.

Foley, C. F., Chen, M., Johnson, M., and Meyer, L. (2009). "Noble Group." HBS Case Study 210-021.

Fort, T. C. (2014). Technology and Production Fragmentation: Domestic versus Foreign Sourcing, Working Paper 13-35, Dartmouth College.

Gans, J. S. and Shepherd, G. B. (1994). "How Are the Mighty Fallen: Rejected Classic Articles by Leading Economists," *Journal of Economic Perspectives* **8**(1), 165–179.

Garetto, S. (2013). "Input Sourcing and Multinational Production," *American Economic Journal: Macroeconomics* **5**(2), 118–151.

Gennaioli, N. (2013). "Optimal Contracts with Enforcement Risk," *Journal of the European Economic Association* **11**(1), 59–82.

Gil, R. (2007). "'Make-or-Buy' in Movies: Integration and Ex-Post Renegotiation," *International Journal of Industrial Organization* **25**(4), 643–655.

Goldberg, P. K., Khandelwal, A. K., Pavcnik, N., and Topalova, P. (2010). "Imported Intermediate Inputs and Domestic Product Growth: Evidence from India," *Quarterly Journal of Economics* **125**(4), 1727–1767.

Gopinath, G. and Neiman, B. (2014). "Trade Adjustment and Productivity in Large Crises," *American Economic Review* **104**(3), 793–831.

Grossman, G. M. and Helpman, E. (2002). "Integration versus Outsourcing in Industry Equilibrium," *Quarterly Journal of Economics* **117**(1), 85–120.

Grossman, G. M. and Helpman, E. (2003). "Outsourcing versus FDI in Industry Equilibrium," *Journal of the European Economic Association* **1**(2-3), 317–327.

Grossman, G. M. and Helpman, E. (2005). "Outsourcing in a Global Economy," *Review of Economic Studies* **72**(1), 135–159.

Grossman, G. M. and Rossi-Hansberg, E. (2008). "Trading Tasks: A Simple Theory of Offshoring," *American Economic Review* **98**(5), 1978–1997.

Grossman, S. J. and Hart, O. D. (1986). "The Costs and Benefits of Ownership: A Theory of Vertical and Lateral Integration," *Journal of Political Economy* **94**(4), 691–719.

Guadalupe, M., Kuzmina, O., and Thomas, C. (2012). "Innovation and Foreign Ownership," *American Economic Review* **102**(7), 3594–3627.

Halpern, L., Koren, M., and Szeidl, A. (2011). "Imported Inputs and Productivity," Working Paper, CEU **8**, 28.

Harrison, A. and Scorse, J. (2010). "Multinationals and Anti-Sweatshop Activism," *American Economic Review* **100**(1), 247–273.

Hart, O. (1995), *Firms, Contracts, and Financial Structure*, Oxford, UK: Oxford University Press.

Hart, O. and Holmstrom, B. (2010). "A Theory of Firm Scope," *Quarterly Journal of Economics* **125**(2), 483–513.

Hart, O. and Moore, J. (1990). "Property Rights and the Nature of the Firm," *Journal of Political Economy* **98**(6), 1119–1158.

Hart, O. and Moore, J. (1994). "A Theory of Debt Based on the Inalienability of Human Capital," *Quarterly Journal of Economics* **109**(4), 841–879.

Helleiner, G. K. and Lavergne, R. (1979). "Intra-Firm Trade and Industrial Exports to the United States," *Oxford Bulletin of Economics and Statistics* **41**(4), 297–311.

Helpman, E. (1984). "A Simple Theory of International Trade with Multinational Corporations," *Journal of Political Economy* **92**(3), 451–471.

Helpman, E. (2006). "Trade, FDI, and the Organization of Firms," *Journal of Economic Literature* **44**(3), 589–630.

Helpman, E., Itskhoki, O., and Redding, S. (2010). "Inequality and Unemployment in a Global Economy," *Econometrica* **78**, 1239–1283.

Helpman, E. and Krugman, P. (1985), *Market Structure and Foreign Trade: Increasing Returns, Imperfect Competition, and the International Economy*, Cambridge, MA: MIT Press.

Helpman, E., Melitz, M. J., and Yeaple, S. R. (2004). "Export versus FDI with Heterogeneous Firms," *American Economic Review* **94**(1), 300–316.

Helpman, E., Melitz, M., and Rubinstein, Y. (2008). "Estimating Trade Flows: Trading Partners and Trading Volumes," *Quarterly Journal of Economics* **123**(2), 441–487.

Hoefele, A., Schmidt-Eisenlohr, T., and Yu, Z. (2013), Payment Choice in International Trade: Theory and Evidence from Cross-country Firm Level Data, CESifo Working Paper Series 4350, CESifo Group Munich.

Holmstrom, B. (1982). "Moral Hazard in Teams," *Bell Journal of Economics* **13**(2), 324.

Hummels, D. (2007). "Transportation Costs and International Trade in the Second Era of Globalization," *Journal of Economic Perspectives* **21**(3), 131–154.

Hummels, D., Ishii, J., and Yi, K.-M. (2001). "The Nature and Growth of Vertical Specialization in World Trade," *Journal of International Economics* **54**, 75–96.

Johnson, R. C. and Noguera, G. (2012*a*). "Accounting for Intermediates: Production Sharing and Trade in Value Added," *Journal of International Economics* **86**(2), 224–236.

Johnson, R. C. and Noguera, G. (2012*b*). Fragmentation and Trade in Value Added over Four Decades, Working Paper, Dartmouth College.

Jones, R. W. (2000). *Globalization and the Theory of Input Trade*, Cambridge, MA: MIT Press.

Jones, R. W. and Neary, P. (1984). "The Positive Theory of International Trade", in R. W. Jones and P. B. Kenen, eds., *Handbook of International Economics*, Vol. 1, Amsterdam: Elsevier, pp. 1–62.

Joskow, P. L. (1985). "Vertical Integration and Long-Term Contracts: The Case of Coal-Burning Electric Generating Plants," *Journal of Law, Economics, & Organization* **1**(1), 33–80.

Joskow, P. L. (1987). "Contract Duration and Relationship-Specific Investments: Empirical Evidence from Coal Markets," *American Economic Review* **77**(1), 168–185.

Jovanovic, B. (1982). "Selection and the Evolution of Industry," *Econometrica* **50**(3), 649.

Kaufmann, D., Kraay, A., and Mastruzzi, M. (2010). "The Worldwide Governance Indicators: Methodology and Analytical Issues,". World Bank Policy Research Working Paper 5430.

Keuschnigg, C. and Devereux, M. P. (2013). "The Arm's Length Principle and Distortions to Multinational Firm Organization," *Journal of International Economics* **89**(2), 432–440.

Klein, B., Crawford, R. G., and Alchian, A. A. (1978). "Vertical Integration, Appropriable Rents, and the Competitive Contracting Process," *Journal of Law and Economics* **21**(2), 297–326.

Knack, S. and Keefer, P. (1995). "Institutions and Economic Performance: Cross-Country Tests Using Alternative Institutional Measures," *Economics & Politics* **7**(3), 207–227.

Kogut, B. and Zander, U. (1993). "Knowledge of the Firm and the Evolutionary Theory of the Multinational Corporation," *Journal of International Business Studies* **24**(4), 625–645.

Kohler, W. and Smolka, M. (2009). Global Sourcing Decisions and Firm Productivity: Evidence from Spain, CESifo Working Paper Series 2903, CESifo Group Munich.

Kohler, W. and Smolka, M. (2014). "Global Sourcing and Firm Selection," *Economics Letters* **124**(3), 411–415.

Koopman, R., Wang, Z., and Wei, S.-J. (2014). "Tracing Value-Added and Double Counting in Gross Exports," *American Economic Review* **104**(2), 459–494.

Kremer, M. and Maskin, E. (2006). "Globalization and Inequality," Mimeo, Harvard University.

Krugman, P. (1980). "Scale Economies, Product Differentiation, and the Pattern of Trade," *American Economic Review* **70**(5), 950–959.

Krugman, P. R. (1979). "Increasing Returns, Monopolistic Competition, and International Trade," *Journal of International Economics* **9**(4), 469–479.

Kuhn, T. S. (1996). *Structure of Scientific Revolutions*, Chicago: University of Chicago Press.

Lafontaine, F. and Slade, M. (2007). "Vertical Integration and Firm Boundaries: The Evidence," *Journal of Economic Literature* **45**(3), 629–685.

Lall, S. (1978). "The Pattern of Intra-Firm Exports by U.S. Multinationals," *Oxford Bulletin of Economics and Statistics* **40**(3), 209–222.

Lanz, R. and Miroudot, S. (2011). Intra-Firm Trade: Patterns, Determinants and Policy Implications, OECD Trade Policy Paper 114, OECD Publishing.

La Porta, R., Lopez-de Silanes, F., Shleifer, A., and Vishny, R. (1999). "The Quality of Government," *Journal of Law, Economics and Organization* **15**(1), 222–279.

Leamer, E. E. (1984). *Sources of International Comparative Advantage: Theory and Evidence*, Cambridge, MA: MIT Press.

Legros, P. and Newman, A. F. (2010). "Competing for Ownership," *Journal of the European Economic Association* **6**(6), 1279–1308.

Legros, P. and Newman, A. F. (2013). "A Price Theory of Vertical and Lateral Integration," *Quarterly Journal of Economics* **128**(2), 725–770.

Levchenko, A. A. (2007). "Institutional Quality and International Trade," *Review of Economic Studies* **74**(3), 791–819.

Li, Z. (2013). "Task Offshoring and Organizational Form: Theory and Evidence from China," *Journal of Economic Behavior & Organization* **94**, 358–380.

Lu, D. (2011). "Exceptional Exporter Performance? Evidence from Chinese Manufacturing Firms," Mimeo, University of Rochester.

Manova, K. (2008). "Credit Constraints, Equity Market Liberalizations and International trade," *Journal of International Economics* **76**(1), 33–47.

Manova, K. (2013). "Credit Constraints, Heterogeneous Firms, and International Trade," *Review of Economic Studies* **80**(2), 711–744.

Mansfield, E. and Romeo, A. (1980). "Technology Transfer to Overseas Subsidiaries by U.S.-Based Firms," *Quarterly Journal of Economics* **95**(4), 737–750.

Mansfield, E., Romeo, A., and Wagner, S. (1979). "Foreign Trade and U.S. Research and Development," *Review of Economics and Statistics* **61**(1), 49–57.

Marin, D. and Verdier, T. (2003). "Globalization and the New Enterprise," *Journal of the European Economic Association* **1**(2-3), 337–344.

Marin, D. and Verdier, T. (2008). "Power Inside the Firm and the Market: A General Equilibrium Approach," *Journal of the European Economic Association* **6**(4), 752–788.

Marin, D. and Verdier, T. (2009). "Power in the Multinational Corporation in Industry Equilibrium," *Economic Theory* **38**(3), 437–464.

Marin, D. and Verdier, T. (2012). "Globalization and the Empowerment of Talent," *Journal of International Economics* **86**(2), 209–223.

Maskin, E. and Tirole, J. (1999). "Unforeseen Contingencies and Incomplete Contracts," *Review of Economic Studies* **66**(1), 83–114.

Masten, S. E. (1984). "The Organization of Production: Evidence from the Aerospace Industry," *Journal of Law and Economics* **27**(2), 403–417.

McLaren, J. (2000). "Globalization and Vertical Structure," *American Economic Review* **90**(5), 1239–1254.

Melitz, M. J. (2003). "The Impact of Trade on Intra-Industry Reallocations and Aggregate Industry Productivity," *Econometrica* **71**(6), 1695–1725.

Melitz, M. J. and Ottaviano, G.I.P. (2008). "Market Size, Trade, and Productivity," *Review of Economic Studies* **75**(1), 295–316.

Melitz, M. J. and Redding, S. (2013*a*). "Heterogeneous Firms and Trade," in *Handbook of International Economics*, Vol. 4, Amsterdam: Elsevier.

Melitz, M. and Redding, S. (2013*b*). "Firm Heterogeneity and Aggregate Welfare," Mimeo, Harvard University.

Midler, P. (2009). *Poorly Made in China: An Insider's Account of the Tactics Behind China's Production Game*, 1st ed., New York: Wiley.

Milgrom, P. (2000). "Putting Auction Theory to Work: The Simultaneous Ascending Auction," *Journal of Political Economy* **108**(2), 245–272.

Miroudot, S., Lanz, R., and Ragoussis, A. (2009). "Trade in Intermediate Goods and Services," OECD Trade Policy Working Papers (93).

Monteverde, K. and Teece, D. J. (1982). "Supplier Switching Costs and Vertical Integration in the Automobile Industry," *Bell Journal of Economics* **13**(1), 206.

Mutreja, P. (2014). "Equipment and Structures Capital: Accounting for Income Differences," *Economic Inquiry* **52**(2), 713–731.

Newhouse, J. (2007). *Boeing Versus Airbus: The Inside Story of the Greatest International Competition in Business*, New York: Knopf.

Nguyen, D. X. (2012). "Demand Uncertainty: Exporting Delays and Exporting Failures," *Journal of International Economics* **86**(2), 336–344.

Novy, D. (2013). "International Trade without CES: Estimating Translog Gravity," *Journal of International Economics* **89**(2), 271–282.

Nunn, N. (2007). "Relationship-Specificity, Incomplete Contracts, and the Pattern of Trade," *Quarterly Journal of Economics* **122**(2), 569–600.

Nunn, N. and Trefler, D. (2008)," The Boundaries of the Multinational Firm: An Empirical Analysis," in *The Organization of Firms in a Global Economy*, Cambridge, MA: Harvard University Press, pp. 55–83.

Nunn, N. and Trefler, D. (2013*a*). "Domestic Institutions as a Source of Comparative Advantage," in *Handbook of International Economics*, Vol. 4, Amsterdam: North Holland.

Nunn, N. and Trefler, D. (2013*b*). "Incomplete Contracts and the Boundaries of the Multinational firm," *Journal of Economic Behavior & Organization* **94**, 330–344.

Olley, G. S. and Pakes, A. (1996). "The Dynamics of Productivity in the Telecommunications Equipment Industry," *Econometrica* **64**(6), 1263–1297.

Olsen, M. (2013). "How Firms Overcome Weak International Contract Enforcement: Repeated Interaction, Collective Punishment, and Trade Finance," Working Paper, IESE Barcelona.

Ornelas, E. and Turner, J. L. (2012). "Protection and International Sourcing," *Economic Journal* **122**(559), 26–63.

Osborne, M. J. and Rubinstein, A. (1990). *Bargaining and Markets*, Waltham, MA: Academic Press.

Pavcnik, N. (2002). "Trade Liberalization, Exit, and Productivity Improvements: Evidence from Chilean Plants," *Review of Economic Studies* **69**(1), 245–276.

Pierce, J. R. and Schott, P. K. (2009). Concording U.S. Harmonized System Categories Over Time, Working Paper 14837, National Bureau of Economic Research.

Puga, D. and Trefler, D. (2002). Knowledge Creation and Control in Organizations, Working Paper 9121, National Bureau of Economic Research.

Puga, D. and Trefler, D. (2010). "Wake Up and Smell the Ginseng: International Trade and the Rise of Incremental Innovation in Low-Wage Countries," *Journal of Development Economics* **91**(1), 64–76.

Qiu, L. D. and Spencer, B. J. (2002). "Keiretsu and Relationship-Specific Investment: Implications for Market-Opening Trade Policy," *Journal of International Economics* **58**(1), 49–79.

Rajan, R. G. and Zingales, L. (1998). "Financial Dependence and Growth," *American Economic Review* **88**(3), 559–86.

Ramondo, N., Rappoport, V., and Ruhl, K. J. (2013). "Horizontal versus Vertical Foreign Direct Investment: Evidence from U.S. Multinationals," Mimeo, NYU Stern.

Rauch, J. E. (1999). "Networks versus Markets in International Trade," *Journal of International Economics* **48**(1), 7–35.

Redding, S. J. (2011). "Theories of Heterogeneous Firms and Trade," *Annual Review of Economics* **3**(1), 77–105.

Redding, S. and Venables, A. J. (2004). "Economic Geography and International Inequality," *Journal of International Economics* **62**(1), 53–82.

Rodrik, D. (2000). "How Far Will International Economic Integration Go?" *Journal of Economic Perspectives* **14**(1), 177–186.

Romalis, J. (2004). "Factor Proportions and the Structure of Commodity Trade," *American Economic Review* **94**(1), 67–97.

Roth, A. E. (1985). "A Note on Risk Aversion in a Perfect Equilibrium Model of Bargaining," *Econometrica* **53**(1), 207–211.

Rubinstein, A. (1982). "Perfect Equilibrium in a Bargaining Model," *Econometrica* **50**(1), 97–109.

Ruhl, K. (2013). "An Overview of US Intrafirm-trade Data Sources," Mimeo, NYU Stern.

Schmidt-Eisenlohr, T. (2013). "Towards a Theory of Trade Finance," *Journal of International Economics* **91**(1), 96–112.

Schott, P. K. (2004). "Across-Product versus Within-Product Specialization in International Trade," *Quarterly Journal of Economics* **119**(2), 647–678.

Schott, P. K. (2008). "The Relative Sophistication of Chinese Exports," *Economic Policy* **23**(53), 5–49.

Schott, P. K. (2010). "U.S. Manufacturing Exports and Imports by SIC or NAICS Category and Partner Country, 1972 to 2005," Yale School of Management.

Schwarz, C. and Suedekum, J. (2014). "Global Sourcing of Complex Production Processes," *Journal of International Economics* **93**(1), 123–139.

Segura-Cayuela, R. and Vilarrubia, J. M. (2008). Uncertainty and Entry into Export Markets, Banco de España Working Paper 0811, Banco de España.

Siddharthan, N. S. and Kumar, N. (1990). "The Determinants of Inter-industry Variations in the Proportion of Intra-firm Trade: The Behaviour of US Multinationals," *Weltwirtschaftliches Archiv* **126**(3), 581–591.

Spencer, B. J. (2005). "International Outsourcing and Incomplete Contracts," *Canadian Journal of Economics* **38**, 1107–1135.

Tang, H. and Zhang, Y. (2012). "Quality Differentiation and Trade Intermediation," Mimeo, John Hopkins SAIS School.

Thomas, J. and Worrall, T. (1994). "Foreign Direct Investment and the Risk of Expropriation," *Review of Economic Studies* **61**(1), 81–108.

Timmer, M. P., Erumban, A. A., Los, B., Stehrer, R., and de Vries, G. J. (2014). "Slicing Up Global Value Chains," *Journal of Economic Perspectives* **28**(2), 99–118.

Tinbergen, J. (1962). *Shaping the World Economy; Suggestions for an International Economic Policy*, New York: Twentieth Century Fund.

Tintelnot, F. (2013). "Global Production with Export Platforms," Mimeo, Princeton University.

Tomiura, E. (2007). "Foreign Outsourcing, Exporting, and FDI: A Productivity Comparison at the Firm Level," *Journal of International Economics* **72**(1), 113–127.

Trefler, D. (1993*a*). "International Factor Price Differences: Leontief was Right!" *Journal of Political Economy* **101**(6), 961–987.

Trefler, D. (1993*b*). "Trade Liberalization and the Theory of Endogenous Protection: An Econometric Study of U.S. Import Policy," *Journal of Political Economy* **101**(1), 138–160.

Trefler, D. (1995). "The Case of the Missing Trade and Other Mysteries," *American Economic Review* **85**(5), 1029–1046.

Trefler, D. and Zhu, S. C. (2010). "The Structure of Factor Content Predictions," *Journal of International Economics* **82**(2), 195–207.

United Nations (2010). "International Merchandise Trade Statistics: Concepts and Definitions".

Van Biesebroeck, J. and Zhang, L. (2014). "Interdependent Product Cycles for Globally Sourced Intermediates," *Journal of International Economics* **94**(1), 143–156.

Vanek, J. (1968). "The Factor Proportions Theory: The N-Factor Case," *Kyklos* **21**(4), 749–756.

Viner, J. (1932). "Cost Curves and Supply Curves," *Zeitschrift für Nationalökonomie* **3**(1), 23–46.

Waugh, M. E. (2010). "International Trade and Income Differences," *American Economic Review* **100**(5), 2093–2124.

Whinston, M. D. (2003). "On the Transaction Cost Determinants of Vertical Integration," *Journal of Law, Economics, and Organization* **19**(1), 1–23.

Williamson, O. E. (1971). "The Vertical Integration of Production: Market Failure Considerations," *The American Economic Review* **61**(2), 112–123.

Williamson, O. E. (1975), *Markets and Hierarchies: Analysis and Antitrust Implications*, New York: Free Press.

Williamson, O. E. (1985). *Economic Institutions of Capitalism*, New York: Free Press.

Wright, G. C. (2014). "Revisiting the Employment Impact of Offshoring," *European Economic Review* **66**, 63–83.

Yeaple, S. R. (2006). "Offshoring, Foreign Direct Investment, and the Structure of U.S. Trade," *Journal of the European Economic Association* **4**(2-3), 602–611.

Yeats, A. J. (2001)," Just How Big Is Global Production Sharing?" in S. W. Arndt and H. Kierzkowski, eds., *Fragmentation New Production Patterns in the World Economy*, Oxford: Oxford University Press.

Zeile, W. J. (1997). "U.S. Intrafirm Trade in Goods," *Survey of Current Business* **78**, 23–38.

Index

www.ingramcontent.com/pod-product-compliance
Ingram Content Group UK Ltd.
Pitfield, Milton Keynes, MK11 3LW, UK
UKHW032037230125
454070UK00003B/100